TURKEY BEYOND NATIONALISM

TURKEY BEYOND NATIONALISM: TOWARDS POST-NATIONALIST IDENTITIES

Edited by Hans-Lukas Kieser

I.B. TAURIS
LONDON · NEW YORK

Supported by the Swiss Academy of Humanities and Social Sciences
www.sagw.ch

Published in 2006 by I. B. Tauris & Co. Ltd.
6 Salem Road, London W2 4 BU
175 Fifth Avenue, New York NY 10010
www.ibtauris.com

In the United States of America and in Canada distributed by Palgrave Macmillan
a division of St. Martins Press, 175 Fifth Avenue, New York NY 10010

International Library of Twentieth Century History 8

ISBN 10: 1 84511 141 9
ISBN 13: 978 1 84511 141 0

A full CIP record for this book is available from the British Library
A full CIP record for this book is available from the Library of Congress

Library of Congress Catalog Card Number: available

Printed and bound in Great Britain by TJ International Ltd, Padstow, Cornwall
From camera-ready copy edited and supplied by the editor

Contents

Introduction

Hans-Lukas Kieser

The title of this book implies that Turkey has been deeply marked by nationalism in the 20th century. In this book we seek to understand Turkey's recent developments and future perspectives by analysing thoroughly what has been and still partly is the impact of nationalist thinking on the country. Nationalism was the mindset of the founders of the Republic in 1923; and even if it evolved in many ways during the 20th century, important principles and assumptions remained valid, or their validity was not openly questioned. Hence we need clear insights, as complete as possible, into what has been the nationalist fabric of modern Turkey.

Underlying the title is the question about the evolution of today's Turkey towards post-nationalism: in other words towards a political spirit that permits the development of a liberal, truly pluralist society where – something which has not been the case for many decades since 1923 – different cultural identities can freely express themselves, and where the state does not feel threatened by such a pluralism.

The Turkish 20th century

Let us take "revolution" as a key term for a short journey through the Turkish 20th century. Since the late 19th century, revolution had been demanded in order to create a "new Turkey", but the word meant very different things to different protagonists. Whereas for the Young Turks who opposed Sultan Abdulhamid, revolution meant the takeover of political power in the first place, after 1911 a broad movement of Turkish ethno-nationalism (or Turkism) among educated Turkish-speaking Muslims arose. They began to understand revolution as systematic social change in nationalist terms. They developed and propagated their new and modern ethno-nationalist thinking in an organization called the Turkish Hearth, an important journal called Turkish Homeland, and through other networks.

Ten years later those Turkists were among the founders of the Republic. They considered nationalism, understood as a secular, partly *völkisch* credo, a modern remedy for the problems of the moribund Ottoman Empire. Unlike the would-be revolutionaries before them, they were ready to anticipate the fall of the multi-ethnic Ottoman Empire on one condition, the awakening or resurrection, as they put it, of the pure, innocent and healthy Turkish nation.

Hence revolutionarism and nationalism have been closely linked in Turkish history since the beginning of the 20th century. On the eve of the First World War, Turkish nationalism, together with a strong faith in contemporary science, took the place of religion and the cosmopolitan Islamic creed among educated youth. The radical nature of Turkish nationalism lies in the fact that as well as being a force for future national cohesion, it had to replace a universalist Ottoman worldview and the Islamic culture which lay behind it.

The Young Turks' Committee of Union and Progress (the CUP), which was at the head of the Empire before and during the First World War, sponsored the Turkist movement, but, still eager to mantain or even to expand the Empire, followed a complex set of Turkist, Islamist and Ottomanist policies. The CUP partly adopted the Turkists' political vision of a nation state in Asia Minor as the Turkist congress in Geneva had outlined it in March 1913.[1] Just before and during the First World War a policy of forcible population displacement made multi-religious Asia Minor a mostly Muslim and Turkish region, a development that was accomplished after the First World War during the so-called National War of Salvation. This time the national movement under Mustafa Kemal Pasha, the later Atatürk, clearly limited its territorial aspiration from the beginning. That corresponded with its military possibilities after the Ottoman defeat in the First World War, and was in perfect accordance with the Turkist vision in Geneva six years earlier.

To sum up, we see three stages of national revolution in the first three decades of the 20th century. First, there was a takeover by young patriotic Muslim Ottomans, officials and officers, as was the case during the so-called Young Turk Revolution in 1908. Second, after 1911, a vision emerged of a total social transformation in ethno-nationalist terms, linked to the vision of Anatolia as the homeland of the Turks. Paradoxical as it may seem, this vision coexisted with the irredentist pan-Turkist dream of a union with the Turkic people in the Caucasus and Central Asia – a dream, we know, that motivated Enver's fatal military campaign against Russia in 1914/15. The third stage was the battle for, and construction of, the Turkish nation-state in the interwar period, called by the Kemalists the "Turkish Revolution" and presented and taught under this title throughout the 20th century. The history of this revolution, the War of Salvation included, has in its Kemalist version formed the sacred core of Turkish nationalist articulation since the 1920s.

The Kemalist revolution exhibits strong personal and ideological continuity with the previous revolutionary movements and their protagonists. Its deep impact on Turkey and the ongoing severe problems with the historiography of the nation-state's founding period (specifically from 1913 to 1938), have to do with this linkage. This also explains why the makers of the Republic identified with the anti-Christian CUP policies in Anatolia of the 1910s, though they claimed to have founded a totally new state in 1923. The Turkish revolution of the interwar period, however, built upon the demographic facts that had been created in the decade before and were set out and recognized in diplomatic terms in the Treaty of Lausanne in 1923. Mustafa Kemal himself declared the same year to Muslims in Adana: "Armenians have no rights at all in this prosperous country. The country is yours, the country belongs to the Turks. In history this country was Turkish, therefore it is Turkish and will remain Turkish for ever. The country has finally been returned to its rightful owners. The Armenians and the others have no rights at all here. These fertile regions are the country of the real Turks."[2]

After 1923, the Kemalist single-party regime imposed far-reaching reforms. Its declared goal was to make the new Turkey a respected nation state on the same level of civilization as those in Europe. The way the founding fathers attempted to do this in reality fitted into the context of the time: forcible social technology, Social Darwinism, undemocratic elitist decision making, *völkisch* nationalism, an anti-liberal stance, and a cult of leaders. Like other European countries Turkey must fathom and recognize these important shadows in its own history, if it really wants to take leave of the spirit of those times.

The contrast between the cures of the interwar period and today's prescriptions for the road to Europe is sharp: here we see the pragmatic implementation of a culture of law in a pluralist framework, closely controlled by international EU commissions; there national sovereignty was affirming itself proudly against an agonizing imperialist post-First World War Europe, and particularly against all those in Asia Minor who were not able or did not want to convert to the enthusiastic, exclusivist belief in Turkishness.

Nevertheless a direct link exists between then and now: the wish to be secular and the wish to be European. There is no clearer sign of this than the centrepiece of the Turkish revolution, the Swiss Civil Code, considered in Europe at the time as the most progressive law, and introduced in 1926 in the young Turkish Republic. But the act and actor of this introduction again were ambivalent; Dr Mahmut Esat Bozkurt, the minister of justice, believed coercion and violence to be an appropriate means of implementing legal progress. The biographical record of this important politician and theorist of Kemalism shows strong anti-Christian and later on anti-Kurdish resentment. Almost naturally, in the 1930s he sympathized with Adolf Hitler.

Apart from the case of Bozkurt, the construction of the new state was highly ambivalent. Article 88 of the 1924 Constitution defined all citizens as Turks, irrespective of their ethno-religious affiliation. Administrative practice and social reality, however, fell far short of this civic understanding, largely favouring an ethno-religious Turco-Sunni and in the 1930s a strongly völkisch understanding of Turkish identity. The Law on Settlement of 1934, for example, which is still in force, limits the right of immigration and naturalization to people "of Turkish descent and culture".[3]

Even though Hitler called himself, like Mussolini, Atatürk's student,[4] Kemalism differs from fascism and Nazism. This is evident in the prudent managment of foreign affairs by Atatürk and his successor Ismet Inönü. It was symbolic that Atatürk appeared in public as a well-dressed British gentleman, instead of a uniformed chief,[5] and similarly there are differences in the form and direction of the respective revolutionary projects. Nevertheless strongly anti-democratic, anti-liberal features were common to all of them. Despite the transition to a multi-party system, no fundamental break took place after 1945, and no attempt to come to terms with the weighty historical heritage of the nation-state's founding period (1913-38) succeeded.

Contrary to western Europe after the Second World War which, with transatlantic help, bade farewell to the previous period of war, revolution and genocide while beginning its common construction, Turkey never got the opportunity to distance itself expressly and officially from its own national myths – perhaps understandably. One needs a reliable, constructive perspective for the future, if one wants to overcome traumas, inflicted or suffered, in one's own history. A purely anti-Kemalist Islamist, Kurdish nationalist or generally anti-Turkish about-turn in the writing of history did not and does not do the job.

Together with most authors of this volume, I believe that there is now a better opportunity to come to terms with Turkish national history than ever before. It is time to say a last good-bye to the Turkish nationalism which is rooted in the inter-war period – although this does not hold good for a couple of its declared, but unattained, goals: equality, democracy, and a modern secular state under the rule of law. The last good-bye concerns the underlying national identity, *Türklük* or "Turkishness", based (among the Young Turks) on Muslim Turkish identity and (for Atatürk and many Kemalists) on an anthropological, ethno-racial identity. If the ethnically and religiously neutral *Türkiyelilik* ("being from Turkey") is not given pride of place as a cornerstone of Republican identity, as a commission has recently proposed, modern Turkey's problematic ambivalence can hardly be overcome. The Report on Human Rights of the government's Commission for Minorities and Cultural Rights[6] was presented in autumn 2004; it raised hot debates and met much opposition in Turkey, thus showing that the road towards a post-ethno-national identity is still a long one. Even though with sometimes wildly varying interpretations, the experience of history and the political imprint of the founding fathers remained an untouchable cornerstone throughout the 20th century in Turkey. Everyone claimed the "biblical corpus" of Turkish nationalism: all the parliamentary parties after the establishment of the multi-party system in 1946 as well as the young revolutionist Deniz Gezmiş (the figurehead of the young leftists after 1968), the authorities who hanged him in 1972, and the speakers of minorities as different as the Alevis and the Jews. Rhetorically at least, they all subscribed to the War of Salvation; to the ideals of the Turkish revolution; to Atatürk as the immortal leader and world history's great revolutionary; and many of them even to Atatürk's highly Turco-centric history of civilizations, the so-called Turkish History thesis.

The corpus of nationalist references lacked thorough critics of its historical value, and it could be used or misused in all kinds of ways. No wonder that despite important attempts at indoctrination, it did not help establish national coherence and stability, as became evident in the second half of the 20th century. The party leaders often used an unprincipled populist nationalism to serve their electoral campaigns and day-to-day politics. Many of them had recourse to Islam or Islamism for the same purpose. Despite its evident contradiction with the Kemalist legacy, a Turkish-Islamic synthesis was established that determined the public space in the last third of the century. This resulted in obligatory Sunni Muslim education at school after the military coup of September 1980.

All these adaptations could not manage to make Turkish nationalism a sufficiently integrative force. Its historical record in the founding period was too anti-liberal, too exclusive. When, after the middle of the 20th century, rural youth began to attend school, they realized their previous exclusion und became politicized. The idolization of Turkishness and its leaders provoked the non-Turkish citizens, particularly the Kurds; privileges for the Sunnis entailed discrimination against other confessions, particularly the Alevis. The social cleavage between those who suffered under the country's permanent crisis and those who turned the same crisis into a profitable affair contradicted republican values fundamentally. The army, though called the guardian of the Kemalist revolution and highly respected for that, appeared increasingly to many as an anti-democratic caste that was particularly privileged because of its geostrategical importance within NATO.

In the 1970s, Turkey was on the brink of a general civil war. At high human and social costs, the military coup of 12 september 1980 recreated some stability. But still the army and the political class did not call into question the ethno-national philosophy of their state. The simple word "Kurd" remained a taboo in the media and the public sphere, until the anti-Kurdish massacres in Northern Iraq and the subsequent mass flight into Turkey made it internationally impossible to continue this course after 1988. But the timid liberalization in the media was not enough to stop the ongoing war between the state and a Kurdish guerilla force whose leaders were sometimes denigrated as Armenians. Turkish nationalism, including its phobias from after the First World War, was greatly reinvigorated in the context of the clash with the Kurds and the end of the Cold War. Even non-militant Kurdish intellectuals were accused of planning to divide up Turkey, working hand-in-glove with the enemy camp in Europe.

Once more the resurgence of the old ghosts of Turkey's founding period could be observed. Turkey reacted with coercion and violence. In the war with unscrupulous guerilla fighters, the security forces systematically depopulated thousands of villages and collaborated with Mafia-like networks and Islamist killers. In reality Turkey was quite helpless. Its inhabitants, above all in the east, suffered very much. The political class failed to offer any perspective which would lead to the abandonment of ethno-nationalist vision of society and centralist visions of the state which were no longer viable.

It is true that Turkey was seeking to be a candidate to the Union for four decades. Hence the EU, which was concerned by massive immigration from Turkey, was asked to share responsibility for the affairs of a country that was knocking at its doors. But the EU was not ready to do this. The USA for its part waas content with the functioning of the strategic partnership. It only began to worry about Turkey seriously when, in 2003, it refused to participate in the military campaign against Iraq.

Against the background of the 1990s, we can speak today of signs of a silent liberal revolution or post-national transformation in Turkey. Why has this come about after the nationalist outbursts and the dismal record on human rights in the 1980s and 1990s? Several factors have contributed to a fundamental change: among them the disillusionment of a growing civil society over the political system that since the proclamation of the nation state has never achieved three important goals: economic welfare, political liberties, and human rights.

At the end of 1999, the EU's decision to accept Turkey as a candidate to join the Union was a high level affirmation of the new perspective long longed-for in a fragmented Anatolian society. This opened the way for pragmatic and innovative solutions to many chronic problems related to Turkish nationalism in the 20th century. With Ebru Bulut (in her chapter on popular nationalism in this volume), one can consider the deep economic crisis of 2001 as the point when Turkish nationalism, seen as the "syntax" of the political system, burnt out. As they had already done during the catastrophic earthquake in 1999, the nation and its representatives appeared weak and dependant on the West. All this led to the fundamental reconfiguration of the political field in the elections of 2002, from which the Justice and Development Party (AKP), led by Recep Tayip Erdogan, emerged as the great victor. All the other traditional parties that had dominated the field since the 1950s were losers, i.e. no longer represented in parliament, except for the Republican Popular Party (CHP).

Turkey today is living through a period of transition which is important not only for the country but also for Europe and the Middle East. Concomitant with the process of emancipation from a dominant nationalism, there are not only political and economical but also enormous historiographical challenges. These should be taken seriously – and not merely among historians – if Turkey's silent revolution is to be successful in the long term.

There is a further challenge. We in Europe and elsewhere are required, not just as scholars, to think through modern history in a markedly interactive, trans-national perspective. For Europe, such a perspective should include the neighbouring country Turkey, with its Ottoman background, much more than our university ivory towers and textbooks have done in the past.[7]

This book

This book investigates the new perspectives of present-day Turkey. Its title suggests an emancipation from ethno-nationalism for the sake of liberal and human rights. Emancipation in this sense requires much political und legal action but also gruelling intellectual and historiographical work. The authors of this book seek to contribute to this work by making Turkish nationalism the subject of sophisticated scholarly consideration and respectful criticism, but decidedly not of fascination. Fascination has been present too long, first in the admiring perception of Turkish nationalism in interwar Germany (due to shared nationalist and revisionist sympathies), and later – partly geo-strategically motivated – in British and American Turkish studies that praised the "modern rise" of an anti-Russian, pro-Western modern Turkish nation state, a NATO member since 1952.

The book has five parts that chronologically and thematically cover about a hundred years from the founding period of Turkish nationalism, at the beginning of the 20th century, to today's post-nationalist challenges in relation to the EU reforms, historiography and collective self-understanding.

Part I deals with the founding period and its enduring ideological weight. Mehmed S. Hanioğlu articulates the groundbreaking thesis that, several years before the Young Turk Revolution of 1908 and the Turkist Movement of the 1910s, Turkism was already the driving force of the members of the Central Committee of the Young Turks' revolutionary Committee of Union and Progess. His text is an excellent historical introduction in the origins of Turkish nationalism.

In my biographical approach of Mahmut Esat Bozkurt, I (Hans-Lukas Kieser) focus on Turkist continuities from late Ottoman to early Republican times. I insist upon the ideological force Turkism possessed for the generation born during the Ottoman *fin de siècle*, and its force of "salvation" providing emancipation from the Islamic Imperial thought that had entered a state of deep crisis in the 19th century. My study points out the profound ambivalence of the modernist project related to Turkism, including Kemalism, since it oscillated between an Occidentalism regarded as universal, and a pseudo-scientific *völkisch* enthusiasm that excluded the ethno-religious Other, if he or she did not or could not convert to the "Turkish ideal".

Hamit Bozarslan in his chapter distinguishes three stages of Kemalism: first the Kemalist movement during the War of Independence as a kind of offspring of the Committee of Union and Progress that "cleansed" "its" Anatolian territory from its Christian "enemies"; second the revolutionary process of the 1920s (after 1923), focused on the personality of Mustafa Kemal, but without a codified ideology; and third, in the 1930s, Kemalism as an elaborated ideology of nationalist revolution, giving the state the right to exert absolute control over society. Kemalism represented "a thoroughly successful experience of integration into Europe, but into a profoundly anti-democratic and anti-liberal

Europe", Bozarslan writes. He concludes by asking whether "Turkey will be able to bid farewell to yesterday's Europe, as the condition of her integration into Europe, or if she will preserve the Kemalist legacy as the essence of her own conception of Europe."

Part II focusses on what happened to the ethno-religious Other under Turkish nationalism. The Armenian Genocide or the coercive Greek-Turkish population exchange are well-known events in the West, but were only the tip of an iceberg that consisted of massive ethno-religious violence, coercion and discrimination during and beyond the Republic's founding period. Based on recently released Ottoman state documents, Fuat Dündar summarizes the CUP's extensive settlement policies during the First World War that also concerned non-Turkish Muslim groups, among them the Kurds.

With special regard to the Jews, Rifat Bali surveys the politics of Turkification during the single party period (1923-50). Turkification affected the non-Turkish Muslims in the first place, whereas the Republic remained ambivalent where non-Muslims – those who remained after the massacres and expulsion before 1923 – were concerned, because it never accepted them as fully equal citizens. Thus despite the pressure and various measures of Turkification, Turkifying the non-Muslims in the sense of integrating them into an egalitarian and secular Turkish nation failed.

This was partly true also for the *dönme*, Jews, mostly from Saloniki, who converted to Sunni Islam in the 17th century. Even if the *dönme* were far better placed than Christians or Jews to assimilate into Turkish society and have access to important posts, dönme identity was "difficult to resolve so long as the question of race surfaced and conceptions of race fed into understandings of the nation", as Marc Baer writes in his chapter. Thus the totally discriminatory implementation of the Capital Tax levy promulgated in 1942 touched Christian, Jewish *and dönme* citizens. Between 1938 and 1945, Turkey deprived several thousand of its Jewish nationals living abroad of their citizenship, thus leaving them at risk of persecution and annihilation, as Corinna Görgü shows. Her study investigates the early Republican policies of naturalization and denaturalization aimed to create an ethnically homogeneous population. This too ist the context of Berna Pekesen's chapter on the Armenian exodus from Alexandretta in the 1930s.

Despite the profound ambivalence of Turkish nationalism towards non-Sunnis or non-Turks, nationalism was and remains, until very recently, the only legitimizing framework within which to make claims in Turkey, particularly for members of non-Sunni groups. They have often proclaimed themselves to be intensely Kemalist citizens as a talisman against the unitary dogma of the Republic, fearing otherwise to be seen as illegitimate Others with particularist claims. This is particularly true until today for the important group of Alevis (non-Sunni Muslims), as Elise Massicard shows in her paper. There is some hope that Turkey's road towards the EU will lead to the recognition of the

Republic's interior diversity surmounting the constant fear of Turkey falling apart.

Part III addresses the post-nationalist historiographical challenge facing today's Turkey: how to come to terms with a complex past while leaving behind ready-made nationalist explanations? These were – partly comprehensible – "products" that made advances possible despite all the shadows. But they served largely to reshape or suppress the memory of traumas inflicted in the nation-state's founding period. Moreover, as Fatma Müge Göcek makes clear in her chapter, the Turkish historical narrative failed to problematize the ideology of nationalism because it becomes totally integrated into it. The same nationalist narrative caused the actions of groups now seen as Others to disappear or be depreciated, including retrospectively their actions in Ottoman times. Göcek proposes an alternative post-nationalist historiographic periodization of Ottoman and Turkish history. According to this periodization, the nationalist period starts with the 1902 Congress of the Ottoman opposition parties in Paris, and not, as does the Turkish master-narrative inaugurated by Mustafa Kemal, with the War of Independence in 1919. 1902 leads us back to a multicultural Ottoman order, but also to the years when the CUP's Central Committee took a strongly Turkist turn. A post-nationalist Turkish historiography thus has to analyse the two decades before 1923, taking a critical stance towards deeply-rooted nationalist prejudices, instead of obfuscating these "most virulent formative stages of Turkish nationalism". For Göcek, a new era toward a post-nationalist period in terms of Muslim-minority relations starts in 1982 with the beginning neo-liberalization under president Turgut Özal.

One very particular formative stage was the slaughter of the Anatolian Armenians during the First World War, a *pièce de résistance* and insuperable obstacle for a narrow nationalist historiography, because, for apologetical reasons, it suppresses the perspective of the victims. Insofar as historiography is an activity dealing with truth(s), it has to take on responsibility. Beyond legal issues, Raymond Kévorkian addresses the question of how to deal with the historical responsibility for the Armenian Genocide. Analysing some court-martials in Istanbul in 1919-20, he points out the problem of the representatives of a society used to understand itself as Sunni Muslims, as the *millet-i hakime* or dominant Ottoman class, and therefore not responsible to anyone but themselves. Instead of stubborn apologetics for key instigators of mass violence like Talat or Ismail Enver, Kévorkian asks the actors of a future Turkish national historiography to bring out the role of Turkish people with civic courage who acted against the anti-Armenian measures of the régime, like Vehib Pasha, Hasan Mazhar and other soldiers or civil servants.

Part IV deals with "Turkey in motion", with the "transformations and post-national challenges" of today's Turkey, particularly with the politics and symbols of the Justice and Development Party (AKP), in power since 2002. Ebru Bulut shows in her chapter how the "traditional" political system was able to

reproduce itself again (for the last time?) in the 1990s, and how it was supported by a revival of popular nationalism against the background of the war in the
Kurdish provinces. Nationalist cohesion collapsed after 1999, with the economic crisis of 2001 playing an important role and thus opening the way for
the reconfiguration of the political landscape in 2002. Günter Seufert reviews
the AKP's religious politics: Does the AKP government still use religion as a
means of nation building, as the "secularist" Republic of Turkey always did
through the Directorate of Religious Affairs (founded in 1924, when the
Caliphate was abolished)? Or are there signs of religion becoming a free factor
of civil society in Turkey? The fundamental problem is, as Seufert states with
reference to the theologian Mehmed S. Aydın, that in Turkey "the omnipresence of debates about religion goes hand in hand with the absence of religion
as a moral language of society", and hence the religions' silence on vital issues
(in marked contrast to the Churches' behaviour in the West). The AKP gov-
ernement itself is not (yet) ready for fundamental reforms of its Kemalist – and
partly Ottoman – heritage of politically controlled religion. It seems to be still
far from conceiving a fundamental reform, if not abolition, of the Directorate
of Religious Affairs (a state institution financed by the taxes of all Turkish citizens, but responsible, until now, exclusively for promoting a Sunni version of
Islam close to the state). Seufert nevertheless believes that a new, more liberal
way of approaching religion, postulated by personalities like Hüseyin Hatemi
from Istanbul University's Law Faculty, or particularly in the form of a "new
Islamic theology", by Mehmed S. Aydın (now Minister of State in charge of
the Directorate of Religious Affairs), "is (…) preparing state and society for
reforms that may become inevitable in the years to come." In her chapter on
"post-nationalist semiotics", Béatrice Hendrich interprets the AKP's emblem,
a shining bulb underneath the acronym "Ak Parti" ("ak" meaning white,
clean). For her, the emblem is "deliberately polysemic and strives to integrate in
one message Islamic tradition, societal reform, technical and cultural progress
and the orientation towards a democratic Europe, instead of making Turkish
nation-building its only goal."

The Kurdish conflict is the real acid test for Turkey's reformist road towards
an open society, as Gülistan Gürbey points out in her chapter. Like all the
authors of this volume, Gürbey judges Turkey's EU perspective positively,
appreciating the steps already taken towards reform. These steps, which can
hardly be reversed, are resulting in a perceptible improvement of the atmosphere even for Kurds in Turkey; most important is the lifting of the state of
emergency in the south-east, so frequently imposed during the 20th century. But
as with the reforms concerning the non-Muslim minorities, the legal framework gives the authorities much leeway for restrictive application in the field
of cultural rights. Gürbey pleads for the EU to make clear what precisely it
understands as minimum standards according to the Copenhagen criteria and
how Turkey can work for a better implementation of the central criterion of

accession, "respect and protection of minorities". The problem of the internally displaced persons, mostly Kurds from the eastern provinces, is still unre-
solved; the solid, civic, pluralist integration of that part of Asia Minor, which
has a particularly bloody historical record since the Armenian massacres, still
has to be carried out. The peaceful solution of the Kurdish conflict is a core
challenge for Turkey, indeed an acid test for its emancipation from a burden-
some ethno-nationalist heritage.

The subject of Part V again is "Turkey in movement", particularly with
regard to its EU perspective. Eugen Krieger traces the story of Turkey's first
steps toward the then European Economic Community (EEC) around 1960.
Joseph Luns, president of the EEC, optimistically declared in 1963 that the
Treaty of Association with Ankara testified "to the profound changes taking
place on our continent". Krieger points out that major motivations for the
Treaty of Association with Ankara in 1963 were security concerns in the context
of the Cold War and the pressure of the USA. The enormous financial aid
repeatedly given in this connection by the West did not promote a development of democracy, but sustained the political and military élites' precarious
management of the country, marked by social unrest, economic crisis, mass
migration and military putsches.

A factor important for the process leading to the reconfiguration of the
political landscape in 2002 was the EU's decision in 1999 to accept Turkey as
a candidate for membership of the Union. Gabriel Goltz examines the intensive reform process that Turkey has undergone since 2002 with regard to the
non-Muslim minorities. He argues that a general lessening of the state's tight
control over the social sphere, as a result of the EU process, has probably
proved to have more positive effects for the non-Muslim communities, contributing to an egalitarian plural society in Turkey, than the tool of minority
rights set out in the Lausanne Treaty of 1923, but largely ignored in the legal
reality of the Republic for the last eighty years and moreover limited to certain
recognized Christian and Jewish groups. Analyzing the interconnection
between national identity, asylum and immigration politics, Kemal Kirişçi discerns the EU as a vehicle of post-nationalist transformation in Turkey. In
recent asylum and immigration policies there are, Kirişçi argues, clear elements
of "post-nationalization" compared with the previous ones rooted in the
Kemalist interwar-period. In these two areas, "Turkish officials are now much
more willing to cooperate with Turkish and foreign non-governmental organizations, western governments, the European Commission and other international organizations, such as the UNHCR in particular." But with regard to
national identity and immigration, the challenge for Turkey – like Israel – to
revise its ethno-religiously-centred approach, replacing it with one that might
be more inspired by civics, is far from being accomplished, Kirişçi concludes.

Basel, June 2005

PART I

TURKISH NATIONALISM:
THE IDEOLOGICAL WEIGHT
OF THE FOUNDING PERIOD (1905-1938)

Chapter 1
Turkism and the Young Turks, 1889-1908

M. Şükrü Hanioğlu

The dominant explanation of the emergence of Turkish nationalism holds that it was a relatively late development, the origins of which lie in the Balkan Wars of 1912-13. According to this thesis, war in the Balkans exposed the bankruptcy of the worn-out ideology of Ottomanism, leading to an abrupt surge in nationalist sentiment among Ottoman intellectuals of Turkish decent. Despite numerous errors in theory and fact, this thesis has proved remarkably resilient. David Kushner's path-breaking study of 1977 on the rise of Turkish nationalism between 1876 and 1908 should have been sufficient to finish off the thesis once and for all, but instead left only an insignificant dent in its armour.[1]

Twenty years later a popular historian of modern Turkey and the late Ottoman Empire could still maintain that "the vocabulary of nationalism scarcely existed in the Turkish [...] language of the [late Hamidian] period" and that the term *millet* in the pre-1908 Young Turk context still referred to "religious communities."[2]

An important reason for the persistence of such easily refutable claims[3] is their affinity to Turkish official ideology in the early years of the republic. Ideology entered scholarship in the 1920's and '30s through the pens of Turkish historians who fully accepted Republican verdicts on late Ottoman history. They reconstructed nationalist history in such a way as to ignore the Hamidian period entirely. Focusing instead on the Second Constitutional Period between 1908 and 1918, they drew a straight line back from the new ideology formulated by the founding fathers of the Turkish republic to its alleged origins under the rule of Ottoman Committee of Union and Progress (hereafter CUP).[4]

From a theoretical perspective, this approach has three major flaws. First, it treats nationalism as a spontaneous ideological and political phenomenon, thereby ignoring precursor, proto-nationalist movements and ideologies that prepare the ground for the emergence of nationalism. An examination of the official and the underground opposition press under Abdülhamid II leaves no doubt that a Turkist movement did emerge during the pre-revolutionary period – although it strove to stay within the bounds of Ottomanism by remoulding it. Second, the prevailing explanation approaches the concepts of

Ottomanism and Turkism in a distinctly essentialist manner. As a consequence, it imagines a false competition between two discrete, monolithic, and unchanging ideologies: Ottomanism on the one hand and Turkism (or Turkish nationalism) on the other. In reality, however, these concepts possessed fluid, blurred boundaries even after the Balkan Wars. Moreover, Turkism often appeared as a new interpretation of Ottomanism rather than a clear-cut break with it; usually, this meant attributing a centrifugal role to the Turkish ethnic group within the Ottoman whole. Third, due to its retrospective approach to history, the dominant thesis perceives a teleological dissolution of Ottomanism into Turkish and other Ottoman nationalisms. But what seems inevitable in retrospect was not so at the time.

In this short article, I analyse the attitude of the Young Turks (and particularly the CUP) towards Turkism, trace its transformation into a nascent nationalist movement before the Young Turk Revolution of 1908, and demonstrate the significance of Turkism in the *Weltanschauung* of the CUP. The discussion focuses on elite perceptions of identity. There are two major reasons for this. For one, the debates recorded in historical sources took place largely between the literate few: intellectuals and political elites. Secondly, although the educated elite amounted to a small fraction of the population of the empire and their published journals were read only by the literate few, they stood at the forefront of the dramatic changes that took place in late Ottoman society. They exerted an influence on the shape of events that far outweighed the relative proportion of the elite in the population. Nevertheless, it is important to bear in mind that the overwhelming majority of the Ottoman populace, caught up in their local identities and concerns, remained largely unmoved by the grand ideals of Ottomanism, Turkism or Pan-Islamism.

The Evolution of Ottomanism as a Concept from the Tanzimat to the Young Turks

Several major factors compelled the Ottoman state to adapt its official ideology in the 19th century: the need to confront European modernity, the challenge of nationalist movements, the necessity of asserting central control over an enormous and fractious empire, and the desire to join the European Concert. The key change involved a redefinition of the concept of equality. The Islamic conception of respect for the rights of the unequal dhimmī was gradually replaced by a notion of equality derived from the French Déclaration des Droits de l'homme et du Citoyen. As Mahmud II is claimed to have said: "Je ne veux reconnaître désormais les musulmans qu'à la mosquée, les chrétiens qu'à l'église et les juifs qu'à la synagogue."[5] The Tanzimat statesmen strove to institutionalise this approach by producing universally applicable legal codes. The implications of legal equality for a social order defined by religion were revolutionary. The new emphasis on an Ottoman identity common to all citizens of the empire crowded out, at least in theory, the hitherto dominant sectarian identities. The "de-religionization" of official ideology and redefinition of a secular homo Ottomanicus was an extraordinarily difficult undertaking. Not only did Muslim resentment swell after 1856 (and with it support for the maintenance of Islam as a pillar of the state-caliphate), nationalism emerged as a powerful competitor to both the religious and the Ottoman orientations within all Ottoman communities. As nationalist separatism increasingly threatened to tear apart the multi-national empire, the remedy of equality between Muslims and non-Muslims (however much desired by the latter) no longer appeared adequate.

The attempts of the Tanzimat to reform the religious communities from within tipped the internal balance of power in favour of new laymen at the expense of the old clerical establishments. Even in the small Jewish community, lacking in clerical hierarchy, the reform proved ultimately unsuccessful when a revival of rabbinical influence produced a bitter clash between the two elements.[6]

In the Greek Orthodox Patriarchate the results were still more damaging, as non-Greek ethnic community leaders launched a struggle for their own independent churches. The influence of laymen within the various communities also gave rise to the development of new educational curricula that tended to foster nationalism. Thus a reform designed to weaken clerical communitarianism and enhance equality between communities ended up cementing a bond between ethnicity and religion, thereby reinforcing the very centrifugal ethno-nationalist forces it was meant to suppress.

Clearly, Ottomanism founded upon the notion of equality among religious communities was no panacea for the internal strife afflicting the Ottoman realm. In order to respond to the challenge of ethnic separatism, during the second half of the Tanzimat era Ottomanism was refashioned as an ideology promoting equality among Ottoman ethnic groups. However, just as the old Ottomanism never succeeded in erasing the traditional dominance of the Muslim *millet*, so too the new Ottomanism could not escape the preponderance of influence exercised by the Turkish element.

The intrusive demand of the imperial centre for a wholesale identity shift from ethnic and religious to supranational and secular, coupled with the push for rapid centralisation of the empire, could not fail to arouse the suspicion amongst non-Turkish ethnic groups that behind the stated goal of "Ottomanism" lay a more sinister aim of Turkification – a process ultimately aiming at suppressing their identities and privileges. Such suspicions were heightened by the increasing employment of Turkish symbols by the imperial centre. İsmail Kemal Bey (Ismail Qemali), a loyal servant of the leaders of the Tanzimat (who, as he put it, "would have done honour to any country in the world") admitted that the reforms, coupled with the harsh measures adopted against recalcitrant communities, "concealed the perpetual desire of the

Turkish chauvinists to bring about the unification of all the races of the empire."[7]

It was no coincidence that during the last decade of the Tanzimat, the intellectuals known as the Young Ottomans, who sought to reconcile Islamic principles with European constitutionalism, in the final analysis advocated a version of Ottomanism grounded in the concept of citizenship and guaranteed by a constitution. Ottomanism, as the Young Ottomans (as well as the future architect of the Ottoman constitution, Ahmed Şefik Midhat Pasha) envisioned it, placed the individual's identity as a citizen of the empire above all other affiliations. Such an interpretation, of course, also tended to reinforce the secular character of Ottomanism.

In fact, many non-Turkish proponents of Ottomanism demanded that government positions be open to all Ottomans. As the organ of the Bulgarian Ottomanists put it: "As long as a career in the state bureaucracy continues to be a birthright of sorts for the Muslims, as long as Christians are excluded from high government office and are barred from lower-level positions in all but rare circumstances, there is no reason whatsoever to hope that non-Muslims will want to study the [Ottoman] Turkish language to any great depth [...] We do not believe it will be possible for all citizens of the [Ottoman] empire to think of themselves as members of the same family until they all have equal access to government service."[8]

Some Jews expressed similar sentiments in reaction to the government's decision not to appoint a Jewish member to the new council of state, arguing that "wherever Israelites are settled they are invariably loyal and useful members of the community, especially in those countries where their rights are fully admitted as citizens."[9]

Thus demands for rights of a secular character, such as equal opportunity employment in the bureaucracy, supplanted customary religious demands (e.g., the call for full implementation of religious equality promised in 1856).

The promulgation of the Ottoman constitution, and the subsequent convocation of a parliament, marked the high point of what might be termed "new Ottomanism". The timing of the announcement – at the height of an international crisis and under heavy European pressure to grant privileges to the empire's Christian communities – was, of course, no coincidence. Indeed, many Ottoman statesmen and intellectuals had come to view Ottomanism (founded upon citizenship) as a powerful tool to resist European demands for privileges for the non-Muslim communities of the empire.[10] If legal distinctions between the religious communities were abolished, so the argument went, the logic behind European demands for equality would cave in. In the event, the implementation of new Ottomanism had to be postponed indefinitely, due to the prorogation of the parliament in February 1878, but at the time it was embraced by some intellectuals as a silver bullet with which to kill off separatism once and for all.

The régime of Abdülhamid II redefined Ottomanism once again, imbuing it with Islamic characteristics. Fearing that a strengthening of the common denominator of citizenship would lead to dangerous demands for representation and would ultimately accelerate separatist processes,[11] the régime reintroduced a determining role for Islam in imperial identity. The return to Islam was also warranted by the demographic changes imposed by successive losses of Christian-populated territories in the wars of the 19th century, and particularly in the Russo-Ottoman war of 1877-78. By bringing religion back centre-stage, the régime reversed the trend towards the secularization of identity set in motion by the Tanzimat statesman. Moreover, in Hamidian Ottomanism, the boundaries between religious, ethnic, and supranational identities were deliberately blurred. The sultan saw his main mission as protection of the Caliphate; to fulfil it he sought to forge Pan-Islamism into a proto-nationalist force, one with which he could hold the Muslim elements of the empire together. Undoubtedly, Hamidian Ottomanism was most attractive to non-Turkish Muslims, such as Albanians, Arabs, and Kurds for whom it provided a real alternative to nationalist orientations. Islamic Ottomanism was naturally least attractive to non-Muslim ethnic groups, whom in practice it threatened with a diminution of status, theoretical legal rights notwithstanding.

The spread of Turkism during this period did not yet exert a marked influence on official ideology. But it was nourished by frustration with official policy. One of the distinguishing marks of the Hamidian régime was the prominence of Muslim Albanians, Arabs, and Kurds in the highest positions of the bureaucracy and court. This policy fuelled the surreptitious growth of Turkist sentiments. Beneath the surface of Hamidian censorship, resentment at the preferential treatment of non-Turkish Muslims – and the denial of just dues to Turks – was simmering. This was almost imperceptible at the time; Abdülhamid II did not tolerate any open discussion of identity. His successors, however, called him to task for spoiling individual Albanians, Arabs, and Kurds, and granting favours to the Muslim components of these communities. The surge of Turkist sentiment under Abdülhamid II reinforced the deleterious impact of the sultan's own Pan-Islamic rhetoric on the bond between citizenship and identity.

Since both ideologies reached beyond the boundaries of the empire to non-citizen constituents, they could not fail to undermine the notion of Ottoman citizenship.

The Young Turks between Ottomanism and Turkism

The origins of the Young Turk movement can be traced back to the founding of the Ottoman Union Society (later renamed the Ottoman Committee of Union and Progress) at the Royal Medical Academy in 1889. Oddly enough, not one of the four founders was of Turkish descent. They did, however, represent a diverse cross-section of the other major Muslim communities of the empire – Albanians, Circassians, and Kurds. Consequently, in its early days the

Committee – as evident from its name – leaned towards the régime's new Ottomanism, which promoted union among Muslim Ottomans. Thus, it was strange but true that the sultan's non-Turkish Muslim opponents (and his supporters within those communities) shared with him a common vision of the future of the state. As summarized by İshak Sükûtî, one of the original founders of the CUP, Albanians and Kurds, among others, must unite with the Turks against the West, for they shared a common goal: to defeat European schemes aimed at detaching their lands from the common fatherland in the interests of Balkan and Anatolian Christians.[12] Indeed, the first overt action of the CUP in 1895 took place in response to an Armenian political demonstration.[13] Key branches of the organisation drafted memoranda advocating the exclusion of Christians from the organisation because of the danger that they might "turn the committee into a Christian committee," "serve as an instrument of European intrigues," "prevent the committee from implementing its policies vis-à-vis Christian [Ottoman] communities," and "prevent the committee from taking the Muslims onto the path of progress."[14] Other branches that opposed an overtly exclusionist policy proposed to withhold secret identity numbers from Christian members, thereby denying them access to secret correspondence while preserving the illusion of inclusion.[15] If the Young Turks were strongly influenced by the official ideology they were in principle opposing, their *Weltanschauung* was similarly influenced by the more surreptitious groundswell of Turkism. The increasing centrality of Turkish nationalist ideas in the Young Turk world view was, contrary to popular conception, a gradual, inconsistent process that was subject to numerous influences.

The major vehicle for the introduction of Turkish nationalist ideas was the penetration of the organisation by a growing body of members of Turkish extraction, who believed in the primacy of the Turks within the empire. The following anecdote gives some indication of their sentiments. One of the prospective leaders of a CUP coup d'état scheduled for 1896 later described his plan: "In the event that Abdülhamid had ventured to resist and ordered the Arab and Albanian divisions at the Chamberlain's office to open fire on the national troops, [self-sacrificing] volunteers would easily have assassinated him."[16]

It is significant that even at this early stage, when the CUP was still operating as a coalition of Muslim Ottomans, he reserves the term "national troops" for Turkish divisions and employs somewhat exclusionist language to refer to the Arab and Albanian soldiers. The privileged status accorded to Turks is also evident in the presentation of the official CUP organ as "a Turkish journal."[17] That the second official CUP organ was named *Osmanlı* (Ottoman) – and that the choice of title was strenuously defended at the time – demonstrates that despite a strong inclination to privilege the Turks, the CUP leadership, at least officially, still wished to portray a more inclusive agenda that remained within the boundaries of the official ideology.[18] In this regard, the decision of a number of Young Turk intellectuals to name their journal *Türk* in 1902 should be considered a landmark. Official efforts to the contrary notwithstanding, the growing acceptance of cultural Turkism within the rank and file of the CUP increasingly pulled the organisation as a whole in a Turkist direction, blurring boundaries between Turk and Ottoman at the expense of the other ethnic groups of the empire. As Tunalı Hilmi Bey, a leading CUP member, put it: "Turk and Ottoman [were] the same."[19]

Until 1902, eminent Young Turks and CUP leaders linked Turkish primacy – if they did so at all – to the political principle of majoritarian rule: "in all civilised, and even in uncivilised nations, the right of governance is always in the hands of the people who form a majority. Can Turkey be an exception to this rule?"[20] As the Young Turk movement evolved, the basis of the argument shifted to more racial grounds, as writers began to emphasize the superiority of the Turks over other, especially Muslim, Ottoman ethnic groups. Five major factors prompted this transformation.

The first factor was the evolution of the Young Turk movement. As the movement, which had begun as a free-spirited student organisation in the royal colleges of Istanbul, came under increasing scrutiny by the authorities, it was forced out of the capital to the fringes of the empire and beyond, where it quite naturally came to reflect the prevailing proto-nationalist ideology of the periphery, chafing under prevailing – or pending – European domination. In later phases, especially after 1905, the local perspective of branches in Crete, Cyprus, Bulgaria, Rumania, and the Caucasus deeply influenced the *Weltanschauung* of the central CUP leadership (and subsequently, the Committee of Progress and Union, or CPU, which emerged in late 1905).

The tradesmen and teachers who led the Young Turk movement in these regions imbued it with a distinctively anti-Christian, and by implication pro-Turkish colour since the supranational Ottoman identity did not carry much weight among Muslim minorities in those portions of the Balkans that were already lost to ethnic nation-states or on the verge of being lost. Their correspondence told a powerful tale of cruel oppression at the hands of Bulgarians, Greeks, and others, while their energetic representation on the CPU central committee by Talha Kemalî ensured that their proto-nationalist outlook reached a sympathetic audience within the organisation's leadership. In fact, so powerful were these local influences, that by the time of the revolution in 1908, the CPU had become the representative of the Turkish Diaspora more than it was the representative of Ottoman Turks.

A second cause for the rise of ethnic Turkish nationalism within the Young Turk movement was the new political possibilities opened up by the Russian Revolution of 1905. Many individual Tatar and Azeri intellectuals, such as Yusuf Akçura and Hüseyinzâde Ali (Turan), joined the Young Turk movement early on. But it was only after the Russian Revolution of 1905, and because of the subsequent freedom enjoyed by Turkic groups under later Tsarist rule, that elaborate organisational relations grew up between the CPU and Turkic groups in the Caucasus, Crimea, and Central Asia. The CPU helped these groups publish journals that envisioned a "Turkish nation" whose "head lies at the Chinese Wall and whose legs reach to the Sea of Marmara and the Mediterranean."[21]

In turn, the main Young Turk organisation was affected by pan-Turkic notions. A leading Young Turk wrote in 1906 that "all regions from the Adriatic Sea to the Chinese Sea have a single faith. The people who dwell there (...) belong to the Turkish race (...) If only those who belong to the Turkish race were united, they would be able to establish the most majestic government in the world."[22] Islam, a religion common to almost all Turkic peoples, could cement this ethnic union, but its role would ultimately be secondary. In this regard, Pan-Turkism contrasted with the sultan's Ottomanism, in which Islam formed the indispensable glue. The most important effect of the stress on Turkish ethnicity was to undermine the notion of identity based upon citizenship, the core of Tanzimat Ottomanism. For example, official CPU commentary on Armenian-Tatar strife in the Caucasus underscored the difficulty of choosing sides, as Armenians were "compatriots" and Tatars were "brothers in religion and nationality."[23] The secret correspondence of the CPU leadership, however, leaves no doubt as to where its sympathies lay.[24]

Third, the monumental Japanese victory over Russia in the war of 1904-5 greatly encouraged the spread of popular race theories. Until then, a major cause of hesitation among Young Turk admirers of pseudo-scientific racial theory was European disdain for the Turks as "a race in the lower part of the racial hierarchy."

Yet here were proud men "of the yellow race" who were "obliterating this slander against nature with their progress in their country, and with their cannons and rifles in Manchuria."[25] It is no coincidence that Yusuf Akçura penned his path-breaking series of articles on the future of the empire in the wake of the early Japanese victories.[26] Sketching the alternatives that lay before the Ottoman Empire, he clearly favoured the pursuit of Turkish nationalism "based upon race."[27] At about the same time, many Young Turks called upon the Turks to follow Herbert Spencer's advice to the Japanese, namely to eschew marriage with Europeans so as to preserve their racial purity.[28] Hence, when Young Turk leaders boasted that their country was destined to become the "Japan of the Near East,"[29] they implied something more than the development of industry.

If events in the Balkans, Russia, and the Far East represented distant sources of inspiration and change for the Young Turk leadership, the impact of the resurgence of French nationalism after the humiliation of 1871 was more direct. As leaders of a movement headquartered in Paris, and whose intellectual medium of communication was French, the Young Turks could not fail to be affected by the tide of French nationalism rising around them, and especially by the irredentist calls of L'Action française for revenge and "liberation" of those parts of the fatherland that had fallen under alien rule. The effects of popular nationalist sentiments were amplified through the teachings of French thinkers such as Albert Sorel and Emile Boutmy, who counted many Young Turk intellectuals among their disciples.

The final cause of the "Turkification" of the Young Turk agenda was the rise to positions of prominence of leaders of Turkish descent in the CUP and CPU. Beginning as a paradigmatic manifestation of the sultan's Ottomanist vision of solidarity among the Muslims of the Empire,[30] the organisation gradually came under the domination of ethnic Turks. There were only a few ethnic Turks among the twenty CUP members who led the movement between 1889 and 1896.[31] In late 1896 the central committee of the CUP included Mizancı Mehmed Murad (Daghistani), Çürüksulu Ahmed Bey (Circassian/Turk), Dr Nâzım (Turk), Dr Şerafeddin Mağmumî (Turk), and Dr İshak Sükûtî (Kurd). Muhammad Qadri Pajić (Herzegovinian) and Ahmed Rıza (Turk) directed the affairs of the two semi-independent branches in Cairo and Paris, respectively, and İbrahim Temo [Ibrahim Themo] (Albanian) led the autonomous Balkan organisation.[32] By early 1907 the central committee comprised Ahmed Rıza (Turk), Sami Paşazâde Sezaî (Turk), Captain Hüsrev Sami (Turk), Dr Bahaeddin Şakir (Turk), Dr Nâzım (Turk), Talha Kemalî (Turk), and secretary to the central committee Lieutenant Seyyid Ken'an (Turk). The establishment of Turkish control over the central committee was both a result and a catalyst of the ascendance of Turkist ideas within the organisation as a whole.

Although over time political Turkism gave way to a more racial doctrine, the majoritarian principle, as well as historical claims (based upon the inherited rights of the descendants of the founders of the state who "had come from Transoxania and shed their blood from here to Transoxania"[33]) continued to serve as justifications for granting a guiding role to the Turks. Two competing visions underlay these justifications. On the one hand were those who, drawing upon nineteenth century racial theory, proposed a Turkish *Herrenvolk*; they explained European descriptions of the Turks as a non-white, Asian race – despite the fact that "most Turks [were] racially European" – "as an argument to drive [the Turks] totally out of Europe and to preclude [their] rule over Christian nations there."[34] Others, on the other hand, saw the Turks as a *narod-patron* leading others on the path to progress: "reasonable Arabs [...] admit that the Arabs do not have among them men able to match the Turkish officers and governors, and that the Turks are superior to other Muslims in the arts of war, administration, and law enforcement."[35] Echoes of the pre-Tanzimat rhetoric of Muslim dominance can be heard in both approaches, particularly in the notion of the voluntary acceptance of an elite group as the natural and beneficent leader of the entire community. Dr Bahaeddin Şakir, who oversaw the reorganisation of the CPU in 1905-6, was alluding to the pre-Tanzimat social hierarchy when he wrote that for the children and grandchildren of the Turks, "who had produced a world-conquering state from a tribe," it was "preferable not to live" if the alternative was "to become a subject nation, and a subject nation as Turks and Muslims."[36] Although nineteenth century race theories could provide no legal basis for Turkish leadership, their perceived scientific character could help sanction Turkish superiority. In this respect, the widespread acceptance of scientism in Young Turk circles went hand-in-hand with the embrace of race theory.

Another important tenet of the brand of Turkism that captivated many Young Turks was anti-imperialism. While recklessly committed to the wholesale adoption of Europe's values, its science and its modernism, the CUP/CPU leadership vociferously opposed European pressures on the Ottoman Empire in the context of the Eastern Question. Explaining that Christian fanaticism and Turcophobia lay at the root of Western attitudes towards Turks and the empire, they rode a popular wave of anti-Western sentiment that had been growing in the empire ever since 1856.[37]

It is this anti-imperialist impulse that explains the otherwise perplexing role of the CPU/CUP in the establishment of Pan-Islamist organisations. Seeking allies against European encroachment, the Young Turks could not ignore the potential for harnessing other anti-Western struggles to their cause. Indeed, similar calculations had motivated the sultan's own Pan-Islamist campaign. So scientists and positivists, who envisioned an ideal society virtually cleansed of religion, threw their weight behind their ideological opposites.

While the Turkism embraced by major Young Turk organisations oscillated between the *Herrenvolk* model and that of the *narod-patron*, and both increasingly strained the boundaries of Ottomanism, a new journal appeared that would redefine cultural Turkism and, in the process, break the shackles of Ottomanism once and for all. The journal, named *Türk,* carried contributions by authors with pen names such as Oğuz, Özbek, Tuğrul, Turgud, Kuneralp, Uluğ, and Uygur. It dedicated itself to the defense of "the rights of the Turks"[38] as an ethnic group and, more importantly, as a race, based upon the notion that "the differences between nations are based upon organic principles."[39] It praised "learned" Turkic groups, such as the Azerbaijanis, for comprehending that they were "racially Turkish."[40] Although the journal rarely referred to the old concept of a union of Ottomans, it did not renounce the reality of a poly-ethnic state, as was apparent in a series of articles on the future relationship between the Turks as the central ethnic group and others, such as Armenins and Jews.[41]

Particularly novel was *Türk*'s attitude towards Islam: "Our affection and regard for Islam are complete; however, our century is a century of revolution [...] therefore we cannot make our journal merely a religious journal [...] we should in any event devote our writings to the moral and material progress of the Turkish world. What should we do, how should we work, that the Turks may never remain behind foreigners and Europeans in the struggle for survival?"[42] Upholding the racial bond between Turks, the journal renounced the primacy of Islam as a uniting force. In place of the glorious Islamic tradition and the inherited virtues of Islam, *Türk* posited the unique history of the Turkic peoples, and the superior cultural values that gave them a special propensity for modernism, as the building blocks of Turkish solidarity. Claiming that "the Turk has acquired all his present vices from the East" and that "had he entered Europe instead of the south, and had he settled in the west, like his Hungarian brethren, he would now have outstanding governance, and prosperity,"[43] the journal's publishers clearly sought to drive a wedge between the Turkish national narrative and the Islamic one. Moreover, they made the alleged natural proclivity of the Turks for modernism – a trait lacking in all other groups of the Orient[44] – into a central pillar of Turkism. The editors of *Türk* heaped praise on the Turcoman tribes who had remained true to their "primal national virtues" and without being "purged of their Central Asian customs," such as the independent role of women in society. In such arguments one can already identify the contours of the future republican narrative.[45]

But culture and history were merely the static building blocks of the new Turkish entity. They were not active agents with which to build a nation. The new force that *Türk*'s founders sought to harness in the service of nation-building was science.

As predicted by mid-nineteenth century *Vulgärmaterialismus*, only a society totally governed by science, would be truly modern. As they saw it, the Turk was a *magnas inter oper inops*. Once he comprehended his innate strength, accepted science as his only guide, and exploited his unique suitability to modernism, he would not only arrest the decline of the empire and save it from destruction, but also turn it into a truly geat power and a formidable player on the international stage.[46] This was obviously a very radical approach in the context of the early twentieth century. Its doubtful applicability to the incurable ills of a poly-ethnic empire riven with separatist strife made it a Château en Espagne in the eyes of many intellectuals of the time.

Many believed that the adoption of such illusions as policy would only speed up the dismemberment of the Ottoman Empire. Later scholarship has also accused the CPU/CUP leaders – many of whom, like Yusuf Akçura and Hüseyinzâde Ali (Turan), contributed to *Türk* – of pursuing an unattainable goal.[47] While these criticisms are perfectly sound, they obscure the tremendous ideological power and extraordinary dynamism that the new gospel of Turkism lent to the Young Turk movement as a whole and to the CPU/CUP in particular. It is worth recounting the evolution of Young Turk thought in some detail in order to see why this was so.

The major Young Turk organisations initially promoted a vision of Ottomanism quite similar to the one proposed by the sultan – hardly a promising basis for an opposition movement. There were other aspects of the Young Turk *Weltanschauung*, such as its strong materialist and positivist undertones, that were scarcely appealing to the masses. The rejection of their call by those

who opted to side with the incumbent sultan rather than split hairs over ideological minutiae forced the Young Turks to appeal to the opposition within
their various target communities. Thus, for example, while the Kurdish chief-
tain Milli İbrahim, whom the sultan made a pasha in 1902, remained loyal to
his father-sultan, members of the rival Bedirhan clan, who had been ousted
from power during the Tanzimat,[48] were inclined to work with the Young
Turks. Similarly, Isa Boletini, an Albanian warlord, remained faithful to the
régime,[49] but Ismail Qemali, whose family had fallen from imperial favour
during the Tanzimat,[50] made common cause with the Young Turks. Yet the
practice of pragmatic politics collided with the increasingly ideological bent of
Young Turk policy. For those disgruntled fringe groups that chose to cooperate with the Young Turk opposition were situated precariously on the margin
between Ottomanism and their respective nationalisms. Although the Young
Turks initially tolerated such nationalist deviations, over time they came to
regard them as essentially separatist. Their allies, in turn, were not particularly
well disposed towards an interpretation of Ottomanism that cast the Turks as
the dominant nation of the empire. They eventually came to consider the
CUP/CPU version of Ottomanism as a thinly veiled excuse for Turkish domination.

As noted above, the quest for allies in the battle against the sultan often led
the CUP to support non-Turkish nationalists. The organisation, for example,
published a bilingual journal, *Kürdistan*,[55] which promoted a form of Kurdish
proto-nationalism.[56] A major CUP leader was extremely proud of "being a member of the brave Kurdish nation,"[57] while another also wrote for *Kürdistan*.[58] But
such alliances with groups promoting a cultural proto-nationalist agenda
turned the CUP into a loose umbrella organisation with no single, coherent
revolutionary programme. At the same time, its attachment to an Islamist form
of Ottomanism similar to that of the sultan forced the CUP to work with the
ulema. In the early days of the movement, the ulema were encouraged to found
CUP branches in Cairo and other cities, and to publish their own journals as
official CUP organs.[59] The assumption was that the leadership of the ulema was
necessary to generate Muslim unity. Yet the Islamic activism of the ulema contradicted the materialist and positivist convictions of the CUP's leaders. This
ideological incoherence, when added to the positivist disinclination for revo-

During the early stages of the movement, non-Turkish supporters of the
CUP expressed themselves without inhibition. Statements such as this were not
atypical: "we the Arabs comprise three quarters of the Ottoman subjects, but of
the ninety thousand officials, eighty thousand are Turks [...] even though it is
a well known fact that the Turks are less wise and inferior administrators."[51]
The Albanian founder of the CUP, İbrahim Temo, once wrote in a letter: "I
especially hate the Turks."[52] Despite such remarks, and despite Temo's work on
behalf of Albanian organisations demanding cultural rights,[53] the CUP valued
his prestige among his Albanian compatriots.[54]

lutionary change, and to the Young Turks' constant fear of unwittingly triggering foreign intervention in Ottoman affairs (on the pretext of protecting various ethnic and religious communities), effectively paralysed the mainstream organisations. The Young Turk movement, in its early days, amounted to weak advocacy of radical change by non-revolutionary means.

The adoption of Turkism by the Young Turks prompted a radical change. The gradual incorporation of Turkism into the Young Turk platform supplied an activist core to the movement for the first time in its history. By acquiring its own powerful engine of revolution, the CPU completed its transition from a weak umbrella organisation of dissidents to a revolutionary organisation in its own right. The problem, of course, was how to reconcile the CPU's new ideology with its inter-ethnic alliances. The obvious solution was to try to sell Turkism as a form of Ottomanism.

In a confidential letter exploring this problem, the CPU defined itself as a "pure Turkish committee."[60] At the same time, the organisation would accept an Armenian candidate, for example, if he "came and said to us 'Look, I am an Ottoman, too; I love Ottomanism and want to serve Ottomanism in accordance with your programme.' We would then say to this Armenian, 'Compatriot, welcome! This is the way if you indeed want to work with us towards the furtherance of Ottomanism.' [...] We would accept a non-Muslim Ottoman into our committee only under these conditions."[61] Not surprisingly, few non-Muslims were prepared to accede to such terms. More generally, the major non-Muslim organisations refused to accept a vision of Ottomanism that seemed to them like a new scheme of Turkification, designed to re-impose the religious domination of pre-Tanzimat times in the ethnic and national terms of the post-Tanzimat era. When approached by the CPU, they called for a union based not upon *égalité individuelle*, but upon *égalité raciale et sociale*, and demanded that the CPU "regard the fatherland as common to all, abandon claims of superiority and hegemony and limit [itself] to being a 'partner' instead of a 'superior.'"[62] The chasm between the competing visions of Ottomanism had grown too wide to be bridged.

In fact, after 1905-6 the CPU (and later the CUP) could not move beyond tactical alliances in its relations with non-Muslim Ottoman organisations. There seemed little logic to strategic partnership – even an alliance based upon common interest and not ideology – as long as the CPU believed that "reform in the Ottoman administration depends upon a rebellion by the Turks, the dominant element in the Empire, and not upon insurrections by a bunch of Armenians or Bulgarians."[63]

Instead the CPU/CUP's greatest rival, Sabahaddin Bey, who headed the League of Private Initiative and Decentralisation, attempted to muster these groups under his banner. Yet his organisation lacked the recognition accorded to the CPU/CUP as representatives of the dominant ethnic group of the empire. Even powerful organisations like the Dashnaktsutiun, who had tried to work with Sabahaddin Bey, were eventually compelled to reach an understanding with the CPU.[64]

The CPU's stance towards non-Muslims was not an extremely radical position in the context of the period, for even the official ideology under Abdülhamid II approached the non-Muslim Ottoman communities in a similar manner. But the rejection of cooperation with non-Turkish Muslim organisations was very radical indeed. It also offered a hitherto absent basis for criticism of the sultan as a non-nationalist cosmopolitan. The régime too felt the Turkist pressure and adapted official ideology accordingly. But it never went as far as many Young Turks. Especially prior to 1906, the radical defence of Turkism by the CUP and many other Young Turks led to strongly worded attacks on non-Turkish Muslim organisations and their leaders; they used the term "vagabonds"[65] to refer to Albanian nationalists, and "Arab gang" for Arab proto-nationalists.[66]

The CPU/CUP, unlike the journal Türk, continued to promote Pan-Islamic ideas through the Islamic Fraternal Society under its control,[67] and by other means. It should be emphasized, however, that the CPU/CUP's Pan-Islamism was primarily a manifestation of anti-imperialism and not of Islam. It was thought that promotion of the unity of Muslims in defence of Istanbul, the seat of the Caliphate, would assist the CPU/CUP in its anti-imperialist struggle against the West, as well as block Albanian and Arab nationalism. In this they did not differ greatly from the sultan, whose Pan-Islamism they nonetheless criticized.[68] This explains how the staunch positivist Young Turk Ahmed Rıza could revitalise a plan,[69] originally initiated by Abdülhamid II,[70] to erect a mosque in Paris. At the same time, the cooperative relationship with the ulema that had marked the early days of the CPU[71] dissolved after 1902.

While Turkism offered a new and coherent revolutionary appeal for intellectuals and officers of Turkish decent, it alienated numerous others. The major shortcoming of the Turkish nationalist prescription was of course structural: mounting a proto-nationalist challenge in a multi-national empire faced enormous obstacles. But then again, so did the attempts at remodelling the empire with a new supranational identity. The CPU leadership, not surprisingly, opted to try a little bit of both approaches, and attempted to straddle the fine line between Turkism and Ottoman supranationalism. This was particularly evident in the two years preceding the Revolution of 1908. The principal line of demarcation was that between culture and politics: Turkism on the cultural level flourished, while Turkism as a political programme was stifled. On the political level, the organisation made a conscious effort to push the Turkism burgeoning in its ranks into the background and to erect a façade of Ottomanism reminiscent of the early Tanzimat ideology. The new doctrine placed renewed emphasis on the ideal of "equality" among Ottomans. Rhetorically, this primarily entailed the replacement of the terms "Turk" and "Turkish" with "Ottoman" in public statements,[72] and the dissemination of propaganda pamphlets bearing different messages to Turks, non-Turkish Muslims, and non-Muslim Ottomans.[73] The decision to make Macedonia the centre of CPU revolutionary activity reinforced the opportunistic motivations behind this policy. Turkism was worthless in the ethnic melange of Macedonia; the Albanians in particular – a pillar of the revolutionary movement – could not be rallied to action by a doctrine of subservience to the Turks. Thus it was that on the eve of the revolution the leaders of the Young Turk movement found themselves returning to an ideology they had almost forgotten and with which they were increasingly at odds – Ottomanism.

If the move back towards Ottomanism increased the chances of forging alliances with other proto-nationalist groups, other CPU policies undermined this potential and ushered in a new era of open conflict between Turks and non-Turks. In 1908, the CPU adopted new regulations that reshaped the committee's policy vis-à-vis those groups that it deemed separatist. Ahmed Rıza, for one, had long thought that non-Turks, "despite being Ottomans," were not as "interested in the maintenance of this [Ottoman] government as Turks" were.[74]

Until 1907, however, such beliefs translated merely into a policy of non-cooperation with these elements. The new obligations imposed by the new regulations transformed non-cooperation into open warfare: "the hindering of those who work towards creating discord because of their racial and religious aspirations is also one of the principal duties of the committee."[75]

This was a declaration of war on non-Turkish nationalists. No longer would the CUP ignore, or even attempt to convert, those who did not share its vision; it would henceforth combat perceived separatists just as it fought the sultan and the external enemies of the empire. The non-Turkish rivals of the CUP, for their part, were not taken in by the new Ottomanist rhetoric either before or after the Young Turk Revolution of 1908. The Turkist inclinations of the CUP leaders were simply too evident. Indeed, as the following vignette illustrates, the *Zeitgeist* at the time of the revolution was decidedly Turkist. Mehmed Rıza Pasha, the former minister of war exiled by the CUP after the revolution, believed his status as a Turk entitled him to preferential treatment. His excited refutation of the charges of corruption levelled against him could not have been more explicit: "Thank God! Again thank God that I am a Turk son of a Turk and a Muslim son of a Muslim."[76]

In such a climate, only communities that harboured no hope of territorial separation from the empire agreed to collaborate with the CPU/CUP. Groups such as the Jews or the Kutzo-Vlachs preferred any version of Ottomanism to the unpromising prospect of minority status in a nation-state. They accordingly gave their full support to the CPU/CUP. Thus it is no coincidence that Salonican Jews participated in the activities of the committee, that Kutzo-Vlach bands agreed to operate under CPU command, or that many Jewish and Kutzo-Vlach representatives were elected to the Ottoman Parliament from CUP lists.

The CUP had no qualms about making Nicolae Constantin Batzaria, a leading Kutzo-Vlach intellectual, first a senator and then a cabinet minister. Contrary to the assertions of CPU/CUP opponents and the British propaganda machine during the Great War,[77] the relationship between the CPU/CUP and these groups had nothing to do with a Jewish conspiracy or Zionist intrigues. In fact, when the Zionists approached the CPU in the wake of the revolution and requested help in settling Jews in the sub-province of Jerusalem, the organisation replied: "The Committee of Progress and Union wants centralisation and a Turkish monopoly (*Alleinherrschaft der Türkischen*) over power. It does not want Turkey to become a new Austria(-Hungary)."[78] On the contrary, Jewish support for the Young Turks signified wholehearted support for the vision of citizenship in a poly-ethnic, multi-religious empire, even one dominated by the Turks. There was little unique, and nothing sinister, about the cooperation between the CUP and Jews. For those communities and individuals willing to accept the CUP's version of Ottomanism, the future could be an inclusive one. But for those who expected further rights or a hyphenated identity it could well be exclusive. Such groups, in the eyes of the CUP, were essentially separatists.

The revolution catapulted the CUP to a position of political power, transforming the organisation almost overnight from a weak opponent of the status quo to a stakeholder in the empire. It was thus not surprising that erstwhile allies, whose separatist inclinations were sometimes tolerated in the interests of overthrowing the sultan prior to the revolution, became arch-enemies shortly thereafter. Following the revolution, the CUP embarked on a course of open confrontation with Albanian, Armenian, and Arab organisations. The number of non-Turkish holders of senior positions in the CUP decreased drastically. For their part, nationalists typically regarded the remaining non-Turkish members of the CUP as wholly Turkified or, worse, denigrated them as lackeys of the Turks. Moreover, the 1908 Young Turk Revolution did not simply alter the power structure at the centre; it also had a profound impact on the ruling order within the various Ottoman communities. The seizure of power in the Ottoman communities by nationalist-leaning avant-garde groups following the revolution thus posed a major problem for the CUP. Where in the past the sultan could work with traditional elites and their pragmatic representatives – such as Albanian warlords, Arab sheiks of leading religious orders, and the Armenian amira class – the CUP now faced recalcitrant revolutionaries – such as the Bashkimi Society, proto-nationalist Arab clubs, the Dashnaktsutiun, and the left wing of VMORO (Vnatrešna Makedonsko-Odrinska Revolucionerna Organizacija). Basing their claims upon representation instead of tradition, these organisations proved far less amenable to patronage and cooption.

As a consequence of these changes set in motion by the revolution, the period of CUP rule from 1908 to 1918, known as the Second Constitutional Period, turned into a bitter struggle between the CUP-controlled centre and the various ethno-religious groups of the empire. CUP-dominated governments sought both to centralise the empire and to impose a heavily Turkish version of Ottomanism on non-Turkish communities that either defended a hyphenated Ottomanism centred on the recognition of cultural rights or pushed for the realisation of their national ambitions through separation. The combination of aggressive centralisation and Ottomanisation tended to push defenders of cultural rights and advocates of separatism to make common cause against a perceived policy of Turkification. This coordinated resistance, in turn, reinforced the Turkist convictions of the CUP leadership.

A careful reading of the publications of the CPU/CUP, its confidential correspondence, and official memoranda, leaves no doubt that the organisation embraced Turkism long before the Balkan Wars. In fact, the Turkism promoted by the journal *Türk* and by some official CUP organs between 1903 and 1908 was by no means less radical than that championed by such avowedly Turkist periodicals as *Genc Kalemler* or *Türk Yurdu* in the Second Constitutional Period. Once it seized power, the CUP tried to reconcile its Turkist beliefs with the political measures necessary to achieve its primary goal of saving the empire. The committee, however, was not prepared to make any substantial sacrifice with regard to its concept of "the dominant nation," which, as described by a prominent journalist soon to become a deputy on the CUP ticket, had become the irreducible bottom line of the CUP: "whatever is said, in this country, the dominant nation is the Turks, and it will be the Turks alone."[79]

Conclusion

Long before the Balkan Wars, Turkism and Turkish nationalism had taken root among prominent Ottoman intellectuals and the leadership of the main Young Turk political organisation. First as a cultural concept, then as a political programme, Turkism gradually conquered the major Young Turk organisations and made a profound impact on their agenda. To be sure, the Balkan Wars were to provide a significant impetus to the rising tide of Turkish nationalism. They proved the CUP's long-standing assertion that, with few exceptions, the non-Turkish communities of the empire inclined towards separatism; demands for cultural rights and recognition were mere pretexts for dangerous nationalist agendas. Yet despite this seemingly incontrovertible verdict, the urge to save the multi-national empire – with all its insoluble contradictions – prevented the CUP from fully implementing the Turkist political agenda even after the Balkan Wars; the fundamental incompatibility of nationalism and empire granted Ottomanism a new lease on life, even under CUP rule. Hence the complex picture that emerges here: Turkism rose to prominence much earlier than is usually assumed, while Ottomanism persisted much later than is commonly held. It was only after the demise of the empire and the establishment of the republic in Anatolia that Turkism came into its own, displacing both religion and rival nationalist formulations as the official ideology of the republic and a vital tool in the process of Turkish state-building.

Chapter 2
An ethno-nationalist revolutionary and theorist of Kemalism: Dr Mahmut Esat Bozkurt (1892-1943)

Hans-Lukas Kieser

Mahmut Esat Bozkurt is the Minister of Justice who, in 1926, introduced the Swiss Civil Code in Turkey. In his preface of the same year to the new Law (a preface which also figures in recent editions) we read these words: "The Turkish nation [...] must at all costs conform to the requirements of modern civilization. For a nation which has decided to live this is essential."[1]

These words briefly caracterize the political thinking of a man whom I propose to call an ethno-nationalist rightist revolutionary. By this I understand a man believing in modern progress, in a nation defined ethnically, and in the necessity of using violence to achieve modernity. In this short biographical study I want to shed light on three stages of Bozkurt's life: first his childhood in Izmir and education in Switzerland; second his official positions in Ankara in the early years of the Republic; and third his political thinking in the 1930s. The concluding part of this chapter is a reflection on what I consider Bozkurt's deep ambivalence. This can be seen in, on the one hand, the dead-end of his ethno-national Turkist credo, partly fed by hatred, which is closely tied to his revolutionary project; and, on the other hand, the open window of his longing for new horizons, a longing that, in the last analysis, I judge able to force open the prison of his radical Turkism.

Student years and membership of the Foyer turc
Mahmut Esat was born into a family of landowners in the little town of Kuşadası, south of Izmir. His father was first president of the municipality of Kuşadası, then member of the Council of the Ottoman province of Izmir. Mahmut attended primary school at Kuşadası and secondary school at Izmir. Turgut Türkoğlu, Mahmut's schoolfriend and later himself a Member of Parliament in Ankara, recalled the young Mahmut's tremendous hatred of all non-Turks.[2] This hatred may partly be explained by his family history. His grand-parents were *muhacir* (Muslim refugees) from the Peleponnese. His grand-father Hacı Mahmut told the boy patriotic stories of painful losses; as

Türkoğlu writes, these awakened in the child his love for his nation and fatherland.³ In 1908, the sixteen-year-old Mahmut entered the University of Istanbul, where he obtained his Ottoman masters' degree in Law in 1912. Thanks to his well-to-do family, he had the means to finance what was then seen as the crowning achievement of an academic training: studying at a French-speaking university in Paris or in Switzerland. Mahmut decided to prepare his doctorate at the University of Fribourg, where he first had to acquire a Swiss master's degree in Law. The place where he mostly lived and had his flat was Lausanne. A few years earlier, in 1911, Turkish ethno-national clubs called *Foyers turcs* had been founded in Lausanne and Geneva. They were in the vanguard of the Turkist movement in Europa and had close ties with the Turkists in the Ottoman capital. In those years, this movement began to win over the majority of Turkish-speaking university students.

It is not clear when exactly Mahmut Esat arrived in Switzerland. He was surely there during the First World War until 1919, and probably entered the country in 1913 or 1914, thus shortly after the international congress of Turkists in March 1913 in Petit-Lancy near Geneva. Important spokesmen of the Turkist movement attended this congress, among them Hamdullah Subhi, the long-standing president of the organization called *Türk ocağı* (ideologically identical with the *Foyers turcs* or *Türk yurdu*; *Foyers turcs* is used in this article as a generic term for both). The proceedings of this Geneva congress were published in 1913 in Istanbul.⁴

The *Foyers turcs* of the diaspora were the formative microcosm which Mahmut Esat entered on the eve of the First World War. He developed his ideas here before he began his political career in Ankara in 1920. This is also true of Şükrü Saraçoğlu, Cemal Hüsnü Taray and many other men who occupied important positions in public life in the early Turkish Republic.⁵

Let me say a few words about this formative microcosm. The goal and "ideal" (*mefkûre*) of the *Foyer* movement was to carry out a salutary social revolution in ethno-national terms. Such a revolution was considered the means to save a Turkish nation that would otherwise perish. The dream of national "rebirth" was associated with the *Foyers*' members' vision of their own nation as the greatest victim in history, particularly of Russian aggression, of European imperialism, and of disloyal non-Muslim citizens of the Ottoman Empire in collusion with Europe. The *Foyers*, however, emphasized the constructive project, not the complaint: the effort required to achieve Western civilization. Their members often condemned their own (Ottoman Muslim) failure; this sometimes went so far as self-humiliation.

The 1913 congress and the publications and minutes of the *Foyers* stressed the particular urgency of educating Turkish men and women, if possible in Europe.⁶ One text already postulated the legal equality of men and women and emancipation from Islam as a basis for ordering society. On the other hand Islam was very much in evidence as a major cultural ingredient for defining

"Turkdom". By contrast, in the 1930s Kemal Atatürk and the Turkish Historical Society he founded wanted to get rid of Islam once for all and base Turkdom exclusively on "scientific", anthropological, ethnographical, and paleological foundations. Pre-Ottoman history was, however, already very important for the historical construction of identity in the *Foyer* turc.[7] The depressing sight of the recent past was offset by a militant visionary belief in Turkdom. The new Turkish identity to be established was considered superior to all other identities. The ardent belief in it, and the project of a "New Turkey" closely tied to it, helped to surmount the difficult present in a declining Empire. During the 1913 congress, hatred, resentment and the call for revenge were all the more forcefully expressed since the Second Balkan War was going on at the time.[8]

At the same congress of Geneva, the participants declared their pride in having created a new national consciousness, in calling themselves straightforwardly "Turks", and, after a great deal of effort, in having destroyed the attitude of understanding themselves as *Osmanlıcı* or members of an Ottoman nation, in the multi-ethnic sense of the term.[9]

Another topic of discussion was what one speaker called the liberation of the economy from the grip of the non-Muslims, a matter of much concern for Mahmut Esat, who later (1922–1923) became Minister of Economy. Like most of his *Foyer* "brothers", he saw the "class struggle" of the peasants and the workers as a struggle against what were called at the congress the Ottoman "Armenian profiteers", the Ottoman "Greek swindlers", and only in the third place the oppressive Turkish landlords. The "class enemy" was closely associated with the ethno-religious enemy.[10] The *Foyer* members talked about the urgency of saving Turkdom in Anatolia from the foreigners, among whom they included the non-Muslim Ottoman citizens! All participants at the Geneva congress were "convinced that only Anatolia could be the Turkish homeland and guarantee the political existence of Ottoman Turkdom", and they "promised to commit themselves whole-heartedly and dedicatedly in the forefront of the struggle aimed at making the Turks the masters of Anatolia."[11]

Though he studied in Fribourg, Mahmut Esat became a member and the president of the *Foyer turc* in Lausanne. He cooperated with his friend Şükrü Saraçoğlu, then president of the *Foyer turc* in Geneva; much later Şükrü became Prime Minister of the Republic of Turkey (1942–46). Şükrü, also a native of Izmir, was linked to the Izmir cell of the Young Turkish Committee of Union and Progress (CUP) that was headed by Celal Bayar, later President of the Republic of Turkey (1950–1960). In contrast to the well-to-do Mahmut Esat, many members of the *Foyers* in Switzerland lived, like Şükrü, on a scholarship awarded by the Ottoman state.

At the end of World War I, when Mahmut Esat was its president, the *Foyer* in Lausanne, helped by friends, began to take the leadership of the movement for the "defence of the Turks' rights" (*Türk hukukunu müdafaa*) in Anatolia, as we can read in the minutes of the Lausanne *Foyer*.[12] Those months were very prolific in articulating visions of a "New Turkey". We do not find among *Foyer* members signs of crisis or despair like those felt among the Turkish Muslim intelligentsia in Istanbul.[13]

Well-known topics re-emerged in the discussion about the Turkish nation-state to be created in Asia Minor: the elimination of Christian influence inside and outside this territory once and for all, but the adoption of the example of the Ottoman Christians in education and economy. In religious matters, the *Foyer* members ascertained that the nationalists should "not hesitate to guarantee our national organization under a religious [Muslim] cover, if necessary", in order "not to alienate the people from Turkism". A long struggle was foreseen against the "religious conscience well rooted amongst us but which harms progress". Polygamy, women's veiling, and arbitrary divorce by men were rejected. In those discussions Mahmut Esat stated that "in religious matters religion has to serve Turkdom, not vice versa".[14]

In the months after the end of the First World War, the nationalist Turkish diaspora in and around the *Foyers* in Lausanne and Geneva produced an important quantity of propaganda literature in defence of the Turkish nationalist position on the future of Asia Minor.

This agitation took place in cooperation with professional journalists and diplomats from the capital close to the CUP, among them Ahmed Cevdet Oran, the owner of the journal *İkdam*, and Reşid Safvet Atabinen, a diplomat and close friend of Javid Bey and Talat Pasha, who later became secretary of the Turkish delegation at the Lausanne Conference, a Member of Parliament in Ankara, and a founding member of the Turkish Historical Society. A main aim of the propaganda was to prove by demographic or other arguments the "Turkish race's" prerogative to found a nation-state in the whole of Asia Minor.

In the Lausanne-based English-language paper *Turkey*, Mahmut Esat and his friends Şükrü Saraçoğlu, Yakup Kadri Karaosmanoğlu and Harun Aliçe protested against British prime minister Lloyd George for his use of the term "Muslim Greeks": "[...] we, who are Turks, from the points of view of blood, sentiment, conscience and all, and are wholeheartedly attached to our nation, we protest against the attributions of Mr. Lloyd George. There is no 'Mohammedan Greek' in our country. We are Turks not only by religion but mainly by race."[15]

In June 1919 Mahmut Esat and Şükrü Saraçoğlu traveled secretly from Switzerland to Anatolia to engage in the guerilla war against the Allies in the region of Izmir. Shortly before his departure Mahmut Esat had completed his doctorate at the University of Fribourg.[16] After the inauguration of the Turkish National Assembly in Ankara in April 1920, Mustafa Kemal called the ambitious young jurist to Ankara. In 1922, at the age of 30, he was made Minister of Economy, and in 1924 he became Minister of Justice.

A Minister in the young nation state

Mahmut Esat returned to Asia Minor in 1919 as the bearer of a revolutionary national project. When, in 1922, he was proposed to head the Ministry of Justice he refused, saying that the situation did not yet permit the radical changes he had in mind.[17]

His long article "The principles of the Turkish revolution"[18] of 1924 glorified the War of Independence as a "holy revolution" to establish the nation's full sovereignty and achieve its final full accession to the community of Western states under the rule of modern law. Through this the Turkish Revolution was giving all oppressed nations, particularly the Muslim ones, a good example, he argued. In a speech in 1930 he called the Turkish Revolution the greatest revolution in world history, and praised the Republican People's Party, the bearer of the Revolution, that "took the material and symbolic wealth [in Asia Minor] from the hands of the foreigners [non-Muslim Ottomans included] and gave it to the Turkish nation."

Many elements of the history of the Turkish Revolution as taught in the universities after 1930 are already in place in Mahmut Esat's article of 1924, except for the veneration of Atatürk. Mahmut Esat deplored the fact that the people was not yet truly sovereign, but he did not question the link between this fact and his own understanding of nation/people as the community of the Muslim Turks, i.e. the religious community formerly ruling in Ottoman times (*millet-i hakime*). He understood that neither the establishment of Turkish sovereignty over Asia Minor nor its Turkification made Turkey a modern democracy; he thus postulated a third revolutionary stage for establishing the people's sovereignty in the political system and the economy.[19] Until his death Mahmut Esat remained marked by the knowledge that Turkey still had a long way to go to become a real democracy, as Switzerland was above all, in his eyes.

When Mahmut Esat became Minister of the Economy in 1922, he said that he was close to the left wing of the CUP.[20] He showed a particular concern for the poorer classes and set up a system of loans for farmers. His first aim, however, was to fully turkify the Republic's economy in accordance with the *Foyer* doctrine, i.e. to oust and dispossess the non-Muslims. This concern was clearly expressed during and after the First Congress of the Economy in Izmir in February 1923, both by him and by the President and *Gazi* Mustafa Kemal.[21]

In 1924 Mahmut Esat was appointed Minister of Justice, and two years later he introduced the Swiss Civil Code into Turkey. He again proved to be revolutionary in this office, this time directing his efforts not against non-Muslims but against the "religious reaction" (*irtica*) that he largely identified with the Kurds. The Kemalists had not accorded the Sunni Kurds the autonomy promised them for their collaboration during the War of Independence. This brought about the great uprising led by Sheikh Said in 1925, that was motivated partly by religion (the Caliphate had been abolished in 1924) and partly by Kurdish nationalism. Threatening the Kurds in particular, the Minister of

Justice declared during a speech on the new Civil Code: "The Turkish Revolution has decided to acquire Western civilization without conditions or limits. This decision is based on such a strong will that all those who oppose it are condemned to be annihilated by iron and fire. [...] We do not proceed according to our mood or our desire, but according to the ideal of our nation."[22]

Later, during the Kurdish uprising of 1930, this prominent Kemalist spoke of the war between two races, Kurds and Turks, and went so far as to say: "All, friends, enemies and the mountains shall know that the Turk is the master of this country. All those who are not pure Turks have only one right in the Turkish homeland: the right to be servants, the right to be slaves."[23]

Mahmut Esat leads us again into the problematic core of the Kemalist Revolution of the interwar period: a revolutionary modernist project; an underlying ethnic, not civic, understanding of nation; and thus a profound tension between the universalistic ambition of the project (to be part of the universal community of civilized states under the rule of law) and the coercive, violent reality of its *völkisch* nationalism. Interestingly, the Minister of Justice took the ethnic and linguistic pluralism in Switzerland as a strong argument for the universal validity of its Civil Code,[24] but he did not take this pluralism, including political pluralism, seriously as the essential context for the very functioning of those laws.

Nevertheless, did the Civil Code not prove to be a stable foundation stone of Republican Turkey, a firm pledge of Turkey's abolition of Sharia and Caliphate? Undoubtedly, the enthusiast nationalist Bozkurt gave lasting and constructive impulses to Republican Turkey. It is true that the Code he introduced became an incontestable pillar of the state and was more and more integrated and adapted to Turkish society.

For several decades, however, a worrying gap existed between the laws and their observance (notably where legal marriage was concerned). There was another problem. The hurried adoption of the Civil Code had to do with a deal at the Lausanne Conference of 1923; only if Turkey introduced such a modern code, would the Western powers accord the Republic full sovereignty and not insist on supervising its tribunals after the abolition of the Capitulations (the legal privileges for foreigners in the Ottoman Empire). Thus the nationalist élite's primary desire for power and sovereignty also influenced the hasty legal revolution in 1926.

Theorizing Kemalism after 1930

Mahmud Esat was Minister of Justice until 1930. His disappearance from the political scene coincided with the closing-down of the extensive *Foyer turc* organization (*Türk ocağı*), i.e. its fusion into the single-party organization of Mustafa Kemal's Republican People's Party in 1930–1931. The *Foyers* had been Mahmud Esat's intellectual home for nearly twenty years; back from

Switzerland he had continued to frequent them. After the *Foyers* were closed
down, intellectual, cultural, and political public life was more then ever controlled by the state and centered on its leader. Mustafa Kemal made great efforts
in those years to promote the Turkish History thesis and the Sun Language theory, both highly Turko-centric visions of human history. In theses endeavours
the former Minister of Justice was not involved. Mahmud Esat continued to be
a Member of Parliament until his death; he was moreover appointed Professor
of the History of the Turkish Revolution at Istanbul University, a new branch
of study that the state began to promote after its university reform in 1933.
Together with Moïz Kohen Tekinalp[25] he then became the most important theorist of Kemalism, an ideology he declared to be of universal validity.
According to this logic, Atatürk was the greatest revolutionary in the world.[26] It
was the time of nationalist superlatives in and outside Turkey. In the 1910s and
1920s, Tekinalp had also been close to the *Foyers* turcs. In 1932 Mahmut Esat for
the first time used the term "Kemalism" (*Kemalizm*).[27] Besides, following the
Surname Law of 1934, Mahmut Esat adopted the surname "Bozkurt", the name
of the emblematic animal (grey wolf) symbolizing Turkdom for the Turkists.

In his book *Atatürk ihtilali* Bozkurt defined revolution (*ihtilal*) as en event
that produced a completely new situation by annihilating and replacing all that
had been before.[28] The setting up of the new fully justified the destruction of
the old and "bad"; seen in this light it legitimized all the violence exercised by
Kemalism. For Bozkurt, Atatürk completely personified the Turkish
Revolution and the Turkish nation. Thus if Atatürk reigned, the nation
reigned, and there was perfect "authoritarian democracy", the chief taking his
authority from the nation/people.[29] In the same paragraph in his book, Bozkurt
asserts that German National Socialism and Italian Fascism are nothing other
than versions of Atatürk's regime. For Bozkurt, National Socialism was the
German liberation movement, analogous to that of the Turks after the First
World War. Thanks to the Turks' success against the "imperialist" powers and
the treaty they imposed at Paris-Sèvres, the Turkish experience, in Bozkurt's
eyes, offered an ideal model of liberation for all nations oppressed by the West,
particularly for those defeated in the First World War. He proudly cited
Hitler's explicit affirmation of this position in a speech in the Reichstag.[30] In
the 1930s, Bokurt's previous quasi-religious *Foyer* cult of Turkdom or
Turkishness (*Türklük*) fused with the cult, equally quasi-religious, of the leader-
saviour Atatürk; Atatürk's career was identified with the War of Salvation
(*Kurtuluş Savası*) of 1919–1922 and the revolutionary construction of the nation
state – in short, with the history of the Turkish Revolution as taught by
Bozkurt.

Conclusion

From his arrival in Switzerland, Mahmut Esat was committed to a national
project that more and more took shape in the formative microcosm of the

Foyers turcs. Asia Minor was to become the homeland of the Turkish nation –
a nation understood as the community of Turkish-speaking Muslims sharing
the same ideal of a strong, modern, and secular Turkish nation-state in Asia
Minor. This was the goal he aimed to achieve, and this was the meaning of the
term "revolution" often used in the *Foyers*. Esat was not much concerned to
save a multinational empire, in contrast to the founders of the CUP and the
"first" generation of Young Turks.

Glorifying the Turkish ethno-nation above all, Bozkurt logically was not
immune to racism and other forms of misanthropy. He frequently made enthusiastic and exaggerated statements like "all for the Turks"; "total Turkism";
"first the Turks, then humanity, and finally the others";[31] and – openly anti-
Semitic – "For me a Turk has more value than all the Jews of this world, not to
say the whole world".[32]

The clear problem with Bozkurt's ethno-nationalism – this is presumably
true of all ideologies of this kind – was his unquestioning essentialist belief in
a collective identity that he took to be a superior and absolute value. Behind
this belief were the traumatic traces of the late Ottoman period, the *millet-i
hakime*'s hatred of the non-Turkish, non-Muslim "other", and the fear of the
Turks' collapse as a political entity.

In the eyes of most European readers at the beginning of the 21st century,
Bozkurt's *völkisch* nationalism undoubtedly appears strange and negative. But
even if often dominant, this was not the only pole of his worldview. His thinking had a schizophrenic aspect. He was incapable of conceiving of "New
Turkey" other than in two contradictory, paradoxical ways. For he almost
always sought to put Turkish society in a universal frame and to think and
shape it according to universal terms that, by definition, cannot be ethnocen-
tric. Thus the blatant nationalist he sometimes was could quite innocently also
express his political views thus: "In a political perspective, revolution or
progress mean making the people as sovereign as possible. For the Swiss it
would be reactionary to adopt Turkish norms. For us on the other hand it is
revolutionary to implement theirs."[33]

Bozkurt's and many Kemalists' exaggerated nationalist thinking had a lasting negative impact on Turkey, because a really civic and pluralist, and thus
democratic, conception of society could not develop out of it. But the other
impact, which had some constructive long-term results, was the will to participate fully in modern "civilization" by accepting norms and values considered
as universal. This is the legacy worth highlighting politically today in a Turkey
on the road towards "post-nationalist" communitarian horizons.

Chapter 3
Kemalism, westernization and anti-liberalism

Hamit Bozarslan

Turkey is the only candidate country for membership of the European Union to have an official doctrine, the well-known Kemalism. As Etienne Copeaux suggests[1], this doctrine, is, at the same time, a "transcendental system" and the basis of the country's Constitution and political culture. So far, however, Turkey's European partners have not considered this existence of an official state ideology as an obstacle to her probable integration. On the contrary, following a half-century long scientific and political tradition, going back to Bernard Lewis[2] and Niyazi Berkes[3], many politicians, observers and Turkey specialists often celebrate Kemalism as the first – and so far unique – successful experiment of secularization and westernization in the Muslim world. The Turkish authorities themselves legitimize their project of European integration as the fulfilment of Mustafa Kemal's world vision and ultimate dreams.

The categories used in the discussion about Kemalism, however, were to a very large extent elaborated *post facto* and do not reflect the self-image that Kemalism, as praxis or as ideology, propagated between 1919 and 1938. Moreover, those categories are almost exclusively ideological ones; they accept the existence of a reified "Muslim world" as an unquestionable reality, which, compared to the progressive, open-minded and civilized West, is supposed to be under the domination of "darkness". Kemalism is thus considered as a successful venture of a civilization-change, a switch from the "darkness" to the "light". Such a reading simply ignores the fact that Kemalism emerged in a political climate in which many European countries vehemently rejected the very idea of "enlightenment", democracy and political liberalism, advocating instead dictatorship and the rule of single parties and sanctified "leaders".

Leaving aside such reified categories as "civilization" and "darkness", that no historian can seriously consider as analytically meaningful, I will in this contribution propose some elements which re-establish Kemalism in its historical context, or rather, contexts. The re-contextualization also entails abandoning the interpretation of Kemalism as a set of dreams and fulfilled projects elaborated by its founder or as a coherent intellectual and political framework existing in his mind and will. My hypothesis here is that, like the other inter-war ideologies, including Bolshevism, Fascism, and Nazism, Kemalism was a product of its own time and a series of factors and constraints, which changed with time, determined its evolution.

During its almost two decades of existence, the Kemalist regime went through three phases, each of them being marked by some specific dynamics. The first period was that of the War of Independence (1919-1922). The second one, going from 1922 to the end of 1930, was that of a "Janus -like" Kemalism, which was at the same time nationalist and the bearer of a project of civilization. The third period, covering the years 1930-1938, witnessed an openly and self-consciously anti-liberal and anti-democratic regime. During this period, Kemalism projected itself into the future as the third pillar of an anti-democratic world, Fascism and Bolshevism constituting the two other poles.

Each period has produced its own paradoxes, contradictions and tensions, which survived up to the death of Mustafa Kemal. The more the Republic of Turkey transformed Kemalism into a sanctified national syntax and Mustafa Kemal into a sanctified "founding father", the more the Kemalist premises became social and political obstacles, preventing her move towards a genuine democracy.

The first Kemalism: the War of Independence

A double and complementary feature shaped the Kemalist movement during its first years, i.e. the period of the War of Independence (1919-1922). As Erik-Jan Zürcher emphasises[4], the Kemalism of this period was, roughly speaking, an offshoot of the Committee of Union and Progress. And, like the Committee during World War I, it had a solid social basis composed of the Kurdish and Turkish *eşraf* (local notables), *ulema* (doctors of religion) and armed bands, who had either participated in the Armenian genocide or were motivated by religious concerns. Together with the resistance to the European (and particularly Greek) invaders, these two factors transformed the War of Independence into a nationalist and religious war conducted against the non-Muslim populations of Anatolia. The new State, which was founded in 1922 under Mustafa Kemal's leadership, and which regarded itself as in historical continuity with the Ottoman Empire, conceived of itself openly as the victory and revenge of "Turkishness" (and therefore of "Islam") over the Christian components of Anatolia. In that sense, the War of Independence completed the process of the religious homogenization of the Anatolian population already undertaken and successfully conducted by the Unionist regime through its extermination of the Armenians. The war and the population exchange with Greece which followed shortly after created "modern Turkey", in the sense that they "liberated" the occupied parts of a territory claimed by the *Mısak-ı Millî* ("National Pact" of 1920) and "cleansed" this territory of its non-Muslim "enemies" and "usurpers".

During this first period, Kemalism can hardly be described as an ideology. Obviously, the Kemalist elite preserved the Unionist political culture and its way of manoeuvring, and ultimately, like the Committee of Union and Progress, it had a social-Darwinist worldview. But it was obliged to combine arguments emanating from Turkish nationalism, socialism, anti-imperialism and Islamism (and pan-Islamism).

It is not surprising that during the war years Mustafa Kemal tried to mobilize the religious legitimization at his disposal in order to create a broad alliance. Religious affiliation was in fact the main criterion of the definition of "otherness", and the Kurds as well as many provincial dignitaries accepted Mustafa Kemal's leadership only because he promised to protect and preserve the *khalifa* and form a new, religiously legitimized state. This alliance and this religious legitimization, however, ultimately linked Kemalism and the nation it "liberated" to "Islam". To some extent, thanks to the war, Kemalism gave Turkey a religious sense, condemning it to become demographically, politically, and culturally "Muslim". In later decades, this historical and organic link between Nation and Religion allowed the Islamist movement to contest the Kemalist policy of secularization and propose their own, dissident reading of the War of Independence. Islamist intellectuals could in fact easily accuse Mustafa Kemal of having betrayed the original spirit of the War of Independence and produced "a history based on lies"[5].

1922-1930: the second Kemalism

The Kemalism of the second period starts with the end of two alliances which made the War of Independence possible: the Turkish-Kurdish alliance (which was replaced by the policy of denial of the Kurds' existence), and the Islamist-Unionist-Kemalist coalition. During this period, the Kemalist government was strong enough to imagine itself as a truly revolutionary regime, without any direct and organic link with the Unionist past or any previous experience encountered in any age of Ottoman history. As a revolutionary regime, and thanks to its voluntarism and enthusiasm, it could develop a syntax of hegemony, specifically based on nationalism; it had at its disposal efficient coercive tools (the repression of the Kurdish revolt of Sheikh Said and of the so-called "liberal" opposition and the *irtica*, i.e. "religious reaction", in 1926, the execution of opponents in 1926).

My assumption, however, is that this revolutionary *élan* did not go hand-in-hand with an ideology, at least, with an ideology that the Kemalist elite could designate as such and try to codify as a written "credo", as was the case with the Fascist and Bolshevik movements.

The entire revolutionary dogma of this period is focused on the personality of Mustafa Kemal, who conceived of himself as an "I-nation"[6] (and as a "*docteur ès histoire*", dictating the only legitimate and authorised historical reading of Turkish past). And this "I-nation" incarnated a war declared on many different kinds of internal "enemies": *irtica*, cosmopolitanism, Turkey's Ottoman and Muslim past, Mustafa Kemal's former companions, non-Muslim Anatolia and, of course, the Kurds.

These "enemies" and challengers however, were deeply rooted both in history and in the People. For instance, according to an opinion poll carried out in 1927 among university students in Istanbul, only 5% of the sample considered the "homeland" and 10% the nation as the most sacred value in which they believed. In contrast, 40% answered the question with "honour" and yet another 40% "religion and the Koran". The Kemalist regime was thus obliged to introduce a radical distinction between the Nation, which represented the "Golden Age" and the "Glorious Future", and the People, which represented the immediate and corrupted Ottoman "past". While the Nation appeared to be a meta-historical entity, incarnated by Mustafa Kemal himself and, marginally, by the elite surrounding him, the People was conceived of as an ignorant mass that ought to be disciplined by revolutionary reforms, and if necessary, by coercion. In the conception of Kemalism of this period, sovereignty did not emanate from the People and was not exerted by it, but solely by the Nation, i.e., the ruling elite (later on, during the third period of Kemalism, the elite would be redefined as a pyramid of chiefs). While preserving Islam as the national religion by default, the revolution became a means of punishing the People for their "archaic" and "superstitious" belief. Nationalism, "Revolution", and "civilization" were thus perceived as power instruments, used by the Nation against the People in order to "discipline" it and elevate it to a "national" level.

This second Kemalism was obviously a Janus-like phenomenon. On the one hand it was nationalist, and nationalism constituted its main *raison d'être*. On the other hand, however, following the legacy of Ziya Gökalp and the Unionist elite, it conceived of "Western civilization" as the sole horizon of the Turkish nation. For the Kemalist elite, "entering into Western civilization" was another name for gaining "strength" in order to engage the "struggle for survival" with other nations, considered as hostile (or potentially hostile) "species". "Civilization" was the very condition of remaining oneself, a Turk and Turkish, but at the same time it meant becoming someone else. The distinction between Nation and People that Kemalism introduced allowed it to organize and manage the consequences of this complex historical operation of remaining oneself and becoming the other.

This Janus-like phenomenon was in itself not paradoxical. In fact, as Fikret Adanir[7] and Mete Tunçay[8] have shown convincingly, the Kemalism of this period was only one of a wide range of European and non-European anti-liberal and anti-democratic movements and experiments. Kemalist "Westernization" did not only signify the adoption or imposition of new ways of being and behaving, dressing and managing the urban space. It also meant accepting the political categories of a non-liberal West (single party rule based on political étatism, social organicism, the use of state coercion against "internal enemies", the aesthetization of force and brutality), as modernity and as tools for strengthening the self. To some extent, the Kemalism of this decade represented a thoroughly successful experience of integration into Europe, but into a profoundly anti-democratic and anti-liberal Europe.

Kemalism was certainly not the only Janus-like regime in the world of the 1920's. However, it can be presented as a singular case, in the sense that it survived this period thanks to the transformation of Mustafa Kemal's legacy into a quasi-religion, with its unavoidably "contradictory verses"[9]. As Taha Parla has suggested[10], notwithstanding their internal contradictions, these verses have constituted the major taboos of Turkish political culture ever since his death. Mustafa Kemal's reading of Turkish history, especially recent Turkish history, is still the only legitimized discourse in Turkey and his "appeal" to the youth to combat the "ignorance, complicity and even treason" (*gaflet, delalet ve hatta hiyanet*) of future "power holders" is often used in order to legitimize any action against the country's elected body. The legacy of the legitimization of the elites' (and the intelligentsia's) intervention against the People to impose the Nation's choices or a project of civilization can explain, at least partly, the military coups and the army's direct and indirect interventions between 1960 and 1997.

The Kemalism of the third period

Many reasons explain the passage to this third period: the short-lived Liberal Party experiment (1930) showed in fact that the Kemalist regime and revolution were highly unpopular across Turkey, and the Menemen "incident" (1930) attested that reactions against it could take on a millenarian dimension. In 1931, some Kemalist intellectuals went to Italy and the Soviet Union in order to study these "revolutionary experiences" and learn the ways in which a revolution could become popular. After these massive "training courses" the Kemalist elite projected itself as the agency of a profoundly anti-liberal and anti-democratic revolution. The review *Kadro* (Cadres), which brought together some former members of the Turkish Communist Party, played a decisive role in this new orientation.

The Kemalism of this third period clearly articulated nationalism and revolution, thus creating a link of causality between the two. The *Türk Tarih Tezi* (Turkish Thesis of History) and the *Güneş Dil Teorisi* (The Sun-Language Theory) were the decisive steps in the nationalization of the Revolution. But they also signified that the Kemalist Revolution was no longer indebted to any other revolution or tradition, either the French Revolution or the Philosophy of the Enlightenment. Obviously, these references were not completely abandoned; but they either ceased to be a source of legitimization of the Kemalist discourse, or, as was the case with the French Revolution, were severely criticised.

During this period Kemalism became an "autonomous" ideology, formulated around its famous Six Arrows (integrated into the Constitution in 1937). Kemalist "secularism", which is widely mentioned as the first successful separation between state and religion in the Muslim world,[11] was only one of those arrows and could not be isolated from the five others: "nationalism", "republicanism", "revolutionarism", "étatism" and "populism". All together, these "Six Arrows" transformed Kemalism into something much more complex and ambitious than a secularizing experiment: an ideology of a "nationalist revolution", such as many European – and non European – countries had already adopted or were about to do so. All the other steps taken during the 1930's (establishment of a Chair of the Turkish Revolution at University level, the progressive and well-known fusion of the State and the single Party, the promotion of Mustafa Kemal to the status of Eternal Chief) were measures to reinforce the Turkish nationalist revolution.

The opposition between the Nation and the People, which marked the second period of Kemalism, was overcome during this period by the redefinition of the state as an organ with the right to have absolute control over society. The consolidation of the Fascist and Bolshevik experiences, carefully studied in Turkey, and the popularity – and later on, the victory – of Nazism, constituted without any doubt important elements explaining the Kemalist move towards the ambition of a total control of the society by the State. The fusion of the State and the single Party (1937) which marked the ultimate manifestation of this control also changed the status of the People. The People ceased to be the simple vehicle of transmission of a corrupted "Ottoman legacy", and in its profound depths, it became the bearer of the Nation's essence – but without being aware of it. The State's (i.e., the "Chief's") conscious intervention was thus necessary in order to reveal this essence to its bearer. The creation of new mass organizations, namely the *Halkevleri ve Halkodalari* (People's Houses and Chambers), the preparation of new schoolbooks, the paying of particular attention to children (as "the State-owned heirs of the Nation", as *Kadro* defined them), the definition of the Turks as a "nation-army", were some of the signs of the Kemalist regime's new orientation.

The policy of Westernization and Civilization of the 1920's was not abandoned during this period: on the contrary, after the "reactionary Menemen incident" in 1930 and the repression of the Nakchibandiyya brotherhood which immediately followed, it was reinforced. More than before, however, the very concept of "civilization" was turkified. The Turks were no longer conceived of as a group that had to adopt a foreign civilization in order to survive, but rather as a group of whose essence civilization was a part, and as the bringers of civilization to others. The Turkish Thesis of History even concluded that all civilizations in world history have a Turkish origin.

The perception that this third period Kemalism had of "civilization" in fact had nothing to do with Mirabeau's definition of civilization as "the refining of manners". It was quite close to the notion of "regenerative barbarism" which was quite popular in the Europe of the 1920's and 1930's. In Turkey, "regenerative barbarism" found its literary expression notably in poetry (such as that of Behçet Kemal Cağlar) and its visual expressions in painting and

sculpture, especially the oeuvre of Heinrich Kippler, who worked for the
Kemalist regime. This new form of "civilization" was synonymous with the use
of force. As a Kemalist author put it: "Now the entire world knows that the
Turks will teach other nations civilization and liberty, if necessary by the bay-
onet and the power of the sword"[12]. In accordance with this interpretation, the
project of the destruction of Dersim (1935-1938) was presented as the "bringing
of civilization" to this "region exploited by feudalism".

After the hesitations of the two first periods, the Kemalism of the 1930 finally gained a coherent form. It introduced the absolute superiority of
"Turkishness" (understood as something in between Nation and Race) and its
revolution; which, in turn, legitimized the pyramidal rule of the Chiefs, headed by the Eternal Chief.

Conclusion

The Kemalism of this third period is hardly discussed (much less defended) in
the current hagiographic literature, which usually insists only on Kemalist secularism or, en passant, timidly comments on a couple of quotations of Mustafa
Kemal. It is also almost totally absent from the debate on the Turkish candi-
dacy. The reason for this silence is obvious: it is simply impossible to reduce it
either to secularism alone or to Westernization, as they are understood today,
and it is almost the exact opposite of even a very impoverished definition of
democracy.

Obviously, Kemalism was a "Westernizing" power and ideology: but the
"West" or Europe were not, and are not, unhistorical entities. The Europe of
2000 shares almost nothing with the Europe of the 1920s and 1930s, which constituted the model for the Kemalist elite. Quite the contrary: the very formation
of modern Europe required the destruction of this former one, which, was
marked by the "brutalization of societies" (George L. Mosse) and social
Darwinism. The question, then, is to know whether Turkey will be able to bid
farewell to yesterday's Europe, as the condition of her integration into Europe,
or if she will preserve the Kemalist legacy as the essence of her own conception
of Europe.

PART II

TURKISH NATIONALISM: THE TRAUMA OF UNITARIST TURKIFICATION AND SOCIAL ENGINEERING

Chapter 4
The settlement policy
of the Committee of Union and Progress
1913-1918

Fuat Dündar

The birth of the Committee of Union and Progress dates back to 1889; it emerged on the policy scene as early as October 1895[1], when the Armenian question was becoming more and more threatening to the unity of the Ottoman Empire and, more importantly, when it started to increase the possibility of the great powers of the day intervening. However it took only two years to disintegrate. Its rebirth was in 1906, in Macedonia; but this time, its composition had changed: while it was composed mainly of students and intellectuals in 1895, thereafter it became an army officers' organization. As for its ethnic structure, it was far from reflecting the Empire's demographic profile, as the majority of its members were Macedonian Turks.

Although one of the decisions taken during its second congress was to launch a "military rebellion in two years",[2] the Albanian revolt speeded up the whole process[3]. On 24 July 1908, Sultan Abdulhamid (1876-1909) re-established the 1876 constitution (*Kanun-i Esasi*). By 23 January 1913, when the attack against the Bab-i Ali took place, the Committee had taken on the responsibility of power, and it established absolute control over the Empire for the next five years. The loss of the Balkans played an important role in this turning point. This loss not only affected the interests of the Empire but it was vital for the Committee leaders' and members' personal interests, for their families were Balkan immigrants.Thereafter, by means of a small secret group within the organization, the Committee pursued a policy aiming at the Turkification of the entire state mechanism, the Islamization and Turkification of Asia Minor's demography and the Turkification of the economy[4].

Each of these aspects of the Turkification policy deserves a detailed analysis. However, the demographic aspect has remained an unexplored area until today. This gap is important and this article seeks to constitute a first step towards filling it.

Before focusing on the Muslim populations, it is worth glancing at the non-Muslims. The massive deportation of the Asia Minor Greek community started with the Balkan wars, and especially in 1914. The Committee's plans for a population exchange to involve 30,000 Balkan Muslims and 120,000 Greeks of Asia Minor could not be carried out due to the outbreak of the First World War. De-Hellenization of Asia Minor took place anyway, however, even if it was restricted at that date to the coastal region only.[5]

Likewise, in the case of the Armenians, the turning point was the Sarikamish defeat. Instead of expatriating Armenians to Russia (which had exiled the Muslims of Iran and the Caucasus), the Committee deported them to the Syrian desert. It was soon to become clear that the real aim of the displacement was to exterminate the Armenian population of Asia Minor.[6] The Jews of Palestine were also affected by this deportation and displacement policy. This, especially Jamal Pasha's own project, was never fully carried out, due to the pressure from the Allies, the USA and also the Germans.[7]

It should be noted here that the documents on this subject can be found mostly in the Ottoman Archives of the Turkish Republic, under the classification folder BOA.DH.SFR (*Basbakanlik Osmanli Arsivleri-Dahiliye Nezareti-Sifre Kalemi*/Ottoman Archives, Ministry of the Interior, Office of Coded Telegrams). Most of them are based on the coded telegrams of the Directorate of Settlement of Tribes and Refugees (*IAMM-Iskan-i Asairin Muhacirin Muduriyeti*), especially those of Talat Pasha.

Unlike the Empire's traditional policy of population settlement, which was based on military and economical considerations, the Committee placed demographic resettlement at the heart of its policy, as displacement and settlement of populations became a vital necessity for putting an end to the territorial losses of the Empire. Furthermore, the massive and fast transformation of the demography of Asia Minor underpinned the Turkification policy. It should be noted here that the Ottoman government's authority over the right of settlement was increased in absolute terms with the introduction of the Law of Displacement (*Tehcir Kanunu*) on 27 May 1915, and the Turkish army was vested with comprehensive powers to implement it.

For this purpose the Committee launched a major restructuring initiative, putting into effect new laws and regulations, including the Law for the Settlement of Immigrants which came into force on 13 May 1913. Under this Law a Directorate was established which would be reorganized as the General Directorate for Settlement of Tribes and Refugees on 14 March 1916[8]. The General Directorate was not only responsible for displacement and settlement issues but also dealt with linguistic and ethnological research on the minorities of Asia Minor, carried out by the Committee's researchers who sat on the Scientific Committee (*Encumen-i Ilmiye Heyeti*) as well. For example, Baha Sait Bey was responsible for Kizilbashes and Bektâshîs; Mehmet Tahir (Olgun) and Hasan Fehmi Hoca for the Ahîs; Asad (Uras) Bey for the Armenians; Zekeriya Sertel for the tribes, sects and Alevis; and Habil Adem for the Kurds and Turcomans.[9]

Of these studies only two, namely "The Kurds" and "The Turcomans", were published in 1918 by the General Directorate.[10] We can see clearly how these publications played an important role in the official ideology regarding the question of the minorities.

While the Committee was carrying out the policy of displacement and settlement of Muslim populations and non-Muslims as well, it often referred to census and ethnographic maps to improve implementation of the Turkification policy. For example Talat Pasha sent coded telegrams to all the provinces and districts on 20 July 1915, instructing them to prepare ethnographic maps and statistical tables of their regions, even including the smallest villages.[11]

After a quick look at the settlement policy of the Committee in general, we can now focus on the policy of displacement and settlement of Muslim populations.

Albanian immigrants who were expelled from the Balkans after 1913 were dispersed from western Anatolia to the interior and eastern Anatolia, in such a way as to constitute less than 10% and sometimes 5% of the total population under Talat's orders.[12]

In addition, the General Directorate published a special order for them, the Albanian Order, requiring that Albanian immigrants should settle in specified regions "mixed with other ethnic groups".[13] The traditional settlement policy of the Arab tribes of the Empire was brutally changed under Jamal Pasha's regime (November 1914 - December 1917 in Syria). Jamal carried out a cruel and selective displacement policy, depending on loyalty to the government, which resulted in the fragmentary settlement of Arab families. The main objective was to suppress Arab rebellion and weaken Arab demography in Syria.

The first large displacement by Jamal Pasha took place in September 1915. The Druze of the Hauran were expelled to Osmaniye; the outcome of this was to restructure the ethnic and religious composition of the Syrian region. When the displacement of Arabs was at its height, the General Directorate published the Arab Order on 23 April 1916, to organize better the settlement of Arab families who were distributed amongst the different Anatolian cities and villages.[14]

On the one hand, Jamal wanted to settle Arab families in the Turkish region where they could be assimilated easily and rapidly[15]; and on the other, he settled the Armenians of Asia Minor in areas of Druze residence[16]. In total, at least 5,000 Arab families were affected by this policy, which was to continue for the next two years.[17]

Until 1913, the Bosnian immigrants expelled from the Balkans were not discriminated against, compared to other Muslims; but after this turning point things changed. They were separated from other ethnic groups and, like the Albanians, they were deported far from the west of Anatolia, to be settled in the interior and eastern Anatolia, where they were supposed to forget "their language, their traditions and their national cultures" easily. However, the

Committee was not as rigid with them as it was with the Albanians, nor were the Bosnian immigrants so numerous and politically well-organized.[18]

The Georgian Muslims, especially the Ajarians, who had escaped from the Russian army at the beginning of the First World War, escaped again in 1916 from Trebizond towards the west, especially to the provinces of Ordu and Bolu. The Committee closely observed their movements and settlement. Local agencies of the Directorate did not settle them without its authorization. For example, according to a coded telegram, the local agencies of Trebizond were required to deport the Georgians from there to Ordu.[19]

One of the Committee's largest operations, after the Armenians, involved the Kurdish population, which included more than one million people over a vast territory. Firstly, the settlement process of Kurdish tribes, which had been continuing for many decades, was stepped up after the displacement of the Armenian population; and secondly the flight of the Kurds before the Russian army would give the Committee a chance to deport them to central and western Anatolia.

A series of coded telegrams sent by the Directorate in May 1916 allows us to clarify the outline of the displacement and settlement policy affecting the Kurdish population. They would by no means be allowed to settle in the south (the Arab area); they were made to settle only in the western region of Asia Minor, and it was ensured that the chiefs, the sheikhs and the imams settled separately from their tribes and communities in the cities, never in small villages where they could be influential.[20] Especially after the retreat of the Russian army from eastern Anatolia, the Kurds who attempted to return to their land were stopped by force.[21] Despite some disobedience by the Lazes, the Committee did not consider them very dangerous. For this reason, they were allowed to settle in coastal regions of strategic importance, in the area inhabited by the Christian population. Moreover, the Committee set up brigades formed of Lazes (just like the brigades of Georgians and other Caucasians) to send to the Caucasus, as they were considered great warriors.[22]

The Circassians were settled along the Baghdad-Hejaz railway in Syria to protect the railway against Arab tribes. Because of this region's desert climate and frequent attacks by the Bedouins, many of them wanted to migrate to Asia Minor. But the Committee did not accept their demands, as they were very important for the security of the railway and major cities such as Mecca and Medina. After the start of the Arab revolt, however, the first convoy of Circassian immigrants reached Urfa in November 1916. Faced with a *fait accompli*, the Committee settled them in Urfa, Diyarbakır, Ma'mûret-ül-azîz, Maras, Elbistan and Mardin, where the Russian army was only about ten kilometres away and advancing rapidly.[23]

The gypsies, both Muslim and non-Muslim, had been living amongst the Balkans immigrants of Albanian, Bosnian and Turkish origin. But the Committee had accepted only the Muslim gypsies, never the Christian gypsies.

Towards to the end of 1917, however, when the Muslim gypsy immigrants increased in number, the Directorate decided to ban even their entry into the Empire. For example, on 18 December 1917, four out of a total of 38 wagons carrying immigrants were not allowed into Ottoman territory because of their gypsy identity.[24]

Another evidence of this discrimination was Article 3 of the General Ordinance on Tribes and Refugees issued by the Directorate on 15 January 1918, prohibiting gypsies from entering the Empire.[25]

Furthermore, the Directorate issued and then sent to several cities and villages the Gypsy Order of 22 December 1917, under which gypsy nomads were forced to work in military factories.[26] Turkish immigrants from the Balkans and those fleeing from the Russian army in the East, as well as the nomadic Turcoman tribes, were the main demographic source that the Committee could draw on in implementing its Turkification policy. In general, the Balkan Turks settled in Thrace, in the coastal region of western Anatolia, in the Marmara region (especially the islands) and in Adana[27]. As regards the Turkish refugees, they settled in the east in provinces such as Diyarbakır, Urfa, Maras, Antep.) and the south-east (like Mosul) and especially along the railway lines as a security measure to guard against attacks by Arab tribes.[28]

With regard to the Turcomans, who numbered around one million, the Committee considered them a means to "reinforce Turkish sovereignty" among the Arab and Kurdish population.[29]

Apart from that, even if the Committee and Jamal Pasha had wanted to settle Turkish colonies in Syria and Palestine, the Arab revolt and the priority accorded to the Turkification of Asia Minor did not permit them to achieve their desire.[30]

Conclusion

This comprehensive transformation of the ethnic and religious composition of Anatolia caused the disintegration of the structure of the Muslim societies as well. The essential aim of the settlement policy was to put an end to the existence of demographically homogenous regions by mixing the Turkish Muslim population with non-Turkish Muslims. In line with the Committee's policy, the directions the displacements took were *grosso-modo* as follows: the Kurds were moved from east to west across Anatolia; the Arabs were moved from south to north across Syria and Anatolia; the Bosnians and Albanians were moved from west to east across Anatolia; the Circassians were moved from south to north across Syria and Anatolia, etc. Certain zones were forbidden to certain ethnic groups. Strategic areas, islands, coastlines, the area along the railway lines and rivers were reserved for loyal elements. Moreover the Committee wanted to destroy the traditional structure of all non-Turkish Muslim populations, and for this reason it separated them from their traditional chiefs, settling them among the Turkish population at such a rate as to constitute less than 10% of the total population. An important point was that the Committee issued separate orders for each specific ethnic and religious group, for which a separate assimilation policy was developed and pursued.

In short, a significant section of the country's population was displaced by the Committee in the space of five years. Here is the estimated breakdown of the displaced population: nearly one million Balkan refugees, approximately 2 million Kurdish and Turcoman nomads[31], 5,000 Arab families from Syria, nearly 1.5 million refugees from eastern Anatolia[32], some Arab refugees from Tripoli and Benghazi whose number is unknown, nearly 400,000 new Balkan refugees, and the Circassians who escaped from Syria. In other words, more than one third of the Muslim population of Asia Minor was transferred to places far away from their original habitat[33]. If we add to this picture the massive reduction of the non-Muslim population, i.e. nearly 1.2 million Greeks[34] and more than 1.5 million Armenians, we can see clearly that one half of Asia Minor's population was affected by the Committee's policy. It is certain that thanks to this policy the movement of National Struggle and Mustafa Kemal found an ethnic and religious composition of the population of Anatolia which lent itself well to the construction of the new nation-state. In other words, the origins of the ethnic distribution in present-day Turkey are to be found in this period, 1913-1918.

Chapter 5
The politics of Turkification during the Single Party period

Rifat N. Bali

This paper analyzes in brief the Turkification policies of the founding fathers of the Turkish Republic towards the country's minorities. It will seek to examine how the chief Republican leaders, Mustafa Kemal and his colleagues, defined the Turkish nation and determined the guidelines to convert non-Muslims into Turkish citizens, and what they considered the indicators of having been Turkified. It will also try to describe the methods they used for speeding up the process and the hidden face of the Turkification project, which was the Turkification of the economy. The term "minority" refers strictly to the non-Muslims, as the term was designated at the Peace Treaty of Lausanne.[1]

The term "Turkification" means the Turkish Republic's project to create a state of citizens enjoying equal rights, who define themselves first and foremost as Turks, their religion being a private matter.[2]

How Mustafa Kemal defined the term "Turkish nation"

According to Mustafa Kemal, unity of religion was not essential for the formation of a nation. For him, a nation was a society formed by persons who (a) share a rich historical legacy, (b) have a sincere desire to live together, and (c) have a common will to preserve their shared heritage. Mustafa Kemal's definition of the Turkish nation did not exclude the non-Muslim citizens, provided that they considered themselves part of the nation, a thought which he expressed in the following statement: "If the Christian and Jewish citizens who live among us today bind their fate and destiny to the Turkish nation because their conscience tells them to do so, then how can the civilized and nobly moral Turkish people consider them as strangers?"[3]

The minimal conditions for becoming a Turk

The various statements of Mustafa Kemal and other Republican leaders declaring that non-Muslim citizens were accepted as part of the Turkish nation always included three minimum conditions: the non-Muslims had to adopt (a) the Turkish language as their mother tongue, (b) Turkish culture, and (c) the ideal of Turkism. In 1925, after repressing the Sheikh Said Kurdish rebellion, Prime Minister İsmet Pasha made a declaration to the delegates of the nationalist organization *Türk Ocakları* (Turkish Hearths.)[4] The forceful tone of his words proved the strong determination of the Republic's elites to Turkify its minorities. These were his words: "Our immediate duty is to make Turks all those who live in the Turkish fatherland. We will cut out and throw away the minorities who oppose Turks and Turkism."[5] Both the Republican People's Party (RPP) and Mustafa Kemal would repeat this message in different forms in the subsequent years. For example, an RPP regulation accepted in 1927 specified once again that "the strongest bond among citizens is the union of language, sentiments, and ideas".[6] Similarly Mustafa Kemal, while visiting Adana in 1931, underlined once again how speaking Turkish was an important criterion for being considered a Turk. He said: "One of the most obvious, precious qualities of a nation is language.

A person who says he belongs to the Turkish nation should in the first place and under all circumstances speak Turkish. It is not possible to believe a person's claims that he belongs to the Turkish nation and to Turkish culture, if he does not speak Turkish."[7]

The person who best understood how to interpret such declarations was a Jewish businessman by the name of Moiz Kohen. Kohen changed his name to Tekinalp and in 1928 published his book entitled *Türkleştirme* (Turkification), which he dedicated to the nationalist organization *Türk Ocakları*. In his book Tekinalp argued that not only Jews but all minorities had to be Turkified if they wanted to deserve the status of citizenship granted to them by the Constitution of 1924.

A chapter of his book includes his address to the Jewish community in the form of ten instructions that the community had to follow to become Turks. They were modeled after the Ten Commandments of Moses, and were in essence a summary of the Republican founders' expectations:[8]

. Turkify your names
. Speak Turkish
. In the synagogues read part of the prayers in Turkish
. Turkify your schools
. Send your children to state schools
. Interest yourself in Turkey's affairs
. Socialize with Turks
. Eliminate the [Jewish] community spirit
. Do your particular duty in the area of the national economy
. Know your constitutional rights

What the Republican elites really wanted was for non-Muslims to disband their "community" structures, melt and dissolve their religious/ethnic identities into the new Turkish national identity, and emerge as Turks of Jewish or Christian faith. These new Turks, sharing a unity of language, spirit and culture with Turkish society at large, would no longer be distinguishable from their compatriots, the Muslim Turks.

What were the main indicators of being Turkified?

Speaking Turkish

The first condition of language unity was to speak Turkish. Obviously the Jewish community, which had spoken Ladino for centuries, could not adopt Turkish as its mother tongue in a matter of a few years' time. For this reason, in the first years of the Republic Deputy Chief Rabbi Becerano stated that Jews would adopt Turkish in a matter of ten to fifteen years' time. In other words he was asking the authorities to show patience and tolerance towards the Jews not yet speaking Turkish.[9]

However Mustafa Kemal and his entourage, who were implementing the Reform Laws (such as adopting the Latin alphabet, fixing Saturday and Sunday as the weekend instead of Friday, accepting the Gregorian calendar, etc.) day by day, did not have the patience to wait for ten to fifteen years. Consequently the "Citizien Speak Turkish!" campaign of the first years of the Republic, which aimed to put public pressure on minorities to convince them to speak Turkish in public, mainly targeted the Turkish Jewish community because of its special situation. Turkish Jews did not speak Hebrew, which the Turkish elites regarded as the Jewish mother tongue. If they had spoken Hebrew, Turkish Jews could easily have argued that according to the rights granted to the minorities by the Lausanne Peace Treaty, they could continue to speak and teach Hebrew freely. However they were speaking Ladino, which was Castillian Spanish mixed with Turkish, Greek, and French words, and also French, which they had learned at the Alliance Israélite Universelle schools.[10]

For this reason they were continuously criticized by the republican elites, in whose eyes Turkish Jews were the prototypes of a minority population which did not want to be Turkified. Not a day went by in the humoristic journals and the daily press without Jews being made a laughing stock in articles or caricatures, whereas such ridicule was rarely aimed at Greeks or Armenians.[11]

Turkification of names and surnames

Another indication of being Turkified was to Turkify names and surnames. The Law of Family Names, promulgated in 1934, made it mandatory for everybody to take a family name. However the law prevented the adoption of names of tribes, foreign races or nations as family names. The Greeks of Turkey would Turkify their names by dropping the "-dis" and "-pulos" suffixes. Most of the Jews would Turkify their names and surnames by finding a Turkish equivalent for each Jewish name.[12]

Participation in campaigns of donations

The most important indicator of having assimilated to the Turkish ideal was the making of donations to non-profit societies such as the Red Crescent, the Turkish Aviation Society, and the Children's Welfare Society, or to campaigns which were initiated after natural disasters in the country. Contributions to such campaigns aimed to convey the following message to Turkish society and the Republican elites, "We are Turks like you. We are together in our happy and sad moments". At the same time it aimed to prevent the slightest criticism that the minorities were not faithful to their fatherland. In fact, when looking at the lists of donors to such campaigns, one can immediately discern that non-Muslims contributed much more than Muslims.[13]

Liquidation of community schools

The principal method for achieving cultural unification was the Turkification of minority schools, which in the Ottoman Empire taught the language and culture of the specific minority groups. In the Turkish Republic, these schools would start to Turkify their curriculum according to the dictates of the Ministry of Education. As a matter of fact, Prime Minister İsmet Pasha, in a speech pronounced in 1925 at the Teachers' Union, made the new national education policy of the young Republic crystal clear. These were his words: "The foreign cultures must melt into this homogeneous nation. There can not be different civilizations in this nation. Each nation of the world represents a civilization. We now clearly propose to those who see themselves tied to other communities rather than the civilization of the Turkish people to join with the Turkish nation. Not as an alloy, not as a federation of civilizations but as a single civilization. This fatherland belongs to this people and to this nation which has been unified."[14]

Methods used to accelerate Turkification

The Republican elites sometimes used different ways and means to speed up the Turkification process. Among them two methods were encountered most often and were most effective.

The first method was to exercise public pressure on minorities via well-known journalists who were at the same time members of the Parliament and of the RPP. These journalists indirectly conveyed the expectations of the RPP leadership for the Turkification of minorities in their editorials, thus prompting public pressure.[15]

The second method was to put pressure on the minority communities to dismantle their centrally-structured community organizations. The most important institutions of the minority communities were the non-profit foundations which ran hospitals, churches, synagogues, schools, and old people's homes. After the Law of Foundations was accepted in 1935, the General Directorate of Non-Profit Foundations had the authority to designate the directors of the minority foundations. These directors imposed from outside, lacking internal support from the community grassroots, could not generate donations as in the past. At the same time, the new law put a freeze on the acquisition of new property, thus blocking the communities' development. These changes resulted in the cash flow of the community foundations being reduced to a minimum, and as a result their structure being weakened.[16]

Turkification of the economy

For the minorities who had lived for centuries as *dhimmis* in the Ottoman Empire, the project of Turkification promised equality, constitutional rights and public participation in building the new Turkish Republic. For this reason community leaders were eager to accept the project and promote it to their grassroots. From the early years of the Turkish Republic, however, certain symptoms hinted at a hidden agenda which was in full contradiction with the aim of transforming minorities into citizens with equal rights. This hidden agenda was the project of Turkifying the economy.

The founders of the Republic, after winning the National War of Independence, wanted to make Turkey fully independent economically. For them, however, "independent" meant making Muslim Turks dominant in the banking, trading and manufacturing sectors. There were two reasons for this: (a) they considered the Muslim Turks as "the true masters of Turkey since they alone had shed their blood for the fatherland", and (b) in the eyes of the Republican elites the non-Muslims represented the last remnants of the Capitulations, a system of economic privileges granted to the European powers which exploited the Ottoman Empire.

In their addresses during the First Congress of Economy in February 1923, both Mustafa Kemal and Minister of Economy Mahmut Esat Bozkurt emphasized that the sovereignty of the Turkish people had to be consolidated with that of the Turkish economy. In the same spirit, Mustafa Kemal's address in Adana to the artisans of that city is also very meaningful. When an artisan complained that the Armenians had the upper hand in all crafts, Mustafa Kemal's reply was as follows: "Armenians have no right in this prosperous country. The country is yours, the country belongs to the Turks. Historically this country was Turkish, therefore it is Turkish and will remain Turkish for ever. The country has finally been returned to its rightful owners. The Armenians and the others have no right to be here. These fertile regions are the country of the real Turks." These words showed without any doubt the intention of the Republican leadership, as they presented the Armenians as foreigners, rather than as Turks.[17]

The first step in implementing the Turkification of the economy was the firing of non-Muslim employees working in foreign companies established in Turkey. This decision aimed to make room for the Muslim Turks returning from the War of Independence and looking for employment. In the 1920s the employees who were fluent in a foreign language and had some commercial experience were all non-Muslims of foreign or Turkish nationality. A quota was imposed to limit drastically the number of employees of foreign nationality that foreign companies could employ. Many employees exceeding the quota were fired and replaced with Muslim Turks. The companies who did not comply were warned that unless they did so, their activities would be suspended. The officials who enforced this decree did not differentiate between non-

Muslims of Turkish nationality and those of foreign nationality. As a result non-Muslims Turkish citizens also lost their jobs.[18]

Another method used in the Turkification of the economy was the interpretation of the term "to be a Turk", a term which was used in the clauses of different legislations, such as those establishing the qualifications for being a state employee or opening a pharmacy. In its application, the term "Turk" was interpreted not as a nationality but as an ethnic and religious identity, and it therefore came to mean "Muslim". The result was that non-Muslims were de facto discriminated against.[19]

Did the executors of the Turkification policy really want to Turkify the minorities?

The Turkish Republic was established as the continuation of the Ottoman Empire, but it denied its Ottoman past since it wanted to establish a new state with new citizens governed not by Sharia Law but by Republican principles. This meant that religion would be a private and not a public affair. But the behaviour of the Republican elites vis-à-vis non-Muslims was quite contradictory to the Republican principles. On one hand they repeatedly stated that they would accept the minorities as real "Turks" provided that they sincerely embraced the Turkish ideal, language, and culture, and on the other hand they interpreted the legislation and the concept of "non-Muslim" in a manner that made it very clear that they considered Turkey as a predominantly Muslim country in which non-Muslim citizens did not have full rights.

Even Tekinalp, the Jewish ideologue of Turkification, admitted that until 1931 there was a significant number of people in Turkey who believed that unity of religion was necessary for the nation's unity and that it was only in 1931, in the Third Convention of the RPP, that this situation was clarified.[20] Indeed, in this convention the RPP defined the nation as "a political and social entity formed by citizens bonded together in a unified language, culture and ideal" and made the following statement for the benefit of its non-Muslim citizens: "We have to declare our ideas very clearly to our Christian and Jewish citizens. Our party totally accepts these citizens as Turks, provided that they participate in the unity of language and ideal. Needless to say, in this new society there is not even a trace of the anachronistic reaya (non-Muslim subjects of the Ottoman Empire) mentality."[21]

In the face of this crystal clear declaration, how can we explain the reasons for the discrimination that existed in daily life and in the application of the various legislations in the Single Party period? My tentative answer is the following:

The most important reason for the failure of the Turkification policies was the Ottoman legacy that the young Republic wanted to get rid of but could not. The Turkish Republic, born from the remains of an Empire run for centuries by Sharia law, was not able to change the collective memory of its elites and its society, even in the period when the principle of secularism was applied in its most rigid form. The Ottoman Empire, until the reforms of the Tanzimat, administrated its non-Muslim communities through the millet system and considered them as *dhimmis*, People of the Book, who were under the protection of the Muslims. The Republican regime, in spite of its declarations that it accepted its non-Muslims as equal citizens provided that they melt into the Turkish national identity, could not forget the years of the Armistice and the National War of Independence. The Republican elites remembered how the minorities cheered the Allied Forces when they occupied Istanbul and the Greek army when it occupied Izmir. They could not forget the famous Grande Rue de Péra in Istanbul, where one could hear Ladino, Greek, Armenian and French, but practically not one word of Turkish. They called İzmir "Gâvur İzmir" (infidel Izmir) because the majority of its population consisted of non-Muslims and Levantines. They could not forget the fact that while a National War of Independence was going on, the minorities living in Istanbul and İzmir were tending their own businesses. All these negative snapshots from the past formed the collective memory of the young Republic's elites and became the main handicap in the successful implementation of the Turkification project.

The Republican regime promised equality and secularism to non-Muslims, but it could never accept them as citizens and continued to view them as *dhimmis*, because of the Ottoman legacy. Furthermore, the memory of the War of Independence, never faded from the minds of the Republican elites, in whose eyes non-Muslims were "strangers whose loyalty was suspect" and not founding members of the Turkish nation since they had not fought in the National War of Independence. The relationship between the Republican elites and the non-Muslim Turkish citizens was somehow a love-hate affair, as they put pressure on them to Turkify on one hand while on the other hand they really did not want to embrace them as loyal citizens with full rights.

This negative legacy of the past would resurface later in the atmosphere of World War Two and recreate the trauma of the years of the Armistice and War of Independence. As a result, the Capital Tax levy promulgated in 1942, which rightfully intended to tax profits earned from speculations and black market operations, would be implemented in a totally discriminatory manner against citizens of the Jewish and Christian faiths and those of Dönme origins.[22]

The discriminatory implementation of the Capital Tax levy would be the last and the unforgettable example of the de facto discrimination against the non-Muslims in the Single Party period. It was, at the same time, the proof of the complete failure of the Turkification policies.

Chapter 6

Depriving non-Muslims of citizenship as part of the Turkification policy in the early years of the Turkish Republic: The case of Turkish Jews and its consequences during the Holocaust

Corinna Görgü Guttstadt

Following the creation of the Turkish Republic in 1923, the focus of the Kemalist policy turned to the Turkification of the population of the newly-formed nation state. A considerable number of studies have been published recently on many aspects of this Turkification, including language policy (*vatandaş Türkçe konuş*), the formation of nationalist organizations (*Türk ocakları*), the creation of a national historiography (*Türk Tarih Tezi*) and forcible resettlement (*iskan politikaları*). However, the policies of naturalization and denaturalization that aimed to create an ethnically homogeneous population have received little attention.

Because of the enormous loss of population during a series of wars (the war in Yemen and in the Balkans, the First World War and the War of Liberation) and the subsequent expulsion of Greeks (and surviving Armenians), the Kemalist leadership was interested in increasing the country's population and encouraged the settlement of immigrants who were seen as capable of becoming Turkish.[1] In particular, Muslims from the Balkans and Turkish-speaking citizens from the then Soviet areas of Central Asia and the Caucasus were regarded as "desirable elements" and they were usually given Turkish citizenship without many formalities.[2] On the other hand, several thousand members of non-Muslim minorities were deprived of their Turkish citizenship (denaturalized). The majority – but not all – were living abroad. Deprivation of citizenship was also used to silence political opponents, e.g. the denaturalization of the One Hundred and Fifty (*150-likler*) in 1924, whose case was published in Turkey last year. "Support for the enemy during the liberation struggle" resulted in several cases in individuals being stripped of their Turkish citizenship.[3]

Laws and decrees approved to ensure the legality of denaturalization

1.) Law No. 1041 of 23 May 1927

This law empowered the Council of Ministers to denaturalize citizens who had not participated in the War of Liberation and had not returned to Turkey prior to the promulgation of the law.

2.) Decision 7559 of the Council of Ministers of 26 December 1928

This decision allowed the denaturalization of women who had not participated in the War of Liberation.[4]

3.) Law No. 1312 on Citizenship of 23 May 1928[5]

Article 10 entitled the Council of Ministers to denaturalize people for various reasons, such as desertion, not doing the obligatory military service or falling into the category of those "... of whom it had become known that they fled abroad and who could not prove the opposite and return within the given time, (...) or Turkish citizens who have been living abroad for five years and have not registered with the Turkish Consulates in question."[6]

4.) Travel and Traffic Decree (*Seyrisefer Tâlimatnamesi*) of 1933[7]

5.) Article 7 of Law No. 2848

This law was passed on 18 November 1935 as an amendment to the *İskan Kanunu* (Law No. 2510) and gave the Council of Ministers the right to determine who "was to be regarded as a Turk because of his culture"[8].

6.) Passport Law No. 3518 of 28 June 1938

This law allowed for the denaturalization of people, in particular if they had not notified a Consulate for five years.[9]

Measures against minorities

In Article 88, the 1924 Constitution of Turkey declared all inhabitants of Turkey to be Turkish citizens, and thus guaranteed legal equality. The discussion on the Constitution, however, made it clear that the Kemalist policy on citizenship differentiated between Turkish citizens and "true Turks".[10]

This attitude was reflected in a number of laws concerning access to professions and education and was aimed at banning members of minorities from participating in the economy - what may be called "economic Turkification".[11]

The legal provisions on deprivation of citizenship were also directed against the minorities. This can be highlighted as follows:

Law No. 1042 (non-participation in the liberation war) was one of the main reasons for the mass deprivations of citizenship in the 1930s and 1940s. It discriminated against minorities who had little opportunity to participate in the liberation struggle. The kernel of what was to become the Army was the *Anadolu ve Rumeli Müdafaa-i Hukuk Cemiyet-i*. Its statute described it as an Islamic organization fighting for the maintenance of the Caliphate.[12]

Only in December 1920 did this force become a regular army (*merkez ordusu*) and on 26 December 1920 was it decided to draft non-Muslims.[13]

A few weeks later, on 2 March 1921, an order was issued to move members of minorities from the army into labour battalions (*amele taburları*). The non-

Muslims who were sent to these units were disarmed, stripped of their uniforms and put to work on road construction and the like. This practice was not only discriminatory, but no doubt it was understood as a direct threat by those in the labour battalions: The practice had been introduced in the First World War and the killing of Armenians in similar units had marked the start of the Armenian genocide.[14]

It should not be forgotten that the majority of Jews had no opportunity to participate in the liberation struggle because they mainly lived in Western Anatolia, Thrace and Istanbul, regions that at the time were under Greek or Allied forces occupation. In addition, it was even difficult to recruit Muslim Turks into the army, because people were exhausted and tired of war. Some sources state that more soldiers died during attempts to desert than from Greek attacks.[15]

This context, and the fact that women and hundreds of people who had either not been born or were babies at the time of the war were also stripped of their citizenship because they had not participated in combat[16], indicates that the laws were designed to deprive unwanted sections of the population of their Turkish citizenship. Inspecting the *Başbakanklık Cumhuriyet Arşivi*, I did not find a single case where the law had been used against a Muslim.[17]

The Travel and Traffic Decree (Seyrisefer Tâlimatnamesi)

According to this decree, only people who had left Turkey with a travel document issued by the Grand National Assembly of Turkey (that is, the provisional government between 1921 and 1923, before the foundation of the Republic) or by the government of the Turkish Republic, were entitled to return to Turkey. All those who had left the country with Ottoman documents or without a valid passport had to apply to Turkish diplomatic representations abroad for permission to return. The applications were reviewed by the General Directory for Public Order (*Emniyet İşleri Umum Müdiriyet*).[18]

Because the provisional government had decided not to give passports or certificates of citizenship to non-Muslims, this decree again singled out members of these minorities.[19] According to Çağaptay, who studied the diplomatic correspondence between the US Embassy in Turkey and Washington, the decree mainly prevented Armenians in the United States from returning to Turkey, while Turks and Jews there got permission, even if they only possessed Ottoman documents. In Europe, the *Seyrisefer Tâlimatnamesi* decree was clearly used against Jews, as can be seen in a letter written by Monsieur Yakar from Paris to Prime Minister İnönü. Amongs other things, Monsieur Yakar complains that the Turkish consulates abroad did not inform Turkish citizens living abroad about laws concerning them.[20]

Quantitative investigation of denaturalization

In his article on various models of denaturalization, Çağaptay cites several examples, but he does not systematically relate the reasons given to the ethnic-religious background or place of residence of the people in question. Having looked at the list of decisions on denaturalization found in the *Başbakanlık Arşivi*, I suggest the following typology:

Under the term *"vatandaşlık"* (citizenship), the list of contents carries 756 entries between 1924 and 1944 relating to people stripped of their citizenship.[21]

In the first years of the Republic, these decisions mostly concerned individuals living abroad, who had either acquired a different nationality or applied to be released from their nationality in order to get a different one. The majority were members of minorities living abroad. In individual cases, Greeks and Jews living in Turkey were stripped of their citizenship.

In these cases, deprivation of citizenship appears to be the legal confirmation of expulsions that took place during three periods: the First World War, the War of Liberation, and the so-called population exchange between Greece and Turkey. One can assume that the decisions were related to the acquisition of the expellees' property. According to Article 8 of Law No. 1312, persons who ceased to be citizens had to sell their property in Turkey within one year. If this could not be accomplished before the deadline the government would handle the sale.[22]

As late as 1928, the 41 decisions on denaturalization concerned individuals, including one married couple and one set of siblings. The 43 denaturalized persons comprised Armenians, Jews, Greeks, Muslims, one Arab Christian and one Circassian. For 19 persons, the reason given for deprivation of citizenship was that they had changed their citizenship without permission; four persons were stated to have done military or other service for another state; three persons were stated not to have taken part in the War of Liberation; one Jew from Vienna asked to be stripped of his citizenship; one Armenian was simply described as belonging to the Armenian people, apparently reason enough to deprive him of his citizenship.

In 1929, the first mass denaturalizations were carried out. Five decisions issued in November 1929 concerned 497 persons who were stripped of their citizenship because they had not participated in the War of Liberation. In the late 1930s, the mass denaturalizations increased significantly. In 1939, 11 of the 18 decisions were mass denaturalizations concerning a total of 729 persons. Five of these decisions could be consulted at the *Başbakanlık* Archives. The decisions did not concern persons who had taken up a different citizenship. Instead, they were based on Law No. 1041 (no participation in the War of Liberation – 208 persons), Article 10 of Law No. 1312 (a total of 107 persons) and two decisions related to 127 peoples presented as "without ties to Turkish culture" (Article 7 of Law No. 2848).[23]

In the 1940s, these mass denaturalizations increased further. 1941 saw ten decisions which deprived 716 persons of their citizenship. In 1942, a total of 703 persons were stripped of their citizenship because they had not participated in the War of Liberation or regularly notified the Turkish Consulate.[24]

1943 marked the peak of mass denaturalizations involving a total of 1,421 persons in 14 decisions. 1,293 persons were stripped of their citizenship either because they "had not taken part in the War of Liberation" (456 persons) or because they had not shown up at the Consulate for five years (837 persons).[25] In 1944, seven decisions deprived 605 persons of their Turkish citizenship. The fact that the vast majority of Cabinet's decisions were not promulgated in the *Resmi Gazette* (Turkey's Official Gazette), as was prescribed, points to the semi-legal character of this policy. From the late 1930s through the 1940s, the overwhelming majority of mass denaturalizations concerned Jews living in Europe. This deprived them of their protection from persecution by the Germans.

Turkish Jews in Europe

At the beginning of the Second World War, some 20,000 Jews from Turkey were living in Europe. About 10,000 of them were settled in France[26]; and a roughly equal number was living in other European countries.

While a number of Ottoman Jews had already moved to various European metropols (Paris, Brussels, Berlin) during the last decades of the 19th century, a bigger wave of migration occurred between 1909 and 1923. This migration had several causes, including the drafting of minorities for military service in 1909 and the ensuing wars that took place, mainly in regions where Turkish Jews lived. However, the main exodus of Turkish Jews to Europe started in the mid-1920's, when Turkey's before-mentioned politics of economic Turkification limited their economic activity.

As Jews in Europe, they were subjected to Nazi Germany's measures against Jews, including the risk of being deported to concentration camps. At the beginning of the Holocaust, Turkish and other foreign Jews belonged to those groups whose deportation to concentration camps was "delayed" for tactical reasons. Foreign Jews were also partly exempted from other anti-Jewish measures, like wearing a star suffering various limitations on their daily life.

From the autumn of 1942 onwards, the diplomatic missions of neutral countries or those allied to Germany were asked to repatriate their Jewish citizens from German-occupied countries (the so-called "Heimschaffung"). The NS authorities contacted the missions of Turkey and other neutral countries and gave them lists of the names of their Jewish nationals who had been detected in these countries.

They informed them that they must repatriate their nationals, or else these Jews would be "subjected to the general measures concerning Jews", i.e. they would be deported to a concentration camp. All those who could not prove their Turkish citizenship were regarded as stateless and therefore left without any protection from the NS anti-Jewish policies. Stateless Jews were among the first victims of deportations, which already started in Germany in November 1941. The deportation of 20 former Turkish Jews, who had unexpectedly been deprived of their Turkish citizenship in the late 1930's from Berlin, is documented[27]. Thousands of stateless and foreign Jews were victims of the big raids in Paris in 1941 and were among the first to be deported from 1942 onwards.

Germany was interested in maintaining good relations with Turkey, which was neutral for most of the war, and took care not to harm ties between the two countries. When the Turkish authorities did not react to German demands to repatriate their Jews within the given period (the first deadline was 31.12.1942), the deadline was extended several times until 31.12.1943 (or 31.1.1944 for France). Furthermore, in many cases, even after Turkish Jews were arrested and detained in camps in several European countries, the Nazis sent lists of these Turkish subjects to the Turkish authorities, asking whether the Turks were ready to claim them as their citizens.[28] The cases of Lazar Rousso and Albert Saül prove that Turkish interventions to rescue Jews with Turkish citizenship were successful. Both of them had been detained during street operations in Paris in 1941 and taken to the concentration camp at Compiegne.[29]

Both Rousso and Saül, were released after protests from the Turkish Embassy in Paris.[30]

Stanford Shaw documents further successful examples of Turkish intervention in favour of arrested Turkish Jews.[31]

Deprivations of citizenship parallel to the Holocaust

Compared with the total number of Turkish Jews in Europe during the Holocaust, the number of rescue attempts appears minimal. Looking at the correspondence between Turkish and German officials documented in the political archives of the Foreign Ministry in Berlin, Turkey's policies were mainly concerned to "... prevent a mass immigration of Jews to Turkey".[32]

This became manifest *inter alia* when Turkey again and again did not meet the deadlines for evacuating their Jewish nationals in territory under German control. Only in February 1943 did the Turkish Embassy in Paris inform the German authorities that it recognized 631 (out of 3,000) Turkish Jews as Turkish citizens; it only asked for get transit visas for 114 persons to evacuate them to Turkey.[33]

In order to prevent the feared "mass immigration" of Jews (who held Turkish citizenship), the Turkish government increasingly relied on depriving Jewish nationals of their citizenship as NS policies became more severe against Jews. My research in archives in Berlin, Prague, Brussels and Paris shows that at a time when Turkish Jews urgently needed the protection of their diplomatic representatives, the Turkish government in fact increased its rate of denaturalizations. Thus, many of the Jews living in Germany and Austria were stripped of their citizenship in the 1930s. The Turkish authorities asked even the NS authorities for help, first, to summon and interview the persons in questions, and later to deliver the decisions on denaturalization. In Berlin and Prague, this was done by the foreigner police, under the ultimate authority of the Gestapo. Thus, the Gestapo was immediately informed about which Turkish Jews were now considered stateless.

Once the deportations of Jews from Western Europe had begun in 1942 and Germany had asked Turkey to repatriate its Jewish nationals, the Turkish government reacted with mass denaturalizations. In 1943 and 1944, more than 2,000 people were deprived of their citizenship. According to the lists available in the *Başbakanlık Cumhuriyet Arşivi*, the proportion of Jews among them was 92% in 1943. Of these, 92% were living in France, and the rest (11 persons) were living in other occupied countries of Europe. The picture in 1944 is almost identical: 83% of the denaturalized persons were Jews and about 90% of them were living in France.[34]

Most of these denaturalizations appear to have been executed according to lists of names that the Germans sent to Turkish missions. The German Embassy in Paris had sent the Turkish General Consulate a list of "some 5,000 Jews" in France.[35] In other occupied countries, the NS officials acted similarly. For example, the four Turkish Jews living in Prague were denaturalized after Germany's inquiry.

Only in spring 1944, when the German defeat was obvious and Turkey started to bet on the winning horse in its foreign relations, did international pressure enable several hundred Jews to be transported from France to Turkey in six trains. Yet even in the spring of 1945, the tendency not to let unwanted Jews into the country dominated the decisions of Turkish officials. On 11 March 1945, 137 Jews of Turkish origin reached Istanbul on the vessel "Drottningholm". They were part of an exchange of civilian prisoners of war between Turkey and Germany, and came from Bergen-Belsen and Ravensbrück concentration camps. Although the ship docked just as Bergen-Belsen was liberated and news about its horrors was published in the Turkish press, Turkey did not allow 116 of the 137 rescued Jews to enter the country. Only after troublesome negotiations did Haim Barlas, representative of the Jewish Agency in Istanbul, reach an agreement that they might leave the ship and be interned in three hotels in Istanbul, with the Jewish Agency covering the costs.

Summary

Between 1938 and 1945, Turkey deprived several thousand of its Jewish nationals living abroad of their citizenship. Although this policy was rooted in the nationalist goals of the Turkish Republic's early years, the continuation of it during the NS period in Europe meant that the Turkish authorities withdrew protection from their Jewish citizens, leaving them at risk of persecution and annihilation. Turkey likes to point to its "outstanding commitment"[36] to the rescue of Jews during the Holocaust and use this as positive propaganda in its foreign relations, including its repeated denials of the Armenian genocide. Turkey has still not clarified the fate of its Jewish citizens. Several thousand Turkish Jews became victims of the Holocaust, but no account of that tragedy or commemorative book yet exists.

Chapter 7
The exodus of Armenians from the Sanjak of Alexandretta in the 1930s

Berna Pekesen

In the Ottoman Empire, which was characterized by ethnic, religious, linguistic and cultural diversity, the formation of the nation state was accompanied by dramatic shifts of population from the start. Not surprisingly, therefore, the emergence of a Turkish national state in Asia Minor, too, saw demographic reorganization of a similar order, that is, the expulsion and resettlement of part of the population. There is hardly a group within the territory of the present-day Republic that was not confronted by this phenomenon at some time. The exodus of Armenians from the Vilayet of Hatay (Alexandretta), which was an autonomous *sanjak* under French mandate between 1921 and 1938, should be seen within this framework.

The topic has been treated rather marginally in historiography. Obviously, there is a tendency to interpret the mass flight from the area in the years 1938-39 as a natural result of former watersheds, such as the deportations and massacres during the First World War, the dissolution of the empire, and the emergence of the new Republic. If the prehistory of the event is taken into account, it is indeed not far-fetched to come to such a conclusion. Furthermore, this exodus took place at a time when it was hardly considered as an extraordinary occurrence, especially since the whole affair was carried out, in comparison with the events of 1920 in Cilicia, in an unspectacular manner. Yet, even though comprehensive monographic treatments are still lacking, some studies have appeared in recent years which, though touching upon the issue only fleetingly, have contributed to the clarification of at least the political circumstances of the population shifts. They provide the starting point for this article, in which I attempt to give a summary of the factors that led to the mass flight of Armenians from the former *sanjak*. In short, this exposition has a preliminary character. Given the complexity of the questions raised, it cannot claim to do justice to all aspects of the issue.[1]

My main interest is to examine the exodus of Armenians (along with Arabs and other groups) from the *sanjak* of Alexandretta (1921-1938) as a product of the widespread ideology of ethnic homogenization during the period. The exodus was also, however, the result of rival claims by Turkish and Arab nationalists to Alexandretta, which was a French mandate territory until its union with Turkey in 1939. Finally, the Western powers, by creating the necessary legal framework for this predictable development, were also involved. The exodus from the *sanjak* must be viewed in the context of their appeasement policy, particularly since they had repeatedly considered compulsory population exchange in the manner of the Greek-Turkish settlement at Lausanne (1923) as the *ultima ratio* in solving ethnic conflicts.[2]

Turkish irredentism and the international setting

At the end of the First World War, Britain and France occupied the Arab provinces of the Ottoman Empire in the Fertile Crescent or established their influence over them. Most of these territories were to be partitioned between the Allied powers according to the secret agreements (Sykes-Picot, 1916) negotiated during the war. The new political order of the Middle East was meant to be drawn up by the Allied peace conference in San Remo and the Treaty of Sèvres (1920). The Ottoman Empire was expected to renounce all its rights over the Arab Middle East and North Africa, while the provinces in the Fertile Crescent would be granted the right of self-determination. Instead, the Allies carved two "A"-type mandates out of Greater Syria: the mandate for the northern half (Syria proper including the *sanjak* of Alexandretta and Lebanon) was awarded to France, and the mandate for the southern half (Palestine and the provinces in Mesopotamia) was awarded to Great Britain. Under the terms of an "A" mandate, individual countries were deemed eventually to become independent, but they were temporarily subject to a Mandatory power until they had reached political maturity.[3] The Grand National Assembly in Ankara refused to ratify the Treaty of Sèvres, the terms of which had been accepted by the Sultan.[4]

Popular opposition to the Treaty of Sèvres developed into a Turkish national movement under the leadership of Mustafa Kemal (Atatürk). After military setbacks against Turkish nationalist forces in southern Anatolia (Cilicia) in 1920-21, the French felt obliged (by the Ankara Accord) to evacuate the occupied districts, maintaining, however, their mandate over the *Sanjak* of Alexandretta. Under French control, several small states had already been formed in Syria: Greater Libanon, the State of Damascus, the State of Aleppo, the Territory of the Alawites, and the Druze state. Alexandretta was added to the State of Aleppo, but was granted a separate, almost autonomous administrative status.[5]

In the Peace Treaty of Lausanne (1923), which established the current boundaries of the modern state of Turkey, Ankara renounced all claims to former Ottoman provinces in the Middle East, including the *sanjak* of Alexandretta, but excluding the province of Mosul, which soon became the object of an international controversy involving the League of Nations along with Great Britain. After a decision by the League of Nations (October 1924) and a later treaty with Great Britain (1926), Ankara was finally forced, albeit against its will, to relinquish its claims to Mosul in return for a ten percent share in the oil produced there.[6] But soon another controversy arose, this time over the *sanjak* of Alexandretta (encompassing the cities of Alexandretta and Antakya/Antioch and their surroundings), of which the mandate had, as already mentioned, been awarded to France by the League of Nations. Seemingly, Ankara accepted this arrangement, but with explicit references to the National Pact, adding that *"une terre turque vieille de quarante siècles ne peut pas rester aux mains de l'ennemi,"* thus insinuating that actually the *sanjak* should have remained within the boundaries of Turkey.[7]

Nonetheless, up to the middle of the thirties, Turkish diplomacy never officially demanded the re-integration of the *sanjak* into Turkey. The Turks quickly abandoned their restraint, however, when the political constellation in Europe began to change.

In Ankara it was now believed that the political climate had become favourable for a renewed discussion of the *sanjak* question. While Turkish-British relations improved in the course of the Ethiopian crisis (1935), and Ankara won a diplomatic victory when the Montreux Convention allowed the re-militarization of the Straits[8], the position of France was successively weakened by the developments in Central Europe, particularly after Hitler had occupied the Rhineland. In these circumstances President Atatürk obviously saw that the moment was favourable for a definitive solution of the *sanjak* issue. With unmistakable pride in having regained full sovereignty over the Straits, he now declared the *sanjak* question to be top on the agenda.[9]

Border rectification and demographic engineering

The *sanjak* of Alexandretta had been a region shaken by crises since the beginning of the twentieth century. The area became the theatre of large scale actions of expulsion and resettlement, and on account of its geostrategic suitability it was regarded by the Young Turk regime as a transit area in the deporting of Ottoman Armenians towards Syria and Mesopotamia. Even after 1918, the area remained caught up in the demographic turbulence caused by the Great War.

The Allies' military occupation hardly eased this situation. The French, who controlled Cilicia between 1918 and 1921, as if to comply with their historic mission as "Protectors of Christians in the Levant", attempted to create an independent Armenian state in that territory.[10]

At least the resettlement of those Armenians living in various refugee camps (carried out in cooperation with the *Légion Arménienne*) was viewed in this light, even though it was undertaken in order to alleviate the refugees' lot.[11] The ill feeling among local Muslim groups soared. In northern Syria and in the hinterland of Antioch a guerrilla war broke out against the French occupation forces, communal clashes leading to massacres and counter-massacres in many places.[12] The Turkish segment of the Muslim population was caught between two enemies; fearing revenge by both Arab and Armenian nationalists, many sought refuge in the Anatolian interior.

As mentioned above, the Ankara Accord of 1921 ended the state of war with France. This entailed not only the French army's evacuation of Cilicia, but also a mass exodus of the Armenian population in the wake of the retreating French troops. Fearing that they would face revenge or persecution if they remained, the majority of both the re-settled and the indigenous Armenian population hurried to find safety in Syria, Lebanon and Palestine, with some choosing to go to Alexandretta, which also remained under French Mandate.[13] The flight of the Armenians also marked the collapse of Franco-Armenian collaboration, and with it the loss of Armenian trust in the French Mandatory power, a mistrust which, as we shall see, was confirmed again by the exodus from 1938 onwards.

But population shifts could also occur legally, in accordance with international law. Arbitrary drawing of frontiers often led to demands for rectification and sometimes even to negotiated exchanges of territory.[14] Thus some Arab towns such as Jisr-ash-Shughūr, Kessab, Bayir and Bassit, which were at first attached to the *sanjak* of Alexandretta, were later partly reassigned to the province of Aleppo and partly to the Territory of the Alawis for economic reasons. One consequence of such a reorganization was that the proportion of Turks in the *sanjak* increased.[15] In turn, the Turkish element had cause for complaint when the Franco-Turkish Treaty of 1937 annexed several towns with a clear Turkish majority such as Bayir, Bucak and Hazine to Aleppo, thereby cutting them off from the *sanjak*.[16]

Similarly, Ankara accused the French Mandatory administration of having settled groups of Armenians in the *sanjak*, thereby manipulating the ethnographic map of the region to the disadvantage of the Turkish element.[17] It appears pointless to list further cases of arbitrarily drawn boundaries; it is certain, at any rate, that the border populations, indigenous as well as newly settled, were pushed back and forth by these measures and, overnight, could find themselves turned into the citizens of a neighbouring state.[18]

These shifts in territory and population played an important role in the 1930s when rival Arab and Turkish claims began to be formulated in respect to the "national character" of the *sanjak* of Alexandretta. The parties involved in the conflict were primarily concerned with delivering statistical "proof" of their own numerical superiority in this territory. At first they demanded certain prerogatives for their respective group, but then, as the crisis continued, either independence or cession of the *sanjak* to Turkey or Syria.

Population statistics of the period, albeit not very reliable, nonethless convey a picture of the demographic structure of the *sanjak*. Generally speaking, the population consisted essentially of Arabs, Turks and Armenians. Yet there was hardly consensus about their relative numerical strength. Published numbers diverge greatly. Turkey claimed that in 1936 the *sanjak* numbered 300,000 inhabitants, of which 240,000 were Turks. This number was, however, strongly contested by the Mandatory power and the Arab side. According to official

French statistics of 1936 the total population (219,080) was made up as follows:

Turks	38%
Alawite Arabs	28%
Sunni Arabs	10%
Christian Arabs	8%
Armenians	12%

Moreover, 954 Circassians, 474 Jews and 130 others were counted.[19] However, classifying the population in the traditional way according to religious affiliation proved to be quite problematic under the conditions of the inter-war period, when nation-building increasingly stressed ethnic descent. While the Arabs were divided into various religious groups (Alawite, Sunni and Christian), the Turkish-speaking population, irrespective of religious affiliation, was considered to form a single ethnic group. This may have served the imperial interests of France in Syria well, but it was certainly welcomed by Turkish nationalism also, which saw itself in an advantageous position in the *sanjak*.[20]

In retrospect, it is hard to gauge the extent to which the political awareness of national affiliation was developed within diverse communities. One can, however, proceed from the assumption that pre-national links and primordial ties still formed the main relational system for individual communities, even after the introduction by the Mandatory powers of concepts such as the modern state. In any case, within the *sanjak* of Alexandretta the legacy of the Ottoman millet system as an ethno-religious form of organization continued to exist.[21]

Contrary to what Arab and Turkish nationalists postulated, religious affiliation remained decisive in the *sanjak* as in some other parts of the Middle East. Thus Sunni Arabs mixed with Sunni Turks of the area because of their common Sunni outlook, and the phenomenon of Arabs turned Turks and Turks turned Arabs was no rarity. No wonder that in the elections of 1938, prescribed by the League of Nations, the Sunni-oriented Turks in the *sanjak*, who had been estranged by Kemalist secularizing reforms, opted for the Sunni Arab bloc. The Alawites in the *sanjak*, much divided in their political outlook, acted similarly. While the majority saw themselves primarily as "Arabs", many Alawite Arabs indicated themselves as Turks.[22]

Arab-Armenian cooperation during the *sanjak* crisis

It would be no exaggeration to state that the aggravation and internationalization of the *sanjak* crisis between 1936 and 1938 gave a decisive impetus to the formation of pan-Arab consciousness in Greater Syria.

Until the 1930s, the traditions of the *millet* system were still respected by the Arab population. The older generation, in particular, who had served the former Ottoman Empire, regarded the Turks primarily as brothers in faith and did not see the conflict over Alexandretta as a threat to their own political existence. This is why they could hardly be mobilized against Turkish aspirations.[23] Only the emergence of an Arab educated elite in the *sanjak* region who could formulate radical demands in opposition to Turkish nationalism brought about a significant shift in this regard. Arab nationalism was, above all, represented by the League of National Action (*'Usbat al-'amal al-qawm'*). The 'Usba stood for a pan-Arab secular programme which had grown partly from the same roots as Turkish Kemalist nationalism, and partly in opposition to it.[24]

This group, which in the course of the crisis became increasingly radical and was supported by most Christians, Arabs as well as Armenians, proclaimed the fight against Turkish nationalism and, above all, the retention of the *sanjak* within Syria, as their goal.

As regards the political orientation of the *sanjak* Armenians, it can be said that their aversion to the Turkish bloc was basically due to the "original" catastrophe of the mass murder of which they were the victims during World War I. Thus most Armenians in the region aligned themselves with various other groups in a united front against Turkish demands, that is to say, they were for the union of the *sanjak* with an independent Syria. In addition to the revolutionary Dashnak and Hunchak parties, which had a strong following in the region, some local groups had also emerged, such as the one led by Dr. Matussiyan in Antioch, which co-operated with the Arab 'Usba movement.[25]

The conclusion of the Franco-Syrian treaty of 1936 envisaged the end of the mandate and the transition of political power to an independent Syrian state. To the *sanjak* Turks, who were supported by Ankara, this turn of events was unacceptable. The idea that they were to be ruled by a people which itself was still under foreign domination was humiliating. Those forces, on the other hand, which opposed the idea of union with Turkey, intensified their struggle to attain the recognition of the *sanjak* as an Arab province. The result was a worsening of the political climate. The press of both sides made the situation more acute by publishing sensational reports and news. Thus from the middle of the 30s onwards, frequent rallies, demonstrations and strikes were organized, which often ended in street clashes. By 1937, bloody battles were already being fought, so that only direct intervention by the League of Nations appeared capable of producing a solution. This, of course, would mean the internationalization of the *sanjak* question.

The Turkish government had already unequivocally expressed its determination to achieve its goals, if necessary by military means. However, Ankara did not yet demand the immediate incorporation of the *sanjak* into Turkish territory, but rather upheld the view that the Turks of the *sanjak* had the right to self-determination. In other words, it asked for complete autonomy of the province, which implied its separation from Syria and the establishment of an autonomous buffer state.[26] In the light of this, it is understandable that the League of Nations resolution of May 1937 was welcomed in Turkey, since it des-

ignated the *Sanjak* explicitly as an "independent entity" (*entité distincte*) separate from Syria, granting the Turkish element at the same time far-reaching
administrative and cultural autonomy. The time had obviously arrived for
Ankara to take concrete measures geared to extending Turkish military, political and economic influence over the area.

The subsequent period saw a systematic Turkification of the administration,
the educational system and the judicial apparatus in the *sanjak* region. This
implied, among other things, that Turks were given or allowed to take over
positions in the civil service, and that public institutions, such as mosques,
schools and hospitals, were segregated.[27]

The policy of Turkifization and especially the hotly disputed elections of
1937 gave rise to a virtual gang war between rival Turkish and Arab factions.
This development culminated in the occupation of the *sanjak* of Alexandretta
by the Turkish army and the proclamation in September 1938 of a republic in
the area under the name of Hatay. Finally, in July 1939, the Republic of Hatay
declared its union with Turkey. In other words, the Ankara government succeeded after all in getting all its goals accepted by the French – a remarkable turn
of events, which was due not least to considerable British support for Turkey
throughout the crisis.[28]

Exodus from the *sanjak*[29]

Simultaneously with the withdrawal of French troops a mass exodus from the
sanjak set in. Not only the Armenian and Arab populations were involved, but
later on also the Greek Orthodox and the Alawites, including even some Turks.
True, it had been quite common for people to flee since the beginning of the
crisis, but in the late 1930s this assumed the dimensions of a real movement.

For example, bloody clashes in the Reyhaniye district had induced several
hundred Armenians to leave the area in the summer of 1937. Similarly, terrified
groups elsewhere also showed a tendency to emigrate around that time.[30] The
reason why such departures had not been more widespread before 1938 should
be seen in the policy of the French authorities, who resorted to various means
in order to prevent any emigration from the *sanjak* which would have severely
compromised them internally and internationally.[31]

But once it was clear that the French would evacuate the province, near panic
broke out and large-scale emigration could no longer be prevented. About 90
percent of the Armenian population, some 22,000 persons, emigrated in the
first ten days after the union of the province with Turkey. They were followed
over time by 10,000 Alawites, 5,000 Orthodox Christians and 12,000 Sunni
Arabs.

The refugees reached the Syrian villages and towns of Badrousiyé, Tartous,
Kessab and Aleppo over land, with other groups departing from Alexandretta
by sea for Latakia, Tripoli and Beirut. Most of them had to be accommodated
in camps which had been hurriedly set up, or in schools or buildings belonging to the Armenian community or other charitable organizations.[32] To judge

from the literature on the topic, the combined effect of a series of factors should be seen as bringing about this spectacular movement. First of all, those non-Turkish groups who tended to view the *sanjak*'s remaining in Syria as an existential question, and were therefore committed to that cause politically, felt at the mercy of their Turkish adversaries, and defenceless against them. Clearly, they feared reprisals, especially in the countryside, once the Turks had become masters. The pronouncedly conciliatory attitude of the Ankara government in this phase, when it appeared bent on winning over at least the "moderate Armenians", could not alleviate the widespread mood of anxiety. The Turkish administration even went so far as to accuse some "Old Turks" of having harassed the non-Turkish population.[33]

France, too, laboured in vain to halt the stream of refugees, not least because of conflicts arising in the Syrian districts which were receiving them. But the refugees seemed not to heed any placatory attempts, for example, the provision that they should stay in Hatay until suitable accommodation had been found for them in Syria and the Lebanon. The majority had left the province before French emigration assistance could be organized.[34]

Evidently, the refugees entertained a deep distrust not only of Turkey but in the meantime also of France, which had not lived up to her responsibilities as a Mandatory power.

Secondly, mass migration from Hatay may have resulted from the fact that the Franco-Turkish agreement of July 1938 did not provide for minority rights for any non-Turkish group in the province. The population was confronted with having to indicate the nationality of their preference within a short period. Theoretically they could opt for Syrian or Lebanese citizenship, but this would have amounted to them being degraded to the status of foreigners in their own homeland, apart from the extra burden of having to apply for passports and visa whenever travelling to or from the province. After a period of deliberation of six months, the entire population remaining in Hatay would automatically be given Turkish citizenship; and, as became evident later on, many left not least in order to evade conscription.[35]

Another factor contributing to the intense unrest among the refugees may have been rumours about an imminent division of the Near East between British, Turkish and Zionist interests, including a Turkish occupation of Aleppo and the Jazira region in Upper Mesopotamia.[36]

Some Armenians had further reservations and fears. In the first place, there was the collective trauma of the massacres they had suffered in the late Ottoman period. The French debacle in Cilicia had only strengthened those fears. The feelings of the Armenian refugees are correctly summarized in the following contemporary report:

"[T]here is too much recent history to make the Armenians believe that they could enjoy a free and happy life as Turkish subjects. The Armenians point out that they have always been distrusted by the Turks as disloyal, they rebelled during the War, those of Musa Dagh defied the Turkish armies and the story of the Forty Days which tells the saga is a lasting shame to the new Turkey. More recently the Armenians, led by the political parties, which cannot forget the short-lived Armenian Republic in the Caucasus, have used every means to prevent the cession of the *Sanjak* to Turkey. This they feel that even a [re-]generated Turkey cannot easily forgive."[37] Indeed, most of the Armenians living in the *sanjak* were already immigrants, victims of previous expulsions and resettlement measures. In contrast to some indigenous Armenians, described in Turkish terms as "moderate"[38], who occasionally co-operated with Turkish nationalists, the immigrants were adamant that they would never again come under Turkish rule.[39]

That such fears were not entirely groundless, the Armenians remaining in Anatolia had learned already. During the 1930s, some Armenians in the eastern provinces were forced to abandon their homes for urban centres in the west under the infamous Law of Resettlement[40]. A policy of linguistic Turkification, tendencies towards ethnic homogenization, as well as assimilatory pressures induced others to emigrate "voluntarily".[41]

Finally, the exodus from the *sanjak* caused "pangs of conscience" among the representatives of the Allies in the Near East. Syrian Arab opinion held the Mandatory powers, France and also to a certain extent Great Britain, responsible for the debacle on the *sanjak* question. They had exercised a decisive influence on the issue by ceding the territory to Turkey and had thereby knowingly accepted the resulting mass exodus. Furthermore, by not showing due consideration for the non-Turkish peoples of the *sanjak*, France had committed a breach of international law. British diplomats were apparently rather uncomfortably aware of these facts, as can be discerned from the following piece of correspondence:

"The French commonly assert that it was British pressure on them to satisfy Turkey and bring her into the Peace Front which made them give way with respect to Hatay. If such is the case the British people, especially Christian folk, should recognise they have a moral responsibility to repair the damage to human lives done by the cession. Like the transfer of the Germans from the South Tyrol, which received scant notice in the Axis press, so this problem has been ignored to a large measure in the democratic press. Britain and France will have no cause to point the finger of shame at other refugee making nations if they do not solve this problem promptly and generously."[42]

Not surprisingly, therefore, both powers strived to save what they could of their reputation by organizing generous humanitarian aid for the refugees. Since France had failed to stop the emigration, it tried at least to facilitate the resettlement of the refugees. France also negotiated a small correction of boundaries between Hatay and Syria according to which three villages inhabited by Armenians were ceded to Syria.[43] Great Britain, too, which participated in the humanitarian efforts to ease the plight of the refugees by furnishing considerable funds, attempted, by bringing its influence to bear on Ankara, to secure compensation for the Armenians who had abandoned property in Hatay.

Conclusion

It is a commonplace that in times of war some movement of populations is almost inevitable. But even the conclusion of peace may result in territorial realignments, with concomitant involuntary population shifts.[44] In the case of the *sanjak*, however, the conflict had much deeper roots. The collapse of the Ottoman Empire and the compartmentalization of its territory created conditions under which the Mandatory powers promoted the establishment of modern nation states. With their arrival on the scene, territorial revisionism assumed new dimensions.

The mandates established in former Ottoman provinces were conceived of as emancipatory projects of nation formation. Yet this process generated new political concepts such as majority and minority population groups.[45]

In this manner, under the cloak of "the national right of self-determination", regionalist or ethno-religious fissures were encouraged. The leaders of such movements were rarely aware that by demanding this right in respect to a specific territory, they were actually preparing the ground for future minorities. Thus neither Turkish nor Arab nationalists envisaged equal rights for groups other than their own in the *sanjak* of Alexandretta.

The international community failed to react to these developments in an adequate fashion – if it did not exacerbate them in several ways. No wonder that forced population transfer after the model of the Lausanne settlement between Greece and Turkey was hailed as a virtual panacea for all similar conflicts ever since.

Western appeasement strategies as they evolved during the inter-war period also had a bearing on the *sanjak* question. As soon as the region became the object of international bargaining, the Great Powers contributed their share to the escalation of the crisis. In this context, even the League of Nations functioned as an instrument of legitimizing the goals formulated by the Great Powers.[46]

Furthermore, as the Mandatory powers involved, France and Great Britain exerted a direct influence on the solution of the *sanjak* question to Turkey's advantage. In the face of the increasingly critical situation in Europe on the eve of the Second World War, they had a strong interest in an alliance with Ankara.[47]

As a concrete result of this bargaining, the British-French-Turkish mutual assistance pact of October 1939 was signed just one month after the Republic of Hatay had declared its unification with Turkey. The mass exodus from Hatay of non-Turkish populations thus appears, with hindsight, to have been a price which the signatories took into account for the sake of a grand design.

Chapter 8
Turkish Nationalism and the Dönme

Marc Baer

The 1923 Treaty of Lausanne called for an "exchange" of populations between Greece and the newly recognized Republic of Turkey. As a result, at least four hundred thousand Muslims of Greece were forced to go to Turkey, and 1.2 million Orthodox Christians of Turkey were sent to Greece.[2] Among those subject to deportation to Turkey was a distinct Salonikan socio-religious group that referred to itself as the "Believers."[3]

For over two centuries the Believers, commonly known as Dönme, a Turkish term for convert, had lived an open secret following their conversion from Judaism to Islam in the wake of the conversion of the messianic rabbi Shabtai Tzvi in 1666. Neither the category "Jewish" nor "Muslim" expresses their religious identity. Unlike Jews, the Dönme ostensibly followed the requirements of Islam, including fasting at Ramadan and praying in mosques, one of which they built. Unlike Muslims, the Dönme maintained a belief that Shabtai Tzvi was the messiah, practiced kabbalistic rituals, and recited prayers in Hebrew and Judeo-Spanish. The Dönme in Salonika saw themselves as a community apart, married only among themselves, maintained detailed genealogies, and buried their dead in distinct cemeteries.[4]

The Athens government considered the Dönme Muslims and refused to allow them to remain in Greece, in part because it wanted to be rid of a significant non-Greek economic element. The estimated ten to fifteen thousand Dönme were compelled to abandon their native Salonika. Once they arrived in Turkey, the Dönme deportees drew considerable public scrutiny, for the group presented a puzzle.[5]

Were they really Muslims, or were they "secret Jews"? Were they Turks or foreigners? The identity of the group was debated in the press and parliament as Muslims were defining who belonged to the Turkish nation. In this paper I analyze the role that the Dönme played in defining the parameters of the discussion about who belonged to the Turkish nation. Two Dönme, Mehmed Karakaşzade Rüşdü and Ahmed Emin Yalman, presented to the anxious public radically different interpretations of their group's identity, the Dönme's ability to integrate into the Turkish nation, and the boundaries of Turkishness. An investigation of the debate about whether the Dönme belonged in Turkey provides insight into the contradictions of the construction of being Turkish, and how the Dönme propelled the issue of their identity into public consciousness while struggling to legitimize their existence in the new republic. By focusing on the Dönme experience, I illustrate the inherent tension of creating a single, homogenizing, and secular national identity from a plural society that had been organized around religious identities. I explore the perceived danger of hybridity and the interrelation of racism and nationalism.[6]

This paper also sheds light on the process through which majorities and minorities are constructed as modern nations come into being. Although the nationalism and loyalty of the nation's core group was assumed to be a given in new states, minorities had to prove their loyalty in order for them to demonstrate they deserved citizenship.[7]

The architects of the Turkish Republic aimed to jettison the organizing principles of Ottoman society — cultural difference, religious identity, corporate autonomy, and communities. By erasing the vestiges of a plural society, they expected shared culture, national identity, equal citizenship, and individuals to become the pillars of the new society. The end of empire spelled the end of the tolerance of difference since the founders of Turkey took upon themselves the task of clarifying identities by disallowing mixed ones. The leaders of the Turkish Republic intended to create a socially cohesive population and a unified economy. They desired a single nation instilled with a new secular Turkish identity acquired through schooling in a Turkish language stripped of Ottoman hybridity and socializing in a culturally homogenized reality.[8]

Citizens were taught to distinguish difference, which was equated with foreignness, from sameness, which meant belonging to the nation. This was based on the assumption that citizens of a nation-state must be the same in order to be treated the same. And as in other nation-states, the existence of previously inconsequential religious groups became problematic. Removing from the public sphere manifestations of religion that did not support the modern state project and restricting them to the private ironically increased the significance of religious identity and made it an issue of public debate.

Muslim anxiety about whether the Dönme could be considered both Muslims and Turks reflects the confusion about who belonged to the Turkish nation and nation-state. Defining who was a Turk had not yet been resolved when the republic was founded. The first constitution represented a voluntarist nationalist ideology.[9] According to the constitution, "the people of Turkey, regardless of religion and race, are Turks as regards Turkish citizenship."[10] Although all people within the boundaries of Turkey were not considered members of the Turkish people or nation, this political notion of being Turkish would allow the assimilation of the major components of Ottoman society.

This was based on the idea that what one is, is a matter of self-attribution. Yet there was an opposing understanding of being Turkish based not on what people do or say, but on what they are. According to an organic view, only those who were of the Turkish "race" or "lineage" and, by extension, only Muslims, could be considered Turks.[11]

This biological and religiously bounded understanding of the Turkish nation did not allow for the assimilation of any (other than some Muslim) peoples, who were reconfigured as Turks. In either definition, there was a distinction between Turks, members of a primordial nation, and Turkish citizens, members of the modern nation-state.

The two contradictory strands of nationalism and the tension between defining identity on the basis of being or becoming Turkish stand out in the debate over the identity of the Dönme. They became a focal point of contention since their existence called into question what it meant to be Turkish, tested the limits of Turkishness, and troubled social and national categories. The Dönme were in a better position than Christians or Jews to assimilate into Turkish society since they were already outwardly Muslims. But their acceptance required a two-phase conversion: they had to first prove their sincerity as Muslims, and then, after being recognized as Muslims, the Dönme were compelled to abandon this accepted religious identity for a secular one. But they faced hindrances in the process of becoming secular, not only because they had to endure a double stripping of identity (Dönme and Muslim), but because they were perceived as a threat on several levels. First, they were foreign, most having arrived from Greece. Second, they were not of the Turkish "race" since they had only intermarried among themselves, descendants of Jews. Thus by blood and lineage they were not Turks. Third, they were rumored to have inordinate financial power, but economic power was to be in the hands of "True Turks" as the state aimed to liberate the economy of non-Muslims and foreigners and create a Turkish bourgeoisie. Finally, their loyalty was considered in doubt. For some in Turkey, the desire of some Dönme to remain in Greece proved their lack of fidelity to the nation. For all of these reasons, the Dönme would have to prove themselves to be loyal Turks by ceasing to work for their own interests and instead act for the good of the new nation. They would have to consciously and publicly identify with Turks in order to integrate, since in theory their subjective choice to assimilate would resolve the problem of how they related to the state and society.

Immediately following their arrival in Turkey, the Dönme faced a wave of controversy. Ironically, the public debate over the Dönme was incited by the proclamations of one of their own, Mehmed Karakaşzade Rüşdü. To him, Dönme could not be considered members of the Turkish race since Turks were Muslims by birth and not by conversion. Befitting the group's international ties, Karakaşzade was a cosmopolitan Dönme trader who owned stores and properties in Berlin and Istanbul. For unexplained reasons he had been banished from the community at the age of fifteen. He also quarreled with some Dönme over loans and payments, and went to court in a dispute over alimony and ownership of properties with his Dönme ex-wife. He may have decided to

take out his anger at these people by castigating all Dönme.[12] At the beginning
of 1924, as thousands of fellow Dönme began arriving in Turkey, Karakaşzade
engaged in a campaign to alert the public of their hybrid identity. He peti-
tioned the Grand National Assembly, met with Atatürk, was interviewed by all
the major newspapers in Ankara and Istanbul, and published an open letter to
the Dönme.

Karakaşzade's "Open Letter to All Salonikan Dönme," which appeared in
the daily *Vakit* (Time) on 7 January 1924, at the beginning of the wave of Dönme
immigration, is a phenomenal statement of racialized nationalism.[13] The author
begins by claiming that the Dönme, despite "taking refuge under the compas-
sionate and pitying wing of the pure and honored Turkish nation," deceived
their "hosts" by not revealing their true identity and distinctiveness. The
Ottoman government should be blamed, he argues, for not impelling them to
have social relations with Turks and allowing them to live apart relying on
mutual assistance. But the time for separateness is past. There is no way to
"explain away our foreignness" after "the great Turkish revolution and victory
that astonishes the world." A new country has been born in which "the hearts
of people living in the lands that this honored Turkish nation rules" beat as
one and their minds all "bear the ideal of being Turkish." Karakaşzade was
astonished that the Dönme continued to maintain separate customs. He claims
five or ten Dönme may openly mix with Turks, but this fact does not absolve
the rest of the ten to fifteen thousand Dönme who maintain a separate and
secret existence. He argues that the Turkish nation will no longer tolerate foreigners: "Do you think Turks will endure and suffer a foreigner to remain? You
are mistaken, gentlemen!"

Karakaşzade explicitly presents organic criteria for membership in the
nation, but finds the Dönme deficient. He writes that in Turkey, "only Turks
truly have the right to live because it is the Turks who defended this soil by irri-
gating it with their blood."[14] While Turks were mixing their blood with the soil,
or becoming one with it, the Dönme, whom he labels "sponging parasites,"
hoarded their wealth and "did not sacrifice even a fraction of their blood, rich-
es, or wealth." This reflected the view of some in the political elite, such as Talat
Pasha, the minister of the interior until 1918, that Armenians, Greeks, and Jews
shared all the benefits of the fatherland, yet bore none of its burden.[15] They
"never participated in war" and "never spilled a drop of blood," but during
times of war continued to make money through trade and lived well. Because
Turks "defended the fatherland," and the Dönme did not, Karakaşzade claims
they should not be surprised that in 1924 people objected to their continuing
their distinct traditions and living "as a parasite."[16]

Karakaşzade develops the host and parasite motif, which was current at the
time: the Turks are the unwitting host to a dangerous parasite that can destroy
them. But the author of the letter trusts the Grand National Assembly, "which
even writes laws concerning wild boars" that damage farmland, since the lead-

ers of the nation will not "be able to support in its breast a clump of foreigners." Karakaşzade uses the metaphor of comparing the Dönme to the filthiest
animal imaginable to Muslims to refer to the damage these foreigners can cause
to the nation's precious soil. He urges the Dönme to either integrate or leave:
"Today there are two alternatives for us: either definitively mixing and inter-
marrying with Turks living under the same law to work in common for the
entire fatherland and nation whether during good times or bad, or to take care
of ourselves outside the nation's boundary in whatever material and spiritual
form." At the end of the letter Karakaşzade asserts the time is right for the
Grand National Assembly, "which is successfully purifying [the nation of] the
filth accumulated over centuries," to "also soon destroy this inauspicious problem."

Karakaşzade tried to shock the Dönme and alarm the Muslim public and
thereby cause the immediate flight or integration of the Dönme. Contradicting
a basic tenet of Islam, he proclaimed that even if the Dönme called themselves
Muslims and acted like Muslims, because of their origins they could not be
considered Muslims. Karakaşzade may have been motivated by an aim to
avenge his community since he had been banished and had financial disputes.
Yet his public declarations and frantic trips between Ankara and Istanbul to
meet with press, parliament, and president speak of a man desperate to prove
his own Turkishness, despite his lineage. He appears as a zealous convert to
being Turkish who is more pious than those born into the religion he urged the
Dönme to join. Ironically, Karakaşzade often vacillates between using the term
"us" and "you" when discussing the Dönme. This pronoun-switching illustrates
the difficulty he faced in defining his own place in the new nation. Yet did he
imagine he could distance himself from being associated with the Dönme by
expressing such loathing for them? His plan was contradictory, for by making
Dönme identity a public scandal, and playing a key role in depicting Dönme
distinctiveness to others, he may have hindered their smooth integration.

Dönme identity was difficult to resolve so long as the question of race surfaced and conceptions of race fed into understandings of the nation. People
asked whether those of alien or non-Turkish or Jewish blood could be received
as Turks if they pronounced a change in conscience to a belief in Turkishness,
whether as part of "pragmatic considerations of survival and stratagem" or
not.[17] This raises the larger question of whether self-ascribed identities or identities imposed from the outside are more relevant. How could minority
attempts at maintaining a hybrid identity and embracing different beliefs and
affiliations be feasible if belonging to the nation meant belonging to an imagined race?[18] Faced with biological requirements for citizenship, how could
Dönme defend and define their place in the nation? Would an argument pre-
senting the Dönme as longtime loyal servants who are already secular be the
more pragmatic path? To overcome the claims made about their racial and religious identity, some Dönme declared that the differences that marked them

were melting away and had practically disappeared. Following weeks of front-page stories, which asked why the Dönme, who differed in race and religion from Turks and Muslims (considered the same), had been allowed to immigrate to Turkey,[19] the newspaper *Vatan* (Fatherland) published an in-depth history of the Dönme. Its author was the Dönme Ahmed Emin Yalman, the newspaper's founder, owner, and editor-in-chief.[20] On the heated question of Dönme identity, the author of the series claims they were just another "backward" Sufi order (*tarikat*), a numerically insignificant sect within the Muslim community that was on the verge of dissolution. The building of a true melting pot was an urgent task to be accomplished "by asking everyone 'are you one of us, or not,'" accepting individuals and groups that could be absorbed, and throwing out "the foreign parts that do not accept assimilation."[21] The author claims the Dönme are becoming "extinct" since they are abandoning a corporate identity, partly through intermarriage. Accordingly, "Those who are truly Turkish and Muslim must be distinguished in public opinion and must be saved from the necessity of carrying on their back the social stain and mark that is only appropriate for those who are not."[22] The Dönme had to understand the true nature of the Turkish body politics and act accordingly by assimilating, for they had no other choice. One could no longer have a hybrid identity. The author asserts that the new generation opposed being members of the "tribe"[23] and knew nothing about Dönme customs. They were born as members of the group against their wish. He claimed, "the two-century existence of this strange society is a thing of the past" since only the elderly had any attachment, although they too viewed the past "as completely extinct" and did not dare mention it to the new generations "who view it as a ridiculous nightmare."[24] Public attention to the group presented an opportunity to "publicly rip the veil of secrecy that has been covering them for centuries, and do away with it once and for all."

Yalman tried to calm the public by asserting that the Dönme were no longer distinct. Yet Yalman was assailed in the press during these decades for holding Turkish citizenship despite being a "secret Jew," not a Turk and not a Muslim.[25] When he was attacked as the grandson of Shabtai Tzvi and for hiding his true identity behind the Turkish label, Yalman defended himself: "You say 'you're not a Turk, you're a Dönme, and you have no right to open your mouth.' Yet for three centuries my ancestors have taken their part in the Turkish and Muslim community, people who always spent their lives serving the state. How many other people could say this?"[26]

He converts his Dönme identity to a point of honor,[27] and by asserting that the Dönme have always served the state proves their loyalty. But this does not refute the claim that they are not sincere Muslims; nor does the assertion solve the problem of Dönme religious or racial identity.

Yalman's efforts strike the reader as those of a person attempting to prevent his own future from being clouded by his upbringing. Like minorities in homogenizing nation-states, Yalman was calling for acceptance and integration.

His strategy was to promote nationality as a conscious political identity using a vision of a Turkish nation-state established on the basis of the equality of citizens who agreed to identify with being Turkish. Yalman used the metaphor of the "melting pot" to represent the process in which individuals would be melted down and poured into pre-existing cultural and social molds modeled on Turks and Muslims. Non-Turkish and non-Muslim elements were to be incorporated into Turkish society as individuals whose identity would disappear, not as groups that could maintain their difference in a plural society. Individuals with fractured identities, such as Yalman, who seek personal salvation through cultural conversion, but find that the society denies the affiliation they desire, become intermediaries between society and the community.[28]

Becoming a citizen of a modern nation-state where nationness is suddenly, powerfully thrust upon people, and "nationalizing nationalisms" work for the interests of the core nation alone[29] tests individual's ability to define themselves as they struggle between externally imposed and self-ascribed identities.[30] The dissolution of the Ottoman Empire and creation of the Turkish Republic witnessed the transition from an empire that granted group cultural rights and promoted multicultural autonomy, but denied civic, political, and social rights of individuals, to a nation-state that granted individual rights, but denied group rights.[31] This change signifies Turkey's adaptation of the civic model of citizenship, which may appear to be more inclusive than the ethno-national, but in practice contains "inegalitarian and exclusionary elements."[32] States can combine both the civic and ethnic models in the way they treat citizens, using inclusionary and exclusionary principles at the same time to allocate different rights and privileges to groups within society.[33]

In its first two decades, Turkey followed both models since it treated those incorporated as Muslim Turks with the civic understanding of nationalism and those considered non-Muslims and non-Turks with ethno-cultural nationalism, maintaining the pre-state division of society based on religious groups, but adding the modern construct of race and modern understandings of religion as determining factors in the formation of national identity. The problem the Dönme faced was that pluralism based upon accepting and maintaining difference was replaced by an attempt to create a nation based upon ideas of race which excluded formerly integral components of the whole. The nation that was the direct successor of the empire was unable in its first decades to sustain the pluralism that had accommodated separateness and multiple identities. No matter what approach the Dönme pursued, their identity could no longer be an open secret. The logic of Turkish nationalism ensured it had to become a "mysterious page of history," a disappearing relic of the Ottoman past.

Chapter 9
Claiming difference in an unitarist frame: the case of Alevism

Elise Massicard

Many movements for recognition have developed since the 1980s in Turkey (Ayata 1997), as elsewhere in the world. Consequently, this period is often considered as a time of liberalization, even more so as it coincided with the end of the military regime. At the same time, however, Turkish State institutions have continued to stress nationalism and national unity, notably because of the guerrilla conflict in the south-east which continued until the end of the 1990s. The question this paper addresses is thus how nationalism impacts and shapes the ways difference is claimed in Turkey and what the prospects are for the success of these claims.

This paper does not deal with nationalism as an ideology. Rather, it considers nationalism in a broad sense, close to what Michael Billig has called 'banal nationalism', i.e. all those unnoticed practices, ideological habits, beliefs and representations which make the daily reproduction of nations possible (1995:8). Banal nationalism refers to all those familiar forms of nationalism embedded in the routines of social life that are taken for granted and serve as constant reminders of nationhood. In the same way, we will deal with nationalism not in an abstract way, but rather with its concrete bearers – which can be State institutions, but also those who make political demands, and the media – and their logics of promoting nationalism.

This paper concentrates on the Alevist movement[1] which appeared in the late 1980s. Alevism seems especially interesting for our purpose, since it does not directly challenge the very principles of the Turkish nation; in a sense, therefore, it differs from Kurdish nationalist and Islamist movements. In this context, how do Alevists claim difference, particularism and recognition? Which constraints – legal, but also discursive and informal – do they face, and how do they deal with them? How do their mobilization in the emigration and the perspective of European integration change this situation and their scope for action?

First, numerous legal regulations have obstructed Alevist demands on an institutional level.

The difficulty of creating an Alevist Party

The Turkish Law on Political Parties stipulates that parties must pursue the "national interest" and avoid addressing different religious or linguistic groups. More precisely, it prohibits *mezheps*[2] from organizing themselves as parties: "The right to found a political party may not be exercized with the aim of [...] making distinctions based on language, race, religion, *mezhep*, or region"[3]. Party statutes may not contain any clause taking into account religious or *mezhep* differences in membership applications[4]. Party names can not contain the names of religions or *mezheps*, nor any corresponding expression[5]. Moreover, the 1982 Constitution stipulated until 2001 that "none of the rights and freedoms embodied in the Constitution shall be exercized with the aim of violating the indivisible integrity of the State with its territory and nation, of endangering the existence of the Turkish State and Republic, of destroying fundamental rights and freedoms, of placing the government of the State under the control of an individual or a group, of establishing the hegemony of one social class over the others, or creating discrimination on the basis of language, race, religion or sect"[6]. The organization of a religious group as a political party is illegal and illegitimate.

There have been two attempts to create Alevi political parties. The first was the Unity Party of Turkey (TBP, *Türkiye Birlik Partisi*) which existed from 1966 to 1980. The second attempt was the Movement for Democratic Peace (*Demokratik Barış Hareketi*) in 1995, which became the Peace Party (*Barış Partisi*) in 1996 and lasted until 1999. It is noteworthy that neither party has really presented itself as an Alevi party. The TBP has often been considered as a party claiming Aleviness, partly because of its emblem, a lion surrounded by twelve stars – a clear reference to Ali and the twelve imams, therefore to Aleviness. However, there was an inner struggle between a more religious and conservative wing led by Cemal Özbey and Hüseyin Balan, who chose the party's emblem, and a more political and leftist one, led by Mustafa Timisi, which was dominant from 1969 on and vigorously refused any Alevi image or identification[7] (Massicard 2005). TBP publications after 1969 clearly indicate it wanted to erase its widespread Alevi image (see for example TBP, 1978: 17 f.). Although certain legal restrictions concerning the organization of religious groups as parties did not exist at that time, it is interesting to note that the party changed its name in 1969, adding "*Türkiye*" before "*Birlik Partisi*", in order to put an end to the rumours that accused it of working for the division of Turkey or on Iran's behalf (Yücel 1998: 66).

Despite the different legal framework, the BP in the late 1990s faced a similar dilemma. In fact, it did not have any Alevi symbol, but the fact that the party programme stressed the recognition of differences and the diversity of Turkey contributed to its Alevi image. "In his speeches, the leader always spoke about multiculturalism, without stressing Aleviness nor Kurdishness. [...] But the media always stressed Aleviness. [...] The media always claimed we were an

Alevi party [...] Our Sunni friends thought they would find portraits of Ali and
the twelve imams on the walls in the party's office. Only when they came to
see us did they realize it was not the case [...] This is because the party chief was
Alevi. In this country, no Alevi was at the head of a party except for Veziroğlu.
All the other party leaders were Sunni. But nobody ever considered those parties as Sunni parties"[8].

Therefore, neither party really fostered an Alevi image because of legal constraints, the illegitimacy of such an initiative, and probably political strategy.
They did not succeed in attracting Alevi votes. But their poor electoral results
show that both parties were not recognized as "universalist" parties either. This
is quite important in a context where national "universalist" parties hardly ever
defend particularist demands publicly, fearing they could lose the support of
the majority[9]. Therefore, Alevist demands are brought into parliamentary
debates almost exclusively by Alevi Members of Parliament, most of the time
speaking in their own name, and are very rarely relayed by parties; thus they can
hardly achieve anything (Massicard 2005a).

Legal restrictions on the demands which a party can formulate constitute
another obstacle to the existence of an Alevist political party: "Political parties
are prohibited from pursuing any aim which contravenes the stipulations of
the Directorate of Religious Affairs (*Diyanet*) which, in accordance with the
principles of secularism (*laiklik*), is part of the public administration in the
sense that it is politically neutral and aims at national solidarity and unity"[10].
The *Demokratik Barış Hareketi* did actually demand the abolition of the
Diyanet, therefore running the risk of being closed. Its leaders then decided to
resign before losing their political rights[11]. When founding the BP, the same
leading party officials did not take up this demand again, but demanded
instead that all religious creeds be taught at school.

Limitations on possibilities for organizing

Another legal constraint influencing the ways Alevists claim to be different and
demand recognition of this are limitations on possibilities for organizing.
According to the 1983 Law on Associations, it is forbidden to form associations
aiming to create in the Republic of Turkey differences of race, religion, *mezhep*
and region, or minorities based on these, and to demolish the unitary State
structure of the Turkish Republic[12]. Moreover, according to the Civil Code, no
foundation (*vakıf*) can be established with the aim to violate the features of the
Republic as identified in the Constitution and the fundamental principles of
the Constitution, the law, morality, national unity and national interest, or to
support the members of a specific race or religious community (*cemaat*)[13].
Therefore, religious groups cannot organize formally as associations or foundations. This does not mean that there are no such organizations, but these
organizations cannot openly express objectives linked with religion. As a consequence, most Alevi organizations avoid mentioning the word "Alevi" in their
name or statutes. Still, most of them express this dimension through circum-

locutions or allusions, for example by mentioning names of figures symbolizing Aleviness, such as Hacı Bektaş or Pir Sultan Abdal. Many, but not all, organizations which have tried to inscribe the term "Alevi" in their name, or objectives linked with Aleviness in their statutes, have had legal problems or have simply not been registered[14]. But the decisions not to register organizations have often been annulled. As a matter of fact, the action brought against the *Pir Sultan Abdal 2 Temmuz Eğitim ve Kültür Vakfı* in 1997 ended up in the court finding against the Foundation in 2000. But the Court of Appeal finally decided in its favour, judging that "serving Alevi philosophy" did not infringe the law.

Thus Alevi organizations have resorted to legal means in the first place as a means of defence. Their appeals have also led to legal developments. In the summer 1999, after a long legal struggle, the Alevi-Bektashi Educational Foundation (*Alevi-Bektaşi Eğitim vakfı*) finally obtained the right to call itself "Alevi" from the Supreme Court. Reforms passed in the framework of harmonization with European Union legislation have also had legal consequences. In 2002, a court decision foresaw the closing down of a group of Alevi organizations, the Cultural Association of Alevi-Bektashi Formations (*Alevi-Bektaşi Kuruluşları Birliği Kültür Derneği*). The prefecture considered that its objectives (including "the construction of cemevi"[15] and "the fostering of cooperation between Alevi-Bektashi organizations") were contrary to the Law on Associations. The Ministry of the Interior then requested that the association change its statutes. Considering that it did not infringe the law and that changing the statutes would destroy the specificity of the organization, its leading officials refused. In February 2002, the association was closed down in accordance with the Law on Associations (art. 5, § 6)[16]. But this case was mentioned in the European Commission's regular report for 2002 (European Commission 2002: 37), and followed up by the German government, mainly because of Alevist lobbying; thus it acquired a European dimension. The organization appealed against the decision at a time when Turkey's projected accession was a burning issue; in the end, it was registered in 2003.

These cases clearly show that legal constraints on the formal organization and articulation of Alevism are tending to diminish. For example, the 2nd harmonization package removed in March 2002 the prohibition for founding an association aiming to protect, develop or expand languages or cultures other than the Turkish language or culture, or to claim that they are minorities based on racial, religious, sectarian, cultural or linguistic differences. However – and this is a very important point for understanding the way activists operate – contradictions remain between different legal texts or between texts and their application, which contributes to the formation of a grey area where many things are not really authorized without being really forbidden. For example, the preparatory laws for the transition to the constitutional changes decided in 1995, which broadened the scope of action for associations and foundations, were only passed years later. In this zone of legal insecurity, activists know that if they act in a given way, they may or may not be sanctioned. This state of affairs still has a strongly inhibiting effect on the leading officials, who know that their organizations can be closed down quite easily by the authorities, and that they personally can be held responsible and incur punishment.

Despite the gradual improvement in the legal situation, Alevist organizations remain in a sense sensitive. Therefore, it is difficult for most of them to make alliances with non-particularist or "universalist" political forces (parties, labour unions, NGOs, etc.), which fear they will de-legitimize themselves if they cooperate with particularist groups or those who demand to have their identity recognized (Schüler 2000). For example, Alevists quite often support or participate in activities like demonstrations or manifestos organized by other "universalist" political actors (for example demonstrations for Human Rights or 1 May manifestations), whereas these universalist political actors more rarely support publicly Alevist claims.

Beyond the limitations imposed by law, constraints of legitimacy also affect the ways in which Alevists act, as well as their discourses and framings.

Specific Framings

"Framings" refer to "action-oriented sets of belief and meanings that inspire and legitimate the activities and campaign of a social movement organization" (Benford, Snow 2000:614). To what extent are activists allowed to pursue their concerns without being drawn into the idiom of an official rhetoric (Seufert 2000:37)? The study of the Alevists' arguments and framings, based on a corpus of articles in the press over some fifteen years (1988-2003), shows that the main framing used by Alevists to defend their claims is that of the Unity of the Nation. How can this apparent paradox be explained?

Facing growing identity and recognition discourses and claims from the 1980s on, State institutions did not abandon the dogma of the Unity of the Nation, which was the main justification for the 1980 coup[17]. On the contrary, they strongly reaffirmed it, most probably because of the armed opposition in the south-east, where the struggles are at their highest around 1990.

Quite rapidly, the growing particularist discourses and claims were interpreted by some politicians and media in terms either of an "identity problem" (*kimlik sorunu*), thus becoming a public issue, i.e. something that "focuses public attention on a name designating an undesirable situation or a threat on well-being" (Edelman 1988:42), or else in terms of a "crisis", mainly in relation to Kurdish nationalism and political Islam. As a matter of fact, both movements not only demand the recognition of particular identities, but directly challenge the official national identity, which is based on the exclusion of both Kurdishness and – more ambiguously, especially after 1980 – (at least political) Islam, which are constructed as relevant Others of a "modern" Turkish nation (Yörük 1997). In the view of State institutions, both movements not only demand the integration of diversity into national identity, but call into question the very definition of the Turkish nation and the principles of Turkish identity.

The reaffirmation by institutions of the dogma of unity can be observed most clearly through an analysis of the language of discourses dealing with difference and particularism. It is easy to observe the frequency of the semantic field of unity (*birlik*), together with terms like *bütünlük* (totality), *birlik ve beraberlik* (unity and solidarity), and their contraries, *bölücülük* (separatism), *bölmek* (to separate), *ayırmak* (to divide). What we may call a "conspiracy tenet" is also well represented, as shown by the frequency of terms like *tahrik* (provocation), *provokasyon* (provocation), *oyun* (trick), *körüklemek* (to stir up), *tezgahlamak* (to foment), *kışkırtmak* (to excite, provoke). This framing by the authorities goes hand in hand with concrete measures. For instance, the Law on the Struggle against Terrorism, adopted in 1991 and interpreted very widely, provides for trials before State Security Courts (*Milli Güvenlik Mahkemesi*), accompanied by heavier sentences than those handed down by normal courts. Separatism (*bölücülük*) is one of the charges which carries the heaviest sentence.

These developments put movements for recognition in a tricky situation, since such charges can quite easily be levelled against them. Therefore, those who put forward demands have to protect themselves from possible accusations of separatism, which can come from State institutions but also political enemies. In order to legitimate himself and his demands, every political actor therefore has to express himself in the name of Unity against those whom he frames as the "enemies of Unity", which are most frequently stigmatized as separatists and declared traitors or internal enemies without further ado. In short, they have to refer to what Etienne Copeaux has called the "obligatory consensus" (Copeaux 2000), i.e. all those national references considered as sacred, like National Unity, the Turkish flag, and the figure of Atatürk. Defending the Republic and its founding values against its enemies is thus the main legitimate means of expressing demands, notably for movements seeking recognition, which are the most exposed to accusations of separatism.

Charles Tilly distinguishes between "reactive" or "defensive" claims (aiming to the redress of grievances), "competitive" claims (i.e. demands of resources claimed by other groups), and "offensive" claims (i.e. claiming rights that have not been exercised before) (Tilly 1978). In the Alevist case, demands to redress perceived discriminations and to restore the neutrality of State institutions, for example to punish slanders against Alevis, can be considered as reactive; demands for the same rights as Sunnis, such as the teaching of Aleviness at school or the free practice of religious rituals, as competitive; finally, the according of official recognition for Aleviness and permission for it to organize itself separately can be considered as an offensive demand. We can say that only defensive claims have obtained legitimacy, if ever, since they can be framed as discrimination against part of the people, thus endangering national unity. But competitive and offensive claims can easily be understood as challenges to national unity. They are not argued and legitimized publicly in the framework of diversity, as would be the case in a multicultural framework or a system accepting diversity, but in reference to the supreme values of the nation, mainly Unity. For example, the Alevist claim for recognition of *cemevi* as places of worship is mostly framed as follows: Alevis, who are loyal Turkish citizens, cannot practice their religion freely, and are therefore discriminated against, which is presented as a threat to national unity. This shows that recognition or particularist claims remain illegitimate *per se,* even if they have become quite common in the last decades. Therefore, the defence of the nation's supreme values in the framework of Turkish nationalism is the only way to gain legitimacy, even (or especially) for identity claims.

Political actors resolve this tension in part by appropriating, but also by reinterpreting, or even misappropriating, key elements of this consensus, be they concepts or symbols (Navaro-Yashin 1998). Unity is affirmed by all, but also redefined by different political actors in order to impose their own vision and division of the world. Every political actor tries to delegitimize his political enemy by accusing him of being an enemy of Unity. In the case just mentioned, all those who oppose the recognition of *cemevi* are said by Alevists to endanger national unity, since they contribute to and reproduce the discrimination of a part of the population: it is not the Alevists claiming recognition who are thus framed as separatists, but the people opposing it. Thus the very category of separatism is no longer the monopoly of the PKK, but it can be applied to any political actor, including the State. The register of separatism is indeterminate: its very definition is at the heart of the debate. The same process is at work concerning other supreme values, like *laiklik* (secularism). For instance, the Islamists argue that Kemalist *laiklik* is not really *laiklik*, but an oppressive control of religion. In order to save the Republic, "real" *laiklik*, which the Islamists claim to represent, has to be implemented. Sometimes, political actors even try to change the content of the obligatory consensus itself, by adding some elements to it or excluding them, as has been the case with Islamists trying to impose civil society as a legitimizing element (Navaro-Yashin 1998).

The framing of unity is used, therefore, to legitimize as well as to de-legitimize, in complex interactions which we do not have the space to go into here[18]. What makes such broad uses and interpretations of this framing using Unity possible is its very flexibility and interpretative breadth. Moreover, this tenet also refers to common and familiar values and representations, spread by schoolbooks and other media (Copeaux 1997).

However, the more this reference to unity is affirmed in diverse contexts and with different meanings, the more it loses any meaning and becomes a mere incantation, somehow similar to the figure of Atatürk. However, even if it loses any concrete meaning, this compulsory framing strongly influences the ways in which discourses are produced and reality is conceived of. In this context, the growing discourses of identity and recognition do not simply indicate the "end of taboos restraining the discourse" (Vorhoff 1998:23) nor the liberalization of discourse and legitimisation[19]. The constraints on the formulation and framing of claims have changed, but they remain strong.

The role of the media

When analysing the framings movements produce, one must also take into account the principal forum where they are reflected, the media. What is the role of the media in this process? It has been argued that the development of private media in Turkey in the 1990s played an important role in the liberalization and spread of discourses of identity (Yavuz 1999).

However, the media may also play a role in the production and reproduction of nationalism (Anderson 1991; Yumul, Umut 2000) and therefore of discursive constraints on movements like Alevism. They are not a mere instrument where discourses of mobilized groups are reflected without any distortion or expressed freely (Neveu 1999). On the contrary, the media contribute to shaping the conditions of the construction and staging of groups and their claims in the public space. Movements struggle with media for the consecration of the public identity of the group they claim to represent, especially for a group like the Alevis, who have to confront a negative public image. This dimension is even more important for the Alevists, since they do not have their own national newspapers nor TV channels, unlike the Kurdish nationalist and Islamist movements, but only specialized, poorly distributed journals, which are read mostly by activists or sympathizers anyway. Therefore, Alevists strongly depend on external media to spread their ideas, representations, and claims.

Obviously, institutional constraints on even the private media lead them to adopt and reproduce the official discourse, notably the discourse on Unity. Let us just recall that the main media are linked to business groups who are themselves indirectly connected to the political field. Besides, commercial media base themselves on common-sense anticipatory frames to provide simple ways of producing meaning. They do this by packaging the abundant flow of confusing information in forms readily consumable by heterogeneous audiences, and by framing them into clear positions (Öncü 1995:54). The notion of global conspiracy, which is the habitual stuff of Cold War narratives and the conventional plot of numerous spy movies, is familiar to wide audiences and constitutes a plausible interpretative scheme (Öncü 1995:66). Therefore, political and identity discourses as reflected by the media may not indicate a monolithic ideological hegemony, but most probably also correspond to commercial media practices which, paradoxically, could contribute to reinforcing the constraints on discourses and the making of demands.

These framing constraints are spread by some private media not only in Turkey, but also in the diaspora. Some European editions of Turkish newspapers[20] contribute to disseminating the national narrative and allegiance to the Turkish Nation (Anderson 1983). This is most notably the case of the Turkish daily with the largest circulation, *Hürriyet*, which often launches campaigns against political actors of Turkish origin distancing themselves from Turkish nationalism and allegiance to Turkey; *Hürriyet* also launched several harsh campaigns against the main Alevist Federation abroad, the AABF (*Almanya Alevi Birlikleri Federasyonu*, Federation of Alevi Communities in Germany) (Sökefeld 2004).

However, interviews with leading Alevist NGO executives and militants also show that, even if this Unity framing has been co-produced by state institutions and the media, it has been taken over and interiorized by the officials and militants themselves. These statements lead to a rethinking of the assumption that a liberation of media as well as political discourses is taking place.

Conclusion

Whereas debates on identity and diversity have indisputably become more widespread in Turkey since the 1980s, difference, and even more particularism, are still illegitimate and stigmatized. Many constraints strongly influence and limit the expression of difference and demands for its recognition. Turkish nationalism remains the legitimizing frame for claim-making, even more so for movements seeking recognition.

This situation can only be understood by analysing who supports banal nationalism and "obligatory" references, and why. It is not only conservative state authorities, but also media (even in the diaspora) – because of political connections but also mere commercial considerations – and political actors, even those in the opposition, who may disseminate Turkish nationalism for their own sake or to legitimize themselves.

The recent mainly legal changes toward more organizational facilities and tolerance of differences are not an achievement of the movements of identity themselves. Rather, they result from the relative depolarization of Turkish political life since the weakening of the guerrilla conflict in the late 1990s and the normalization of political Islam. They also result from the perspective of accession to the EU and the external constraints associated with it. And, last but not least, they arouse much resistance. The very fact that many of these changes have been initiated by the perspective of EU accession or external pressure fosters resistance, as was shown recently by the very controversial public debate on the Minority Report following the 2004 EU Commission Report on Turkey's progress towards accession.

PART III

THE HISTORIOGRAPHICAL CHALLENGE

Chapter 10

Defining the parameters of a post-nationalist Turkish historiography through the case of the Anatolian Armenians

Fatma Müge Göçek

In Greek mythology, Mnemosyne or Memory was the mother of all the Muses, including Clio, the mother of History. When modern historiographers discuss how History came into the world as a discipline, they often evoke this myth of origin and then proceed to the controversies that developed after the birth, for the child grew up to usurp many of the functions of the mythical grandmother. If one of History's functions is indeed to get societies to remember their pasts, what does contemporary Turkish society remember about 1915? It is the dismal answer to this crucial question that necessitates not only a critique of current Turkish nationalist historiography, but also its eventual replacement by a post-nationalist one.

In this article, I attempt to start to develop such a post-nationalist Turkish historiography. After undertaking a discussion of the discipline of historiography, I criticize current Turkish historiography particularly in relation to two of its inherent elements, the hegemony of nationalism and the hegemony of the year 1915. I then propose the possibility of an alternate 'post-nationalist' historiography that seeks to eliminate these hegemonic elements.

The development of historiography as a discipline

The development of historiography, namely the analysis of the specific forms of thinking and writing about history (Fuchs and Stuchtey 2002), in 19th century Europe was embedded in the project of modernity. The discipline faced interrelated empirical and theoretical problems from its inception, however. Empirically, its embeddedness in the project of European modernity generated problems in the construction of historical knowledge. And theoretically, the licence it assumed in the processes of thinking and writing about history created issues in the interpretation of historical knowledge.

Theoretically, the main problem with historiography emerged during the phase of the 'thinking and writing' of history, in that it was through this

thinking and writing that the elements of *memory*, namely ways of remembering the past, and *narrative*, namely placing that which was remembered in the
form of a story were introduced into historiography. Hence, while historiography proceeded in the form of a scientific discipline treating empirically verifi-
able historical facts or events, it necessarily required the intervention of imagi-
nation, first to confer with memory to select some facts in preference to others,
and second to order the actors and events in a particular manner so as to create a coherent story. In the process, then, a fictional element entered into the
historical narrative.

Scholars increasingly drew attention to the inherent biases this fictional element in historiography might contain. Hayden White, for instance, stressed the
pre-modern form of historiography as he noted in particular (1978: 123) that
"prior to the French Revolution, historiography was conventionally regarded as
a literary art. More specifically, it was regarded as a branch of rhetoric and its
'fictive' nature generally recognized ... many kinds of truth, even history,
could be presented to the reader only by fictional techniques of representation." This emphasis on the fictive and the fictional in historiography was further developed by Michel de Certau, who in turn accented the discursive aspect,
stating that (1988: xxvii) "Historiography (that is, 'history' and 'writing') bears
within its own name the paradox – almost an oxymoron – of a relation established between two antonymic (?) terms, the real and discourse."

Historiography as such, according to White and de Certau, contains fictive
and discursive dimensions; even though it indeed engages in history writing, it
does so with plenty of interpretive license. Their analysis in turn of the dynamics of this interpretive license highlights the significance of the current historical *context* within which the particular historiography is constructed; it is after
all the present that informs and reforms the past in accordance with its own
ideological interests. The post-modern projects of deconstruction White and de
Certau engaged in did not attempt to dismantle the past through factual contradiction, but rather analyzed the context within which the facts were situated
so as to tease out the ideological underpinnings of a existing accounts.

Empirically, the positivist notions of scientific objectivity that emerged during 19th century modernity attempted to instill in historiography claims of factual fixed historical truth, thereby overlooking its constructed nature. Yet in
the aftermath of the two World Wars, especially as the human tragedy of the
Holocaust made people aware of how much evil humans are capable of bringing upon themselves, scholars started to approach these historical narratives
critically to reveal the ideologies they concealed in the name of objectivity.
Once those ideological underpinnings became evident, scholars then started to
pay increasing attention to the significance of a historical context, and especially of the impact of wider sections of the population and their social and
economic conditions on how knowledge is constructed. Contemporaneous
political trends were particularly influential in affecting the manner in which

historiography narrated particular historical events and the actors involved in them. The most significant ideological underpinning of modernity revealed by these critical deconstructions was the one which had wreaked so much destruction in the first place, namely nationalism.

During the course of the 19th and 20th centuries, the main components of historiography, namely its time frame, selection of historical events, and historical sequencing, were all employed to legitimize nationalist projects. The people were mobilized as they were alerted to selectively remember particular historical events in their pasts in relation to particular periods of time. It was especially with historical sequencing that certain historical facts became deliberately, systematically, even intentionally highlighted, while others were suppressed and still others fabricated. A historical sequence constructed in this manner did not induce discussion, in that it did not present an argument about history but rather bluntly stated it as uncontested historical reality (Bolle 1987: 261-262). By imagining a past that did not exist, historiography thus acquired the characteristic of a national myth. As past historical events became endowed with special meaning and significance for the present, this national myth also reinforced the power and authority of those currently in power.

Yet probably the most significant dimension such a nationalist historiography acquired was, as one scholar has noted (Ben Yehuda 1995: 282-283), its moral character: nationalist historiography became suffused with "an attitude of sacredness, a high degree of symbolization, a dimension of morality in the form of an instructive lesson ... a simple narrative where the good and bad are clearly differentiated." The historical narrative was also frequently adjusted to fit the moral theme and lesson so that the myth continued to be credible, consistent and coherent. It should be stressed here that historiography employed in this manner was not interested in understanding the past, but rather in imposing upon the past the moral interpretation contained in the national project, which clearly identified the good and the bad before it even started to engage in any historical analysis. Nationalist historiography thus "meant to create attitudes, stir emotions, and help construct particular social realities conducive to the purposes of those transmitting the myth ... Myths become particularly important in times of beginnings – for example, in the early stages of a process of the formation of a nation (Ben Yehuda 1995: 283)."

It is ironic that the moral tone inherent in the nationalist historiographies of the 19th and 20th centuries was ultimately challenged by what nationalism brought upon humanity in the name of modernity, namely the Holocaust. It was the portrayal of this dark side of modernity and the ideologies it fostered through the violence of the Holocaust that enabled scholars first to engage in criticism of the project of modernity and then to start to deconstruct the nationalist historiographies it harboured. Yet such deconstruction brought with it another epistemological quandary. The subsequent writing and rewriting of the Holocaust (Young 1988: 15) revealed that when such a uniquely violent event as this was brought into the historical narrative, it either became normalized and integrated as a historical event within historiography, thereby losing its particularity, or instead ended up monopolizing the historiography and rupturing it in such a manner as to render scholarly analysis almost impossible. The trauma of the Holocaust, though powerful when unmediated, unframed and unassimilated, was revealed anew when it was written into the historical narrative. Some scholars have argued (Young 1988: 37) that this epistemological problem could be resolved to some extent if, in the first place, scholars turned to the information on the violent event of the Holocaust not for evidence but for knowledge, and then, in the second place, made a separate decision as to when to act or not upon this knowledge.

Existing hegemonies in current Turkish historiography

When current Turkish historiography pertaining to the Armenians is critically analyzed within the context of the literature on historiography reviewed in the previous section, Turkish nationalism and the violent events of 1915 emerge as the two elements that need to be critically examined and deconstructed. Hence one can argue for the need for a post-nationalist Turkish historiography solely on the grounds that the application of the contemporary criticisms of historiography to the Turkish case reveals two hegemonies, namely 'the hegemony of nationalism' and 'the hegemony of 1915'. The domination of the ideology (read Turkish nationalism) and the event (read 1915) that have infiltrated much of the existing scholarship on Turkey remains unexamined, as scholars approach historical sources uncritically and often accept textual rhetoric as historical reality. Yet such histories epistemologically manipulate the role and significance of certain social groups (read Sunni Turks) at the expense of all others, through their selective employment and deployment of history. In so doing, they eliminate outright certain possible choices and trajectories (read non-nationalist solutions) not only from history but also, by implication, from scholars' analyses as well. They thus introduce a certain historical determinacy whereby the nationally triumphant groups (read the now secularized Turkish elites) always soar to historical success against all odds, and the vanquished (read the rest of Turkish society including all the minorities) seem doomed to failure. A case in point is the process through which the point of origin of the official historiography of the Turkish Republic was constructed.

The hegemony of Turkish nationalism

I conjecture here that it was the famous Speech (*Nutuk*) delivered by Mustafa Kemal in 1927 at the Second Congress of the Republican People's Party, which he had founded and now led, that laid the foundation stone for the official historiography of the Turkish Republic. In that speech, Mustafa Kemal narrated his own historiography of the Turkish War of Independence for three days straight; his historiography eventually became that of the nation. The first sentence of Mustafa Kemal's speech in fact declared the starting point of his own historiography – and therefore, by implication, of all the official historiographies thereafter as follows: "I landed in Samsun on the 19th day of May, 1919." The ensuing text not only covered the events from the year 1919 onward, but did so from the vantage point of 1927, four years after the establishment of the Turkish Republic and the suppression of various revolts throughout Anatolia. It is noteworthy that at the particular historical juncture when Mustafa Kemal took to narrating his version of this new nation's past, all the minority groups in Turkey, including the Armenians, had already been very effectively marginalized. Given these epistemological parameters, it was virtually impossible within the confines of Turkish nationalist historiography predicated on such a historical framework ever to recover and fully recognize the agency of such ethnic and religious groups in Turkey.

And the ensuing Turkish nationalist discourse neatly categorized these ethnic and religious groups according to strictly maintained boundaries of inclusion and exclusion. It defined the Turkish secular elites, who were included, as historically triumphant and then proceeded to integrate their norms and values into society as 'historical reality.' The nationalist ideology also idealized the emerging Turkish secular elites, as it simultaneously allocated them exclusive determining power over the course of Turkish history and also cleansed them of all the vices they had ever engaged in by censoring history; it thus presented the Turkish elites morally and metaphorically as 'white.' By the same token, Turkish nationalist ideology articulated and narrated the excluded minorities as the vanquished, and then proceeded to attribute to them the exactly opposite characteristics: the excluded were stripped of most of their agency, and the very little they were permitted to exercise was of course depicted within parameters defined by the triumphant group, thereby appearing totally subversive and immoral. Turkish nationalist ideology thus embellished history by selectively employing only those historical events that portrayed the excluded minorities in a negative light, thereby impregnating them with vice. It ended up representing Turkish minorities morally and metaphorically as 'black.' And if scholars, themselves socialized within the Turkish nation-state where such an ideology was predominant, did not treat this highly selective representation of Turkish history critically, their accounts ended up contributing to the maintenance of Turkish nationalist historiography. By so doing, these scholars directly or indirectly reproduced historical actors as either black or white, with no consideration at all either of the possible intermediate shades or of other colours.

The hegemony of 1915

The hegemony of 1915 refers to how the historical events that resulted in the ultimate removal and destruction of the Armenians from their ancestral homeland by the Turks was endowed with a particular historical narrative in which this unfortunate event was a natural outcome. 1915 thus attracted all existing Turkish historiographies to itself with insurmountable force and, in so doing, obliterated all critical historical analysis, eliminating all events, institutions and social groups that might have suggested that another outcome was possible. In the particular case of official Turkish historiography, which was predicated on an unfortunate denial of the extent and intentionality of the Armenian massacres of 1915, the historical events before 1915 were thus selectively retold in a way that both legitimized what befell the Anatolian Armenians, and also took pains to demonstrate that the same fate, if not worse, befell the Turks as well. Hence the Anatolian Armenians of the Ottoman Empire were portrayed in history as an initially wealthy and contented 'loyal' social group who turned ungrateful and treacherous mostly at the instigation of the Great Powers; the same Powers were also narrated, by the same stroke of the pen, as aggressors against the Turks in attempting to wrest the Empire away from its 'rightful owners.' As a consequence, both the Turks and the Armenians were depicted as suffering 'equally' during the First World War, which was brought upon them by the Great Powers. In all, then, 1915 was expanded to subsume both the subsequent and the consequent historical events, and giving them a moral dimension which involved all humanity.

In official Turkish historiography, both the hegemony of Turkish nationalism and the hegemony of 1915 ended up dramatically limiting the historical repertoire of scholars engaged in research into Turkey's past. The official use of history thus portrayed very selectively the social conditions of the Ottoman Empire, the agency of various social groups within it, the repertoire of choices these groups had, and the range of historical events they encountered. Given this state of affairs, I argue here that it will not be possible for official Turkish historiography to make any significant empirical and methodological advances without reconstructing its framework through engaging in critical analysis. I propose to reconstruct such a historiography by reconsidering in particular its periodization, so that this periodization is not based solely on the nationalist history of the Turks that came to seem natural and eventually emerged as hegemonic, but rather on the intersections of the experiences of both the Turks and the minority groups, in this case the Anatolian Armenians, of the Empire.

The alternative periodization of a post-nationalist Turkish historiography

The alternate periodization of a post-nationalist Turkish historiography, as it is proposed here, needs to comprise, in relation to the Ottoman *millet* and imperial structures, the following stages: (i) the Formative Period, 1453-1639; (ii) the Institutionalization Period, 1639-1834; (iii) the Reform Period, 1834-1902; (iv) the Nationalist Period, 1902-1982; and (v) toward a Post-Nationalist Period, 1982-2004.

I. The Formative Period, 1453-1639

Even though the origins of what became the Ottoman Empire could be traced to the establishment of the Ottoman principality in the Iznik region around 1299 and even the interaction of the semi-nomadic Ottoman Turks with the non-Muslims residing in Anatolia a century earlier, it was probably with the conquest of Constantinople from the Byzantine empire that the Ottoman Turks started to develop not only the ideal but also the realization of an imperial structure populated by social groups from multiple ethnicities and religions. It is thus then that the first outline of a policy regarding the conditions under which non-Muslims were to exist within the confines of Ottoman lands started to form (Braude and Lewis 1982).

According to this policy, the non-Muslim minorities were organized into religious communities termed *millets*, where the Greek, Armenian and Jewish communities comprised the main categories. Each *millet* community was organized around its religious institution and headed by its particular elected religious leader, who oversaw the internal administration of the community and was legally responsible for it, especially in terms of the payment of communal taxes, to the Ottoman Sultan. Under this arrangement, even though the non-Muslim minorities possessed economic rights, they lacked significant social and political rights in that they could not bear arms, travel on horseback within cities, or hold administrative office, except when appointed by the Sultan. Since their civic rights were based on their religion, they also could not marry Muslims without undergoing religious conversion and, if they chose to do so, they lost their legal rights within their own communities. As a consequence, during this formative period, given the conditions under which they functioned, the Ottoman minorities ended up becoming active and prominent in the one sphere – the economic one – where they faced a minimum of restrictions. They thus specialized in particular professions and utilized their multilingual skills, especially in inter-imperial trade.

The fact that the Ottoman minorities suffered restrictions in relation to their social interaction with the rest of the population, however, produced significant repercussions throughout society. The Ottoman social system, as it was established, ended up integrating the superiority of the Muslims, in that no such social political, social or economic restrictions were placed upon them; they could bear arms, hold office, and also live in a society that operated within the Islamic legal framework. In short, one can claim that during the formative period, the social system allowed the Ottoman minorities to coexist peacefully with members of other religious communities – a quite advanced state of affairs, given the persecutions of religious minorities throughout Europe but one which, in the last instance, favoured the Muslims. 1639 marks the end of this formative period because of a change that then occurred in the particular position of the Armenians within the empire: it was with the treaty of 1639 between the Ottoman and Safavid Empires that the location of the Armenians in the Ottoman social system became finalized (Libaridian 2004: 13).

I should comment here on how this periodization differs from that currently provided by Turkish nationalist historiography. The latter's portrayal of this period is one of continuous peace where it was 'Turkish magnanimity and

Muslim benevolence' that granted rights to the religious minorities living in the Turks' midst; the narrative thus imputes the agency of religious minorities by implying that they in turn became and remained peaceful 'out of gratitude.' Hence the moral tone of benevolence on the part of the Turks and gratitude on the receiving side of the minorities is already established. Turkish nationalist historiography then proceeds to carefully select and frequently mention other contemporaneous historical events with the intent to demonstrate the superiority of the Ottoman treatment of minorities over others; one such event which is frequently mentioned involves the violence inflicted by the Spanish Inquisition upon religious minorities, resulting in their death or deportation. That the Ottoman Sultan welcomed such minorities into his empire further strengthens the nationalist narrative. Hence the initial positive moral tone set by the domestic treatment of the religious minorities in the Ottoman Empire is extended to establish moral superiority over contemporaneous European empires.

In developing the above-mentioned narrative, Turkish nationalist historiography thus selectively highlights the favourable dimensions of the minorities' existence in the empire. Yet, in so doing, it also fails, again selectively, to mention other aspects of Ottoman minority existence. Specifically, Turkish nationalist historiography underplays or keeps silent about the obligations the Ottoman minorities had to fullfil in return for what they received, namely the additional taxes they were obliged to pay, and also the legal, social, political and administrative restrictions they faced within Ottoman society because of their religion. In addition, Turkish nationalist historiography assumes the natural dominance of the Ottoman administrative perspective, as it too treats the Ottoman minorities as one undifferentiated, rather stereotyped, social group; it thus fails to take into account, for instance, the internal dynamics and divisions of the religious minorities such as the ones that existed between residents of the capital and inhabitants of the provinces, or the inter-communal strife among them, that was also present from the outset. Also overlooked at this particular historical juncture is the tension that existed between the Ottoman Muslims and minorities because their interests often came into conflict. The absence of these factors in Turkish nationalist historiography idealizes and thereby dehistoricizes the relationship between the Muslim and minority communities; in so doing, it indirectly sets the stage for the later mythification of Muslim and minority relations. It is therefore no accident that with the advent of domestic strife in 19th century Ottoman society, this selective representation 'naturally' leads to blame for the social strife being placed on the ungrateful Ottoman minorities and their treachery.

II. The Institutionalization Period, 1639-1834

This period focuses on how Ottoman social structure started to take shape as the now established relations between the Muslims and minorities were reproduced over centuries (Göcek 1996). Even though the Ottoman Muslim and minority communities indeed coexisted relatively peacefully, they continued their transformation not as one social unit, but as two separate communities, one Muslim and the other non-Muslim, that evolved within themselves and in quite limited interaction with one another. Hence the initial legal separation based on religion became institutionalized in the Ottoman social structure, creating a very strongly defined and maintained bifurcation: as the Ottoman subjects subsequently practised their religions within their own communal spaces, their social networks and networks of communication developed most strongly with each other rather than across the divide; as the same subjects could not marry or inherit across the religious divide, their transfer of knowledge, wealth and resources also occurred within their own communities, separately from one another. In particular, the restriction placed upon minorities, as non-Muslims, of not being allowed to bear arms excluded them from the Ottoman military profession which became the exclusive domain of the Muslims. Even though this restriction proved quite advantageous to the Ottoman Muslims during the Empire's expansion, in that it brought them not only material wealth but higher social standing as well, it nevertheless started to work to their disadvantage in the late 18th and 19th centuries when the Empire stopped expanding. As the Ottoman army then started to face increasing defeats, the Ottoman Muslims manning the military not only failed to acquire wealth and status through warfare, but began to lose their lives at alarmingly high rates.

What limited Ottoman imperial expansion during the same historical period was the rising West. It was the emergence of European powers now equipped not only with the products of the industrial revolution but with new military warfare techniques that established a strong position on the borders of the Ottoman Empire. This Western transformation, which disadvantaged the Ottoman Muslim subjects, provided new opportunities for the Ottoman non-Muslims. Because of the European economic expansion consequent on the industrial revolution, European trade with the Ottoman Empire escalated and the Ottoman minorities, who had for ages been directed to specializing in trade and the economy at home, acquired, unlike their Muslim counterparts, increased advantages because of their linguistic, cultural and religious affinities with Europe. The Ottoman sultans made use of the skills of some Ottoman minorities by appointing them to significant administrative posts, often relying on either their domestically developed economic skills or their linguistic skills; hence many ended up heading Ottoman economic institutions or engaging in diplomacy with European powers on behalf of the Ottoman Sultan. Yet, the minorities manning these high-level administrative posts differed from their Muslim counterparts in one significant respect: the Ottoman Sultan often established control over the Muslim office-holders by marrying them to women from his own household, so as to guarantee their loyalty, or the Muslim office-holders were able to resist the Sultan's control by networking with their powerful relatives or passing their advantages on to their children. Since the

Ottoman office-holders from the minorities were located socially outside of such family and marriage networks, their hold on the power they acquired was much more precarious position and often did not extend beyond their own lifetime.

The political developments in Europe in the form of the Enlightenment and the ensuing French Revolution also affected the Ottoman social structure and with it, the Ottoman Muslims and minorities, in quite different ways. The most significant outcome of this Western political development was undoubtedly a discussion of the rights of individuals as citizens rather than as Imperial subjects. A world where rights were preordained was gradually replaced by one where individuals operated in a society within which they acquired contractual rights and responsibilities to become citizens of equal standing. As such, these citizens wanted to make the societies they lived in their own and, when prevented from doing so, they undertook revolutions to realize their visions – which are often termed 'visions of modernity.' It is no accident that the penetration of these European visions into the Ottoman Empire occurred indirectly through education and directly through the Ottoman minorities who had both the closest economic contact with Europe through trade and also often sent their sons to Europe to be educated, so as to sustain the economic advantage they had been able to build up in the Empire. And not surprisingly, the Ottoman minorities became conscious of and increasingly dissatisfied with their position within the Ottoman social system. After all, the Ottoman minorities and Muslims coexisted within an overarching Imperial culture and their language, music, architecture and arts had been influenced by one another through the centuries.

For instance, Armenian architects built mosques, Greek musicians composed musical pieces, and Jewish artisans created clothing. Yet while all that was produced by Muslims and minorities created the Ottoman public space, the cultural ownership often ended up getting attributed to the socially, politically and legally dominant Muslim community. What the Ottoman minorities produced was only theirs privately; because of the societal restrictions placed upon them, they did not have as much claim on public ownership, and no particular space of their own within the Ottoman public sphere other than their carefully defined communal space. Even though the Ottoman minorities increasingly participated in the creation of the Ottoman public space, they were not publicly recognized as a part of it; instead, they were obliged to retire to the privacy of their own communal space.

Hence, as a consequence of these political and economic developments in Europe and the concurrent Ottoman internal transformation, the positions of Ottoman Muslims and minorities became affected in different ways. The interaction between the external and internal dynamics affected the Ottoman minorities more favourably than the Muslims. While the Ottoman minorities were advantaged by the economic developments, the new political ideas increasingly highlighted their disadvantaged location within Ottoman society. The Muslims increasingly lost the advantages of their normalized dominance in society as Ottoman Imperial expansion tapered off and they too became dissatisfied with their location within society. It was in the next historical period that both social groups, especially the younger generations educated in Western-style institutions, turned to reforms in an attempt to redefine their locations; both parties noted that the problems were embedded in the existing Ottoman social system, both identified the preordained nature of Ottoman Imperial rule as the possible origin of such problems, and both started to work for the introduction of an Ottoman constitutional government that would, in theory, ensure them larger public space for increased political participation.

Once again, I need to comment on how this periodization diverges from the narrative provided by Turkish nationalist historiography. In the nationalist narrative, there is no differentiation of the formative and institutionalization periods of Ottoman social structure in relation to the lives of its Muslims and minorities. Ottoman history is instead divided into the 'classical period', that covers the whole of the roughly five hundred years (1299-1839) preceding the 19th century European impact, and the ensuing 'reform period' of about eighty years (1840-1922), that articulates the Ottoman transformation occurring as a consequence of this impact until the foundation of the Turkish Republic. The lack of differentiation of the Ottoman classical period produces two consequences: it further dehistoricizes the societal locations of Muslims and minorities by ignoring the transformations they underwent in the course of the four centuries; how the disparate locations of the Muslims and minorities gradually become embedded in the Ottoman social structure, and how the two religious communities produced a deeply embedded structural divide, are overlooked. It also mythifies the characteristics of Ottoman minorities by treating them as unchanging over the course of the centuries, whereby the initial nationalist assessment of Muslim benevolence and minority gratitude continues unchallenged.

As a consequence, the only source of change the nationalist historiography highlights is not internally generated, but externally enforced by the expanding West. The increasing involvement of European powers in the Ottoman Empire is therefore interpreted negatively as the intervention of these powers in Ottoman internal affairs in general and their pressuring for reforms favouring the Ottoman minorities in particular. The interaction also assumes a moral character as it is clearly defined, in line with nationalist rhetoric that categorizes all as being either good or bad for the nation, while the latent intention of Western powers is to weaken and destroy the Ottoman Empire from the start. The economic and political impact of Europe is also selectively highlighted in relation to the unrest it produces among the Ottoman minorities alone; the negative impact of the European transformation on the location of the Ottoman Muslims in relation to the minorities is overlooked. The Muslims enter nationalist rhetoric only in terms of the increasing tension between the Ottoman Sultan who holds on to his power and the newly emerging Western-style educated Muslims who want to share that power.

It is within this epistemological context that the historical analysis of the reform period, the period of visible Western European impact on the Ottoman social structure, commences. From the outset, however, Turkish nationalist historiography treats the Western impact on Ottoman Muslims and minorities as two independent, rather than interdependent, phenomena, thereby ideologically reading into the text their subsequent failure to transform peacefully along the same lines.

III. The Reform Period, 1834-1902

It was toward the middle of the 19th century that both the Ottoman minorities and the Western-style educated Muslims started to process and interpret the political, social and legal ideas generated in Europe within the dynamics of Ottoman society. Especially the younger generations of both the Ottoman minorities and the Muslims observed the West, where they increasingly received their education, and most importantly, in order to reproduce the military and economic success of the West, started to establish educational institutions in the Ottoman Empire along similar lines. In the educational and social reforms they undertook, the Ottoman minorities were primarily supported by the emerging class of merchants and tradesmen who benefited from the increasing economic and trade relations with Europe, while the Ottoman Muslims were helped by the Ottoman state. The disparate nature of this support had varying effects on the Ottoman social structure: the reforms pertaining to the Ottoman minorities were successful mostly when undertaken by the minorities themselves and, as such, they remained confined within the boundaries of the minority communities. The reforms carried out by the Ottoman state, which targeted in theory both the minorities and the Muslims, mostly succeeded in the case of the Muslims but failed to overcome the institutionalized structural divide in society between the Muslims and the minorities in practice. Still, the reform period was marked by intense efforts among all parties, namely the Ottoman state administration and the existing Muslim elites, the minorities with their local governance structures, and the Western-style educated Muslims with their new political visions, to reform the empire into a form that would fit all their needs.

The Ottoman imperial administration spearheaded the reform efforts (Armaoğlu 1964) by undertaking administrative legal reforms approximately every two decades (1839, 1856, 1876) to ensure equal rights for the Ottoman Muslims and the minorities. The persistence of these efforts shows several things, I think. First, it reveals how deeply ingrained Muslim-minority inequality was in the Ottoman social system; even after three unsuccessful tries it was not overcome. Second, Muslim dominance in the Ottoman social system was clearly so deeply ingrained that each time the reform efforts had to be introduced as alleviating problems with the social locations of *both* the Muslims *and* the minorities, whereas in essence they attempted to bring the status of the minorities up to the level of the Muslims.

According to the first Ottoman Reform Proclamation, the *Tanzimat*, which was promulgated on 3 November 1839, the individual rights of both the Muslims and the minorities of the Empire were recognized together equally for the first time. What is noteworthy in it is the novel legal treatment of both social groups under a single decree which was bound to highlight the legal inequalities existing between the Ottoman Muslims and the minorities, especially when they were placed side by side rather than being treated as two structurally entirely separate categories. The following Ottoman Reform Proclamation, the *Islahat*, promulgated on 28 February 1856, further attempted to negotiate and bring about equality between the Muslims and the minorities of the Empire. As noted above, the need to proclaim a second reform approximately two decades after the first suggests how profound was the structural adjustment to the Ottoman social system required to alleviate the sources of inequality: these extended from equal opportunity in recruitment to educational and administrative institutions, to equal representation in the courts, and to equal opportunity for membership in provincial assemblies. These reform proclamations had to be followed by a third almost two decades later when, on 23 December 1876, a more drastic legal reform, the *Meşrutiyet*, was undertaken with the declaration of the Ottoman constitutional system and the formation of an Ottoman National Assembly. Even though European powers interpreted this Ottoman move as a pre-emptive move to relieve the European pressure placed upon the Empire for reforms, it nevertheless did permit all subjects some degree of representation in an assembly and led to the first elections in the Empire. I think that the Ottoman state did indeed try to reform the empire along Western lines in an attempt to capture European patterns of imperial success, but it failed when it was unable to overcome the deep structural divide that had developed in Ottoman society between the Muslims and the minorities. The difference in societal reaction to these state-initiated reforms was noteworthy in that there were strong generational differences in reception among both the Ottoman minorities and the Muslims. Most of the younger generations in the Ottoman minority communities welcomed the potential improvement to their legal status and their closer integration into the larger Ottoman society that these reforms implied, but they were frustrated with the slow pace at which the reforms were executed and the resistance they faced both within their own communities and also from Ottoman Muslims. The older generations in these communities predicted that these legal reforms would increase the sense of loss of communal identity, as their communities became more and more integrated into Ottoman society at large; they wanted to retain their special language, legal system, local practices, and special privileges even when these sometimes brought with them practices of exclusion

from the larger society. The reactions of the Muslims were also complex; those
younger generations of Ottoman Muslims educated in Western-style institutions embraced the Western European ideology of the brotherhood of all men
under equal rights in theory and in principle; they therefore realized and supported these reforms as a necessary component of modernity. As their dominance in the existing system came naturally to them, they were not yet aware
how this equality would directly affect their lives in practice. The older generations of Ottoman Muslims protested vociferously, stating that they did not
want to destroy a system that had worked so well for so many years, and some
even proclaimed that they did not want the Ottoman minorities who had been
subordinate to them for so many centuries to be elevated to the same legal status as theirs.

The Ottoman minorities participated in the Ottoman state-initiated reforms
as individuals and in the reforms of their own local administrations as groups
(Artinian 1970). Probably the reform initiated by the state that had the most
influence on the Ottoman minorities was the 1839 Ottoman Reform
Proclamation, in that it enabled the establishment of mixed tribunals in the
millets. Previously, the local administrative bodies of the Ottoman minorities
had been dominated by the power of religious leaders, but this reform created
space for lay members in these tribunals who in turn introduced new ideas and
reforms into their particular *millets*. The participation of the laity in religious
affairs dynamized all three minority communities of the empire, namely the
Jews, Greeks and Armenians (and the Syrian Orthodox). Moreover, the concurrent changes in the Ottoman taxation system also contained in the reform
edict enabled Ottoman minority merchants and artisans to participate more
fully in their local *millet* administration, thereby providing increasing support
to the reformist elements and their new ideas. It was also during this period
that the first stirrings of nationalism were felt, as Greece was established as an
independent state in 1830 and all the communities struggled with the issue of
defining their identities within an Imperial framework in a world still structurally dominated by empires. The ensuing rebellions in Wallachia, Moldavia,
Montenegro and Serbia in the 1850s, and the increasing influence of the
Russian empire in the Balkans and the north and north-east in the 1890s put
the Ottoman Empire more and more under pressure for reforms to improve
the rights of its Christian subjects.

The interpretation by Turkish nationalist historiography of this period of
Ottoman reform is marked by a deep ambivalence. For while it has to recognize
and legitimize the Western ideas and institutions of reform that later provided
the founding stones of the Turkish Republic, it must criticize the Western powers who instigated those ideas and institutions. Nationalist historiography
therefore treats the recipient elements of Ottoman society selectively; it does
not recognize any differentiation within the Ottoman minorities because it
treats them as one stereotyped unit of analysis that has no agency of its own,

and so their reaction vis-à-vis the reforms is interpreted in terms of how they fell under the influence of Western powers to turn against the Ottoman Empire. The contributions of those minorities who helped Westernize Ottoman society are also overlooked. In relation to the Ottoman Muslims, those older generations that reacted adversely to the reforms are dismissed as 'traditional religious' elements that did not have the interests of the Empire at heart. In so doing, nationalist historiography also obfuscates and dismisses the most significant criticism of reform advocated by this group, that it eliminated the natural dominance of Muslims in Ottoman society. The only Ottoman group that emerges triumphant with its agency unscathed is the young Ottoman Muslim reformists, as these were the intellectual forebears of the Turkish nationalists. In this case too, however, the nationalist historiography treats historical facts selectively by employing the most significant methodological fallacy of nationalism: the rhetoric of the Muslim reformists is treated as historical reality. Even though the Ottoman Muslim reformists did pay lip service to legal equality in theory, their record becomes much more chequered when one analyzes the degree to which such reforms were carried out in Ottoman society. As I noted previously, there was significant structural resistance to the application of reforms.

By overlooking the discrepancy between the rhetoric and reality of reforms and by treating the rhetoric as reality, Turkish nationalist historiography manages to portray the impact and reception of reforms much more favorably than they actually were. In the narrative of nationalist historiography, if problems with reforms did exist, the culprits were either the Western powers who applied too much pressure or the Ottoman minorities who wanted too much too soon; the reactions of the Ottoman Muslims are overlooked. Hence it is only the agency of reform-minded Ottoman Muslims that is recognized within Ottoman society.

IV. The Nationalist Period, 1902-1982

Even though the seeds of the nationalist period were sown earlier, during the latter half of the 19th century when many rebellions occurred in the Empire, from the Balkans to Syria, Lebanon to Jeddah, I propose the historical event of the 1902 Congress of the Ottoman Opposition Parties in Paris as the starting point or origin of the nationalist period because it was then that political parties belonging to the Muslims and minorities of the Ottoman Empire met in Paris to discuss their common future if there was to be one. As participants in the Congress, they all had a fair chance to become significant players in determining the future of the Empire and history had not yet eliminated some for the benefit of others.

If the 1902 Congress as a starting point is compared with the starting point of nationalist historiography, the Turkish War of Independence in 1919, it becomes evident that two social factors were eventually dropped from nationalist historiography. The first factor to be eliminated was the ideology of nationalism that had started to take shape among some of the Young Turks; it disappeared in the ensuing Turkish historical narrative by becoming totally assimilated into it. The second factor to be lost was the multi-cultural, multi-ethnic structure of the Ottoman Empire reflected in the various groups participating in the Congress; it was gradually marginalized in Turkish historical narrative as these groups lose their agency to survive except as the 'Other.' It should also be noted that these two elements were intimately connected as well: the gradual marginalization of the ethnic and cultural groups was justified and legitimized by the escalating nationalist rhetoric embedded in the same narrative. The physical removal of these groups, often by force and violence, accompanied this symbolic disappearance. When one approaches the events of 1919 from such a standpoint, it becomes evident that in that particular period, those who had committed themselves to fight a War of Independence, including Mustafa Kemal, were already ambivalent about where ethnic and religious minorities of the empire would fit into the ensuing state they aimed to establish in their fatherland. In addition, two such minorities, namely the Anatolian Armenians and Greeks, had already been uprooted once from their ancestral lands for the good of the 'homeland' upon the orders of the Committee of Union and Progress. Yet this initial uprooting could only be brought into the narrative through an already ideologically mediated historical framework.

Any discussion of the historiography of the nationalist period needs to include the interventions of two historians, Erik Zürcher (1992) and Gerard Libaridian (1978), both of whom contest Turkish nationalist historiography from different vantage points. Zürcher provides a very articulate discussion of how Turkish historiography is based on a celebration of the foundation of the Turkish Republic and how the version of history presented by its founder, Mustafa Kemal, has therefore often been accepted without much criticism (1992: 238-9). He himself analyzes the social background, organizational characteristics and ideology of the Union and Progress leaders and the leaders of the newly founded Turkish Republic in order to demonstrate the significant continuities that existed between these two groups (1992: 241-7). The striking parallels that exist in the historical phases of these groups' transformations lead Zürcher to propose a historiography covering three parallel phases: 1906-1908 and 1919-1922; 1908-1913 and 1922-1925; 1913-1918 and 1925-1945. This in turn leads him to conjecture that "modern developments in Turkey, especially the changes which took place after World War II" can best be understood if the Kemalist movement is interpreted as a continuation and extension of the Young Turk one (1992: 250-252). I fully concur with his argument and suggest 1982 as the end of this period, because the subsequent introduction of neo-liberal reforms altered the social, political and economic landscape of Turkey.

Libaridian commences his article with a commentary on the historiography of the Armenian massacres proposed by Gwynne Dyer which he criticizes on the grounds of its inability to distinguish the standpoint of the society from that of the state, its failure adequately to periodize different historical phases, and once again its incapacity to contextualize events within the periods when they occurred (1978: 79-82). What is most pertinent, however, is Libaridian's criticism of reading the political formation of modern Turkey into the history of the Ottoman Empire. He argues (1978: 83-4) that such a reading reduces Ottoman history to the history of the Turks, and equates the interests of the Ottoman ruling class with those of the subjects, thereby obviating the need to discuss critically whether those interests corresponded to the needs of the very diverse groups of subjects. Hence nationalist historiography, as such, reduces Ottoman history to the narrative not only of the Turks, but particularly of the Turkish elite. I also concur that one needs to be wary of the nationalist rhetoric of 'representing the nation', for although many groups during this period did indeed talk and execute many violent acts on behalf of the nation, they were often small groups of leaders who assumed such roles without being popularly elected to them.

Let me now articulate the parameters of this nationalist period. The events of 1902 present a different framework, one where nationalism and its destructive treatment of minorities has not yet left their marks on the historical narrative. In 1902, the historical repertoire of the Congress still included all the ethnic and religious groups of the Ottoman Empire, and the ideology of nationalism was one among the many that were feverishly discussed. Such a point of origin would enable one to map out the many possible paths of social transformation that Turkish nationalism eradicated by suppressing, deporting or eliminating various ethnic and cultural groups in the Empire. It would also capture the agency of such victimized groups as they attempted to resist this nationalism on its own terms. In 1902, the Ottoman social groups still came to the Paris Congress as groups within an empire, but they demonstrated both there and soon thereafter that peaceful coexistence was to prove impossible, because the Muslim-Turkish element was not willing to forego what it regarded as its natural dominance in the Ottoman social structure and the *millet* system had generated a Muslim-Christian divide that was beyond repair. The environment was too polarized for the various social groups to come together to act in unison, for they had been separated communally for so long. It was at this Congress that the Young Turk movement started its transformation from an intellectual endeavour into a political entity, a process which eventually produced the 1908 revolution, when the Committee of Union and Progress, formed by a segment of the Young Turks, seized power from the Ottoman Sultan.

The period as a whole was thus marked not only by the nationalisms of the Ottoman minorities, but also by the nationalism of the dominant Muslim group directed against them, that eventually wrought havoc on them, through forced deportation in the case of the Armenians, forced population exchange in the case of the Greeks, and gradual attrition in the case of the Jews. From the

point of view of the history of the Muslims and minorities, the founding of the
Turkish Republic in 1923 was not a very significant turning point, in that the
minorities retained their rights according to the Lausanne Treaty, while their
acquisition of the rights and responsibilities of Turkish citizenship remained
mostly limited to responsibilities rather than rights. Even though they *rhetorically* acquired full rights, they did not do so in practice. This state of affairs is
demonstrated by the following incidents all instigated by the Turkish state at
intervals of about a decade. Before and during the Second World War, the
Turkish Jews were forcibly deported from Thrace to prevent their possible collaboration with the enemy, all three minorities forcibly conscripted into the
army to work as labourers, and soon thereafter targeted to pay a Wealth Tax
(*Varlık Vergisi*) that literally wiped out all their resources; a decade later, the
state surreptitiously set street mobs on to the minorities in Istanbul to destroy
their shops, houses and churches (6-7 September 1955); and still another decade
later, during the Cyprus events in 1963-64, the minorities were forced to emigrate, and only allowed to take savings not exceeding the equivalent of $100. It
is at the end of this nationalist period that the minorities were almost totally
destroyed and the path of destruction wrought by Turkish nationalism was
nearly complete.

By mapping out the nationalist movement from its Ottoman inception to
its Republican phase, this period brings narrative coherence to the historical
events, it also connects the trauma of 1915 with its nationalist aftershocks into
the 1960s. This periodization of course differs dramatically from the nationalist historiography, which refuses to recognize the significant historical continuities between the Ottoman Empire and the Turkish Republic and in so doing
fragments the narrative history of state-sponsored prejudice and violence
against the minorities in the name of nationalism. The exclusion of 1902-1922
from the nationalist historiography blots out the most virulent formative
stages of Turkish nationalism that proceeded almost totally unchecked under
the Young Turks. With the foundation of the Turkish Republic in 1923 and the
ensuing radical Westernization the Kemalists set on foot, Turkish nationalism
became neatly enfolded – and hidden – in the Western civilizational project.
Turkish nationalists gained much more international recognition and respect
as ardent Westernizers and pursued their national projects under this guise.
Their sustained prejudice and violence against the religious minorities in
Turkey were also justified in the name of this civilizational project; all social
groups who criticized state projects were immediately accused of obstructing
Turkey's path through Western civilization toward progress.

V. Toward a Post-nationalist Period, 1982-present

The advent of the new era toward a 'post-nationalist period', in terms of
Muslim-minority relations, starts in 1982 with the neo-liberalization of the
Turkish economy, media and communications under the Turkish President
Turgut Özal. This liberalization process created pockets of public space not

controlled by the Turkish state where social groups finally started to discuss the societal transformations on television on their own terms. The political oppression forced upon society by the military at exactly the same time may even have helped this societal implosion along by getting people focused on 'non-political' topics such as identity formation. It was also during this period that a substantive amount of Armenian, Greek and Jewish minority literature was translated into Turkish, and memoirs of members of the minorities also made their appearance for the first time. Even though the Turkish state was literally forced into this neo-liberalization due to its changing location in the world political situation at the end of the Cold War, the result was nevertheless that new plots of public space not controlled by the state were created in Turkey. Whether these plots have the potential to transform into political space capable of empowering minorities in Turkey remains to be seen.

The official Turkish minorities of Jews, Greeks and Armenians are currently so decimated in number that they no longer possess their former social, political and economic significance. The Turkish state recognition of, and apology for its policies of prejudice and violence against these communities would therefore have symbolic significance at best. The most significant unofficial minority, the Kurds, is still not fully recognized by the Turkish state in terms of its rights. Yet the rights of all social groups in Turkey vis-à-vis the state – as opposed to their responsibilities, which they have always been forced to fulfil – have recently become significant on the national agenda in relation to Turkey's impending European Union membership. The recent public discussions around these and other social issues and the often violent reactions of nationalist elements, however, have demonstrated how deeply ingrained and integrated nationalism still is in contemporary Turkish society. The next decade in Turkey will witness the attempts of the liberal elements in society to counter the nationalist hegemony and bring in what may hopefully be termed, in dominant-minority relations, the 'post-nationalist European period'.

Chapter 11
Facing responsibility for the Armenian genocide? At the roots of a discourse that legitimizes mass violence

Raymond H. Kévorkian

The research conducted by Taner Akçam which T.A. has been conducting for many years into the objective reasons that paralyse contemporary Turkey when it comes to face the responsibility of the genocide committed by its founders, have laid the first foundations for any reflection on this topic. Akçam has made it clear that by scrutinizing this question, one touches the very foundations of the Republic of Turkey established by Mustafa Kemal, which is, as Erik Jan Zürcher had repeatedly shown, the continuation or outcome of the Young Turk experience.

It would be irrelevant here to analyse anew the ideological basis supporting the project of "ethnically homogenizing" Asia Minor conceived by the Committee of Union and Progress (İttihad ve Terakki Cemiyeti). The studies by Şükrü Hanioğlu and Hamit Bozarslan have revealed that the system the Ittihadists built up aimed at excluding "foreign entities", to create a sort of *Lebensraum*. However, no one can ignore how much the Ottoman heritage, independently of the novelties introduced by the Young Turk ideology, influenced and still influences Turkish public opinion in its perception of the Other. The transfer of sovereignty and responsibility from the dominating Ottoman group to the dominated Turkish group took place almost naturally. This transfer did not destroy the legitimacy and superiority that this group was convinced it possessed when dealing with the other groups of people constituting the Empire. We believe that this strong feeling of legitimacy and property played a major role in the collective implementation of persecutions against the non-Turkish Ottoman population and still plays a major role until today in the rejection of any form of responsibility. This self-perception allowed the production of a discourse legitimizing violence committed by the dominating group against a dominated one, which precludes any feeling of guilt and reveals a true inability to face responsibility for misdeeds committed. While today limited elites are aware of this, they are prevented from acting in consequence by the mass of public opinion, which still believes in the legitimacy of violence when it is perpetrated by the State against dominated groups. The aim of this article is to scrutinize this precise and essential topic and find some preliminary answers to the question raised here, drawing on debates sparked off by the crimes committed in the War, the inquiries that the government ordered, and the criminal trials of members of the Young Turk elites organised after the debacle provoked by the First World War, that is during the short period after the Armistice of Moudros from November 1918 to May 1919. During this time the impact of the defeat allowed some limited avowals which, however, most often still have an undertone of a discourse legitimizing mass violence.

As far as the trials themselves are concerned, their scope and goal should first be defined. These court actions have been so far presented by Turcologists as a result of pressures by the Franco-British victors. An examination of the Archives of both the British High Commissary Commission at Constantinople and the Intelligence Service of the French Navy shows that the victors first thought of establishing an "international court", whose composition and functioning were discussed between British and French lawyers. As is well known, the Young Turk networks facing them still remained almost untouched, with local clubs and supporting personalities among the government and the military who had been organised for years; even after the Armistice, Sultan Mehmet VI Vahidettin had a hard time imposing a Cabinet that was not under the thumb of the Ittihat, or its new incarnation, the Teceddüd Fırkası. The Young Turk circles probably thought that cosmetic measures and the removal of leading personalities would suffice to let the Ottoman Cabinet appear acceptable to the Allies. The Sultan and some Liberal circles adopted a more realistic approach, demanding a minimum purge so that Western diplomacy would not be indisposed and the image of Turkey to be presented at the coming Peace Conference would be less debased. It seems that the Liberals' strategy consisted not only in starting legal proceedings as soon as possible in order to get rid of their Young Turk opponents, but also in putting up the following defence: not denying the violence committed against the Armenians, and the Greek Orthodox, Syriac and Chaldean Christians, but holding only the Central Committee of the CUP responsible, thus dissociating it from the Ottoman State and the government. By so doing, they opposed the Young Turk line that consisted in denying all responsibility, while from the start relativizing the involvement of the Ottoman administration in these war crimes.

In other terms, even the Liberal wing, decimated by the Ittihad after 1913, did not at any point plan to take it upon itself to acknowledge its responsibilities, even at the most favourable moment. The fear of break-up of the Ottoman lands may have had a certain effect, but one should not ignore the pressure of Turkish public opinion, about which the press of the time provides us with a quite precise image. The press unanimously developed a single discourse, putting the blame on the victims and legitimizing so-called "administrative meas-

ures" made inescapable by the Armenians' "collective treason", best illustrated by the catastrophic situation of the Ottoman Empire.

The Constantinople criminal trials are still insufficiently known. They are
closer to these of Leipzig, at which a German court tried criminals of war, than
to those of Nuremberg. Examining them, we are confronted with the question
whether States are able or not to judge their own citizens for mass crimes which
their own administration have organized.

The construct of a legitimizing discourse and the debates in the Ottoman Parliament in November 1918

Before scrutinizing the Young Turk discourse in front of the different institutions established after the Moudros Armistice, it may prove useful to evoke one
of the rare occasions on which the leader of the CUP, Talât, expressed himself, one year before the end of the war. The appointment of Mehmet Talât
as Grand Vizier on 22 January 1917 is a turning point in the history of the CUP.
After letting subservient Ministers and Grand Viziers take care of routine public affairs, the CUP openly took over, appointing its own leader at the head of
the Ottoman Government. In its move towards the construction of a new
Turkey, the CUP had the opportunity to draw up a balance of its political
action at its annual congress that was chaired by Midhat Şükrü, its Secretary
General, and held on 24 September 1917 in Istanbul. The composition of the
new committee appointed by the Assembly does not reveal major changes. The
General Council elected to its committee: Musa Kâzım, Said Halim (former
Grand Vizier), Hayri Effendi (Şeyh ül İslam), Haci Adıl (vali [Governor]) of
Edirne, organizer of the deportations out of Thrace, in autumn 1915), İsmail
Enver (Minister of War), [Giritli] Ahmet Nesimi [Sayman], Ahmet Cemal Paşa
(Minister of the Navy), Cavit (Minister of Economics), Halil [Menteşe]
(Minister of Foreign Affairs), Ahmet Şükrü (Minister of Public Education),
Mustafa Şeref, Hüseyin Cahit (Vice-President of Parliament) and Atıf Bey
(CUP Delegate, and later Vali of Ankara and Kastamonu, whose Armenian pop-
ulation he had deported or massacred).[1]

The Central Committee too remained stable. The party renewed the appointments of Mehmet Talât and Midhat Şükrü, Secretary General, as well as Dr.
Nâzım, [Kara] Kemal (Minister of Supply, in charge of the creation of
"Turkish companies"), [Yusuf] Rıza (working in the Trebizond area), Ziya
Gökalp (the ideologue of the Committee), Eyup Sabri [Akgöl] (a fedayi [militant
risking his life for the cause] and member of the Central Committee uninter-
ruptedly from 1908 to 1918), Dr. Rüsûhi (working in Azerbaijan and the Van
region), Dr. Bahaettin Şakir (Head of the Special Organization [S.O.]), and
[Filibeli] Ahmet Hilmi (Vice-Head of the S.O., in charge of operations in
Erzurum).[2]

The only noticeable promotion within the supreme instance of the party was
that of [Filibeli] Ahmet Hilmi, Dr. Şakir's right-hand man. The total membership of the Central Committee was again ten. All the members known to have

been opposed to the extermination of the Armenian population were in office within the Bureau of the General Council as well as the Central Committee. Even Cavit, who had distanced himself somewhat from it at the beginning of the War, was reintegrated in the Bureau. The opposition of party functionaries to anti-Armenian measures should be qualified, since it is documented by testimonies written *ex post facto* by some of the main characters.[3] One can also surmise that the Armenian question was then, by the beginning of autumn 1917, considered as solved and that the most prudent did not any longer feel compelled to keep their distance.

The speech Talât delivered can only provide us with slight indications about the internal debates, because it was to be published on the following day.[4] Right away, denying the obvious, Talât again repeated the official thesis about the conditions of the Ottoman involvement in the War: "The aggression of the Russian Navy in the Black Sea and the attack on land against our borders forced us to embrace the cause towards which our historical destiny was impelling us, and to side with the Central Powers."[5]

Concerning the central point of the accusations levelled at the Empire, that is, State violence, Mehmet Talât felt compelled to devote more than half of his speech to the measures taken by the Ottoman Empire against its non-Turkish subjects. Since his words are at the same time a track record and a justification, they deserve precise scrutiny. "Our enemies are saying everywhere that we ill-treat belligerent subjects and enemy fighters and that we have committed all kinds of atrocities against our Armenian and Jewish subjects. But fortunately, in many places, people have started understanding the hatred and malevolence of these items of news that we ourselves and many neutral personalities have refuted in the name of humanity and justice." According to the Grand Vizier, the slanderous nature of the accusations levelled against his country were revealed by Ambassador Abraham Elkus and Consuls Jackson and Bordon.[6]

Assertions like these, that were in fact contradicted by these diplomats' dispatches, were an integral part of the Young Turk justification system, which systematically aimed at calling foreigners as witnesses. It did not matter whether they had in fact observed the contrary of what was alleged. In the present case, Talât's allegations were all the easier to make as these diplomats had left Turkey after the United States went to war and thus were no longer able to contradict them. Talât's appeal to "humanity" and "justice" reveals another feature of the Young Turk leaders: they used values ideologically alien to them in order to convince their partners of their moral modernity. In other terms, the Young Turk regime never took upon itself to face its own ideology of exclusion through violence, always hiding behind "the necessities of war". Needless to say, these mechanisms are still at work today.

While the main Ittihadist leaders embarked on a German destroyer in the night of 1 to 2 November, 1918 ?, the Arab MP for Diwaniya, Fuad Bey, tabled a motion in the Ottoman Parliament that the Ministers in charge during the war be brought before the High Court of Justice.[7]

For the first time the matter of the Young Turk Government's responsibility was referred to the Ottoman Parliament, which had been convened on 10 October 1918 and was still constituted predominantly of deputies originating from the CUP.

Besides Fuad's motion, the Young Turk group had to face the five-point request made by fourteen deputies, among who were two Armenian survivors and two Greeks. The subject of the petition was the misdeeds committed by the Ottoman Government in wartime: the extermination of one million Armenian Ottoman subjects, the expulsion of 250,000 Ottoman Greeks and their being stripped of their properties during the war, the massacre of 550,000 Ottoman Greeks from the Black Sea region at the end of the conflict and the assassination of Ottoman deputies. Directly targeting the war crimes committed against civilians by the Young Turk regime and involving the responsibility of the Ottoman State, this petition was rejected in turbulent debates that lasted many sittings.

Nonetheless, Fuad's motion was adopted; in it eight out of ten charges implicated the CUP and the Young Turk Ministers in:

    a. the illegal monopolization of the State administration;
    b. the decision to involve the Ottoman Empire in the conflict;
    c. the secret agreement with Imperial Germany;
    d. the misappropriation of public funds;
    e. the imposition of censorship;
    f. the publication of false news about military operations and other subjects.

The two main charges that more or less directly related to the extermination of the Ottoman Armenians and the violence committed against the Greeks and Syrians – the fifth charge about the Provisional Law on Deportation and the tenth evoking the establishment of the Special Organization and its criminal activities – were vaguely worded, without ever referring to the main victims, while concentrating, especially the first one, on the judicial window-dressing engaged in by the Young Turk Government in order to legalize its crimes. An analysis of the Ministers' declaration in front of the Fifth Parliamentary Commission reveals this trick aimed at avoiding excessive direct publicity for mass murders and the mention of the victimized group by name.

Despite the obvious advantages of Fuad's motion, the Young Turk majority at the Parliament opposed, or pretended to oppose, it, before adopting it on 4 November 1918 as the future basis of its activities. Replying to the motion (takrir) tabled by the few minority deputies still present, which asked the Government about its own attitude towards the crimes committed by the previous Cabinets, the Minister of the Interior, Fethi Bey [Okyar], said that the victims were not only Armenians, Greeks and Arabs but also Turks, and that the Government would do its best to alleviate injustice and repatriate deportees to their homes.[8]

By so doing, he was laying the foundations of the attitude adopted by the defendants and adhered to by successive Turkish Governments in the following months and years; it can be summed up as follows:

  a. we all suffered during the war
  b. we will correct abuses
  c. we will punish the culprits
  d. we will prevent similar things happening again.

In the face of such an approach bearing the seeds of official denial, the Armenian Members of Parliament took steps to compel the Government to face its responsibilities. After the adoption of Fuad's motion, Mattheos Nalbandian, MP of Kozan, and five of his colleagues, officially asked the Government about its attitude to the adoption and implementation of the Provisional Law on Deportation (27 May 1915) and the Law on Abandoned Properties (26 September 1915). Their initiative was all the more justified as the text of the decree was sent to the Presidency of the Parliament a few days after it was promulgated, on 26 May 1915, but handed to the MPs once the so-called deportations had already been carried out.[9]

There was, of course, a surrealistic touch in the fact that Armenian Ottoman MPs, most of whose important colleagues had been assassinated, had to stand before this Parliament, many of the members of which were directly involved in the extermination of the Ottoman Armenians and, to say the least, had grown richer at the deportees' expense, in order to raise an issue that no one really wanted to hear about, and whose minimal formal formulation had to fit the requirements of the time.

At the following sitting devoted to this question, on 18 November 1918, the Cabinet had changed and the CUP leaders were no longer ministers. A vote of confidence in the new government had to be passed as a matter of course. Armenian deputies, especially Artin Boshgezenian, who had been very prudent in their former speeches, decided to bring up the question of the mass murder of their fellow Armenians and to twist the knife in the wound. In a marathon speech, Boshgezenian first recalled that the Empire would be invited to the Peace Conference, that it would be preferable not to go without offering something, and that the Turkish people would appear there as defendants. Acrimonious protests were then heard, to which the speaker responded by inviting the audience to listen to him, even if it meant he would be beaten up afterwards. "We are today face to face with an important crime, one of the saddest and bloodiest pages of Ottoman history [...], the Armenian massacre [...]", he continued, observing that the Empire as a whole was considered responsible for these deeds, that however many Turks, especially the inhabitants of Konya, and even some local governors had disobeyed the Government's orders and had tried to protect Armenian deportees, the government had implemented its scheme using the governors, the local military authorities, the gendarmerie, *çete* (gang) troops and civil servants at large, and that it would thus be difficult to put the blame for the events only on the Young Turk officials, all the more so as in many places the local population had participated in the violence along with the çete. The Armenian MP then requested that no one any longer encourage those "people without honour" who were still organising provocations and denying all these crimes outright, while they in fact were the criminals. He concluded that the heart of the matter was the way they would be treated, that the fate of Turkey depended on their being judged, and that they should be arrested, whereas most of them were still at large and unpunished.[10]

For the first time, a deputy had raised the question of the Ottoman Armenians' extermination publicly – with some oratory precautions. This was no small achievement in a society whose concepts of justice and legal practices were quite remote from European standards. The very idea of indicting the Ottoman State was still inconceivable to most people. The reactions of some Kurdish and Turkish deputies, who repeated the official Young Turk argument about the so-called treason of the Armenians in order to justify the punishment inflicted on them, and who considered these events as rather unimportant, revealed the inability of Ottoman society to grasp the real scope of the mass murder which had just been committed in its name. Hoca İlyas Sami, a Kurdish tribal chief and inspector of the CUP at Mush, reacted in the same way, while his later indictment revealed his major role in the murder of 70,000 to 80,000 Armenians in the Mush region.[11]

The sitting of 9 December 1918 is also interesting. It started with the reading of a motion (*takrir*) submitted by Dikran Barsamian, MP for Sıvas and former member of the Ittihat, and Kegham Der Garabedian, MP for Mush, who had just passed away after a long illness to which he owed his life in 1915. Though dated 5 November 1918, this motion is an answer to the speech of İlyas Sami, formulated by someone who knew him well. It expressed astonishment at the total number of Armenian victims presented by the Muslim colleagues, 100,000 people, when that figure had already been reached in the coastal area of the Black Sea alone, from Samsun to Trebizond.[12] The takrir also reminded the MPs of the way Armenians in the Mush plain had been assassinated.

The sitting of 11 December 1918 should have been devoted in theory to the violence perpetrated against the Ottoman Greeks, especially in Tekirdağ, Edirne and Ġatalca, but it quickly shifted to the Armenian case. The famous poet and MP for Mossul, Mehmet Emin [Yurdakul] asked to be allowed to speak at the end. He observed that the violence, the Armenians' extermination for instance, which had been committed by a gang of criminals, could not be attributed to the Ottoman Government, and even less to the Turkish nation that was in fact the first victim of the conflict, and that it was thus inconceivable to put the blame on his nation.[13] He thus expressed the Parliament's major preoccupation, namely to clear the Ottoman State's name and attribute all crimes, which he however acknowledged as matters of fact and did not deny as many of his colleagues did at the time, to a group which had dragged the Empire into war. He here makes a slight concession, compared to the usual discourse of Young Turk circles, which should be taken seriously. During the same sitting, the MP for Trebizond, Mehmet Emin (not to be confused with the former MP), declared that he personally had witnessed the murdering of some Armenians from Samsun where the mutesarif (district governor) had organized their drowning off the Black Sea coast and that he had been told that the Governor of Trebizond, Cemal Azmi, had done the same in his vilayet.[14]

This testimony, directly implicating the local authorities in the organization of the massacres, set a precedent. For the first time a member of the Ottoman Parliament, and a lawyer at that, expressed himself without self-censorship.

On the following day, 12 December 1918, the Parliament examined the matter once again. Efkalidis, the MP for Tekirdağ, questioned the government, focusing in his speech on the events that had taken place since 1913, and that all had in common that they were either denied or at least interpreted tendentiously. First came the expulsion after 1913 of 500,000 Ottoman Greeks, explained as voluntary departures to join the Hellenic army; this was accompanied by the looting of their property. Second, there was the deportation of the Ottoman Armenians, presented as a punishment similar to the one the English practised in Ireland. Third, the violence suffered by the Ottoman Armenian and Greek populations was minimized with the argument that the Turkish population had also had many victims, whereas the former were Ottoman subjects assassinated by their authorities, while the latter were soldiers fallen at the front or civilians fleeing war zones. Determined to shake his Turkish colleagues, the Ottoman Greek MP concluded by asking them whether they were simply trying to convince themselves or whether they believed they could deceive the whole world.

This speech took place while violent debates in the capital opposed editors of Young Turk newspapers to the Liberal, Armenian and Greek ones. The following speech, by the MP for Kazan, Mattheos Nalbandian, equally aimed at responding to the newspaper articles which used the same arguments as the Young Turks. These were that "they had betrayed us", that "we had to take administrative measures to remove these potential traitors from war zones" and that "some abuses were committed in the implementation of these measures, but we punished the culprits as soon as we were informed".

M. Nalbandian established a chronology of these events for the first time. He began by speaking about the arrest and execution of all the Armenian elite in the capital as well as in the provinces; then he evoked the systematic deportation of all the Armenian population, wherever they were living, and he described the annihilation of caravans in the Black Sea, the Tigris and Euphrates rivers and the Syrian Desert. Questioning his colleagues, Nalbandian said: "Sirs, these things are no tales from the Arabian Nights. These are facts as they happened, for which our prestigious Assembly should express its regrets and weep." The MP mentioned then that his own family had been deported, that he owed his own survival to the intervention of Halil Bey, who was chairing that day's sitting but was then the Ottoman Minister of Foreign Affairs, and that during his trip to Constantinople he had witnessed unimaginable scenes: women and elderly people dying on the roads and children snatched from their mothers. He had opened his heart about all this to Halil Bey on his arrival in the capital. Turning to the poet Mehmet Emin [Yurdakul], he asked him how he could assert that those responsible for these horrors numbered no more than three or five and that the Turkish people was a victim; after all, it was the dominant nation within the Empire, while the Armenians were among the subject nations.[15]

Hoca İlyas Sami spoke next. This time, the deputy of Mush was on the defensive, in contrast to his previous speech in which he accused the Armenians of insurrection in order to justify the crimes. Belonging himself to religious circles, he first exposed the argument of his social group's active benevolence towards minority populations, taking as an example – a rather dubious one – the Armenian massacres of 1895-1896. He asked for the war context to be taken into consideration and for the reasons leading to the violence against Ottoman Armenians to be examined. He thus moved one step forward, admitting the crimes committed against the latter. He no longer mentioned the accusations of massacres committed by Armenians against Turks that had been a leitmotiv of his first speech: "I am compelled to tell the truth. Yes, the eastern provinces were turned into cemeteries." However he added: "It is not the right time to settle accounts"; this would have to be done "once the fatherland's wounds had been dressed."

The new Minister of the Interior, Mustafa Arif Bey, who attended the debates, concluded the sitting with these words, which once again revealed the consistent effort to dissociate the Young Turks legally from the Turkish nation: "Your Honourable Assembly, together with the Government, confirms that some events linked to this matter did take place. Nobody asserts that these did not happen. But I think that if, among millions of Turks, we go as far as admitting that 100,000 were implicated, it is not acceptable to consider the entire race responsible for the misdeeds that they commited [...]."[16]

The Fifth Ottoman Parliamentary Commission and the war crimes
Simultaneously with the above-mentioned debates, the Ottoman Parliament decided to create a fact-finding commission, known as the Fifth Commission. It proceeded, on the basis of the 10 points of Fuad's motion, which had been voted by the Parliament, to the hearing of ministers of wartime Cabinets who

still were in the capital. As far as we are informed, the minutes of these hearings were not immediately published in the official gazette of the Ottoman Parliament, but forwarded to the Martial Court that took over legally in a way. However the British (SIS) and the French (S.R. Marine)[17] Intelligence Services followed the procedure, which lasted from November to December 1918, most carefully. Thanks to them, we have at our disposal the entire minutes of fifteen ministers' examinations, besides the official publications of the Ottoman Parliament used by the Armenian American historian V. Dadrian. These documents show best the ministers' conception of their responsibility in the "abuses" committed against the Ottoman Armenians.

As far as the proceedings of the Fifth Commission are concerned, one has to underline right away that the ministers that could be examined were the least implicated in these crimes.

In one of the first hearings, on 24 and 25 November 1918, the Commission examined Cavit Bey, the former Minister of Finance, who had resigned at the beginning of November 1914, as soon as the Ottoman Empire got involved in the war. This enabled him to describe the circumstances of the Ottoman involvement in the conflict and to guarantee that "the Russian aggression was a made-up story" and that decisions were taken at Said Halim's and not in the Cabinet.[18] Replying to a question asked by the MP for Ertuğrul, Şemşettin Bey, about the conditions of the general call-up in the Empire, he asserted than this was not decided about in the Cabinet, but that it was Enver who took the initiative, having each minister separately sign a draft of an Imperial *irade* [decree], the signing and publication of which took place only after its public proclamation.[19] As far as the provisional deportation laws were concerned, he said they were "contrary to the rules of law and humanity and also to the letter and the spirit of our Constitution" and "they turned our country into a realm of tragedy." Cavit stressed that he was no longer in the government "at the time of the Armenian affair. [...] I was in no way and never in favour of it, and every time I had the opportunity I drew my colleagues' attention to this issue."[20] He emphasised that after he was reappointed, in 1917, he applied "the laws and decrees about the abandoned properties of deported Armenians broad-mindedly. I even obtained from Talât Pasha the authorization for Armenians and Arabs to go back to their homes [...]. I was thus not a Minister when these laws were first implemented".[21] Showing all his capacity to act, he concluded that he wrote to Talât when the latter was appointed Grand Vizier and received the following answer: the new Cabinet "would be careful to enforce the absolute respect of all individual rights and ensure all Ottomans benefited from all the rights granted in the Constitution. The Armenian and Arab questions would be solved as far as the state of war allowed, for the time being, and thoroughly, shortly before peace was made."[22]

To the last question asked by the Chairman of the Commission "about the role of administrative chaos in the crimes, and the alleged participation in them by gangs that made attempts on the freedom, life, honour and property of the population" (thus alluding to the Special Organisation), Cavit Bey replied categorically: "This was not the Government's work."[23] While seemingly dissociating himself from his colleagues of the Young Turk Central Committee and refraining from denying the criminal schemes against the Armenians, of which he claimed to have disapproved, Cavit cynically insisted that he even contributed in 1917 to re-establishing the rights of Ottoman subjects who had died more than a year earlier or were surviving in inhospitable countries a thousand miles away.

On the day before, 23 November 1918, Halil Bey, the acting Chairman of the Parliament and former Minister of Justice, appointed on 11 October 1331 [1915], had been examined.[24] He first denied that a provisional deportation law had ever existed and then acknowledged that it had been promulgated before he was appointed a member of the cabinet. He remarked too that like the Minister of Religious Affairs, he "did not record any proceedings of conversion forwarded from the provinces (*vilayets*)." When interrogated about the Special Organization, Halil Bey in turn asked: "In which regions were these gangs organized?" thus implying that he did not remember such an organization ever having been created. When reminded that criminals had been released and recruited with the agreement of the Ministry of Justice, he replied that he had not been appointed before November 1915.[25]

The first accused heard, Said Halim, Grand Vizier until spring 1917, could not shelter behind a late appointment to assert that he did not know anything. The only high-ranked member of the wartime cabinets still in Constantinople, his evidence is essential. Asked about his responsibilities in public affairs, Said Halim tried against all the evidence to appear as powerless: "The Grand Vizier chairs the Cabinet, but they listen to him if they please to do so. They can turn a deaf ear to him under the pretext that the Parliament alone can put a question to them [...] No one ever asked for my opinion."[26] Questioned about "certain provisional anti-humanitarian laws on the transportation of families living in the border areas or close to strategic positions", he repeated the official thesis: "This law was passed to insure the army's safety while it was fighting."[27] MP Ragıb Bey observed: "Martial courts could condemn and exile certain people. But does the law say that it is legal to chase women and children out of their homes and execute them?"

Said Halim ended by coming out with this remark: "You really want to speak about the Armenian question? [...] The Vice-Generalissimo [Enver] and the commanders declared that the Armenians' presence constituted a danger for the army and proposed to transport them elsewhere. But there was no order to kill them. Only the implementation was wrong [...]". Another step had already been taken, but MP Ragıp Bey pushed him further: "But were you not informed that atrocities were happening while it was being carried out?" The Grand Vizier again played his role as a man of straw, showing obvious signs of amnesia: "As for the rest of the story, I only heard about these atrocities when everything was over [...]. Only the Ministry of War will be able to provide you with explanations for its motivations. There you will receive information, because I cannot say anything that might convince you. All that has slipped my memory."

The President of the Commission then noted that the law had been adopted at the Cabinet and that "the motivations should have been presented then. Was this point discussed in the Cabinet?" Halim's memory faltered again and he ended up saying: "Yes, this is all that I know. When I arrived at the Grand Vizierate, I undertook to conduct reforms in the six *vilayets* [eastern provinces]. When the final talks with the foreign ambassadors about the laws to be implemented by the governors were about to be held, war broke out. Hence the important reforms the Imperial Government intended to conduct were blocked. It was all too natural that the Government, that was firmly resolved to insure prosperity and happiness for all its Armenian subjects, should continue after the war the reforms initiated earlier. Consequently, the right thing would have been to wait calmly for the end of the war. Unfortunately nothing of the sort happened. Fact-finding commissions were set up after the massacre of the Armenians. Once their task was done, these commissions came back to Constantinople. Although I often insisted, the Ministry of the Interior did not want to hear about their results."[28] He then said he had "been horrified to learn of the two [Arab and Armenian] affairs", the euphemism used to speak of the extermination of the Armenians and the crimes perpetrated against a part of the population of Syria and Lebanon.[29] The subsequent part of the hearing, devoted to the dissimulation of military defeats and territorial losses, deserves some attention, because it records the Ottoman authorities' methods of manipulation, like the announcements in the press of the appointments of new *valis* [Governors] in Erzurum and Baghdad: "How was it possible to appoint *valis* in places taken by the enemy? [...]", as one deputy asked.[30] To the tenth question, which was on the Special Organization, Said Halim replied: "[...] As soon as I was informed about the existence of such an organisation, I took steps. It stopped functioning. [...] I told to Enver paşa that it was reprehensible[...]"[31]

The next accused, Ahmet Şükrü Bey, the former Minister of Public Education (1913 – 1918), was a little known though high-ranking member of the Young Turk Central Committee, close to the medical doctors Bahaettin Şakir and Nazîm.[32] His hearing, on 12 November, best illustrates the defence of the most radical and implicated Young Turks.[33] To the first question about the circumstances of the Empire's involvement in the war, he replied without turning a hair that the Ottoman Black Sea fleet had been attacked by the Russians, which obliged the Commission Chairman to recall that everyone knew the opposite in fact had taken place. Şükrü Bey then evoked "the events in Van, Bitlis, Karahisar, Şarki and the Black Sea coastal regions" in order to justify the deportation law, claiming that he knew nothing about the "misdeeds attributed" to the Special Organization.[34]

The Commission proceeded with the hearing of the former Minister of
Trade and Agriculture, and then of Foreign Affairs, Ahmet Nesimi Bey, on 12
and 13 November.[35] As far as the deportation law was concerned, the former
Minister gave the classical justifications, such as alleged Armenian collaboration with the Russians and the Armenians' regular spying on army operations;
he added, exceeding all bounds: "Arms, bombs, independence flags and many
other preparations for a revolt were discovered little by little everywhere. [...]
Some people insisted on our taking extraordinary measures. [...] Some people
declared that if we did not resort to this measures, our army would be caught
between two fires. [...]So the law in question was a military precautionary measure. [...] Some time after the promulgation of this law, I went to Karlsbad on
my physicians' recommendation, and I stayed there from July to the end of
August. Consequently, I was absent from Constantinople during most of the
time when the events under examination occurred. On my return I heard that
some thoroughly bad people had committed all kinds of excesses while this
measure was being implemented."[36]

MP Râğıp Neşaşibî (Râghib Nashâshîbî) then asked Ahmet Nesimi:
"According to you, was the deportation applied to everybody, women, and children or only to fighting men?" His answer reveals the capacity the Young Turks
had to interpret events according to their needs: "[...] As far as women are concerned, some people had assured that it would be even worse to leave them
alone in their villages [...] Moreover, some people had said that they were spying and some of them had been arrested. However, the law had left this point
to the free judgement of those who would implement the measure, taking military requirements into account. Furthermore, I want to say tell my Armenians
colleagues this: my ideas and feelings are well-known. If you do not know about
that, you can find out. I fought to prevent such a measure from being taken.
[...] If abuses have been committed, and if the deportation took place outside
the war zones and without it being necessary militarily, the culprits deserve
punishment." With this hearing the procedure thus moved one step further.
Although MPs were not very curious, they sometimes succeeded in putting the
ministers ill at ease. By revealing that he had fought against "such a measure",
Ahmed Nesimi gave people to understand that the issue had been debated within the Cabinet or the Young Turk Party. The following part of this sentence
indicates too, though cautiously, that this "measure" was implemented "outside of war zones and without it being necessary militarily". The last point in
the hearing was the Special Organisation, about which Ahmet Nesimi said "he
did not know that such gangs had been created."[37]

The hearing on 10 November concerned İbrahim Bey, the former Minister
of Justice.[38] He too asserted from the start that the Russians attacked first.
About the deportation law, he recalled that after the events of Erzurum,

Şabinkarahisar and Bitlis, and "proclamations by the Armenian Committees, the Government had no choice but to promulgate a law on deportations. Then the Cabinet needed to take a decision about the sum to be subtracted from the migrants' assets, for the deportees' supply and comfort [...]." A new element was thus introduced; without admitting that the deportation law was discussed in the Cabinet, but by mentioning a decision for the "deportees' comfort" with humorous cynicism, İbrahim Bey, gave the audience to understand that debates had indeed taken place about the fate of the Ottoman Armenians, without revealing further details. He went even further, though, by alleging that a fact-finding commission had been set up, including civil servants and members of the judiciary, whom he himself had appointed, "among them Asim Bey, President of the Criminal Court, a very honest and upright person, and Nihat Bey, first assistant of the Attorney General. [...] These commissions were connected with the Ministry of the Interior, to which they had to forward their reports." Enlarging on this answer, MP Râğıp Neşaşib" even asked: "How could military commanders allow themselves to massacre people?". But the President sharply called him to order: "The hearing is not about the massacres. We are talking about the law." As Minister of Justice, he was then asked whether the laws had been forwarded to the Council of State and which ones had been promulgated without respecting this procedure. But İbrahim Bey too was struck by amnesia. He was also asked whether the Cabinet had taken a decision "about the deportations and other atrocities. Because this point is of major importance and the responsibility lies with all the ministers." To this the former minister replied: "The emergency treatments that were inflicted during the implementation of the deportation law happened without the Cabinet's knowledge." But Râğıp Bey did not give up, evoking the case of Dr. Reşit Bey, *vali* of Diyarbekir, "who was brought here because there were serious charges against him. But 15 or 20 days later he was appointed *vali* of Angora. This appointment was, no doubt, decided by the Cabinet." Once again İbrahim Bey "did not remember well".

The author of the ten-point motion, Fuad Bey, then entered the debate, recalling: "There are two of these provisory laws which are of extreme importance: the first about the abandoned properties, and the second authorizing death penalties to be carried out without a decree (*irade*)". He received the following answer: "There was indeed a law about the abandoned properties, but its aim was to save them and preserve them from looting".

Harun Hilmi refocused the debate on the war zones where military commanders "were authorized to carry out punishments the way they wanted [...]. But numerous persons were deported and executed in regions which were not war zones". Hilmi tackled İbrahim Bey over the reaction of the Government: "When these events were known about, didn't deliberations take place at the Cabinet in order to put an end to them?" İbrahim Bey merely answered: "What was not spoken about there! Nothing official!" He then observed, however, as a justification that: "the Ministry of the Interior had published documents on the atrocities committed by Armenians against Muslims in the eastern vilayets. [...]" As far as the Special Organisation was concerned, İbrahim Bey asserted that he knew nothing about it: "Nor did the Cabinet know anything. We were completely ignorant of its aim and activities. I know strictly nothing about that and besides I am not obliged to know anything." Certainly irritated by the accused's dilatory answers, İlyas Sami pronounced: "To most of the questions we asked to him, İbrahim Bey replied that he ignored the facts or that they occurred after his term in office. [...] Yet such an event as the fall of Erzurum commits the whole Cabinet. Ömer Naci Bey started the implementation of the measures planned about the Special Organization. It is quite odd that İbrahim Bey, who belonged to the Cabinet when these facts occurred, only heard about them afterwards." Unwittingly, the MP for Mush had just broken the law of silence and explicitly mentioned the name of the first responsible of the Organization in Erzurum. When, slightly later, he was asked why under such conditions he had not resigned, İbrahim Bey ended up admitting: "I remained a member of the Cabinet in order to hinder the misdeeds of this nature which I was informed about as much as possible. You can be sure that when I say we ignored the Special Organization, I mean that no decision was taken in the Cabinet."[39]

One of the last ministers heard, on 27 November, the former Constantinople Chief Commissioner and Minister of the Interior in 1917-1918, İsmail Canbolat Bey, should have shed a new light on these matters. It was under his authority that the Armenian elite of the capital had been rounded-up in the night of 24 to 25 April 1915. But in reply to all the questions about the deportation law, he merely asserted that at the Cabinet meeting on 4 August 1917: "I took the decision to have them brought back to their homes and no one uttered any objection. The implementation of this measure had even started; the Direction of Migrants had started the necessary preparations. The order had already been given to allow deportees from Samsun and its surroundings to return."[40] These administrative measures concerning people who had departed this life represent a variant on the official discourse, nourishing the illusion that the deportations were not definitive.

Most certainly the initiative taken by the Ottoman Parliament and its Fifth Commission had the merit of sparking off the beginning of a debate about the crimes committed against the Armenian population, but the Sultan and Tevfik's Cabinet were quickly convinced that no justice could be done by a Parliament composed as this one was – even including notorious criminals. Now, with the Peace Conference in sight, it was necessary to start the trials against war criminals before the Allies did it themselves. Moreover, the Cabinet could not get any law passed by this Parliament. The Sultan therefore decided to dissolve Parliament on 21 December 1918 and to organize elections. In this way, he took the task of judging the Young Turks away from the Legislative and

so brought about the removal of the MPs' parliamentary immunity. This triggered off the immediate arrest of no less than twenty-four of them.[41] On 21
December, the Minister of Foreign Affairs, Mustafa Reşit, addressed the
Parliament in response to a motion of no confidence tabled by Hüseyin Kadri
in the name of the Hüriyet Perveran Party. He insisted especially on the fact
that the previous governments were being shown up "in the light of Diogenes'
lantern" and that the scope of the atrocities committed against the Armenians
was being discovered, "atrocities, as the Minister put it, which have filled
mankind with indignation: the country was handed over to us transformed
into a gigantic slaughterhouse." "Here is an official admission" concluded a
Constantinople French-language daily.[42]

The contribution of the administrative fact-finding commission, known as the Mazhar Commission

Even before the dissolution of the Parliament, as as 23 November 1918, a fact-
finding commission was set up by the Sultan. In fact, it even seems that the
Council of State discreetly but directly obliged Sultan Mehmet VI to promulgate a firman establishing this Commission; it was to sit on the premises of the
Department of Public Safety. It was to be chaired by Hasan Mazhar Bey, the
former *vali* of Angora.[43] As soon as it was set up, the Mazhar Commission started collecting facts and testimonies, especially concentrating its inquiry on civil
servants implicated in the crimes committed against the Armenian communities. According to Vahakn Dadrian's findings,[44] the Commission's task was
based on paragraphs 47, 75 and 87 of the Ottoman Code of Criminal Procedure
and it had vast investigative powers, since it was empowered not only to institute legal proceedings and search for and seize documents, but also to arrest
and imprison suspects, with assistance from the Criminal Investigation
Department, and even other State services.

   Among the documents collected by the Mazhar Commission, the most sensational is indubitably the written testimony sent on December 5th 1918 to
Hasan Mazhar by General Vehip Pasha, a high-ranking military member of the
CUP and former commander-in-chief of the 3rd Ottoman Army, in whose
province the most systematic massacres occurred, especially in the slaughter-
houses of the Kemah gorges, close to the Gölcük Lake and in the Kanlı Dere
mountains, close to Malatya. The General concluded his Summary of
Convictions as follows: "The deportations of the Armenians took place in complete contradiction with humanity, civilisation and the Government's honour.
The massacre and extermination of the Armenians and the sacking and looting
of their properties are the result of decisions taken by the Central Committee
of the CUP; it was Dr Bahaettin Şakir Bey who trained gangs of butchers to
slaughter human beings and he too who urged them to carry it out. The administrative authorities [that is the *valis* and *mutesarifs*] obeyed Bahaettin Şakir's
directives. As a matter of fact, all the disorders and troubles in the Third Army
were set off by Bahaettin Şakir Bey's underhand dealings. Driven in a special

car, he moved from one centre to another, delivering the decisions taken and
the directives to the various local sections of the Union and Progress Party and
the local authorities in the same places by word of mouth. [...] The atrocities
were committed according to a scheme conceived in advance and were organised absolutely intentionally. First they were directed by the delegates of the
Union and Progress Party and its main offices, and secondly they were implemented by local government officials who had become the submissive tools of
this lawless and unscrupulous organisation's desires and aspirations. [...] All
these activities were dictated through oral instructions and not one written
document remains. The Army and the Turkish element have nothing in common with these crimes and atrocities and did not take part in them."[45]

This sharp appraisal, partially published in the judicial supplement of the
Official Gazette (*Takvim-ı Vakayi*), is the most complete avowal of the general
scheme elaborated by the CUP, but also a unique case. Moreover, the Young
Turk networks did not forgive Vehip Pasha for having broken the law of
silence, best illustrated by the hearings of the Fifth Parliamentary Commission.
He was interrogated on Wednesday 3 December 1919 by the fact-finding commission of the specific court martial for high-ranking officers,[46] which unanimously decided to institute legal proceedings against him and remand him in
custody.[47]

The Young Turk discourse in front of the Istanbul court martial

Courts martial started to be set up in December 1918, but they were apparently
hotly debated; indeed Tevfik's Cabinet resigned on 3 March 1919 because he
did not wish to institute a special Court to try the Ittihadists. Most probably
he was subjected to strong pressures by Young Turk leaders. As early as 8 March
1919, the Sultan ratified the jurisdiction of a new court martial with expanded
competences.[48] According to the daily Sabah, the Court defined different categories of accused who should be tried separately on charges of "massacres and
illegal personal profit":

a. the real planners of the crimes against the Armenians
b. those working in the shadow of these real planners, such as the
   [other] members of the Central Committee of the CUP
c. the members of secret organizations, such as the Special
   Organization, and also high-ranking army officers and prisoners
   who had been released on purpose
d. the members of parliament who did not protest against, and even
   acquiesced in, the crimes which had been committed
e. the journalists who applauded and encouraged the crimes, stirring
   up public opinion with provocative and mendacious articles
f. those who took advantage of these crimes to enrich themselves
   illegally
g. the cohort of Pashas and Beys who officered these crimes[49]

The criminal trials of the Ittihat's Central Committee, in April-May 1919, should have been the king pin of the legal proceedings in 1919-1920. But two main obstacles deprived these criminal trials of their substance: first, the absence of the main party leaders, who had fled abroad and second, the arrest of the other accused by the British and their deportation to Malta. Mehmet Ziya Gökalp, the party's ideologue, was among the all too few Central Committee members heard by the court martial. We have at our disposal the minutes of his hearing. His attitude deserves precise scrutiny. Asked by the commission's chairman about his action as the director of the periodical *Yeni Mecmua*, founded by his fellow party member Bahaettin Şakir, and more precisely whether he "had written articles advocating that Turkey's programme should be Turanism", Ziya Gökalp confirmed that he had expounded his ideas on Turanism, which he considered "advantageous for Ottomanism". When the chairman asked whether this "did not discontent the non-Muslim elements", Ziya Gökalp expressed his party's motivations: "Those elements were always longing for their autonomy. Turanism should have left the other nationalities free, but reinforced the Turkish element. [...]" Confronted with the judges, however, the ideologue denied having supported the "exclusion" of the Armenians. When several telegrams received by the Central Committee about the deportations and the Committee's links with the Special Organization were read out, he was compelled to agree that "when it was necessary, the Committee provided support." He was then asked to confirm "that the deportations were decided within the Central Committee, which exerted pressure on the Government [...], and that massacres and lootings did take place", and to explain whether "the Committee ordered them". Ziya Gökalp answered that Committee members "were informed afterwards and that we complained to the Minister of Home Affairs. Inquiries were made, but it still went on."[50]

In conclusion

The examination of the inquiries and trials organised by the Fifth Commission of the Ottoman Parliament, the Mazhar Commission and the Istanbul court martial clearly reveals that even in the most propitious period for such collective introspection, the accused and witnesses expressed themselves only with the utmost aversion about the crimes committed against civilian populations during the war. If General Vehip Pasha is an exception, we can say on the whole that all the accused, at whatever level of responsibility, denied any personal participation, while admitting that the violence did take place! The memoirs of Talât, Ahmet Cemal, Midhat Şükrü, and other high-ranking Ittihat members do not say anything different, insisting however on the Ottoman Armenians' "treason" and the legal and administrative nature of the measures taken against them that gave rise to "abuses".

Today, Turkish diplomats and politicians still use the Young Turk discourse in their statements, with minor changes, or, when it proves impossible for foreign circles to accept, they refer the issue to historians. In fact, it seems that

Turkish society, especially the young generations, know almost nothing about these events, or only what school textbooks allow them to read. Generally speaking, it is the very conception of history, what İsmail Beşikçi calls the "Turkish thesis of history" that is at the core of the debate. Obviously, facing responsibility for the Armenian genocide would imply a thorough reappraisal of official attitudes, a lengthy educational process that would run counter to all that has been said and written until now, and a revision of the discourse about the "inner enemy" which is still in use, though now directed against Kurds and Alevis. In other words, the accusatory discourse aimed at other sections of the population, which is fuelled by the authorities and the majority of the media, needs to be questioned.

One may say that Turkish nationalism, which is still deeply impregnated with the Young Turk ideology, is at stake today. No one can plan to alter it by decrees, but current political practices show that the Turkish State has a major role to play in modifying the political discourse formulated at the beginning of the 20th century. Specialists of Turkish nationalism know that at the start it was a form of reaction to the Ottoman Empire's incapacity to reform itself and liberate itself from the burden and humiliation of the Great Powers of the time. They also know that a bad answer was found for a real problem.

The recent reform of Turkish law, which has introduced penalties for citizens who "declare that the Armenian genocide did indeed take place during the First World War", is likely to prevent academics and members of the civil society from conducting research and working to inform the public, while they are aware that this issue signs away the future of democracy in their country. If the extermination of the Ottoman Armenians now belongs to history, other groups still living in Turkey remain under threat from the Turkish State that continues to demonize them and reject them as "foreign bodies".

While it still honours such leaders as Mehmet Talât or İsmail Enver, Turkish society remains faithful to a violent and criminal past. If personalities like Vehip Pasha, Hasan Mazhar and many other officers and civil servants who refused to commit or give their support to the mass crimes were rehabilitated, it would discover in its midst people that nurtured other aspirations and advocated more respectable models.

Translated from the French by Hervé Georgelin

PART IV

TURKEY IN MOTION:
TODAY'S TRANSFORMATIONS
AND POST-NATIONAL CHALLENGES

Chapter 12
The social grammar
of populist nationalism

Ebru Bulut

From the early 1990s, nationalism was gathering momentum in Turkey. *Populist nationalism* and a nationalist syntax became the structuring elements of daily political life and, above all, of hegemonic party leaders' and state elites' discourses. Nationalism, however, is not merely a discourse of the 'top' directed to the 'bottom'. In the 1990s, its impact could easily be observed at both the political and the popular levels. Thus, it is important to distinguish *populist nationalism* from *popular nationalism*, by which is meant the exacerbation of nationalist feelings and the increased attachment to the idea of the nation in every-day representations, discourses, and practices which could be observed during the 1990s.

The rise of popular nationalism interacted with the rise of political Islam and the Kurdish nationalist movement, both represented as threats to national unity and territorial integrity. On the other hand, popular nationalism also reverberated profoundly with populist nationalism. Indeed, nationalist populist discourses of the elites (political, but also bureaucratic and military) developed into a "syntax of hegemony"[1] in the 1990s that ensured the political system as a whole reproduced itself.

However, it seems that nationalism such as the Turkish political scene experienced during the last decade reached its paroxysm towards the end of 1990's and started its decline thereafter[2]. To understand this evolution, one needs to take into account the impact of the economic crisis that Turkey underwent in February 2001. This crisis led to a reconfiguration of the political system where the ruling political parties of the 1990s were ousted from the active political game. This reconfiguration has allowed a series of political reforms towards democratization with a view to joining the European Union. In the present context, popular nationalism does not appear as the main obstacle hindering political liberalization. Nevertheless, as Turkish social grammar is still deeply impregnated with nationalism, one has to be cautious concerning future developments.

The principal aim of this essay is to understand the popular dimension of nationalism, i.e. the everyday shapes that nationalism takes in Turkey, and its place in the common ideas and form of everyday discourse about politics.

My assumptions in this essay are based on fieldwork in Kadıköy and Bağcılar, two Istanbul neighbourhoods, as well as on long-term observation of the political events in the 1990s. Even if the data collected from the fieldwork are incomplete, it can allow scholars/observers to proceed to an insightful sociological reading of the political events and developments of this decade. Therefore, my ambition in this essay is to articulate the findings of my fieldwork with the analysis of the political situation of the last decade in order to grasp the relationship between popular and populist nationalism.

I will concentrate on two topics. First, I explore the political system in the 1990s, its mode of reproduction and the conditions in which popular nationalism has strengthened. Second, I will argue that since the 2001 economic crisis, nationalist mobilization has weakened and the political reproduction with support of nationalism has exhausted. Therefore, I will analyse this demobilitzation and its reasons. Finally, I will discuss the place of popular nationalism in the new configuration after the economic crisis of 2001.

The reproduction of the political system in the 1990s

During the last decade, a succession of political crisis has marked the Turkish political landscape. These crises have been politically staged by different agents in the political system. Therefore, a nationalist syntax based on enmity has become the main instrument for the reproduction of the political system[3]. At that time the Turkish political arena witnessed the rise of Kurdish nationalism and political Islam. Kurdish nationalism claimed the recognition of another entity beside the Turks in Turkey. Moreover, the PKK (Workers' Party of Kurdistan), the leading Kurdish actor, had started an armed struggle which progressively gained popular support among the Kurdish population and strengthened particularly after the Gulf War (1991). In this context, the military appeared as the undisputed actor combating the Kurdish movement. Concurrently, political Islam posed a second serious challenge to the Turkish polity. The electoral successes of the Islamist party demanding the widening of the boundaries of secularism provoked anxiety among the state elites and a part of the population as well. Added together, these dynamics contributed to enlarging the military's room for manoeuvre and allowed them to claim the title of guardians of the endangered territorial unity or "secularism under threat". Thus, this context left little room in the decision-making process for governments.

This "subordination" of the political class to the military, however, cannot be explained solely by the political turbulences of this decade. Unable to find significant solutions to the growing economic and social problems, the major political parties experienced a progressive loss of legitimacy, while military elites found a favourable context to spread their views. In order to compensate for their lack of legitimacy, they drew closer to bureaucratic and military elites and placed themselves in a "cartel system"[4]. In this context, throughout the nationalist crises, the nationalist populist discourse imposed itself as a syntax of hegemony based on the imperative of national unanimity, the designation of an enemy and the denunciation of all protests as treachery. Branding the Kurdish movement and political Islam as foes, this syntax focussed on them as threats to the constitutive foundation of the nation. These crises were not completely artificial or invented, yet some events or debates were presented as the disclosure of the conspiracies of "separatists" or "Islamists"[5]. The succession of these crises in the last decade permitted the establishment of a permanent state of emergency and mobilization which, in turn, allowed the political system to be reproduced in the same form or without any radical upheaval. Obedience and the imperative necessity to postpone all other socio-economic or democratic demands were put forward as the only ways to overcome the conspiracies and dangers threatening the country. The radical alternative challengers of the state (Kurdish politicians, Islamists, or even liberal intellectuals) were stigmatized as a threat to the country's security.

This not only gave non-elected military, civil and judicial bodies the opportunity to reinforce their position and their capacity to intervene in the political sphere. It also provided the political parties of the "cartel system" with the opportunity to stay in the political competition, despite their lack of popular legitimacy.

The foundations of power

Nationalism ensured the reproduction of the political system because, in the context of the 1990s, it was able to gain the consent of the majority. Obviously, the Turkish state resorted to coercive measures to maintain public order or marginalize movements considered as hostile. Nevertheless, coercive measures by themselves are not sufficient for the actors to maintain their power in a political system like that of Turkey. According to Vincent Descombes, "the problem of power is not merely a question of force or of strategy; it is the problem of opinion. Power exists and is able to do what it is able to, only if it ensures itself a form of *consent*"[6] from the majority of its "subjects". So, one must ask not only how this power is reproduced, but also investigate the locus and foundations of its legitimacy.

Meta-political values such as Kemalist principles[7], national unity and territorial integrity, the republican project and the idea of a strong Turkish state are accepted as principles constitutive of politics and not as historically and politically determined categories[8]. In the 1990s, the legitimacy of cartel agencies stemmed from their ability to shift all political problems to the meta-political level where these constitutive values of the state were at stake. The transfer to the meta-political level makes it conceivable to appeal to "the nation" to mobilize in the name of national unanimity insofar as its very existence is at stake. In the 1990s, Kurdish and Islamist movements as well as their demands were presented as an offshoot of the collaboration between internal and external enemies and thus not at all representative of the opinion of "loyal" Kurds or "devout" Muslims. This interpretative framework is in keeping with the pattern of conspiracy theories, which evoke threats to national unity, territorial integrity and the principle of secularism. Whenever debates criticizing the official ideology proliferated and intensified, the threats hanging over Turkey were brought on to the agenda as the country's essential preoccupation.

As the legitimacy and authority of the state elites stem from the guardianship role of meta-political values, shifting political problems to a meta-political level allows these elites to involve themselves in the political game. Their presence and intervention in political life is legitimate and carries "authority", *provided that* their declarations concern meta-political values.

The role of these non-elected bodies is not just constitutional; they consider themselves - and are also considered by the majority of the population – the ultimate guardian of the Turkish state. Even though they constitute an essential part of the Turkish polity, they stand above the political field. During the 1990s, non-elected bodies and particularly military elites were able to participate in the production and maintenance of meaning; they offered schemes of interpretation[9] structured around the imperative loyalty to the nation threatened by enemies or conspiracies and the obedience/betrayal paradigm, that makes taking sides obligatory, leaving no third choice.

The remarkable feature of the last decade is not the very existence of these schemes of interpretation but that they became increasingly hegemonic as political parties were moving closer to non-elected bodies. However, although non-elected bodies became crucial actors in the context of the 1990s, they never entirely controlled the political configuration. They were never able to dominate the political field completely, that is, to influence the electoral competition directly or to prevent, for instance, the Islamic party's coming to power. In other words, the last decade did not witness the domination of a single actor but a dynamic political configuration which led to the establishment of a hegemonic bloc structured by the interaction of non-elected bodies with governments formed by cartel parties.

Popular nationalism: mobilization and social grammar

As I have already emphasised, popular nationalism is the approval of, and participation in, the nationalist populist discourses based on the existence of enemy figures – specifically, in the 1990s, Kurdish nationalism and political Islam. It was the response of the majority to the appeals alerting it to "conspiracies aimed at the Turkish state, its nation and its homeland as a whole".

To be sure, nationalist discourses and the appeal to mobilization never gained the support of the whole population. But a *majority consensus* based on national unity and the idea of the imperilled nation stems from them: all social protests were smothered and all alternative positions marginalized and de-legitimized. This mobilization sometimes crystallized in collective actions such as demonstrations, or the protestations following the assassinations of Kemalist intellectuals and the Susurluk affair[10]. However, it is important not to focus only on collective actions. In order to understand the extension of nationalism as the social grammar, one has to consider mobilization not as an ensemble of specific actions but as a continuum which includes actions, sentiments, even silences (non-protestation). It is less a *mobilization for action* than a *mobilization of consensus*[11]. In other words, it is also an unspecified and diffuse phenomenon that embraces the national flag being hung out of windows as well as mass demonstrations and especially the fact that the idea of "the nation in danger" dominated and submerged all other political issues. In the 1999 parliamentary elections, this nationalist mobilization reached its peak with the historic upsurge of the radical right *(Nationalist Action Party, MHP)* and the victory of the nationalist left *(Democratic Left Party, DSP)*. The results were significant in demonstrating that the nationalist discourse had its feedback on the popular level.

Nevertheless, popular nationalism in the 1990s was not only the domain of populist nationalism. Nationalism also profoundly marked social grammar. On the one hand, it manifested itself as the common use and presence of national symbols in everyday life, not necessarily related to politics, like the omnipresence of the national flag or Atatürk's portrait in domestic spaces, shops, offices or on car number-plates[12]. Simultaneously, in the 1990s, pretexts to sing the national anthem multiplied, even before pop concerts or at the beginning of fashion shows[13].

On the other hand, nationalism imposes itself also as a form of problematization in the Foucauldian sense, that is, a way of identifying and posing the problems through which not only politics but also the world become intelligible and meaningful[14]. In other words, and this is what I particularly stress, it is a form of representation that determines what counts for an intelligible and meaningful description of reality. I refer here less to what individuals are saying or thinking (the content of their thoughts) than to the categories and discursive rules on the basis of which they think, talk or act. Political issues were problematized in the meta-political register – i.e. involving the very existence of the nation with reference to core values and the obedience/betrayal paradigm – but a wide part of social life was as well. One could observe this behaviour, for instance, when parents denounced a teacher because of his insulting Atatürk or the citizens denounced the destruction of Atatürk's statue, in order to punish those responsible for these acts. Another striking example was the rescue team AKUT's[15] visit to the Atatürk mausoleum after their intervention following the 1999 earthquake. This visit's aim was to declare their loyalty to the Kemalist revolution, to swear to serve the strong Turkey of future and to be young Turks worthy of Atatürk.[16]

Thus, the omnipresence of national symbols, their appropriation as a sign of loyalty to the nation and this form of problematization largely exceed the simple obedience to the hegemonic bloc. The reference to Atatürk is not only proof of one's loyalty to the ultimate values of the nation, but it is also the key mediator of all kinds of relations to politics. So popular nationalism is not only linked with political questions but also constitutes a "social institution" in the Maussian sense[17].

From my point of view, the popular nationalism of the last decade can be understood through the correlation between (a) *the importance attached to meta-political values* (national unity and territorial integrity, the Republican project, Kemalist principles and the idea of a strong Turkish state), (b) *the approval and meaningfulness of nationalist discourses* (conspiracies and threats to constitutive values), and (c) *the social grammar* observed through the omnipresence and appropriation of national symbols as well as ways of speaking or thinking.

Undoubtedly, popular nationalism was stimulated and instrumentalized in the 1990s. But this doesn't imply that it was elaborated and imposed from outside. Popular nationalism in the 1990s was neither totally constructed by dominants and used as an instrument, nor a social or cultural essence (as if a majority of Turks were "naturally" nationalists). It was an historical and instituted order (values, categories, rules ...) through which actions or discourses were made intelligible and meaningful. Popular nationalism was not the result of populist nationalism; it was rather a response to it. But it was, above all, the social context that enabled nationalist discourses to unfold.

Limits of nationalist syntax: demobilization

On 19 February 2001, a violent altercation between the President of the Republic and the Prime Minister drove the country into the deepest economic crisis in its history. Following this economic crisis, the reproduction of the political system through nationalism seems to have reached its limits then. In this respect, it constituted a breaking point.

First of all, the 2001 crisis weakened the nationalist mobilization of the 1990s, causing what I will call *nationalist demobilization*. Following the crisis, neither the Kurdish question nor political Islam appeared to be a vital preoccupation. It seems that economic concerns had destroyed the importance of these questions. Just before the November 2002 elections, some prominent actors of the political class as well as Salih Kanadoglu, the public prosecutor of the period, branded the AKP[18] and the pro-Kurdish HADEP[19] as dangers. These warnings failed to generate crisis or massive mobilization. In the same way, in December 2002, Prof. Necip Hablemitoglu's murder (well-known for his commitment to Kemalism and his studies of political Islam) did not receive any echo, even though an Islamic journal was branded as responsible. In comparison, three years before that, Prof. Taner Kislali's murder, also a herald of Kemalism, had provoked a huge demonstration during his funeral.[20] Furthermore, in this period, a diplomatic initiative on the Cyprus issue met with relative indifference: the prospect of a solution was formulated as a "loss" for the nation, but this loss was regarded as a trifling matter while Turkey was in serious economic straits.

I do not imply that the Kurdish issue or political Islam no longer represent a threat to national unity or territorial integrity in some people's eyes. I also do not mean that Turkey's context is favourable for reaching a peaceful political settlement of them. The issue at stake here is the contrast between the omnipresence of these questions in the former period and the relative lack of these concerns after the crisis.

This demobilization stems from the economic crisis which brought to light the Turkish state's weakness. But it also crystallized what I will call the symbolic elimination of enemy figures.

The weakness of the state

The call on the IMF for a massive new standby emergency aid package after the 2001 crisis revealed the Turkish state as impotent, dependent on the West and unable to find a remedy on its own. This generated a feeling of loss of sovereignty. The state's weakness was also perceived in relation to some previous factors. First of all, there was the 1999 earthquake, where the state appeared totally inefficient in managing an extraordinary situation. A second element was the debt burden and the long-term supervision exerted by the IMF on the country's economic policy. Finally, the European Union had laid down certain conditions *sine qua non* for probably attaining full membership (regarding human or minority rights, the Cyprus question, and recognition of the Armenian genocide). Furthermore, the health problems of the Prime Minister of the period, Bülent Ecevit, who was physically declining, were a factor complementing and corroborating the image of weakness at a symbolic level. The idea of dependence was also reinforced by the presence of Kemal Dervis, former vice-president of the World Bank, considered as "an American bank", had entered the government. Although it was the Turkish government who reached out to Dervis after the crisis, this initiative was usually described as being imposed on the government by the United States.

The state's weakness was explained by the inefficiency of the political system, ascribed to heterogeneous and unstable coalitions that had governed the country for about a decade. It would not be wrong to assert that the words "coalition" and "inefficiency" were considered almost synonymous. This showed itself in the desire for a bipartite or presidential system, thought to be more efficient and more stable. The desire was more precisely for a system where a single party would obtain a sufficient majority in Parliament to form a government alone. In this way, the ruling party would be able to apply its programme, irrespective of the outcome. This partly explains the AKP's coming to power with an overwhelming majority in Parliament.

The theme of the weakness concerned less the state's ability to intervene for the good of its citizens than its perceived impotence vis-à-vis Western countries. The register of problematization was located less at the political level than at the meta-political one. In other words, governmental policies' inefficiency was not the vital issue, but the the nation itself was perceived as being weak. On the other hand, one could observe an overestimated belief in Turkey's potential to become a worldwide power. In this phantasmagorical view, the Western countries were preventing this possibility from occuring.

Apart from the rumour that Kemal Dervis was not "invited" by the Turkish government but "nominated like a governor" by the United States, rumours about the country's natural resources, rich in oil and all other necessary mineral deposits (especially boron), were circulating in daily conversations.

The most elaborate one was that a secret article of the Treaty of Lausanne signed in 1923 after the War of Independence prevented Turkey from exploiting all of its reserves until the early 2000s. According to this rumour, the economic crisis of 2001 was provoked intentionally at the end of this time to prevent Turkey from becoming a world power once more and to prolong its dependence on the West.

These conspiracy theories could be dismissed as delirium but their recurrence and ordinariness in everyday conversations is evocative. In general terms, the idea of the state's weakness goes hand in hand with the elaboration of conspiracy theories that explain the impotence of the Turkish state. The difference between these theories and those observed in the 1990s is that the conspiracy is not linked directly to the "internal enemies", Kurds or Islamists, but henceforth concerns the West as the actor aiming to weaken the country, if not to destroy it.

Symbolic elimination of enemy figures

Another factor of nationalist demobilization is the disappearance of enemy figures. In fact, the Turkish polity itself symbolically eliminated these figures through which nationalist mobilization was carried out in the 1990s. This elimination, unintentional without any doubt, occurred through a long process which started in 1997, in the case of political Islam, and in 1999, where the Kurdish question is concerned. The 2001 crisis crystallized those former processes. Since then, the meta-political register has become impossible.

Demobilization concerning the Kurdish question stems from the perception of it solely as a problem of terrorism represented by the PKK. As he embodied the whole Kurdish movement, Ocalan's arrest in February 1999 was perceived as the solution to this problem. However, its importance had already been declining since 1997, while the military had branded political Islam as a threat greater than Kurdish nationalism during the historical MGK[21] meeting on 28 February 1997. Moreover, the fragmentation of the PKK and its unilateral ceasefire after its leader's arrest, promoted considerably the idea of its disappearance as a significant enemy. Ocalan's arrest symbolically marked the elimination of "Kurdish terrorists" as a peril. Since the 2001 economic crisis this issue has not seemed to be a rallying factor at the social level.

The mobilization against political Islam also reached its limit through the symbolic elimination of this trend as an enemy. The elimination started at the MGK meeting on 28 February 1997. The Council directed the government led by the Islamist party[22] to struggle against the Islamization of the country and to strengthen its secular character. Three months later, the government resigned. Afterwards, the Islamic party's marginalization continued without the army directly intervening. Indeed, like all social institutions, the Kemalist polity fashioned its own anthropological types[23]: persons bearing its official ideology and sharing a common mindset (the military elites, professors, academicians, the bureaucratic elites and particularly the judges). The MGK's recommendations started a period often called the February 28 process in which all the state elites waged a constant struggle against Islamist party's ascent to power. The signal given by the army also sparked off the involvement of the bureaucratic elites. The Constitutional Court in January 1998 pronounced the closing-down of this party and a five-year ban on its key policy makers, including its chairman Erbakan, taking an active part in politics[24]. This dissolution gave rise to a new Islamist party, the Virtue Party, whose political life was not long either; it was closed down in June 2001.

Ever since, for the first time in its history, political Islam in Turkey has faced fragmentation into two political parties. The first one, the Party of Felicity (SP), declared its loyalty to traditional political Islam, while the second, the Justice and Development Party (AKP) was founded by young reformists and claimed to break with this tradition. This new party, led by its charismatic chairman Recep Tayyip Erdogan, assumed power after the 2002 elections. The February 28 process did not prevent the AKP's victory and perhaps indirectly contributed to it.

At a social level, even though the AKP still represents a threat in some people's eyes, for the greater part it is believed that the party will not overstep the limits imposed by the February 28 intervention. This remark, constantly repeated particularly during the 2002 election campaign, suggests that the "limits", implemented progressively since 1997, have apparently contributed to the normalization of political Islam. And it is a fact that the AKP, the modernist fruit of political Islam, bears the marks of this normalization. Drawing lessons from the past, it renounced the core references of political Islam and claimed a conservative-democratic ideology, inspired by Germany's Christian Democracy. Traditional right-wing politicians were welcomed into the party. Emphasis was put on the party's determination to pursue economic and political relationships with Western countries. The headscarf issue was passed over in silence during the 2002 election campaign (except at the last moment). Furthermore, during its government, the AKP's constant retreats concerning the secularism issue[25] (for example about reforms of the educational system[26]) have fostered the idea of its normalization. Even if the headscarf issue has provoked tensions at the highest level of the state[27], the AKP has not or cannot insist on the legalization of the veil in the university system. On the contrary, the party has consistently refused to clash with non-elected bodies and laid emphasis on the importance of its consensus-seeking policies[28].

On the other hand, the February 28 process showed that state elites are in a position to refashion the political landscape and limit political Islam's room for manoeuvre, without taking power directly. Furthermore, the February 28 intervention is perceived as marking a definitive threshold which no political party can cross. Thus, this intervention eliminated political Islam as an enemy figure and in the same movement opened up new horizons for it. From this point of view, the military's effort to oust political Islam from power has paradoxically contributed greatly to the relative normalization of AKP and its real electoral success.

Combined with the symbolic elimination of the two potential enemies of the 1990s, the rupture generated by the 2001 economic crisis is the decisive factor behind the absence of mobilization against Kurdish terrorism and Islamist reaction, in other words, behind nationalist demobilization.

Conclusion

The 2001 economic crisis shed light on the Turkish state's weakness and crystallized the symbolic elimination of enemy figures. These factors seem to have had a decisive impact on nationalist demobilization. In this respect, emphasis needs to be put on *social fatigue*[29] as a factor that has prompted demobilization. During the 1990s, nationalist mobilization overwhelmed and subordinated all economic problems and demands of democratization. However, as the country plunged into the most serious economic depression of its history in February 2001, the "sacrifices" which were made in order to avoid chaos, to attain stability and to protect national unity were considered vain. In other words, *social fatigue* can be explained by the shock provoked by the economic crisis which has generated the idea that sacrifices have failed to achieve their goal, a rich, stable and strong state, able to impose itself on the international order.

However, it should be noted that non-elected bodies, and particularly military elites, have always remained firmly legitimate in their guardianship role of the Kemalist project, republican values, national unity and territorial integrity. Nevertheless, as a result of the symbolic elimination of enemy figures, the authority of non-elected bodies is now confined to the meta-political register. Politics is relatively clearly demarcated from meta-politics and no more ground down by it. Moreover, the November 2002 elections led to a reconfiguration of the political field. Except for the CHP, all political parties of the cartel system were ousted from the political game. The AKP's coming to power with an overwhelming majority has generated a stabilization of the political system, sought but not achieved from the late 1980s on.

Not only is the agency of non-elected bodies now largely limited, but the current power configuration does not allow "cartelization" and hence the establishment of a hegemonic bloc. Nevertheless, while the foundations of the 1990s mode of political reproduction have disappeared, the social grammar remains firmly marked by nationalism: national symbols and a form of problematization articulated to various conspiracy theories are still omnipresent.

But, with the end of the era of political crises and the disappearance of the Kurdish movement and the Islamists as threats, social grammar does not appear as a source of mobilization. Obviously, demobilization plays a part in the broadening of the political system and in fostering possibilities of democratization. Political liberalization attempts led by AKP for about two years have not generated crises, even though tensions between the two poles of power are not negligible. Even if, in the current socio-political configuration, popular nationalism does not represent an obstacle to structural reforms of the political system, its substantial mark at both meta-political and infra-political levels invites caution concerning current political transformations.

Nationalist demobilization signifies not the end of popular nationalism but its non-articulation with the current political configuration. Even if the AKP could succeed in introducing all the reforms it would like, this will not necessarily lead to the end of popular nationalism in Turkey. Moreover, the structural reforms do not stem from a deep dynamic of democratization and an acknowledgement of Turkey's heterogeneity. Rather, they aim at satisfying the conditions laid down by the European Union. Therefore they are still regarded as formal obligations for full membership. In the political field as well as on a social level, the requirements of the EU are not really considered as stages on the path of democratization but continue to be perceived as concessions. Besides, democratization and other reforms essentially become instruments in the wrestling match between the government and non-elected bodies. In reality, their applications and governmental policies do not really corroborate the assumption that the mentality underpinning these reforms has changed radically.

Chapter 13

Religion: nation-building instrument of the state or factor of civil society? The AKP between state- and society-centered religious politics

Günter Seufert

Introduction: recent quarrels about the Directorate of Religious Affairs

In June 2003, the Justice and Development Party (AKP) majority in the parliamentary budget commission decided to place 15,000 new posts at the disposal of the Directorate of Religious Affairs, which is one of Turkey's two governmental institutions for the administration of Muslim religious life.[1] The decision caused an outcry from the secular mainstream media, and the Republican People's Party (CHP), the Kemalist caucus in parliament, accused the government of infiltrating state bureaucracy with Islamic fundamentalists, infringing the principle of secularism and falling just short of violating the Constitution. Criticism extended to the Directorate itself, exposing it as one of the most inflated state institutions, exceeding most other ministries in terms of its budget and the number of civil servants it employs.

Obviously, the irritation was spurred on by the ruling party's Islamist past, notwithstanding the fact that the privileged position the Diyanet enjoys is not the result of AKP policy. Quite the reverse, it was particularly the periods of thoroughly secular rule which brought the Directorate into existence and, later on, enhanced its status and possibilities. The Diyanet was founded in the heyday of secularizing reforms by the same law that abolished the Caliphate and led to the closure of the religious schools.[2] The institution was granted constitutional rank in the aftermath of the first coup d'etat in 1960 and in 1971, the year of the second putsch, the Directorate's prayer leaders and preachers were made civil servants. Moreover, the law governing political parties that forbids expressing the demand for a change in the Directorate's status, freezing the current situation, was passed in the aftermath of the last military takeover in 1980. Yet, there is at the same time a long tradition of secular complaint about the Diyanet. Particularly the parties that share the secularist legacy of the CHP periodically accuse the Diyanet of religious conservatism and neglecting Turkey's Alevi citizens.[3] Sometimes the need for a religious bureaucracy in a secular state is itself questioned. None of these parties, however, has proposed any motion to change the situation until today. The picture is even more complex. Although the allocation of state resources to the Diyanet and sometimes its sheer existence as a religious bureaucracy are criticized, any attempt to loosen the ties that bind the institution to the government and to turn it into a non-budgetary institution meet with harsh protest.

Six months prior to the alarm about additional posts for the Diyanet, the AKP's minister in charge of the institution, proposed the devolution of the Directorate, which is today under the direct control of the Prime Minister, to the President of State. Such a move reduces the government's possibilities for instrumentalizing religion, he said. In addition, he looked forward to the institution being granted autonomy at a later stage. His ideas met with great suspicion. The AKP government was accused of relinquishing state control over religion, granting unlimited scope to sectarians and religious radicals and in the end risking the rise of separatism in the name of religion. The Directorate thus appears to be a very sensitive issue. Its present situation is not appreciated but neither are plans made to upgrade or downgrade it.

The Directorate and Turkish-style secularism

The key to understanding the riddle may be found in Article 136 of the 1982 Constitution, which was imposed by the military. The precept enjoins the Directorate, firstly, to act according to the principle of secularism and, secondly, to pursue national unity. The early Republic endorsed the French understanding of secularism and made great efforts to replace religion by secular worldviews, particularly science and nationalism. Republican reforms were not limited to outlawing religiously-motivated politics, but also forbade religious education in public and in private. Thus Turkish-style secularism did not only settle for "objective secularization" – which means that "sectors of society and culture are removed from the domination of religious institutions and symbols". To the contrary, the state also aimed at "subjective secularization", acting to ensure that its citizens "look upon the world and their own lives without the benefit of religious interpretations."[4] To do away with religion completely, however, was neither possible nor intended. Considerable sections of the élite possessed an entrenched Muslim self-understanding, and the War of Liberation against European invaders of Anatolia had been fought by an alliance of different ethnic groups of one Muslim nation.[5] In the early Republic, Islam served as a common denominator for Turks and Kurds as well as other non-Turkish Muslim groups, and, thus, as a tool for forging a united and unitarian Muslim Turkish nation. To combat religious reactionism, which aims at reversing Westernization, religion has had to be limited and controlled. On the other hand, Islam has formed the basic component of civil religion[6], uniting the nation, producing common ground, and adding a cosmological dimension to secular nationalism. It has had to be fostered, privileged and even granted a kind of religious monopoly in the public sphere.

Employing Islam for nation-building purposes has required keeping a fragile balance between the exploitation of Islam, plainly practised again after 1980, and the maintenance of an entirely secular orientation. Despite its internal ideological contradiction, the ensuing understanding of Islam, set out in the Directorate's publications and the textbooks for obligatory religious instruction in schools amongst others, provides for the sanctification of the Turkish Nation and the Turkish Republic as its State.[7]

The AKP and the Directorate of Religious Affairs

The AKP's stance towards the religious bureaucracy is twofold. On the one hand, the party endeavours to staff state services with graduates of Preachers' Schools and Faculties of Theology. The term Islamicism is not applicable to this policy. Right-wing parties from Adnan Menderes (who served his first term of office as Prime Minister in 1950) up to Süleyman Demirel (whose last term of office as Prime Minister ended in 1993) implemented the same strategy for transferring state resources to the religiously-engaged segment of society and preserving conservative morality.

In agreement with all other right-wing parties, the AKP also counters political demands to put the Alevi creed on an equal footing with Sunnism, bringing forward theological considerations. In line with Sunni Muslim scholars, who enumerate what is missing in Alevi beliefs, AKP members of parliament and even party chief and Prime Minister Recep Tayyip Erdogan himself refuse to reconsider the factual monopoly of Sunni Islam in state institutions.

On the other hand, there is a timid and circumspect but continual effort to question the perspectives on religion that have long been taken for granted, to redefine religion's role in society and to rethink the given form of the institutionalization of Islam. The debate is instigated from the top, namely by Mehmed S. Aydın, Minister of State in charge of the Diyanet. The 61-year-old professor of Philosophy of Religion was elected a Member of Parliament in November 2002 on the AKP ticket. Aydın represents a considerable current amongst the younger Sunni ulema in Turkey's Faculties of Theology. He started the discussion as early as October 2002 in a theological journal unknown to the wider public.[8] Since his appointment as Minister, however, he has carried the debate into TV studios, the columns of the daily press and even on to the pages of life-style magazines. Like the conservative intellectual and public figure Ali Fuad Başgil[9], almost fifty years ago, Aydın discerns a crisis of confidence between the secular Republic and large parts of conservative society. According to Aydın, religion is rendered unable to fulfill its true function in society as long as it is a politically disputed issue. In modern society, a variety of issues like the economy and social justice, bribery and preservation of the environment can be dealt with only by enlisting the active commitment of broad segments of the population. In an overwhelming Muslim society, in Aydın's eyes, the single individual can only be successfully addressed by referring to a general moral discourse whose meaningful and cosmological base is religion. In Turkey, however, the omnipresence of *debates about religion* goes hand in hand with the absence of *religion as a moral language* of society. This is why society remains silent on vital issues – a silence which is not to be concealed by the clamour of party wrangling.

However, in Turkey today, according to Aydın, Islam itself is not equipped to work along these lines. Aydın views modern theology on one hand as an effort to link burning issues of society to the public's moral self-understanding and on the other as the transformation of conservative religious morality into new contexts. In this sense, according to him, a modern Islamic theology has yet to be forged in Turkey. To improve upon the present situation, the understanding of religion in general and of theology in particular must be upgraded intellectually. Aydın sees the granting of institutional autonomy to the Faculties of Theology, and with them to the Directorate, as a necessity, since autonomy is vital for any intellectual production.[10]

Secularization in – and outside – the religious framework

The disapproval for Aydın's proposal to rethink the Diyanet's status follows from the Republican tradition of secularization outside of the religious framework. The strategy of subjugating religion, marking it out and replacing religious world views instantly and directly by secular ones, is based on a particular evaluation of Islam and Muslimdom. In this perspective, Islam appears as an entirely ossified and intellectually inert body of teachings, hopelessly enmeshed in irrationality and superstition, entirely imbued with patriarchal traditions and fanaticism. Thus, any efforts at reinterpretation, reformation and conciliation between religion and modernity are bound to fail. There seems to be no possibility to shift from concrete and irreducible religious norms that rule behaviour directly to more general values that require interpretation and are thus capable of opening the way to a more ethical understanding of religion. The pious, on the other hand, appear as a gullible mass inclined to reactionism, a social group whose moves must be carefully observed.[11] Instead, Aydın and his fellow thinkers maintain a plea for *secularization inside the religious framework*. A steady process of interpretation and reinterpretation of Islamic teachings will reconcile the Muslim understanding of Islam with values current in the global discourse. According to Aydın: "Islam disposes of a great sensitivity to individual rights and freedoms", and "of immense historical experience in cultural pluralism, rationalism, religious tolerance and other (universal) values".[12] It is the duty of the learned to make the believer aware of that fact and ensure the assertion of these values in society.

From norm to value, reading the Quran against the background of historical consciousness and gender equality

Turkish Muslims have carried out considerable preparatory work in this connection. A religious consultation, summoned by the Directorate in May 2002, investigated the place of women in society, amongst others issues. The consul-

tation arrived at conclusions contrary to the wording of certain Quranic verses but entirely Islamic, according to the participants. The position of women is
revealing of the self-understanding of a conservative community and serves as
a powerful lever for Islamist movements. It is also revealing of the attitudes of
Westerners, who make the place of women in Islam the touchstone for the com-
patibility of Muslimdom with human rights. Muslim conservatives, Islamists
and Westerners critical towards Islam – all three groups in unison refer to the
Quran, that literally allots only half of a man's share of an inheritance to
women, counts the witness of two women equal to that of one man and makes
women subject to men's orders, to be punished in the case of disobedience.
The consultation of theologians issued a diametrically opposed statement, qualifying the Quranic verses concerned as reflections of historical circumstances
and without value as a reflection of Islamic principles. In the consultation's
view, the Quran accepts men and women as ontologically equal, since their relation to God and their capacity for both piety and redemption and sin and corruption are entirely equal and identical. Accordingly, statements of the Quran
on worldly matters contrary to this principle are to be attributed to the particular historical conditions of the Revelation and may not claim timeless validity.[13] A new generation of theologians at the Faculties of Theology backs this
approach. They see the text of the Quran as containing an abundance of norms,
rules and explanations given in specific situations. It is inappropriate to gener-
alize single Quranic decisions formulated in particular contexts. Instead,
Muslim scholars have the task of reaching general conclusions and principles
that reflect the intentions of the Quran as a whole.[14] In this way, the changing
understanding of the Quran in the course of history is brought into agreement
with its timeless validity and – while religious norms need to be (re)interpreted
– religion can be aligned with secular modernity and thus with secularization,
inside the religious framework.

A new image of the Turkish Muslim

This new perspective on Islam is coupled with a new appraisal of the Turkish
Muslim. In an interview given almost two years before his appointment as
Head of the Directorate, Ali Bardakoğlu claimed a significant difference
between Turks and other Muslim nations in the understanding of Islam. As he
put it: "Asked what Islam and Sharia means to him, a man from Saudi Arabia
will repeat: having a thief's hand cut off. Asked what Islam and Muslimdom
represents for him, a Turk will answer: sincerity and moral conduct."[15]

A people with this frame of mind – Bardakoğlu seems to argue – will not use
additional religious knowledge to breed intolerance, but will expand its already
quasi-humanist orientations. In his words: "Greater knowledge denotes a variety of alternatives; it instills the qualification of one's own perspective and the
consideration of opposing views. Those with little knowledge tend to be dogmatic. It is a widely-held opinion that the enhancement of religious knowledge
leads to religious radicalism; but the radicals have only a little knowledge of

religion."[16] "No need to fear the Turkish Muslim masses", runs Bardakoğlu's implicit appeal to the country's secular elite. Moreover, religious education is presented as a step to individualism, because individuals who are better educated religiously will question religious leaders, be it the shaikhs of traditional brotherhoods or Islamist party chiefs.[17]

The dialectics of a liberal society and a liberal understanding of Islam
Why have Turkey's Muslims failed to realize this liberal and pluralistic potential of Islam? Why do they – to speak with Thomas Luckmann – stick to "specific historical forms" of Islam, neglecting the "elementary forms" of Islam,[18] that is, the key teachings and intention of their religion? To answer this question, Aydın develops a twofold argument. After its initial phase, marked by Revelation and the establishment of the community, Islam, like other religions, lost the immediacy of spirituality and transcendentalism, and the believers took refuge in laws and norms that had a deceptive concreteness. The Muslims thus lost their capacity for self-criticism. However, it was self-awareness and self-criticism that brought about the proud periods of Islamic history. Islam's faith, intellectual traditions and teachings thus in principle allow for renovation and renewal. However, as crucial as the teachings of a religion for its capacity for intellectual revival are the overall conditions of state and society. Religion, according to Aydın, is closely interdependent with other symbolic systems of meaning, like philosophy, politics and societal discourses as a whole. In Turkey, he claims, a first glance at the mindset and the intellectual climate of state and society reveals a lack of criticism, individualism, independence and autonomy, and as a corollary, a poor state of intellectual production. He concludes: "Given this lack of dynamism in non-religious fields of society, one can hardly expect individualism, a critical attitude to dogmatism and self-criticism in the realm of religion."[19] This state of affairs takes a concrete form in the state control of religious institutions, their lack of intellectual autonomy and religious scholars being on the government payroll.

It is interesting to note that the minister in charge of State Islam, appointed by the erstwhile Islamist leadership of the AKP, views religion almost entirely as a mirror image of society. He shares this secular understanding of religion with Ziya Gökalp, the nationalist theorist of Turkish modernization in the early years of the Republic. Gökalp argued from the dependency of religious life on society to advocate decisive shifts in the interpretation of religious law and dogma, and to open the door to a more secular understanding of Islam.[20]

However, referring to 'society', Gökalp did not have in mind the inhabitants of the Empire and later the Republic who were not really familiar with his nationalist ideas. Rather he thought of an idealized Turkish Nation, whose approval of equality, progress and rationalism was beyond any question. To bridge the gulf between the actual inhabitants and the idealized nation, according to Gökalp, the state had to work out a new understanding of Islam and teach it to the people.

Aydın, instead, presumes that large sections of the populace long for more civic modernity and are eager to transcend the limits set by the omnipotent state. Convinced of the strength of secular currents amongst Turkey's religious academics today, he timidly argues for a gradual retreat of the state from religious matters and the loosening of the state's grip on Islamic institutions. Gökalp used a secular understanding of religion to develop a unitarian version of Islam along the collective paradigm of nationalism. Aydın presents a more individual and liberal understanding of religion, at the expense of direct state control over Islam. Gökalp was the chief ideologist of nationalism; Aydın considers the changing requirements of post-national globalization.

Secularism in Turkish society and attitudes towards the Directorate of Religious Affairs

This conclusion, derived from public statements and ongoing discussions amongst the modern ulema, may be questioned and even rejected as simplistic and naïve. One should not, however, underestimate the impact of 200 years of cultural and political modernization that started in late Ottoman times and accelerated during the Republic. For the last 80 years or so, the positive sciences have faced no competition in Turkey's schools and universities in explaining the world, society and mankind, and even in the Faculties of Theology secular frames of reference are widely used. And even those who teach in them are not untouched by processes of (subjective) secularization. Muslim intellectuals increasingly 'understand' the faith against the background of secular orientations like equality, progress and nationalism and more recently also from the perspective of feminism and the environmentalist movement. Being anxious that crude politicization may destroy Islam's spiritual potential, Turkish Muslim intellectuals for several years have implicitly acknowledged the modern distinction between the secular world and the religious one[21], and argue for the protection of the latter.[22]

Appreciations of the Diyanet in society, by contrast, vary widely. Like every criticsm directed at the state, criticism of the institution and Turkish style secularism is mostly articulated at the margins. Christian communities complain of the disadvantaged status of their communal foundations. Alevi spokesmen demand official recognition for their version of Islam, as well as to be put on an equal footing in regard to financial aid. Outspoken atheists are few in number[23], and only a handful of irreligious individuals, together with some liberals of Sunni background and Muslim intellectuals, argue for a virtual separation of state and religion, proposing that the Diyanet be closed and/or its functions be devolved to mosque communities and other religious organizations. Disregarding the problematic nature of Turkish-style secularism sketched above, the bulk of the population takes no offence at the existence and functioning of the Diyanet. Only one in four see a discrepancy between the principle of secularism and the Diyanet's task, and three out of four say the state control of Islam prevents the radicalization of religion and religious movements. Almost the same ratio, however, is suspicious that governments may instrumentalize the Diyanet. According to more than half the population, the Diyanet only supports one version of Islam, ignoring other forms of Muslim belief.[24]

These results of a study carried out inside the religious bureaucracy – so to speak – are confirmed by a circumstantial research about the religious attitudes of Turkey's population. There, even more, 82% to be precise, argue for the perpetuation of the institution. Again, however, a large majority (70%) argued for the religious bureaucracy's theological scope being extended and supported the integration of Alevism in the Diyanet's work.[25] The research, additionally, confirms Minister of State Aydın's talk of a crisis of confidence between state and society over religion. 42% of the interviewees expressed the conviction that the state exerts pressure upon religious people, and 53% of those complaining cited the rules regarding the headscarves as a case in point.[26]

The relation of state and society regarding religion thus shows traces of ambiguity. The overwhelming majority agree with Turkish-style secularism and with the state organizing religious life. The majority of Turkish society may thus be described as level-headed, ready to identify with the state and accepting it as an arbiter in religious questions. The Turkish mainstream does not demand abstract religious liberty; instead, it endorses the tutelary role of the state. From the margins, however – and these margins may be rather wide – there is considerable dissatisfaction with the given situation. From a "Sunni Muslim Rightist" perspective, for want of a better term, the state is accused of exerting political pressure on the religious conservatives. This criticism, however, seems not to be motivated by a politicized understanding of Islam but rather evokes notions of religious freedom and even civic sense, if one bears in mind the essentially tolerant attitudes towards non-Muslims and non-believers. If this were not the case, the demand formulated from a more "Alevi Secularist Leftist" perspective for a more comprehensive approach to Islam would not be supported by far more than two thirds of the population.

This picture indicates that some initiatives are needed from the new AKP-appointed officials in the religious bureaucracy. This holds good for creating a new image of the Turkish Muslim, and for asking the state to adopt a more liberal perspective towards the religiously committed. And it is also true for the endeavour to arrive at a more indirect reading of the Holy Scripture and a more pluralist, individualistic and intellectual understanding of Islam.[27]

In fact, a notable part of Turkey's population questions the established public system of religion that only allows for one version of Sunni Islam, outlaws civil Sunni Muslim actors in religious matters, balks at recognition of the Alevi creed, and grants non-Muslim communities no possibility of organization as a church (or equivalent). However, at the political level, this disagreement with the one and only national version of religion expresses itself not as a quest for pluralism but as the struggle of two competing, and mostly antagonistic, discourses. The entrenched cultural and political split in Turkey's politics transfers the multi-layered discontent with the organization of religion into a quarrel between "Muslim conservative" forces demanding democracy, and "secular progressive" forces, focussing their attention on the Islamist threat. Why then does the AKP, a political party, already viewed suspiciously by the secular elite as having a hidden religious agenda, bothering with the Diyanet's work? The answers which come to mind are connected, first, with internal politics, particularly the situation of the party itself. Second, foreign policy and especially the process of Turkey's struggle for EU-membership must be taken into account.

Internal reasons for the AKP government to reconsider Republican secularism and traditional state policies towards religion

The AKP's new approach towards religion accords with the party's policy in other realms such as the economy and overall democratization; it aims at decentralization, liberalization and the general limitation of immediate state intervention. However, no single step has so far been taken in line with the considerations and discussions which have been initiated. Again, one version of Islam is propagated, this time a more liberal, individualistic, and pluralist one, but the status of the Diyanet has not been discussed, let alone changed, nor is there any sign of accepting non-state Muslim actors, such as Alevi communities, or non-state Sunni associations as partners in intra-Muslim religious dialogue.

A look at the political situation of the AKP government may provide some explanations for this somewhat incoherent policy of the party towards the Directorate. Among its possible targets are the Kemalist political rivals. To favour individualism in religious matters creates common ground with the Kemalist discourse upon religion. Besides, individualism, a global value, effectively counters the Kemalist ideology's criticism of Islam in general and the AKP's Islamist past in particular. To present Islam as compatible with modernity and the Muslim masses as ready to accept a depoliticized and primarily ethical version of Islam takes the wind out of the sails of the Kemalists, who gather widespread societal support by referring to the "entrenched reactionary qualities" of Islam. Another target group is the Islamist section of the AKP's own political tradition: The team of Recep Tayyip Erdoğan and the current Foreign Minister Abdullah Gül were already arguing against the politicization of Islam in 2000, when they were members of the Virtue Party (Fazilet Partisi, FP). Instead, they stressed issues of personal commitment and religious freedom.[28] To emphasize individual approaches towards religion fits into this strategy of depoliticizing Islam.

The New Theology is thus functional for the strategy against both Islamist remnants in the AKP (and in Muslim circles critical of the AKP) and against the Kemalist élite. It is, however, difficult to assert the same thing about any practical reform of the Directorate of Religious Affairs, any change in its status, and any integration of Alevi communities, let alone the readmission of non-state Sunni circles like the Sufi orders or the recognition of other religious movements.

However, the abandonment of political Islam has also been coupled, at least partly, with a more critical look at the politics of the nation-state in general. Muslim intellectuals that were and/or still are advisers/members of Erdoğan's team have spoken at length about the Islamic state being in accord with the nation-state. Both types of state cherish an official ideology that favours one group of society ("the Turks" or "the Muslims") against other groups, and both types of state are, thus, condemned to rule unjustly.[29]

External reasons for a new policy towards the institutionalization of Islam

As secularism is viewed as the cornerstone of the Republic, there is good reason – at the domestic level – for adopting a measured modus operandi concerning any step towards reform. On the level of foreign policy, however, considerable urgency exists. The revised Accession Partnership document asked Turkey to "establish conditions for the functioning of these (religious, GS) communities, their members and their assets, the teaching, appointing and training of clergy, and the enjoyment of property rights in line with Protocol 1 of the European Convention on Human Rights."[30]

In writing these lines, the Commission primarily had the non-Muslim minorities in mind, and four Christian communities of Turkey sent a joint letter, dated 23 September 2003, to the Human Rights Committee of the Grand National Assembly in which they called upon the state to grant "... first and foremost recognition of the legal personality of all Christian patriarchates and churches and the removal of all legal obstacles to such recognition ..."[31] Legally the non-Muslim communities of Turkey exist only as a family of foundations for the administration of real estate like church buildings, hospitals and schools. Turkish law forbids the establishment of religious foundations and associations.[32] This regulation applies to both the non-Muslim and the Muslim population. As far as the Muslims are concerned, it goes hand in hand with the Directorate of Religious Affairs' monopoly in governing Islam. As far as non-Muslims are concerned, the regulation justifies the limitations on Christian and Jewish communities whose members factually lack legal equality with Muslims and are not viewed as proper Turkish citizens. In recent time, suspicions have grown that the existing state monopoly over Islam presents an obstacle for the legal recognition of any religious community and may thus become a stumbling block for Turkey's relations with the European Union.[33] Even if a quick solution is found for the legal position of the Christian minorities, it will remain difficult to justify to pro-Muslim circles that minority religious communities are granted rights denied to the country's religious majority. Moreover, the European Commission's 2004 Regular Report speaks for the first time of the Alevi community as a "non-Sunni Muslim minority", thus reinforcing fears that Turkey may be forced to change the entrenched relationship of state and religion.[34] In this context the AKP's New Theology at least questions the state's monopoly over the definition of Islam and may thus prepare public opinion for practical reforms of the religious bureaucracy that may become necessary in the process of Turkey's accession to the European Union. In public, the Directorate still denies any need to change its policy towards non-Sunni groups, particular the Alevis. The most recent statements of its head, Ali Bardakoğlu, in the light of the European Commission's assessment of the Alevis as a religious minority still insist on the possibility of eradicating religious differences in society by teaching the "right" Islam. The harsh reactions of the Head of State, Ahmet Necdet Sezer, and of the Vice Commander of the General Staff, İlter Başbuğ, towards the EU's statement and homegrown initiatives to recognize linguistic and religious pluralism reveal the limited political leeway of the AKP government and together with it the Directorate of Religious Affairs in this issue. In private, however, their exists a clear consciousness of the need to bargain and establish dialogue with Muslim subgroups not recognized officially, including the Alevis' organization.[35]

Already in spring 2004 the Directorate of Religious Affairs asked the Faculties of Theology to comment about how its work might change in the perspective of Turkey's membership of the EU. The 3rd Religious Summit of the Directorate in September 2004 focused on the modification of the services it provides for Turkish Muslims in the European diaspora according to the dominant discourses concerning the relationship between state and religion in Europe.[36]

Steps in the same direction are also being taken outside the Diyanet. Well aware of the need for reform of the religious bureaucracy, the Political Bureau of the Foreign Ministry's Secretariat General for the European Union asked academic jurists to make recommendations for the reorganization of the religious bureaucracy. As a result, Professor Hüseyin Hatemi, from Istanbul University's Law Faculty, drafted a bill that foresees the granting of the status of body corporate to the indigenous non-Muslim communities such as the Greek Orthodox Patriarchate, the Armenian Orthodox Patriarchate, the Syrian Orthodox Patriarchate and the Rabbinate. These new bodies corporate will be supervised by a new Ministry of Religious Affairs, which will also be in charge of two Directorates of Religious Affairs, one for Sunnism and one for Shi'ism that will serve as a framework for integrating the Alevi communities.[37]

As far as the traditions of popular Islam among the Alevis are concerned, Hatemi argues for their institutionalization at the level of organizations of the civil society.[38] Hatemi's considerations are in no way related to the ongoing discussions in the Diyanet. They are, however, a response to the same challenges from abroad to Turkish-style secularism. The New Theology and the questioning of the given form of institutionalization of religion are thus preparing state and society for reforms that may become inevitable in the years to come.

Chapter 14
Post-nationalist semiotics?
The emblem of the Justice and
Development Party AKP

Béatrice Hendrich

"If we were still fighting the war of becoming a nation, how could we become a member of the EU? Turkey has already overcome these problems, it has already become a nation. Now, Turkey has to open up to the world."[1]

The emblems of political parties in the Republic of Turkey consist of two parts: the icon and the party name's abbreviation. The crucial part, in both size and semantics, is definitely the icon. This is not a recent effect of the "iconic turn", but the strength of a graphic tradition connected, among other factors, to the still problematic status of illiteracy in Turkey and the Turkish and Ottoman visual culture of the tuğra and the coat of arms. Elements of these ancestors we will find again in the party emblems.

The "mother of all Turkish republican parties", the Republican People's Party, encouraged this tradition by choosing a semantically heavily loaded icon: six white arrows, symbolizing the six Kemalist principles, on a red background. The understanding of this emblem is culturally restricted: it is only readable at all embedded in the history of the early Turkish republic. So the party emblem as well as the whole process for deciding for this emblem stands in for the process of building a *nation* called the *Republic of Turkey*. The message is arbitrary: it is dynamic in the sense that the arrows, the principles, are meant to symbolize the progressive and revolutionary aspects of the party and state ideology. It is static in the sense that the goal of the development is already fixed: it is to build a Turkish Nation, nothing less but nothing more.

The Justice and Development Party AKP (Adalet ve Kalkınma Partisi) under its leader Tayyip Erdoğan decided for a rather puzzling emblem, a shining bulb underneath the acronym Ak Parti, when it was founded in summer 2001. This emblem continues the graphic tradition but transgresses it, first by using such a different icon, and secondly by playing with the references between icon and acronym. The emblem is deliberately polysemic and strives to integrate in one message Islamic tradition, societal reform, technical and cultural progress, and the orientation towards a democratic, plural Europe, instead of making Turkish nation-building its only goal. This signals a distinct shift in Turkish political ambitions and Turkey's relations with the outside world, that will receive further attention in the article at hand.

The election of 2002 – a decisive step in Turkey's political history?

Since the national elections of 2002, Turkey's national assembly has experienced an unusual structure. With the exception of the one-party period at the beginning of the Republic, the Great National Assembly of Turkey (TBMM) has always consisted of several smaller and bigger parties. Governments could only be built by the means of coalitions; everything could change every day. But in 2002, the representatives of only two parties entered the National Assembly, those of the Republican People's Party (Cumhuriyet Halk Partisi), now the only opposition party, and those of the Justice and Development Party (AKP), in the West known almost solely by her head and current Prime Minister, Recep Tayyip Erdoğan. Even if it is rather too early to call this development a historical change, it does offer us a key chance to explore. I argue that the semiotic study of party emblems over time offers a significant window on to these changes and their portents.

The Republican People's Party

The main opposition party in the National Assembly at present is the CHP, the heir to a grouping of Republican and Kemalist, sometimes termed "Social Democrat", parties beginning with the People's Group (*Halk Fırkası*, HF), which was formed in 1923. The People's Group and its successors were not only the dominant political organization of Turkey from 1923 to 1945; its emblem, the (wavy) red background with the six white arrows was and still is a referential template for a great number of Turkish party emblems. The six arrows became part of the Republican Party emblem in 1931, symbolizing the six principles finally accepted by the 1931 party congress (when the party was still named *Cumhuriyet Halk Fırkası*). (The principles themselves, later called "*Atatürk ilkeleri*" (Kemalist principles), became part of the national Constitution in 1937.)

The image on the left comes from the current homepage of the CHP;[2] the text underneath is entitled "*Bayrak Talimatı*" (explanation of the flag). Unfortunately, the homepage itself does not give an exact date or source of the *Bayrak Talimatı*.

It is even not clear where the historical text ends and the modern explanations and graphical instructions (how to draw the arrows) start. The talimat and the flag were most likely created between 1931 and 1935, beginning with the above mentioned Congress and ending with the decision to call the fırka a Party. The *Bayrak Talimatı* describes the meaning and the origin of the arrows as follows:

"The six arrows represent the main features of our party. The idea, to show the speed and the progressiveness seething in the party's soul with the aim to elevate the nation, was the reason to accept the arrows as the party's sign. There are several types of arrows. The arrows at the party's flag match the Turkish arrows discovered during the researches carried out by our national museums."[3]

The six features or principles are, as the *Talimat* explains: Republicanism, Nationalism, Populism, Etatism, Secularism, Revolutionism. Here I would like to dwell on the second principle, nationalism.

Although nationalism was a main ideological principle and a driving force in political discussion and action leading to the foundation of the Republic of Turkey, there is no one canonical form of it.[4] Not only did different groups and parties promote different understandings of nationalism, but we can see wide variations within a single party. The feature common to all varieties is the conviction that nationalism is the appropriate answer to any political or societal question in Turkey, and that Turkish nationalism is by definition a positive and non-negotiable value. The dogma-like nature of the Kemalist principles is one reason for the long-lasting character of this belief.

In a students' textbook,[5] the second principle is defined in the following way: "[...] Turkish nationalism is an unifying and completing (*bütünleyici*) principle. It is a psychological bond that comes into existence by means of social and cultural actions. This principle provides national unity and completeness, and plays a strengthening role in movements, ideas and actions concerning national goals."

The recent[6] CHP home page also gives a description of the principles. Thus: "The Republic of Turkey is not established on the basis of religion, language, race, or ethnic origin, but on the basis of political consciousness and ideal togetherness (*ideal beraberliği*). Nationalism should not be restricted to race. [...] The understanding of the CHP's nationalism is to defend unconditionally the unity and security of all citizens who form the Republic of Turkey, the independence and sovereignty of the country, and the territorial integrity and rights of Turkey."[7]

Before the national elections of 2002, Faruk Birtek described the CHP as "fanatic nationalist" in the interview mentioned at the beginning. (The National Movement Party MHP he called "radical nationalist").[8] As proof of this attitude, Birtek quotes the "frightening phrases" of Deniz Baykal, head of the CHP, such as "The process of nationalizing is not yet completed".To sum up: more then 60 years after the icon with six arrows was first designed, the CHP uses it exclusively as its party emblem.

This could be a traditionalistic attitude, but in the case of the CHP the visual continuity seems to match the ideological. The non-racist but defensive anti-imperialist and explicitly unifying (homogenizing) nationalism of the 1930s[9] has survived until the present.

Some trends in party emblems

The emblems of the communist parties in Turkey adopt the set of symbols common to communist parties worldwide: red and yellow as colours, stars, hammers, cog wheels and so forth, as motifs. The rightist racist parties, mostly enterprises of Alparslan Türkeş, prefer one or more crescent moons on a red background. The social democrat and/or Kemalist parties, looking to compete with or replace the CHP, demonstrate continuity by the use of arrows or arrow-like beams, as the People's Party (*Halkçı Parti*, HP) of 1983 did. The rightist Muslim parties, which until 2001 were almost exclusively led by Necmettin Erbakan, also used the crescent moon, but in combination with a second motif. Also popular among parties of all ideological stripes are animals (deer, bees, birds) and Turkish landscapes.

The decision to carry on with the semiotics of a former party or to create a totally new icon depends on various considerations. First, if a party in Turkey is banned by the decision of a court or some other institution, the political leaders – or their front men – will try to set up a new party under a different name and with a more or less different emblem. If the political and legal situation is not too precarious or tense, it makes sense to use an easily decipherable emblem, one that only changes the graphical structure but still keeps the former motifs. But this may turn out a too risky endeavour and immediately cause a new ban. The law of 1981 on the dissolution of political parties explicitly forbade the use of "names, emblems, symbols, rosettes etc."[10] of banned former parties. To avoid this risk, the continuously banned and re-established Kurdish parties change their main motif each time: a rose, a deer, a butterfly. Only the ending of the party's name "EP" remains.

The situation is different if the newly founded party is not the successor of a banned party but came into existence as a result of a political schism or as a new and independent movement. Then the creation of a different emblem may intend to demonstrate a political change or the newly founded party's return to the "right way".

The emblems of the Islamist/Muslim parties after 1980

In 1983, Necmettin Erbakan set up his first party after the coup d'état. Besides other features, the Welfare Party (*Refah Partisi*; RP) was an outspokenly anti-European and Islamist party. Despite its aggressive rhetoric and its obviously anti-democratic behaviour, the party survived until January 1998; with the help of the other "democratic and secular (*laik*)" parties, Erbakan reached the summit of his career, becoming Prime Minister in 1996. The party emblem combined the above-mentioned crescent moon with a wheat sheaf of the same size as the moon, and with the party's abbreviation "RP" in rather small letters. The Welfare Party was followed by the luckless and somewhat glamourless Virtue Party (*Fazilet Partisi*; FP), banned in June 2001. Its emblem repeated the RP's emblem of a crescent moon, almost unnoticeably altered in form and position, and five lines with a heart at the end, giving the impression of the for-

mer wheat sheaf. After the banning of the FP in the summer of 2001, the political picture in Turkey changed drastically. In July 2001, the next Erbakan party,
the *Saadet Partisi*[11] (SP), which still exists and is headed by Recai Kutan, was
founded. The party emblem again showed the crescent moon, this time not red
but white, and five Turkish (not communist) stars. One month later, Recep
Tayyip Erdoğan, former mayor of Istanbul and an active member of the
Welfare Party, together with other former RP members like Abdullah Gül, now
Minister for Foreign Affairs, founded a second Islam oriented party competing
with the SP, the Justice and Development Party. At the founding congress, a
completely new party emblem was decided on, the shining bulb with the
party's acronym "*Ak Parti*" at the bottom. The Turkish public reacted with
puzzlement and also much irony to this strange emblem, which in the first version was un-professionally designed. Jokes concerning the bulb started to cir-
culate immediately. Newspapers titled "The harsh light of the naked bulb"[12] or
"Here is the bulb. Where is the enlightenment?"[13]

Probably one of the most severe criticisms could be read in a newspaper ideologically rather close to the AKP's orientation, *Zaman*: "What is the reason
for this aesthetic poverty, this mediocre design? [..] I don't blame those who
like the emblem; but I am angry about the low expectations concerning the
(taste of the) masses among those who accepted the emblem because it got good
statistical ratings."[14]

The polysemic emblem of the Justice and Development Party

It is possible that the bulb was not the original creation of Erdoğan and
friends, nor a spontaneous idea of the party congress. According to the statement of a *Saadet Partisi* member, the bulb was already in use in 1989 during a
Welfare Party campaign, together with the slogan "bright tomorrows".[15] On the
other hand, Erol Olçok claimed the bulb was part of the campaign explicitly
prepared for the AKP by his company.[16] Be that as it may, in the given political
context, Edison's modest bulb together with the party's acronym turns out to
be a rather complex emblem, offering several interconnected ways to read it.
The first point to pay attention to is that the emblem does not make use of any
motif of the former Islamist/Muslim parties. This could be due to the fact that
the AKP was founded *after* the Saadet Partisi and had no choice but to use a
different symbol. But as we have seen in the examples above, if the party
founders had intended to demonstrate continuity in the Erbakan spectrum,
they could have made some minor changes in size and colour and claimed to
be the "real" (*öz*) successor of the Virtue Party. So the message of this emblem
is: "We are different, we are new!" (If the bulb really was used long before in a
campaign of the Welfare Party, all the better. For the politically interested and
well informed, this offers a hint of the party history.)

Among more general considerations,[17] the AKP, heading for power, had one
particularly good reason for contrasting itself with the whole Erbakan enter-
prise: Not only had the Welfare Party been banned by a Turkish court in 1998,

but also the European Court for Human Rights had dismissed Welfare's claim against the ban only two weeks before the official founding of the AKP.[18] To stress its independence from the Welfare or Virtue Party at this moment seemed to be the appropriate message to Europe from a party that reached out for EU membership so decidedly as the AKP did from the very beginning.

I would now like to demonstrate some aspects of the referential relation between the icon of the shining bulb and the party's acronym "*Ak Parti*". It is important to realize that this party has three names: AKP, *Adalet ve Kalkınma Partisi, Ak Parti*. AKP is the widely used abbreviation, but obviously not the name favoured by the party itself or by the agency in charge of its PR. AKP is a technical abbreviation, according to the internationally used system of party abbreviations, but it does not carry any particular meaning. It arouses no firm connotation or association. Quite the reverse is true for the acronym *Ak Parti* situated beneath the bulb. "Its message is very strong. It is a local (Turkish) term. [It means] our forehead is clean (*ak*), our face is clean, permitted (*helal*) according to the religious law like our mother's white (*ak*) milk. [...] [Choosing this name] we did the right thing. But the media mispronounce it. In our statutes, our name is not AKP but *Ak Parti*. They call it AKP because they want to break its communicative force", according to the above-mentioned Erol Olçok.[19] That means the party's correct name is "Clean Party". But the tricky thing is the various meanings of "*ak*" – "white", "clean", "sinless" – in combination with the visual message of the icon. The different possible readings of the whole emblem are intended to provoke the interest of particular recipient groups, to arouse different connotations (and memories).

"*Ak*" deliberately contains a moral and a practical aspect. It refers directly to Tayyip Erdoğan and his image as an incorruptible politician, both being "clean" himself and cleaning up his environment, an image he achieved during his time as mayor in Istanbul (1994-1998). Also, an incorruptible and transparent administration and legal system is what the AKP promises the people.[20]

Together with the shining bulb and slogans in use such as "Open to brightness, closed to darkness", or "forward to a bright tomorrow", "*ak*" indicates the concept "light" in its differing senses in different cultural spheres. It refers both to the European Enlightenment and the prominent place of light in Muslim theology. Enlightenment is a key concept of the new party ideology. A memorandum entitled "Conservative Democracy" stresses the importance of the European Enlightenment for the development of a society, it refuses the traditional criticism of conservatives concerning the devastating results of the Enlightenment, and it opts for a pragmatic third way: "What Turkey needs is the ability to create a modern conservatism, taking account of the dimensions that provoke political or philosophical (negative) reactions, but focusing on the current societal circumstances we live by. From that point of view, it will be more meaningful to criticize not the Enlightenment itself or the necessity for it but the negative aspects we have seen in the French case."[21]

To include the notion of Enlightenment in the party emblem and in written documents is a clear and strong message towards Europe, but also to the (more or less religious and conservatively oriented) intellectual clientele that had been put off by Erbakan and his Islamist nationalist rhetoric.

In religious discourse, "light" enjoys a prominent place both in the Qur'an and in mysticism. To give only one example, a very important verse of the Qur'an runs: "God is the light of heaven and earth. His light is like a niche with a lamp in it."[22]

Now, we turn to the party's second official name: Adalet ve Kalkınma Partisi, the Justice and Development Party. Here "Justice" is a positive term by definition. A true Muslim ruler has to secure justice for everybody. Justice, the improvement of the whole legal system in Turkey, is longed for and bitterly needed by the whole people. The "Recommendation of the European Commission on Turkey's Progress towards Accession" again and again stresses the importance of a functioning legal system and some more major changes in the law as conditions *sine qua non* for accession.[23]

The above-mentioned memorandum of the AKP "Ak Parti ve muhafazakar demokrasi" points to the two sources of human rights: "The first documents to state the human rights were the Habeas Corpus (1670), Bill of Rights (1678), American (1776) and French (1789) Constitutions. But the norms that brought the religion of Islam a long time before that may be as well evaluated in this frame: 'Whoever killed one person has killed the whole humankind.' (Holy Qur'an 5/32)."[24] Finally, "development" is the most all-embracing term: economic, scientific, technical, and social development is a goal to be achieved by the efforts of the Turkish state, of private companies in an open market, of all individuals, and of course by means of EU membership.

Despite these considerations, to some the bulb seems an outdated metaphor. But I would contend that if we consider the economic and technological reality of today's Turkey, the bulb retains its vitality through the very openness of its meaning. Indeed, there are still villages and slum-like quarters in Turkey waiting for electricity, there are citizens of the Republic of Turkey too poor to purchase a new bulb, and the street lighting of Istanbul continues to break down.[25] The political scientist İhsan Dağı stresses the fact that the AKP, following the positive Istanbul experience of Erdoğan, gives more importance to "direct service to the citizens", to the direct approach to the daily problems of ordinary people, than to ideological rhetoric. "However right, great, and holy an ideology might be, it does not contribute to the solution of problems like roads, water(supply), and the sewage system."[26]

Nationalism

As we have seen, the AKP's emblem allows for multiple readings and a healthy amount of criticism, but it does not suggest an explicitly nationalist symbolism. In the history of the Republic of Turkey, this already means something. It is inappropriate to prove the party has an anti-national stance; the whole party rhetoric fits into the common Atatürk-Nation-Independence rhetoric with a dash of religious vocabulary added. The bulb, in particular, matches the positivist developmental worldview of the early Republic. But the nation, national (or Ottoman) history and the War of Independence are no longer the pivot of political ideology and practice. If we take a look at attitudes concerning EU membership, even at first glance (quite literally if we look at the parties' Internet sites) we can see the CHP's reluctance concerning further negotiations between Turkey and the EU Commission. We find much there of the old anti-imperialist rhetoric, talking about pitfalls and lies in the statements of both Erdoğan and the EU,[27] but no documents or strategic papers. The AKP's homepage, by contrast, provides direct links to all documents concerning the negotiations. Furthermore, what is at least a religiously *oriented* party possesses other foundations upon which to establish a party identity – not necessarily a religious one – besides this one and only raison d'être, the nation.

In short, this new party emblem continues the visual tradition of establishing the composition of an icon and an abbreviation, but it transgresses this tradition first by using such a different icon, secondly by using a message-bearing acronym instead of a technical abbreviation, and thirdly by playing with the references between icon and acronym. The emblem is in some respects readable even for those who do not know the details of the history of the Turkish Republic. The six arrows of the Republican People's Party may need to be explained to the colleague in the European Parliament; the bulb is funny but understandable (even if the European colleague only gets half of the message). This emblem is deliberately polysemic, striving to integrate Islamic tradition, societal reform, technical and cultural progress, and the orientation towards a democratic, plural Europe.

Chapter 15

The urgency of post-nationalist perspectives: "Turkey for the Turks" or an open society? On the Kurdish conflict

Gülistan Gürbey

The term post-nationalism cannot or can hardly be exactly defined. It sounds as though it is associated with post-Communism or post-Socialism, although these only refer to the transformation processes in the former Soviet Union and the Eastern European countries after the end of the Cold War and do not indicate the establishment of a certain type of regime.

All in all, is the term post-nationalism not confusing rather than a useful construct? What do we mean by post-nationalist perspectives? Is this a way to address the efforts to give up the ideology of nationalism? If that is the case, what comes next? In the face of world-wide political and economic globalization processes, can we speak of an incipient stage of overcoming nationalism and the idea of the nation state? What political alternatives are offered by the globalization process?

We can rightly say that the process of globalization is advancing. However, it is somewhat problematic also to speak of nationalism and the nation state vanishing. On the contrary, although frontiers are increasingly disappearing in international politics and economics, nationalism and the nation state continue to exist. Both were and are capable of adapting to the situation without being completely destroyed and fundamentally questioned in the process, which means that the idea of nationalism also seems to survive this global transformation process. Even 9/11 did not fundamentally change this. On the contrary, the mighty, powerful nation state is rather more in demand now. The changes affect, in the first place, the conception of nationalism and the relationship between state, individual and society, and, second, the internal power structures of the nation states or the political system respectively.

What does the term post-nationalism mean in relation to Turkey? The term itself sounds promising and expresses a vision rather than an existing or developing situation. And it is just as difficult and problematic to specify what post-nationalism is in the Turkish context. However, what can be stated with certainty is that Turkey is also part of this increasingly politically and economically globalised world and that it, therefore, is influenced by the effects of this process; thus we can speak of a transformation process in terms of Turkey. The pivotal issue we face here is: how does the world-wide globalization process influence a) the Turkish understanding of nationalism and the nation state, b) the internal power structures, in other words the political system, and c) the development of society?

The transformation process in Turkey's politics and society – the end of which is not in sight – has been induced by internal and external factors. The worldwide globalization process and the prospect of joining the EU are the most important external factors. Internal factors are, above all, the evolving civil society, the increasing presence in the media of politics and society as well as the parts played by economic and political pressure groups which see their interests best protected in a functioning liberal, rule-of-law based democracy as in the West. It can be observed that developments or processes in modernization and liberalization go hand-in-hand with deeply-rooted ideologies. It is, therefore, rather difficult to predict what the outcome of this transformation process will be.

Where does the Turkish conception of nationalism and the nation state stand at the moment? How has it changed under the influence of the external and internal factors mentioned?

The prospect of joining the EU and the reforms needed put the Kemalist doctrine of a homogenous state and nation to a serious test. This is most clearly reflected in the internal arguments between the proponents and opponents of the reform process. The opponents, mainly represented by the elites in the military and legal authorities as well as certain political circles, are trying to prevent an easing or liberalization of the homogenous state-and-nation doctrine resulting not just from political convictions. Notions of threats and the phobia of the nation state falling apart play an important part, too. In contrast, while the AKP government, which has an Islamic tradition, and its predecessors opposed membership in the EU for a long time, now it displays a clear intention and interest in continuing the reform process without interruptions. In concrete terms this is illustrated by a host of reform measures that have been adopted within a short time span. The position of the proponents and of the AKP government has certainly been strengthened by the positive recommendation the EU Commission expressed in its Progress Report of 6 October 2004.[1]

A liberalization of the doctrine of the traditionally homogenous conception of the state and nation seems to be most difficult. What does this doctrine boil down to? The Republic was supposed to become a modern nation state and was, therefore, linked to the Turkish nation. In accordance with the Zeitgeist, the nation was to be homogenous in terms of language, religion, culture and ethnicity. In other words, the strict concept of the nation state defines the Turkish nation as the sum of all its subjects, despite their ethnic origin, and thus negates the existence of ethnic, religious and language minorities and the protection of minorities (except Jews, Greeks and Armenians) in its legal foundation. This conception of the nation is based on the attempt after the collapse of the Ottoman Empire to establish a nationally and culturally homogenous unified state on the territory of the Turkish Republic, with the help of a new and integrating ideology, Turkish nationalism[2]. Any articulation of cultural differences was, and still is, perceived as a threat to cultural and national unity and rejected vehemently. Based on the Kemalist definition of the Turkish nation and the postulate derived from it that everybody is equal, any expression of an identity other than Turkish has been illegal and persecuted. The Kurdish population has been most affected by this. State, nation and culture are considered a unity[3] and protected conclusively by the Constitution. The principle of the indivisible unity of territory and nation which secures the rule of a centralist and unitarian state and its ideology forms the second component from which the Kemalist concept of the nation cannot be isolated. This unchangeable principle of the Constitution is infringed when minorities are given cultural autonomy, for instance, or rights to self-government. Fundamental rights and freedoms are curtailed in favour of this principle, which consistently crops up in many legal provisions and laws such as the Penal Code, the Anti-Terror Act and the Party Act.

It is still difficult to speak of a fundamental change in the traditional conception of state and nation as a result of the process of reform. The pivotal elements of the traditional conception are still protected by the Constitution, and thus the aforementioned principle of the indivisible unity of territory and nation can still be used to curb fundamental and civil rights, as it is not sharply defined. Its sphere of validity is indefinite and thus it still hangs over the entire system like a sword of Damocles. Below this level things are in motion; the claim to cultural, ethnic, religious and language homogeneity is losing its artificial substance. Nowadays, this heterogeneity is being admitted and decreed as a necessity. Yet, the reforms permit it only in the private sphere, no matter what the existing problems and hurdles are in putting these decrees into practice. What long-term effects this limited relaxing of the conception from homogeneity in the direction of heterogeneity will have for the persisting traditional foundations of nationalism remains to be seen. However, we can already say now that what has been experienced in everyday life will soon be normality and the process of change will be more and more irrevocable; those moves cannot be reversed. In the end, the adherence of the Kemalist elites to the traditional foundations means that the process of change or relaxation can only be furthered in line with them. In other words, the Turkish conception of nationalism takes good care that allowances are made for certain requirements and processes of transformation, without running the risk of losing or destroying the central elements and foundations.

This example from Turkey illustrates yet again that no ideology other than nationalism has managed to change time and again and still continue to exist.

*Can one speak of a change in the authoritarian internal power structure
in Turkey as well as the Kemalist conception of state, individual and
society in the face of the determining external and internal factors?*
While the central dogmatic and traditional elements in the conception of
nation and nationalism continue to exist, the foundations of the state tradition
continue to exist too. They are based on the imperial character of the Ottoman
Empire: the State is an independent body superior to society and politics. It is
sacrosanct. In today's political and social reality this conception is reflected in
the terms "*derin devlet*" (the profound State) and "*devlet baba*" (Father State).
While the former indicates the lack of definition of the omnipotent State (the
invisible yet omnipresent power apparatus) the latter expresses hopes for the
services it should render. The individual serves the State. In the Kemalist
Republic this idea of the State is embodied by the state apparatus, i.e. the top
echelons in the administration, judiciary and military. Since the State is not a
political instrument but rather politics serves the State, this conception of the
State is authoritarian – a notion which was not alien to other countries in
Europe till the early 20th century either.

In Turkey this has led to certain spheres of policy being regarded as "*Devlet
politikasi*" (State policy). Politically legitimized actors have been prevented
from implementing, entrusting it to the hands of the State apparatus. This
mainly applies to all aspects of the internal and external security of the
Republic. In public awareness these spheres are not primarily a domain for
legitimate political actors but rather tasks for the military (and bureaucrats in
the foreign ministry). As self-appointed guardians of Atatürk's Republic and
its principles, the military leadership claimed and still claims a say and rights
in all matters relevant to home and foreign affairs despite its lack of any parliamentary legitimization and responsibility. The acceptance of the military as
an independent and legitimate political actor in the political system goes back
to a founding myth of modern Turkey and also has other historical roots.

Now the prospect of joining the EU also has implications for the uncontrolled power of the military in the political system. Especially in the internal
dispute between proponents and adversaries of EU membership, the issue of
curbing the power the military enjoys has played a special part since this also
focuses on strengthening civilian politics. The reform of the National Security
Council provides for limiting its influence to that of an advisory body, putting
a civilian bureaucrat at its head and reducing its secretariat. Without a doubt
this move is important for strengthening the civilian authority, yet more efforts
are required to overcome the uncontrolled hegemony and domination of the
military in politics and society which has developed in the course of history.

Against the background of the defects in the political system just mentioned,
Turkish democracy must still be called a defective democracy. The liberal
democracy based on the rule of law which has mainly evolved in affluent
OECD countries is the yardstick for this assessment. The reforms under way are

important, though, for democratization and liberalization. But we cannot yet speak of a liberal democracy under the rule of law, especially because of the massive practical obstacles to their implementation. Furthermore, the political and social process of internalizing the spirit of the reforms is still in its infancy and will still require a considerable length of time.

On the Kurdish conflict – the acid test

In the context of the reforms ushered in, the pivotal issue is whether and to what degree they will bring about changes in the traditional Turkish policy towards the Kurds and lead to improvements in the Kurdish population's political and cultural rights.[4]

First we must note that the Accession Partnership papers do not directly refer to the Kurdish conflict. Neither the words "Kurdish/Kurd" nor "minority" are included. The Progress Reports speak of "cultural rights", " the cultural rights of the Kurds" and "minority" in general and "the situation in the South-East" in particular. This elaborate approach, avoiding calling a spade a spade and only indirectly referring to it, signals that the EU endeavors to take Turkish interests into consideration. The EU primarily regards the Kurdish conflict in Turkey in the light of general human rights and a democratization of the country. Accordingly, it does not call for measures aiming to grant group rights but rather for reforms implementing human rights and bringing about democratization. From the EU point of view, this includes granting individuals human and civil rights and also cultural rights, as well as improving the economic and social situation in the South-East.

Even though the Kurds are not explicitly mentioned in the accession partnership, it must be pointed out that the demands mentioned also apply to the situation of the Kurdish population.

It was, and continues to be, of pivotal importance to Ankara to avoid any explicit mention of the Kurds and the cultural and political rights to be granted to this group of the population. Ankara has managed to achieve this goal; nevertheless, the fulfilment of the Copenhagen political criterion for accession (regard for and protection of minorities) is the real acid test for decision-makers in Turkey.

From the Turkish perspective, it is necessary, in the first place, to keep the regulations in the adaptation measures concerning "regard for and protection of minorities" as restrictive as possible in order a) not to jeopardize the foundations of the conception of state and nation and b) not to recognize the cultural independence of the Kurds. Against the background of the perceived threat to the unity of the state, an institutional recognition could lead to separatist tendencies So the reforms should be set out in such a fashion that they cannot be read as a regulation specifically for the Kurds, ruling out the possibility of cultural independence for the Kurds as a group and making it considerably more difficult to implement individual rights. The extension of individual cultural rights, however, has implications for the situation of the

Kurdish people in Turkey. The focus in terms of cultural rights is mainly on the free use of the Kurdish language in education and the media. Reforms to this end now permit the broadcasting of programs in languages other than Turkish both by the state-run radio and TV station TRT, as well as private nation-wide radio and TV stations. Since June 2004 TRT has for the first time broadcast programmes in Bosnian, Arabic, Circassian and Kurdish (Kurmanji and Zaza). At the moment news headlines, documentary films, music and sports programs are put on the air. The new decree which allows private nation-wide radio and TV stations to broadcast in languages other than Turkish is still being interpreted rather restrictively since strict time limits are fixed: on TV the maximum is 4 hours a week or 45 minutes a day, on radio it is 5 hours a week or 60 minutes a day.

The condition for radio or TV programmes at local and regional levels is that a listener or viewer profile be established by the Higher TV and Radio Council RTüK. In addition, children's programs are still banned, and respect for the indivisible unity of the state still hangs over this granted freedom like a sword of Damocles. This principle often serves as a basis for suspending or withdrawing broadcasting licenses.[5]

One of the important results of the reform process is the lifting of the state of emergency in the South-East of the country. All in all, this step must be regarded positively. Nevertheless, it has not led to any improvement in the precarious situation of internally displaced persons. The EU Commission points this out in its Turkey Progress Report and stresses that serious efforts are necessary to solve the problems of the internally displaced persons, push ahead with the comprehensive socio-economic development of the region and generally further cultural rights.

The reforms now mean that parents can give their children the names they desire. The Kurds, too, can make use of this freedom. However, there are still problems with giving Kurdish names. Lawsuits are brought time and again about naming. In September 2003 a circular narrowed the terms and validity of this reform, outlawing the use of names with the letters q, w and x, which are used in Kurdish spelling.

The amendments to the Party Act, according to which banning parties has been made more difficult, have not resulted in any substantial improvements for pro-Kurdish parties. This is illustrated, amongst other things, by the fact that since the reform in March 2003 the pro-Kurdish HADEP has been banned on the basis of Section 169 of the Penal Code (support for a terrorist organization) and its 46 members have been barred from political activity for a period of five years. Moreover, proceedings have been started to outlaw DEHAP and HAK-PAR. Finally, it must be said that violence against members of pro-Kurdish parties is still the order of the day, as is illustrated by the case of two HADEP representatives who disappeared in 2001 after visiting the Silopi police station.

In July 2002 the Turkish parliament ratified the International Pact on Civil and Political Rights as well as the International Pact on Economic, Social and Cultural Rights. However, Ankara included a proviso expressing reservations about the right to education and minority rights. It says that the right of ethnic, religious and language minorities to exercise their own culture, their own religion and the use of their language will be based on the stipulations in the Turkish Constitution and the Treaty of Lausanne of 1923. Since Kurds are not acknowledged as a minority under the Treaty of Lausanne (unlike Armenians, Greeks and Jews), the Kurds are thus deprived of the political and cultural rights provided for in the international treaties agreements.

The following conclusions can be drawn about the implications of the reforms for the situation of the Kurdish population. Firstly, all in all the reforms have led to more individual and cultural freedoms, which the Kurds as individuals can make use of, as a rule. Especially because of the fundamental problems encountered in implementing the reforms, it is too early to call them historic in the context of policy towards the Kurds. Despite the reforms, the Turkish policy towards the Kurds is still full of contradictions. The treatment of the Kurdish language illustrates Ankara's efforts to prevent any official recognition of this language or of the political and cultural rights of the Kurds, and to render any progress towards furthering the reforms difficult by introducing complex regulations in laws and decrees. The contradictions show that Turkish policy on the Kurds still vacillates between traditional dogmatic rules and tendencies towards liberalization. They also reflect that there is still no consensus among the state establishment about a substantial change of the traditional policy towards the Kurds, which is mainly based on denial and repression.

Secondly, even if the reforms are put into place successfully, which is especially important for the situation of the Kurds, the fundamental question still remains whether or not the reforms (just like individual rights, but not group rights) are really adequate to meet the needs of the Kurdish population and, above all, take into consideration the deeply-rooted desire for autonomy among the Kurds which has developed over time and the historical and psychological dimensions of the conflict. A regulation of this conflict on the level of individuals alone leaves out the extraordinary importance of its dimensions. Regarding more extensive cultural and political autonomy for the Kurds as a group, based on both institutional recognition of Kurdish identity and political representation and integration, the reforms can only be called insufficient.

Thirdly, for the EU the general question arises whether it considers the conflict about political and cultural rights settled for good and is content with the result, in view of the reforms put in place so far, or whether it should make more effort towards achieving a better implementation of the political criterion formulated in general terms of "respect for and protection of minorities". For it is mainly due to the lack of definition of the Copenhagen criteria and the varying national practices within the EU concerning the protection of minorities that there is no objective way of measuring when this criterion for accession has been fulfilled. This leaves much room for interpretation. The definition of minimum standards and the decision whether or not they have been met hinge primarily, therefore, on political considerations. An objective assessment of the degree of fulfilment is possible neither from the EU's perspective nor from the Turkish one. This fact allows Turkish decision-makers much leeway in their interpretation and implementation of this criterion. The danger is that they may interpret and practise it rather restrictively in the spirit of the Kemalist doctrine of the homogenous conception of state and nation.

All in all, there is an urgent need for the EU to act to fill the lacuna and work towards a better implementation of this criterion for accession. One step towards this end is to set out to the candidates for accession in every detail and unambiguously how the criteria should be read and fulfilled. This applies to Turkey as to the other candidates. Aside from a number of clearly-defined demands, such as the abolition of the death penalty, the ratification of both UN Conventions or the lifting of the state of emergency, it remains unclear when, in fact, a situation tantamount to fulfilling the criterion of "respect for and protection of minorities" has been reached. Turkish decision-makers still face the great challenge of at last displaying the political willpower to break with the homogenous conception of state and nation in favour of a substantial and continuous democratization and liberalization of the country, so as to provide an appropriate settlement for the historically-rooted conflict over the political and cultural rights of the Kurdish population. To this end it is all the more important that both the EU and the Turkish decision-makers find a way of involving those directly affected, namely the Kurds, with all their interests and wishes, in this reform process, so as to achieve a European-Turkish consensus on the objectives of the political regulation of this still latent conflict and the ways and means to achieve it. So far no efforts have been made in this direction.

Quo vadis Turkey?

The prospect of joining the EU and the EU policy of setting conditions have had a unmistakably democratizing effect in Turkey. That is why this motor of democratization has to be kept going and constructive accompanying measures provided. An open society will depend on the degree to which the sprit of the reforms has been internalized. The more the set of democratic values has been understood politically and socially, the closer Turkey will get to the virtues of an open society. The two processes are interdependent. The reforms in this context are important as they aim to bring about a clear improvement in the democratic standards of Turkish politics and society, in the fields of democratic institutions, the rule of law, human rights and the protection of minorities. Only when the Kemalist doctrine of state, individual and society is interpreted in the light of democratic values or replaced by the image of a liberal democracy under the rule of law as the basis for actions in Turkish politics and society will the foundation of an open society have been laid. Too much emphasis on national Kemalist principles still prevails in the country's national education system and political culture. Generations has been "collectively" socialized on the basis of this set of values. Therefore, the demand to focus more on democratic values and principles in the Turkish educational system remains rather important. While abstract democratic values in society and politics meet with a considerable degree of approval, there are quite fundamental deviations at the level of implementation when it comes to the Kurdish conflict, homosexuality and the death penalty. It is all the more important that the current collective socialization based on dogmatic national values is replaced by a continuous collective socialization founded on a democratic set of values.

Instead of a summary, I want to stress that Turkey still vacillates between dogma and liberalization in the process of transformation. Even though this process has taken on dynamics of its own and can therefore hardly be turned back, the country's elites are still confronted with the major challenge of displaying the political will to break with the homogenous conception of state and nation in favour of substantial and continuous democratization and liberalization. This is indispensable if the defects in the political system are to be overcome and a collective socialization in society with democratic values is to be established. External constraints, such as the prospect of joining the EU in particular, will continue to play a pivotal role along with internal ones.

PART V

TURKEY IN MOTION: THE EU PERSPECTIVE

Chapter 16
Turkey's fragile EU perspectives since the 1960s

Eugene Krieger

In view of the controversy surrounding the current European debate[1] over Turkey, it is easy to forget how much disagreement already marked the 1959-1963 negotiations leading to Turkey's acceptance as an associate member of the European Economic Community (EEC). The basic difference is that the earlier discussion took place outside the public eye, in the ministries of the member states and in the bodies of the EEC. With the USSR making massive offers of aid at the time in an effort to disaffect Turkey from the Western camp, it was taboo within the EEC to voice fundamental criticism of Turkey in public.

A historical look at the earlier discussion is likely to help inject greater objectivity into the frequently emotional arguments being fielded in Europe today. I therefore propose to present the positions of the various protagonists in the former EEC on the question of Turkey's association with the organisation. I shall begin with the views of the supranational bodies of the organisation, the Commission and the European Parliament. The focus will then turn to the discussions in the Council of Ministers and with that to the opinions of the governments of the individual EEC countries. Given the complex, protracted nature of the decision-making process and the limited space available to me in the present context, I shall be concentrating primarily on Germany and France. Their two governments tended to represent opposing poles in the association talks, the other members states usually following one side or the other.

A difference of views within the EEC

Although its members came from the various EEC member states, the EEC Commission was eager for Turkey and Greece to become associated quickly. The political aspects of partnership with the two Aegean countries were far more important to them than any economic reservations about low standards of economic development, particularly in Turkey. Commission member Rey went to the heart of the matter when he emphasised that the EEC should not view differences between Greek or Turkish and European economic development as an insoluble problem. The Community had to remain open to all potential candidates for association and could not adopt overly stringent economic criteria for their linkage with the Common Market.[2] He regarded the successful conclusion of association talks with Greece and Turkey as a test of the EEC's oft-invoked readiness to take an active part in development aid for developing countries. His statements were manifestly prompted by the Commission's fears that, competing with the Communist camp for the favour of the developing nations, the EEC was in danger of isolating itself, which posed a potential political and economic threat to Western Europe. Consequently the Commission consistently urged the national delegates to the Council of Ministers to comply with the substance of Turkey's wishes with regard to EEC association.

The European Parliament, too, was unanimously for associating Turkey and Greece. The parliamentary records of the time make clear that only countries governed according to free and democratic principles were considered eligible for partnership with Europe. That is why, at the beginning of the Sixties, Turkey and Greece were the EEC's only potential southern European candidates for association, with the option of full membership later on. For, in contrast to the Communist Party dictatorships in Eastern Europe or the right-wing dictatorships in Spain and Portugal, the two Aegean states were governed on the incomparably superior basis of a parliamentary democracy, which the EEC was intent on reinforcing by way of economic support. At the time, Turkey's deficiencies with regard to human rights or the protection of minorities did not yet play a role in European perceptions.

This stance found support above all from the Adenauer government. West Germany made no secret of its conviction that, as the most important Middle Eastern bastion against Soviet expansionism, Turkey possessed enormous strategic importance to the West. The Bonn government viewed both West Germany and Turkey as peripheral countries in a precarious, endangered position on the frontier between NATO and the Warsaw Pact.

In the face of the Soviet threat, Adenauer felt West Germany and Turkey shared a common fate. Under-Secretary of Foreign Affairs Carstens, for his part, was not really counting on a direct military attack by the Soviet Union. Khruschev had spoken of a peaceful rivalry between the two blocs. This, in Carstens' view, concealed Moscow's goal of conducting the conflict with the West by way of infiltration and subversion. He considered the so-called "peaceful co-existence" of the two blocs as, in actual fact, a covert worldwide civil war in which moral resistance, ideological persuasion and economic potential were the decisive weapons.[3]

This standpoint was also shared by members of the opposition party. Thus in 1959 SPD Bundestag members in the Foreign Affairs Committee called for the introduction of a new Western Marshall Plan underwritten by the USA and the FRG. The hope was that coordinated financial aid for developing countries would prevent the almost 1 billion people in the Third World from turning to Communism.[4]

But in the view of the West German government, the major recipients of German aid were to be the developing countries currently engaged in negotiations with the EEC: Turkey and Greece. As Adenauer saw it, Turkey in particular was in no position to stand up to the Communist challenge on its own. He therefore wanted the West to help accelerate the industrialisation of its ally. A further point in favour of supporting Turkey was the fact that Ankara consistently championed Bonn's interests at the international level; Turkey had, for instance, advocated West Germany's admission to NATO and defended the West German government's stance on the question of a divided Germany.

It was against this background that, during the 1959-1963 association negotiations, the Adenauer government consistently endorsed the rapid affiliation of Turkey with the EEC on the most favourable terms possible for the country. Bonn received the strongest backing in this endeavour from the governments of the Benelux countries. In Adenauer's view, Turkish association with the EEC represented defence aid for another Western frontline state like itself, which should be prevented at all costs from being weakened.

Like the members of the European Commission, representatives of the West German government officially termed Turkey a European country that would, subsequent to associate membership, become a full member of the Community. On the other hand, certain unofficial West German government documents raise doubts in the present-day mind about whether this may merely have been opportunistic rhetoric. It is hard to shake off the impression that Bonn had, in actual fact, allocated to Turkey the role of a military province to be bought and maintained by the West – in which case emphasising Turkey's European identity would have been no more than a means of reinforcing Turkish loyalty to the West.[5]

Let us now turn to the European positions critical of Turkey during the association talks. Neither President de Gaulle nor his successor Georges Pompidou fundamentally denied Turkey's strategic importance to the West. But France was also intent on pursuing an independent security policy in Europe and the Mediterranean that would operate outside the NATO framework – an agenda that put considerable strain on relations between Paris and Washington. This was bound to impair France's relations with countries like Turkey, which entertained close military links to the USA. The minutes of meetings of the Council of Ministers and the committees attached to it therefore never find France advancing security arguments as a reason for Turkish association. The representatives of the French government consistently focused on the economic and financial problems of allowing Turkey to become a member of the EEC.

Italy, too, harboured serious economic reservations in this regard. Rome feared that Turkish agricultural exports would present competition for Italy's own Mediterranean produce in the Common Market. But it was above all the French government that reversed its stance on Turkish association several months after negotiations began. Initially, the French Foreign Ministry had hoped that Turkey would offer a new market for French exports, but serious doubts soon surfaced about Turkey's potential for economic development and whether, in view of its high budget deficit, the country could ever be put on a sound economic footing. The longer association negotiations went on, the less viable France considered Turkey, in comparison with Greece, as a prospective associated partner.

While Italy underpinned its critical stance towards Turkey with the purely self-serving rationale of agricultural protectionism, the representatives of the French government developed a wide-ranging and differentiated catalogue of critical arguments against Turkey under the immediate impression of the association talks. These arguments were often elaborated only in highly confidential French diplomatic documents and were never discussed during the meetings of the Council of Ministers. Nonetheless, they undoubtedly influenced the decision-making behaviour of the French government, which, together with Germany, had the strongest influence on the content of the agreement with Ankara.

As early as September 1959, there was talk in the French Ministry of Trade and Industry of the threat Turkish agricultural exports might pose to the French and above all the Algerian farming industry. France was therefore ready to approve the lowering of EEC customs barriers on Turkish exports only on condition that Ankara agreed henceforth to limit grain production.[6] France's strong misgivings made themselves particularly felt in the question of European financial aid for Turkey. The French authorities were highly disapproving of Turkey's efforts to obtain new bilateral economic development loans in the capitals of the EEC countries all the time. Having already been granted a $50 million loan by Italy in June 1959, Turkey had subsequently tried to repeat the same manoeuvre in Bonn. Soon, so the French government feared, Turkey would be submitting a corresponding request in Paris. A memorandum of the French Ministry of Trade and Industry dryly noted that Ankara viewed the EEC as a "Club of the Rich". It was therefore a consistent policy of the Turkish power elite to try again and again to obtain further loans from the European partner states, thereby pushing the national debt to irresponsibly high levels.[7]

France contended that this contravened the rules established in 1958 in the framework of the OEEC. In view of the catastrophic state of Turkish finances, North America and several EEC countries had decided to extend a $100 million development loan to Turkey. But the French felt that this had also been done to avoid further bilateral loans to Turkey. France was unwilling to offer Turkey any additional financial aid, especially since Greece, the other association partner, also needed financial aid and it was vital to keep the overall costs for the two partnerships in mind. Paris was reluctant to commit itself unreservedly to the American brief of stabilising the Aegean states: to do so would have made

France feel it was subordinating its own policies to Washington's security objectives in the eastern Mediterranean. In contrast to West Germany, which was willing to grant new supplemental bilateral loans to Turkey, the French Ministry of Trade and Industry demanded that the EEC also take into account the financial costs of further prospective association partnerships in North Africa. Behind this demand lay France's attempt to channel the financial strength of the EEC in the direction of its own interests. As a result of the Algerian War of Independence, the French claim to leadership in West Africa had become uncertain. With the help of the EEC, French influence in Africa was to be perpetuated, even after the end of the country's direct presence as a colonial power. But this plan would be undermined if the EEC concentrated its capacities for development aid too firmly on the Aegean. Thus one of France's key objectives in the association talks with Ankara was to restrict financial aid for Turkey to a minimum.

French criticism of Turkey grew when, at the end of 1959, it became clear that, despite the financial aid granted by the OEEC, the Turkish budgetary crisis was mounting, while at the same time the Menderes government was making ever more vocal appeals for further loans. At the beginning of December, the Turkish government requested an additional $200 million in annual financial aid from the EEC on top of the aid payments already being made by the OEEC.

At this point the French ambassador to Ankara, Henry Spitzmuller, pronounced the advocates of far-reaching development aid for Turkey — such as West Germany or the United States — to be boundlessly naive and unfamiliar with the Turkish "character". In a confidential letter to Foreign Minister Couve de Murville, he wrote: "C'était en effet mal connaître les dirigeants d'Ankara que de croire qu'ils ne chercheraient pas à tirer le maximum de profit d'un appui qui leur apparaissait tout naturel. Leur pays n'est-il pas la sentinelle avancée du monde libre dans une région endemiquement névralique? Ménage-t-on ses encouragements au soldat qui défend, bouclier en main, des centaines de kilomètres de frontières hostiles?"[8]

France felt that, in the context of the Cold War, the Turkish government was only too skilled in giving stereotype responses to the OEEC's hesitant reminders of the need for financial discipline and economic reform; Ankara knew only too well that, once the Western partner nations had taken the first step, there was no going back.

Whereas the practical constraints of the Cold War were prompting the Adenauer government to defend Turkey's Western orientation, Paris was trying to prevent the EEC from becoming an economic instrument of Washington and its foreign-policy interests. France therefore became even more irate when, at the end of 1959, West Germany's Minister of Economic Affairs, Ludwig Erhard, announced that Germany would be granting new loans to Turkey on top of the OEEC aid. France felt that this would inspire Turkey to come knocking on all of Europe's doors again, "car son appétit demeure solide".

Critical voices of this sort could be heard from France throughout the association talks. In a confidential note to the French Foreign Ministry, the various French ambassadors in Ankara described the Turkish elite as driven by self-serving financial motives and eager to exploit the Cold War situation. French diplomats implied that the Turkish government was not seriously interested in fundamentally reforming the budget and the ailing, largely state-owned manufacturing sector. Ankara, they felt, had realised only too well that Western Europe regarded Turkey's economic weakness as a threat to Western security and that, as a result, the EEC was ready to extend ever more aid. Particularly distasteful, from the French standpoint, was that the Turkish government seemed to view itself as so vital to both sides, and so courted by West and East, that it expected the EEC to buy its favour.

It was this abuse of European good will that France wanted to put a stop to. Consequently, during the negotiations the representatives of the French government consistently demanded that the EEC lower its customs barriers with Turkey only if Ankara was ready to reciprocate in kind. First Turkey would have to prove that it took the conditions of the EEC Treaty seriously by carrying out concrete economic reforms. The EEC took due account of the grave reservations of France (and Italy) by ultimately excluding automatic progress in the association process from the agreement. Any decisions concerning further steps could be taken only if the Association Council, composed of delegates of the member states and of Turkey, was in unanimous agreement. This gave individual countries like France the opportunity, from here on, to block or suspend the association process, should they so wish. Moreover, the French government openly announced that the burden of future financial aid to Turkey would be left largely to the Federal Republic of Germany and the USA.[9]

The French government's critical stance towards Turkey contrasted starkly with De Gaulle's warm approval of the association of Greece with the EEC. But to explain the reasons for France's far stronger objections to the association of Turkey as opposed to Greece, it is, in my opinion, not enough to cite arguments such as Franco-American tensions or French reservations about the underdeveloped Turkish economy. The confidential notes written by members of the French diplomatic service during the negotiations show that, in the view of the French Foreign Ministry, Turkey was culturally not a part of Europe. French observers regarded this as substantiated by the behaviour of their Turkish negotiation partners. The basic attitude imputed (by Ambassador Spitzmuller) to the Turkish government in financial questions was regarded as contradictory to European practices: "L'avidité des Turcs n'a d'égale que leur superbe." The interest of the Turks was limited to the quest for new sources of money; on all other subjects, the Turkish negotiators were inadequately prepared.[10]

The French point of view on Turkey was summarised by French ambassador Michel Huré in 1962, when he wrote: "Géographiquement et ethniquement asiate, tout au moins pour une bonne part, séculairement musulmane, enlisée dans des traditions qui remontent au régime tribal, engourdie dans l'analphabétisme de ses masses, la Turquie se veut, depuis Atatürk, occidentale, laïque et, désormais, authentiquement démocratique."[11] Turkey, so it was felt, expected some sort of consecration from Brussels in its bid for acceptance into this exclusive club of nations, and regarded the complex contents of the Treaty of Rome and other modalities of accession as entirely secondary — particularly as, given the country's totally divergent cultural background, Turkish diplomats often did not understand them in the first place.

These sources prove that France already had cultural reservations about Turkey at the start of association talks, though they were not yet expressed openly

The official positions of the EEC in conjunction with the signing of the Ankara Treaty of 1963

What remains to be asked is in how far the divergent standpoints of the member states were voiced in the official statements of the EEC representatives. The speeches of the representatives of the EEC at the signing ceremony of the Treaty of Association in Ankara on 12 September 1963 are particularly instructive in this regard. Joseph Luns, President of the EEC Council of Ministers and Foreign Minister of the Netherlands, played down the differences between the member states. He did, however, acknowledge French scepticism about Turkey's development potential by demanding thoroughgoing economic reforms.[12] In view of French insistence on the reciprocal lowering of customs barriers, Luns also emphasised that Turkey must fully accept the basic principles of the Treaty of Rome.

Otherwise, the speech was clearly dominated by the need to present the Treaty of Association as evidence that Turkey was part of the "free world" and (Western) Europe. Luns's remarks largely reflected the security-motivated aim, in the face of the Communist challenge, of wanting to keep a country like Turkey firmly allied with the West.

The conclusion of the Treaty of Association with Ankara was represented as the start of an irreversible process leading to Turkey's full membership in the European Common Market. Luns, like Walter Hallstein, President of the Commission,[13] referred to the later accession of Turkey to the Community as the ultimate goal of Turkish association. And yet, Article 28 of the Association Treaty only envisaged the "possibility" of examining the potential admission of Turkey at a later phase of association. Evidently the presidents of the Commission and the Council of Ministers were intent on arousing the impression that the Community was unanimously in favour of working towards Turkey's full membership. But this clearly contradicted the actual situation in the EEC. In the global competition with the Eastern bloc for the favour of the

developing world, Turkey's association with the Community was to demonstrate the openness and good will of the EEC to other countries wishing to
become associated.

In their speeches, Luns and Hallstein tried to posit a clear EEC foreign policy trajectory. The high expectations this awakened on the Turkish side have
retained their effect to the present day. In view of the grave reservations already
privately harboured by a number of EEC governments at the time, there was
some risk involved in Luns and Hallstein's awakening these hopes. If disagreement about Turkey within the EEC ever became public, the EEC would
lose credibility. It was therefore as a clear sign to Europe's "Turkey sceptics"
that Luns closed his speech with the urgent message with which I should like to
conclude the present paper: "The identity of Europe is based on its diversity. It
was with the intention of preserving this diversity that the European integration movement was born and must continue. Europe's aura and influence
would be weakened if our unification process ceased to take this diversity into
account. After the Treaty of Rome and the Treaty of Athens, the Treaty of
Ankara testifies to the profound changes taking place on our continent. Today
I welcome the new state that will join us in our endeavours."

Chapter 17
The non-Muslim minorities
and reform in Turkey

Gabriel Goltz

Since 2002 Turkey has undergone a very intensive process of reform. Driven by
the will to start membership negotiations with the European Union (EU), the
country, especially under the government of the Justice and Development Party
(AKP), has sped from one reform to another. Although there are undoubtedly
shortcomings in the implementation of them, these reforms have created a climate in Turkey that allows a more controversial discussion of the country's
future political shape, which will reflect the plural character of its society.

Still, especially in the bureaucracy a strongly nationalist, unitarian concept
of society, which denies the existence of different ethnic or religious groups,
continues to prevail. While the widespread understanding of the term "Turkish
society" does not include the non-Muslim communities which are predominantly seen as "local foreigners with Turkish citizenship";[1] Kurds and Alevis,
for their part, have been integrated into the "Turkish-Sunni" majority, their
Kurdish or Alevi identity for long denied.

Hampered by the prevailing implicit, and sometimes explicit, mistrust of
these "local foreigners", the reforms concerning the non-Muslim communities
have consisted so far of piecemeal changes in existing laws or regulations with
limited positive effects on the communities' lives. Nevertheless, the liberalization of the social and political environment through the ongoing reform
process, as well as the rising interest in these questions within the EU, give the
non-Muslim communities a better opportunity of applying pressure to achieve
further improvements – provided that Turkey does not veer from its reforming
course.

The present article does not aim at enumerating the problems non-Muslim
communities suffer from in Turkey one by one. Rather, it will glance at significant reforms concerning recognised non-Muslim minorities[2] which have been
carried out up to now and discuss their limited character. Further it will bring
out parameters of Turkish policy towards minorities which still prevents a comprehensive reform in this sphere. However, the reform process has not yet come
to an end. Thus a final evaluation of it cannot yet be presented. Instead, a final

paragraph will hint at agents of change who might push Turkey towards a (more) "post-national", plural society.

Limited Reforms

Only a few of the non-Muslim communities' demands have been addressed during the EU adaptation process in Turkey since 2002. The "congregational foundations" (*cemaat vakıfları*) of the recognised non-Muslim minorities have been mainly concerned by the legal reforms, specifically their right to purchase real estate and dispose of it, together with an option, limited in time, to (re-) register real estate that already belongs *de facto* to them but had been under threat of seizure, especially since a decision of the Turkish Supreme Court of Appeal in 1974.[3] In addition a regulation concerning the procedures and principles in the elections of executive boards of congregational foundations has been issued.[4] Last but not least the building law has been reformed by replacing the term "mosque" by "place of worship". Through this change, churches and synagogues have gained de jure the same status as mosques as far as the allocation of public real estate to those who want to build a place of worship is concerned or the provision of water and electricity free of charge.[5] On the administrative level, the Higher Council for Minorities, which met in secret, whose membership was secret and whose decisions were binding, is said to have been dissolved at the beginning of 2004[6].

Other areas, such as the selective official recognition of non-Muslim communities as minorities according to the Lausanne Treaty of 1923, the absence of a legal status for the patriarchates and the rabbinate of the recognised minorities, the impossibility of opening institutions of higher education for the clergy and religious officials, the compulsory presence of vice-Directors "of Turkish origin" (*türk asıllı*) in minority schools[7] – to mention only a few – have not been addressed yet in any reform project, and nor has the fact that recognised non-Muslim minorities do not receive a share of public funds earmarked for religious services.[8]

On the other hand, even the reforms which have been implemented concerning the congregational foundations have only had a limited effect. The regulation covering the (re-) registration of the foundations' real estate leaves out the properties seized by the state in the past. Moreover, a great number of applications for the registration of real estate that already belongs to the foundations nominally have been send back because of "documents lacking" or have been rejected.[9]

Although congregational foundations have been granted the right to purchase real estate, a foundation itself can still be seized, because the Directorate General of Foundations retains the right under certain circumstances to take over the administration of congregational foundations and turn them into *mazbut vakıflar* (sequestrated foundations which are administered directly by the Directorate General of Foundations)[10] Despite all the reforms, the decision in the case against the foundation which administers the former Armenian

Theological College, Surp Haç Tibrevank (Holy Cross Priests' Seminary), is still pending.[11] Moreover, the Directorate General of Foundations is still struggling to take over the Greek Orthodox orphanage on the island of Büyükada.[12]

Among the circumstances from which the Directorate General of Foundations derives its legally defined right to take over the administration of congregational foundations are irregularities in the boards of these foundations, for example if the board of a foundation has not been or could not be elected in the time foreseen by the law. But, because of the decrease in numbers of non-Muslims especially in Turkey's eastern provinces and some districts of Istanbul, the condition to hold an election could not be fulfilled, for voters as well as candidates have to be registered in the district where the foundation is located. This problem has been dealt with in the above-mentioned regulation of June 2004 concerning the procedures and principles in the election of executive boards of congregational foundations. However, it has not solved the problem entirely. The electoral territory may be extended but only up to the neighbouring district and only following approval by the Directorate General. Nevertheless, the situation has improved, for the number of board members needed for foundations located in districts where only a very limited number of non-Muslims live has been reduced by this regulation.[13]

One of the reasons why only a limited improvement could be recorded on the ground has been the reluctance of an incrusted bureaucracy to implement the reforms. This is certainly true, but as Etyen Mahçupyan of the Turkish think-tank TESEV points out, causes for failure are already to be found in the reform laws and the law-making process itself.[14] Besides the fact that the relevant administrative authorities responsible for applying the laws – in the case of foundations the Directorate General of Foundations – are usually reluctant to do so, the laws themselves are formulated in vague terms and leave the bureaucracy far-reaching powers of discretion in many areas. Instead of formulating concrete rights which could then be claimed, almost every new right which is granted is made dependant on approval by the relevant state authority, which empowers the bureaucracy to interfere in the internal affairs of the minority groups.

Here are three examples. The law and regulation on the right of congregational foundations to purchase real estate leaves the Directorate General of Foundations the power to decide whether the foundation needs the property or not. If not, the act of purchase will not be approved. Even though the foundations are given the right to use real estate for aims other than religious ones, the criterion of "need" which the Directorate General has to decide upon is not defined.[15]

Secondly, as mentioned above, according to the regulation for the elections of foundations' boards the election territory may be extended into the neighbouring district – but again only following approval of the Directorate General, without defining the grounds on which approval will be decided.[16]

A rejected draft regulation on the election and duties of the Armenian Apostolic Patriarch in Istanbul may serve as a last example. Opposing the liberal draft regulation, the Ministry of the Interior insisted upon the responsi-bility of the Council of Ministers, in the sense that the Patriarch to be elected must have the support and trust of the Turkish state and the necessary abilities and education to fulfil the duties of his office. In case the Armenian Apostolic community elects the "wrong" Patriarch, the state has the power to interfere and prevent him being enthroned, as was tried during the election of the present Patriarch.[17]

The publishing of a draft of a bill on foundations, issued by the Prime Minister's office in October 2004[18] and the following resistance of the Directorate General of Foundations and the responsible state minister Mehmet Ali Şahin to introduce amendments asked for by the European Commission, the Turkish Foreign Ministry, the Turkish Secretariat General for the European Union and civil society organisations shows once again the deeply rooted unease and reluctance of the Turkish bureaucracy to loose its hold on the society in general and the non-Muslim communities and its organisations in particular. The process up to the publishing of the draft bill had triggered hope because of the involvement of civil society and representatives of non-Muslim minorities in its making. However the draft bill once published caused disappointment for most of the demands had not been taken into account. Thus, the Director General of Foundations, Yusuf Beyazıt, had refused any demand for restitution or compensation to be given to the congregational foundations for formerly sequestrated real estate while the Directorate General of Foundation continued selling sequestrated real estate to third persons. After the European Commission and representatives of the EU member states had expressed serious concerns, state minister Mehmet Ali Şahin reacted angrily: "Whenever they speak of freedom of religion, real estate comes to their mind." He too excluded any accommodation in the question of compensation or restitution on the side of the Directorate General but proposed an amendment abolishing the right of the Directorate General to take over self administered congregational foundations (*mülhak vakıflar*) in order to administrate them directly (*mazbut vakıflar*). This alone would be an important improvement. Still, one has to wait and see how far these proposals for amendment will be taken into consideration when the bill is drawn up.[19]

The Treaty of Lausanne versus an open society

The limited scope of the reforms carried out so far and the slow withdrawal of the state, which only reluctantly cedes its control over society in general and non-Muslim minorities in particular, show how heavily two internal parameters of the Turkish policy towards minorities, Turkish nationalism and the state principle of laicism[20], still weigh.

Nationalism, with its religious (Sunni) and ethnic (Turkish) connotation, resulted in the Turkish policy of homogenising the society. With non-Muslim

minorities being located outside Turkish society and thus seen as local foreigners or else a potential danger, former policy towards them aimed at aggra-
vating their situation. After the "deportation policy" (tehcir), as it was officially called, the deportation and the mass murder of Armenian and Syrian
Orthodox Christians during the First World War and the Greco-Turkish population exchange (mübadele), other measures such as special taxes (varlık vergisi) in the 40s, pogroms in the 50s and 60s, the seizure of the property of congregational foundations from the 70s on and the restrictions in admitting children to minority schools have been an outcome of this policy towards the
minorities, resulting in a steady decrease in their numbers together with those
of their churches, schools, and foundations. The widespread denial and neglect
of the cultural heritage of these minorities are only a further facet of this long-
term policy of homogenization.[21]

With regard to the principle of laicism as the second internal parameter of
the Turkish policy towards minorities, one has first to consider the understanding of laicism in Turkey. It does not mean the separation of the state and
the majority religion, Islam. Edging religion and its symbols out of the public
sphere, the Turkish notion of laicism also implies a tight control of Islam,
achieved by "nationalising" it through state institutions such as the Presidency
of Religious Affairs, the Ministry of Education, and the Directorate General of
Foundations – all this after Islamic institutions were stripped of their power
during the first period of the Turkish Republic.[22]

Just as the Turkish state has established control over the Islamic institutions,
it disputes the rights of non-Muslim religious communities to exist as
autonomous institutions independent of the state. Thus, foundations or
schools of non-Muslim minorities are subjected to tight state control. The closing down of institutions of higher education such as Surp Haç or the
Seminary at Halki is to be seen in this context. In line with this policy, the
Turkish state refuses the non-Muslim communities a legal status as religious
communities. Hence the Greek Orthodox and Armenian Apostolic
Patriarchates do not enjoy the status of legal entities. Not being nationalised
through state institutions as Islam is, they continue to exist in a legal grey area.
Every demand of the non-Muslim communities to be granted a legal status as
communities or the right to open autonomous institutes of religious higher
education is refused by the Turkish authorities on the grounds that it would
run counter to the principle of laicism. If the majority religion, Islam, does not
dispose of this freedom why should minorities enjoy it, the laicism argument
runs. Another facet of the refusal of legal status is the concern that Muslim
communities could derive for themselves rights to independent and
autonomous institutions, on analogy with the rights to be granted to non-
Muslims.

As mentioned above, the status and rights of non-Muslim minorities are laid
down in the Treaty of Lausanne which is still valid in Turkish law. However,

Turkey grants minority status only to certain non-Muslim communities and, with regard to these recognised minorities, it does not fully grant the rights laid down in the treaty. In this connection, what role may this Treaty play in the future discussion on minority rights in Turkey?

The fact is that for 80 years the legal reality in Turkey has ignored important elements of the Treaty of Lausanne. Thus, the treaty might be used as an argument in order to improve the situation of non-Muslim communities but it seems unlikely this argument will be successful. Moreover, the Treaty of Lausanne should be understood not only as a source of rights for non-Muslim communities but from another perspective as well – as a document codifying the nation-building process in Turkey which had begun in the 19th century. In the Turkish Republic non-Muslims were henceforth minorities, vis-à-vis the *millet-i hâkime*, the ruling (Muslim) nation. As a result of a long process of rising nationalisms and nation-building in Turkey, non-Muslims ceased to be an authentic part of Turkey's social fabric, in the eyes of the Turkish majority, becoming instead an external element attached to Turkish society by an international treaty.[23] How negatively connotated the term "minority" (*azınlık*) is, is shown in the present debate, in which Kurds and Alevis reject this designation and call themselves part of the majority, an "original and constitutive element of the Turkish Republic"[24]. Another aspect of the discussion about the Treaty of Lausanne is raised by secular citizens of "non-Muslim origin" in Turkey. Some prefer to derive their rights (language, schools etc.) from membership not of a religious community but of an ethnic one.

For these reasons, the Treaty of Lausanne seems not to be a means to achieve a plural society in Turkey. Nonetheless it can still be used as an argument in order to improve the situation of the non-Muslim communities. But, as mentioned above, it is not likely to be an effective tool, in view of the dominant interpretation of it and long-standing legal practice in Turkey.

On the other hand, the Turkish state itself is now on the defensive, because of its former inefficiency, economical and political crises, and corruption. The state's withdrawal from areas of society and a lessening of its tight control over the social sphere could have positive effects for the non-Muslim communities.[25] In this process Turkey's integration into the European Union plays an important role. Seen as an external anchor of stability, it may permit the state to withdraw from areas it is accustomed to control. At the same time the European Court of Human Rights (ECHR) is a powerful tool to strengthen the citizens' position vis-à-vis the state. Turkey, as signatory to the European Convention on Human Rights, accepts the ECHR rulings, hence legal practice in Turkey will be increasingly linked to supranational law and institutions.[26]

Seeds of Change Towards Post-Nationalism
One has to admit that in a variety of areas that could not be mentioned in the present article Turkey has undergone considerable changes up to now. Especially in the legal sphere one reform after the other has been introduced.

At the same time, it is not surprising that the widespread understanding of non-Muslim minorities as local foreigners and a potential danger, which is deeply rooted in the collective memory, will not vanish with a few changes in laws and regulations. In addition, every step the ruling conservative pro-Islamic party AKP takes in the direction of widening religious freedoms (including for Muslims) is interpreted by the Kemalist elite as proof of its supposed hidden agenda to undermine the principle of laicism. Thus, especially in this field, far-reaching changes are not very likely in the short term.

However, the reforms to adapt to the EU in recent years have created circumstances which allow a more open debate on sensitive issues and even taboos, bringing fresh air into the closed world of official doctrines that have long weighed upon society.

After the legal reforms, the judiciary is considered to play a crucial role in the transformation process. The before mentioned decision by the Supreme Administrative Court (danıştay) on the equal status of mosques, synagogues and churches and its rejection of the Directorate General of Foundations' taking-over of the foundation which administers the Greek Orthodox orphanage on the island of Büyükada[27] are an important turning point for rights of minorities have been – so far successfully – defended against the state bureaucracy. Moreover, the same court overruled a decision of the Turkish media watchdog RTÜK which had fined a Christian missionary radio accusing it of destroying the Turkish unity by "Christian propaganda". In contrast, the 7th chamber of the Supreme Administrative Court decided – among others on the grounds of the European Convention on Human Rights – that missionary activities are subject to religious freedom as well as freedom of opinion and of expression. Being send back to a local court, the case is still pending.[28]

The growing interest in studying the history and culture of non-Muslims in Turkey may be seen as a grass root starting point for undermining the unitarian concept of society prevailing in Turkey. Institutions such as the History Foundation (Tarih Vakfı), the Turkish Foundation of Social and Economic Studies (TESEV), publishing houses like İletişim, Aras, Belge or the newly founded Birzamanlar, private universities such as Sabancı University, activities connected with human rights initiatives, for example the Commission against Racism and Discrimination of the Human Rights Association may be the first seeds of a changing understanding of society and its history. Civil initiatives like History for Peace, which was partly co-ordinated by the Helsinki Citizens Association, or the Human Rights in Textbooks project of the History Foundation are examples of civic actions which aim not only at changing the content of present school curricula but also at developing a different style of education in order to raise a critical and open-minded new generation.

As far as public opinion is concerned, in September 2004 the Human Rights Advisory Council of the Prime Minister's Office, a consultative body made up of NGO representatives, published a report on minorities in Turkey challenging the dominant Turkish position. This report, although non-binding, caused violent reactions not only among state representatives and politicians but also in wide sections of the media and society. Even though the Council has been changed in the aftermath, after having its official quality denied, for the first time a post-nationalist understanding of society and minority had moved from the edges of academic research into the very centre of political debate. Nonetheless the debate in its aftermath showed how deeply rooted unitarian, nationalist worldviews in Turkey still are.

Chapter 18
National identity, asylum and immigration: the EU as a vehicle of post-national transformation in Turkey

Kemal Kirişci[1]

Turkey is going through a massive political transformation. Undoubtedly, the desire to join the European Union is an important, even if not the sole, factor behind this transformation. Does this transformation amount to a "post-nationalization" of Turkey? This is a difficult and very complex question to answer. It is true that in the specialist literature Turkey has been recognized for a long time as a country whose elite has emphasized and nurtured a homogenous national identity that left no or very little room for ethnic and religious diversity.[2]

It was so that long ago that Kurds were considered to be "mountain Turks", and the public use of Kurdish or other ethnic languages was not permitted. Furthermore, Turkey was immersed in a political culture that mistrusted the international community, in particular Europe and the United States.[3] There was a constant concern about maintaining Turkey's territorial integrity and national sovereignty. This left little room for international cooperation, let alone engaging in a regional integration project of the kind evolving in Europe.

Yet, in the course of the last few years Turkey has embarked on a series of political reforms that have culminated in the EU decision to open accession talks with Turkey in October 2005.[4] I would submit that the EU would have not reached such a decision had Turkey not manifested elements of a post-national state. The European Union, with its shared sovereignty and multi-layered decision-making process, is often referred to as a post-Westphalian, post-national entity.[5] The expectation that candidate countries meet the Copenhagen criteria before qualifying for membership can be seen as a kind of initiation process to become post-national. The member governments, the EU's own institutions and to a large extent the European public await and expect this. Clearly, it would be difficult to reduce the "post-national" qualities of the EU to a black-and-white picture. Furthermore, it would be possible also to argue that one can talk about different degrees of "post-nationalization" within the EU and across the EU. Yet, I assume that the more the EU has become supra-national in a certain policy area, and the more EU member countries advocate common values over national interest and national identity, the more the EU can be said to be post-national.

One particular policy area where states have traditionally been very jealous to protect their sovereignty has been immigration. They have been very strict in controlling who can and cannot enter the country. Looking at a country's immigration policy can also reveal a lot about that country's attitude towards its own national identity. After all, "who you let into the country very much determines who you are". Countries such as Australia, Canada and United States have traditionally defined themselves as countries of immigration. Their policies over the decades have evolved considerably. This evolution has tended to reflect the manner in which they have defined their own national identity. There was a time when these countries' policies encouraged only white European immigration. However, at least for the last four decades they have become much more multi-cultural and adopted policies encouraging diversity in respect to immigration. Germany and Israel, on the other hand, are examples of two countries that have traditionally restricted immigration into the country to a specific group of people. Germany, until very recently, refused to consider itself to be an immigration country. In spite of millions of "guest workers" coming and settling in Germany, the authorities were very reluctant to support or encourage their integration into mainstream society. Policies were based on the idea and expectation that these people would actually one day return to their countries of origin. Instead Germany accepted and very quickly granted citizenship to immigrants of German descent. Israel in that sense very much resembles Germany, as it permits the immigration and settlement of Jews alone. Israel's immigration policy is very closely tied up with its national identity as a Jewish state.[6]

Traditionally, Turkey has been known as a country of emigration. What is less well known is that Turkey, like its predecessor the Ottoman Empire, has also long been a country of immigration and asylum. From 1923 to 1997, more than 1.6 million people formally immigrated to Turkey and well over half a million refugees have sought asylum of one form and another in Turkey since the Second World War. I would argue that one way of testing whether Turkey is now really becoming "post-national" is to examine its asylum and immigration policies. Who Turkish authorities have actually let into the country with the intention of settling in Turkey and whom they have discouraged from entering or from staying on permanently would reveal a lot about how the authorities have defined Turkish national identity. In turn, the manner in which these policies are or are not evolving would make it possible to address the question whether Turkey is "post-nationalizing" or not.

Traditionally, Turkey's immigration policy has resembled very much those of Germany and Israel.[7] Turkish policy once encouraged and allowed the arrival and settlement of immigrants who were defined as of "Turkish descent and culture". The overwhelming proportion of immigrants came from the Balkans. They were Turks, in the sense that they spoke Turkish, or else they were members of Muslim communities closely associated with the Ottoman Empire such as Albanians, Bosnians, Circassians, Pomaks and Tatars. On the other hand the majority of refugees who were not of "Turkish descent or culture" that entered Turkey individually or en masse were given only temporary asylum and subsequently were either resettled in third countries or repatriated. Only a tiny proportion of them actually remained in Turkey. Currently, Turkey's policies are probably short of qualifying as post-national, but they are becoming more post-national then they once were. Some of the policies related to immigration have already been changed. The EU has played an important role in this, even if there is still a long way to go. At the same time the reality on the ground is changing. "Foreigners" are appearing in Turkey increasingly, from the Central Asian and Slav suit-case trader to the African street peddler, from the Armenian or Moldavian nanny to the Russian sex-worker, from the illegal Afghan, Iranian and Pakistani migrants in transit to expatriate professionals and European pensioners, from an increasing number of foreign students, sportspersons and artists to foreign brides and grooms. The social reality surrounding Turkish society is changing. Naturally, government at national and local level as well as the public itself is being forced to adjust. This is occurring at a time that Turkey is discovering its own diversity both ethnically and religiously. However, does all this amount to a "post-nationalization" of Turkey?

The argument I am going to propose is that the more Turkish policies resemble EU policies, the more we can talk about a "post-nationalization" of Turkey. However, a word of caution must also be sounded. First, EU "common" asylum and immigration policies remain controversial, are resisted in many countries and are far from perfect in terms of being post-national. Yet, the EU also manifests elements of "post-nationalization" in the area of asylum and immigration that can indeed be used as a bench mark against which it might be possible to assess Turkey's performance.[8] Second, it would be wrong to ascribe the transformation that Turkey is going through solely to the European Union. Some of it is also a function of the sheer weight of a world that is changing, even if undoubtedly the prospect of EU membership is a very important inducement to transformation and reform.

This paper is divided into four sections. First, I will offer a brief general description of the evolving EU common asylum and immigration policy. Second, the paper will demonstrate the nature of traditional or old immigration into Turkey and its relationship to efforts to develop a homogenous Turkish national identity. The third section will describe briefly the nature of new immigration into Turkey and the government's efforts to respond to this new form of immigration, followed by a section that examines the role of the EU in the "post-nationalization" of Turkish policies as well as the limits to "post-nationalization". Finally, I will argue that the emergence of new immigration and the EU's influence is actually having an impact on state behaviour towards and societal perception of the given Turkish national identity. In conclusion I will argue that recent Turkish asylum and immigration policies and the manner in which they are evolving suggest a certain degree of "post-nationalization" of the Turkish state.

European common asylum and immigration policy

European integration has come a long way since its inception back in 1952. The adoption of the Treaty on the European Union in 1991 has opened the way for policy areas well beyond economic issues to be moved eventually into the realm of some form of supra-nationalism and hence become post-national. Issues concerning who can and cannot enter the territory of a state remain jealously guarded, even in the EU. Nevertheless, the effective implementation of free movement of people within a borderless EU has induced member countries to recognize the need to communitarize immigration and asylum policies. The Amsterdam Treaty of 1997 commits EU members to adopting common policies in these areas by 2004. This commitment was reiterated at the Tampere meeting of EU governments in 1999. In this context, the Schengen Agreement that entered into force in 1995 has become part of the EU acquis and hence common law for thirteen of the fifteen current member states. The Agreement ensures the implementation of a borderless Europe and adopts a common visa policy for third-country nationals. The European Commission has been authorized to issue a number of binding directives on, for example, reception centres for asylum-seekers and illegal migrants, standards for family reunification and residence rights of third-country nationals. Although the EU may still seem a long way from introducing a fully-fledged common immigration policy, the basic outlines and norms that would govern such a common policy seems to be pretty clear.[9]

The emerging common EU asylum policy is intended to respect the 1951 Geneva Convention Relating to the Status of Refugees and will develop a common definition of a "refugee".[10] The policy already defines common principles for the reception of asylum-seekers and is working towards harmonizing status determination as well as the economic and social rights granted to asylum-seekers. Current common policy also includes the Dublin Convention of 1990, which identifies the duty of the country of first asylum within the EU to perform status determination. This is, however, accompanied by an expectation that burdens will be shared among member countries with respect to the cost of implementing this Convention and particularly with respect to the integration of recognized refugees. Common policy also requires that asylum-seekers whose cases are rejected have access to an effective appeal procedure. Many EU governments are also implementing the practice of defining "safe" countries of origin. This is a list of countries whose nationals are considered to be safe from persecution. Asylum applications from such countries are either considered to be manifestly unfounded or else are put through an accelerated status determination procedure. Furthermore, some EU governments also implement the practice of "safe countries of first asylum" outside the EU territory. In this case asylum-seekers are returned to such countries through which they have transited. There are also countries that have been implementing policies hindering the ability of asylum-seekers to reach them to seek asylum. Such practices include carrier sanctions, that is, the practice of fining airlines that carry potentially undocumented passengers or passengers without a proper visa to enter the country of destination. These are controversial practices that attract criticisms from refugee advocacy groups and appear to fall short of constituting a basis for the emerging common policy currently being developed by the European Commission.

No European Union country considers itself an immigration country like Australia, Canada or the United States. Yet, in practice large numbers of immigrants enter and live in the EU. Each member country has its own specific immigration policies. The details of these policies vary from country to country significantly. Nevertheless, there is an effort to develop a common EU policy. The common immigration policy is still a long way from being adopted. However, a number of common basic principles are emerging. One of them is the right of an immigrant to acquire permanent residence status after fulfilling a predetermined reasonable number of years of residence. This is in contrast to the practice which keeps the immigrant in uncertainty about the future, not to mention the inconvenience of each year dealing with the bureaucracy of yearly renewals. Another emerging important right is that of family reunification. Some progress has already been achieved with respect to adopting broad principles guiding family reunification. Another principle is the right for permanent residents to enjoy similar privileges concerning free movement, employment, social security and rights of residence as EU nationals do. Some progress has also been achieved in this respect. Certain countries also grant immigrants political rights, such as the right to participate at least in local elections and government. Most importantly there is a shared view within the EU that a common immigration policy should be non-discriminatory. In other words, an immigration policy is needed that does not discriminate in favour of one or other group on the basis of ethnic origin, race or religion.

The last principle is particularly important because Germany's traditional immigration policy, in a manner very similar to the Turkish one, favoured the immigration and integration of people of German ethnic origin. After the end of the Second World War and the onset of the Cold War West Germany adopted legislation encouraging the immigration of Germans from East Germany and the Soviet Bloc, particularly Romania and the Soviet Union. These people were known as the *Aussiedler*, descendents of German settlers. In contrast to the Aussiedler, the millions of "guest workers" that came and settled in West Germany were never really seen as immigrants. Hence little effort was made to integrate them. The absence of efforts at integration had dire consequences socially and politically, engendering resentment especially among immigrants who failed to integrate and certain sections of German society. It is only after the arrival in power of the Social Democrats under Gerhard Schröder in 1999 that the German government became more willing to recognize the existing reality and correct the bias in favour of German descendents in existing legislation and immigration policies. The new legislation makes it more difficult for the *Aussiedler* to immigrate to Germany and introduces measures to facilitate the integration of current immigrants by making the acquisition of German citizenship easier then was in the past. The new legislation has clearly been influenced, among other factors, by the norms on which the EU wishes to base the development of its 'common' immigration policy.

There are many who argue that European immigration and asylum policies are increasingly aiming to keep asylum-seekers and immigrants out of Europe. They argue that Europe is trying to create a Fortress Europe. The rise of right-wing anti-immigrant movements has played an important role in this. Yet, on the other hand, it is also possible to argue that the EU is moving towards a policy that is based on the rule of law, equality, multi-culturalism and civic norms rather than ethnically driven considerations. Furthermore, increasing priority is given to opening the way for immigrants to participate in politics and enjoy the right to vote and be elected to office, at least at the local level of government. Even if this 'common' policy is still far from having been adopted, and considerable governmental resistance continues to exist to the ideas and policy recommendations developed by the European Commission, the direction appears to be one that is moving away from a nationally-based narrowly defined policy.

Turkish national identity construction and traditional immigration policy[11]

In the case of immigration into Turkey it is possible to talk of a major difference between traditional or old immigration and more recent immigration. Traditional immigration into Turkey typically consisted of immigration from primarily Balkan countries and was governed by legislation and practices that very much reflected the nation-state building concerns of the Founding Fathers of the Turkish Republic. Exclusive priority was given to encouraging and accepting immigrants who were either Muslim Turkish speakers to start with or were considered by the officials to be people belonging to ethnic groups that would easily melt into a Turkish identity.[12] This is very much a reflection of the way the definition of Turkish national identity evolved and the manner in which this influenced or was mirrored in immigration policy.

The Founding Fathers of the Turkish Republic had envisaged a typically civic definition of citizenship and national identity. This was reflected in a conspicuous manner in the 1924 Constitution of Turkey. According to Article 88 of this Constitution, all citizens of Turkey, irrespective of their religious or ethnic affiliations, were defined as "Turks". However, the practice, especially from the late 1920s onwards, developed very differently. Concerns about the territorial and political unity of the country in the face of Kurdish rebellions and Islamic fundamentalist uprisings against secularism played an important role in deviating from this civic understanding of national identity to one emphasizing homogeneity and "Turkishness". The identifying features of "Turkishness" were not solely Turkish ethnicity but the ability and willingness to adopt the Turkish language and membership of Sunni Muslim ethnic groups closely associated with past Ottoman rule. Hence, Bosnians, Circassians, Pomaks, Tatars and so on were definitely included in this definition while Gagauz Turks, who are Christian, and members of other Christian minorities, Alevis and unassimilated Kurds were excluded. Initially, Albanians were also excluded on the grounds that they had too strong a sense of nationhood. However, subsequently many immigrated to Turkey and assimilated into "Turkishness". Furthermore, the international context of the time, which strongly emphasized national homogeneity and unity practically all over Europe, influenced the Turkish elite too.

This definition of national identity was clearly reflected in Turkey's immigration, settlement and, for example, employment legislation. The major piece of legislation governing immigration into Turkey is the Law on Settlement (No. 2510) of 1934. In a most conspicuous manner the Law limits the right to immigrate to Turkey only to people of "Turkish descent and culture". Similarly, Turkish laws from the same period traditionally severely restricted employment opportunities for non-nationals, while positively discriminating in favour of non-nationals of "Turkish descent and culture". The Law on the Specific Employment Conditions of Turkish Citizens in Turkey (No. 2007) of 1932 reserved certain jobs and professions for Turkish citizens. Furthermore, the practice that developed in the 1930s and 1940s was one that closed some of these professions, not to mention public sector professions such as employment with the security forces and the judiciary, to Turkish citizens belonging to non-Muslim minorities.[13]

This practice of giving priority and privileges to people considered to be of "Turkish" ethnicity survived well into recent times. As late as 1981, the then military government introduced a law (No. 2527) enabling foreigners of Turkish descent facilitated access to employment in Turkey, including jobs in the public sector usually reserved for Turkish citizens. Law 2007 from 1932 was rescinded only when the new Law on Work Permits for Foreigners (No. 4817) was adopted in February 2003.

Traditional immigration also included refugee movements into Turkey. The overwhelming majority of these refugees came from the Soviet Bloc during the Cold War. During that period, in close cooperation with United Nations High Commissioner for Refugees (UNHCR), Turkey received refugees from the Communist Bloc countries in Europe, including the Soviet Union. Such refugees, during their stay in Turkey, enjoyed all the rights provided for in the

1951 Geneva Convention. However, only a very small number were allowed to stay on in Turkey, often as a result of marriages with Turkish nationals. The others were resettled out of Turkey. Turkey also experienced mass influxes of refugees in 1952, 1988, 1989 and 1991. The influxes in 1952 and 1989 involved Turks and Pomaks from Bulgaria. They were generally permitted to stay and settle in Turkey. On both occasions the government adopted special policies to facilitate their integration into mainstream Turkish society. In contrast the 1988 and 1991 influxes involved primarily Kurdish refugees. Here Turkish policy was characterized by a preference for repatriation and/or resettlement; these two mass influxes were very much seen as potential threats to national security. In the latter case Turkey embarked on an energetic effort to convince the international community to create a "safe haven" in northern Iraq to ensure the speedy return of the refugees. In the case of the estimated 20-25,000 Bosnian Muslim refugees that came to Turkey between 1992 and 1995, a generous policy of temporary asylum was introduced that gave these refugees access to education, employment and health care, falling just short of proper integration. An overwhelming majority of these refugees subsequently returned home. A similar policy was also adopted for the approximately 17,000 Kosovar refugees from the crisis in 1999.

The state's preferred national identity definition is also reflected in respect to asylum policies. According to Law 2510 only asylum-seekers of "Turkish descent and culture" can acquire a fully-fledged refugee status with the ultimate possibility of settling in Turkey. This is also reflected in the manner in which Turkey has adhered to the central international legal instrument on refugees, the 1951 Geneva Convention. Turkey was among a group of countries who took an active role in the production of a definition of the term "refugee" and was among those countries who pushed for the introduction of a geographical and time limitation to the Convention as expressed in Article 1.B(1)(a). Accordingly, Turkey accepted to be bound by the terms of the Convention only for refugees fleeing persecution in Europe as a result of events prior to 1951. In 1967, when signing the 1967 Additional Protocol relating to the Status of Refugees, Turkey accepted to abolish the time-limit but chose to continue to maintain the geographical limitation.

This geographical limitation has been a central characteristic of Turkey's asylum policies. This in practice has meant that Turkey is under no legal obligation to grant refugee status to asylum-seekers coming from outside Europe. It has, however, allowed the UNHCR to receive asylum applications from such persons as long as these persons are resettled outside Turkey if recognized as refugees. In this way a form of temporary asylum is granted. On the other hand, as mentioned earlier, refugees from European countries have been expected not to remain in Turkey or integrate either. Here too considerations of national identity have played an important role besides factors such as economic and social ones.

New immigration and responding to the sheer weight of reality

More recent or "new" immigration into Turkey is a product of roughly the last two decades and over the last few years it has become much more conspicuous.[14] It has become complex because only a very tiny portion of it involves immigrants of the traditional kind. Legal immigration from the Balkans, for example, has dropped to a trickle. If anything there is an interesting trend in which a growing number of refugees and immigrants from Bulgaria are returning to seek their Bulgarian citizenship. The democratization and liberalization or for that matter the "post-nationalization" of Bulgaria over the last decade or so has helped to improve the status of the Turkish minority in the country. This is attracting immigrants and refugees back. Bulgaria's pending accession to the European Union constitutes an additional motivation for this trend. Furthermore, there are also a small number of former refugees from Western Thrace that are seeking to reacquire their Greek citizenship as Greco-Turkish relations improve. Against this, there are also an increasing number of Albanians, Bosnians, Chechens, Pomaks, Azeris, Turkmens, and other Turkic people that in the past could have enjoyed immigrant status but are now being allowed to stay in the country only in a gray twilight zone between legality and illegality.

Another group of immigrants who benefit from a relatively liberal visa policy are the nationals of Armenia, Georgia, Romania, Ukraine, the Russian Federation and Iran.[15] Among these people there are those that enter the country as tourists but engage in economically lucrative activities ranging from petty trade to domestic work and prostitution and often overstay the duration of their visa. Furthermore, there are also immigrants that enter the country illegally. Some of these illegal migrants seek employment and stay in Turkey, while an important proportion of them try to cross the country in an attempt to reach western Europe. It is very difficult to estimate the numbers of illegal immigrants in Turkey. However, figures ranging from one million to 150,000 are often cited.[16] To these groups one must also add trafficked persons, particularly women. These are persons that have either been coerced or deceived into traveling to Turkey for prostitution purposes and remain in Turkey against their wish. Furthermore, there are also an increasing number of nationals of EU member states and their spouses engaged in professional activities who settle in Turkey, particularly in Istanbul, as well as retired people in some of the Mediterranean resorts. This too constitutes a relatively new phenomenon in terms of immigration into Turkey; the numbers involved are estimated to be around 100,000 to 120,000.[17]

Lastly, there are the asylum-seekers and refugees increasingly coming from countries of Africa, Asia and the Middle East. This pattern began to emerge in the early 1980s. The change of regime in Iran and instability in the Middle East as well as Africa and South-East Asia has led to an increase in the number of asylum-seekers in Turkey. For a long time the government allowed the UNHCR considerable leeway, on condition that these asylum-seekers would be recognized and resettled outside Turkey. However, the growth in the number of illegal entries into Turkey and of rejected asylum-seekers stranded in Turkey led the government to tighten its policy. This led to an increase in the number of deportations and attracted criticism from refugee advocacy and human rights circles. Subsequently, the UNHCR in close cooperation with Turkey succeeded in developing a new system of asylum procedures that today handles approximately 4,000 to 4,500 asylum applications a year. Refugees continue to be resettled outside Turkey.[18]

These immigration- and asylum-related policies of Turkey are under pressure to be reformed. The sheer volume of immigration into Turkey, coupled with the challenges and problems that it poses, is partly creating this pressure. Officials are faced with having to address and find solutions to these problems. Often the solutions require the need to go beyond well-established practices and policies. A case in point is the way in which for example local authorities in Antalya and Alanya have been adopting policies that try to address the needs and complaints of European pensioners. Their efforts have included facilitated services for obtaining residence permits, granting the right to establish churches and also to issue work permits for priests – a practice that is hardly conceivable without some degree of "post-nationalization". Perhaps an even more telling example of "post-nationalization" is the decision of the Ministry of the Interior and the Gendarmerie, traditionally two very conservative institutions in Turkey, to seek to cooperate with a non-governmental organization (NGO) to address the problems associated with the trafficking of women.

Officials from the Ministry of the Interior, subsequently joined by the Gendarmerie, were able to make arrangements in September 2003 with an NGO, the Human Resources Development Foundation (İnsan Kaynaklarını Geliştirme Vakfı , HRDF) and the Directorate General of the Status of Woman to provide social assistance to victims of trafficking until their return to their countries of origin could be arranged. This development in itself is indicative of the transformation that Turkey is going through and constitutes an example of the close cooperation developing between the bureaucracy and civil society in Turkey. During the NATO summit in June 2004, a major additional breakthrough was achieved when, in the presence of the US Secretary of State Colin Powell, a protocol was signed between the municipality of Istanbul and the HRDF. This protocol improves the protection to be offered to women victims of trafficking. The HRDF also set up a mechanism enabling it to receive instant information about trafficked women apprehended by the police. The police, together with the HRDF, cooperate closely with the authorities and NGOs of the countries of origin of trafficked women to ensure them safe repatriation. The HRDF has held a conference in September 2004 on combating trafficking in women, with the participation of officials and representatives of NGOs from a number of Balkan countries. Furthermore, the Ministry of the Interior has also instituted the practice of granting humanitarian residence permits of up to six months for victims of trafficking.

Another example comes from the area of asylum. The Turkish government had earned a notorious reputation for violating the principle of *non-refoulement* (i.e. not sending asylum-seekers or refugees back to their country of origin or to a situation where they may face death, torture or degrading treatment). Many Western governments and human rights as well as refugee advocacy groups criticized Turkey bitterly for this in the mid-1990s. Often, the Turkish authorities would not allow these organizations access either to themselves or to Turkey. Today, government agencies cooperate very closely with Turkish as well as foreign non-governmental organizations and international organizations such as the UNHCR. This cooperation has even involved an organization such as the International Catholic Migration Commission running training seminars for the Turkish police on asylum law. A few years ago it would have been unthinkable for the Turkish Police actually to acquiesce in a programme run by an NGO, let alone an international one bearing a religious name. In December 2004 the UNHCR organized a major consultation meeting on Turkish asylum policies, with a large number of Turkish NGOs and government agencies taking part. The meeting actually involved an open debate and discussion over a pending Turkish asylum law. Until a few years ago it would have been unthinkable for non-governmental organizations to quiz and question an official vigorously on an issue regarded as sensitive for the national interest and security. Lastly, and most fascinatingly in the context of the European Commission's twinning projects, some foreign government officials share offices at the Turkish Police Headquarters in Ankara, preparing projects aiming to help Turkey harmonize its laws with those of the EU.

Turkish society is becoming accustomed to living with foreigners as well as with Turks who would not easily fit into the traditional narrow definition of a Turk. Sports are an area where this manifests itself most conspicuously. Currently, there are a large number of foreigners active and visible in various branches of sport in Turkey. They include Turks who are clearly of foreign descent. Turkish society is becoming accustomed to seeing names in the national teams that are not obviously classic Turkish ones. The most prominent of such names is naturally Elvan Abeylegesse. She is the women's world record holder of the 5000 meters event and represented Turkey at the Olympic Games in Athens. She is of Ethiopian origin and after she broke the world record there was actually a debate in the media about her "Turkishness". Interestingly, many commentators and members of the public defended her "Turkishness" against those who argued she was not a real Turk. When, during the Olympics, she did not perform as well as she was expected to, an outpouring of support for her came from the public. Similarly, the public has been quite happy with the fact that the Turkish national volleyball team that ran a very successful European championship competition in 2004 included a Russian, Nathalie Hanikoğlu.

The national Olympic Teams in 2004 and 2000 included a number of athletes with names that traditionally would not be associated with "Turkishness".[19] I would argue that these developments themselves are also a reflection of a society that is evolving beyond the traditional definition of Turkish national identity.[20]

The European Union, the "post-nationalization" of Turkish immigration policy and its limits.

Turkey's aspiration to become a member of the EU is undoubtedly one of the most important factors behind the changes that are taking place in relation to the redefinition of national identity in general and the reconsideration of immigration policies. A major turning point was achieved at the Helsinki European Council in December 1999 when the EU extended applicant status to Turkey. Subsequently, the EU issued an Accession Partnership document which detailed the reforms to be adopted to meet the Copenhagen political criteria, enabling accession talks to start, and the legal harmonization needed to ensure eventual membership. Among the long list of elements are some which fall within the domain of the justice and home affairs pillar of the EU. They include measures pertaining to immigration and asylum. In turn Turkey issued its initial National Program for the Adoption of the Acquis in March 2001. Since then, the Turkish government has introduced a long series of reforms. Some of them have had a profound impact on the state's approach to national identity. In this respect the most important reform has been the one that makes it possible to broadcast and to receive education in native languages other than Turkish. This is a critical development in terms of graduating from an understanding of a national identity that emphasizes homogeneity to one that acknowledges Turkey's cultural and ethnic diversity.

Even though in a limited manner, some of these reforms have also touched upon issues related to immigration. Legislation that opens the way for some improvements, particularly in the area of employment and settlement procedures for foreign nationals, including asylum-seekers, has been put into place. Legislation has also been passed to improve combating illegal migration and the problem of trafficking in human beings. A commitment has been made to lift the geographical limitation with respect to the implementation of the 1951 Geneva Convention.

The cooperation with respect to improving Turkey's asylum procedures and preparing the country to develop a fully-fledged capacity for status determination has already been mentioned. It would be difficult to account for all these developments without recognizing that a certain change in "hearts and minds" has occurred in the state apparatus and among bureaucrats. This, I would argue, is also a manifestation of an understanding of national identity that is evolving from emphasizing homogeneity to recognizing diversity. Furthermore, it is also a manifestation of a state of mind that is much less suspicious of the outside world and of constant foreign plots to weaken Turkey's unity and homogeneity. These can be seen as manifestations of "post-nationalization". But clearly there is still a long way to go.[21]

Turkish practice is still far from meeting the minimum standards that the EU is in the process of adopting in these areas. The Turkish asylum system has improved significantly over the last few years.[22] Most importantly, all administrative decisions concerning asylum decisions have been open to judicial review since 1997. These court rulings have been supportive of the rights of asylum-seekers and have severely restricted the government's ability to carry out deportation orders in violation of the principle of *non-refoulement*. (This is the principle that prohibits governments to send back a recognized refugee or an asylum seeker back to his country of origin without hearing the case and concluding it.) Although in this respect Turkish practice is now much closer to the European one, the most critical deviation remains the geographical limitation to the application of the Geneva Convention. EU *acquis* require every member to have in place the capacity to carry out their own status determination procedures and also to be able to integrate those asylum-seekers that are recognized as refugees and remain in the country. All candidate countries have had to go through these adjustments and develop the capacity to implement the 1951 Geneva Convention in full.[23]

Turkey is required to make these adjustments before membership. Such an adjustment, however, would mean a major departure from a well-established practice. Yet the government, both in the *National Program for the Adoption of the Acquis* of 2001 as well as the updated one from July 2003, is committed to lifting the geographical limitation as long as the right conditions are put into place.[24] These include the development of an institutional capacity to manage and receive asylum-seekers and perform status determination. In this regard, a draft asylum law is in preparation, even if it may only be in its very early stages.

However, the unwritten issue with respect to the lifting of the geographical limitation hinges on the EU's credibility in the eyes of Turkish officials. Their greatest nightmare scenario is one in which they would find themselves lifting the geographical limitation without Turkey's membership being taken seriously by the EU. Many Turkish officials, as well as a large proportion of public opinion, do not trust the EU and do not believe that it is serious about Turkey's membership.[25] Therefore it is unlikely that Turkey will take any concrete steps to lift the geographical limitation until it is convinced that the EU actually means business. Many officials would consider the opening accession negotiations or the fixing of a clear date as an important confidence building measure. This is one major reason why the draft law on asylum is still pending.

A second critical issue in this respect is burden-sharing. Turkish officials are concerned that Turkey, because of its geographical location, risks becoming a buffer zone or a dumping ground for the EU's unwanted asylum-seekers and refugees. Hence, in this case it will expect reliable burden-sharing measures to be put into place. One such measure will be based on the expectation that EU member countries continue to accept refugees for resettlement from Turkey. This will be particularly critical at a time when Turkish officials perceive a tendency in Europe in the direction of creating a Fortress Europe, in other words a Europe that tries to complicate access to the EU for asylum-seekers, if not deny it to them. This creates a major credibility problem. Many Turkish officials fail to understand why they are expected to raise standards and introduce more generous policies when Europe itself is closing its doors.

The EU also expects Turkey to develop a capacity to house asylum-seekers in reception centres. The practice so far in Turkey has been to assign asylum-seekers whose dossiers are being processed to satellite cities. In these cities asylum-seekers and their families live by their own means and on their own, rather than being housed in a camp. Refugee advocacy groups consider this system to be more humane than one based on reception centres. The development of an administrative capacity to process application as well as to provide social services and humanitarian assistance will also constitute a major financial challenge. The EU's willingness and ability to extend financial assistance to Turkey will be a critical factor. The EU's image in this regard is a very poor one as it has failed to meet many of its financial obligations towards Turkey. Hence, inadvertently the EU is also slowing down reform prospects in this area that would help to readjust Turkey's current asylum policy from one emphasizing national security and identity concerns to one stressing civic and international legal standards.

Traditionally, Turkish migrants have benefited extensively from family reunification program in EU countries. Since legal labor migration to Europe stopped in the 1970s this has been the only legal way outside the asylum path for Turkish nationals to enter and settle in EU countries such as Germany. Immigration into Turkey through family reunification has occurred through the existing immigration procedures based on the Law on Settlement, restricting immigration to people of "Turkish descent and culture". Nevertheless, in the early 1990s in an attempt to prevent the immigration of Bulgarian Turks from Bulgaria the authorities refused to allow family reunification.

At the time there were numerous heartbreaking stories of families being broken up. Though this situation has drastically changed since then, Turkey currently does not have provisions for family reunification in relation to the new immigration trends. This will be an area requiring the development of new legislation and a new outlook on immigration. It will also require the introduction of a completely new approach to who can immigrate to Turkey. In other words, the country will have to overhaul completely its Turkish-centred approach to one that will be more "civic-driven". This would meet European-type standards of immigration regulations and allow individuals and families wanting to establish themselves in Turkey the opportunity to have their applications processed.

An area where Turkish practice is at considerable variance from the emerging common European policy is immigration. The Settlement Law of 1934 that discriminates in favour of immigrants of "Turkish descent or culture" is still in force. Since 1996, consecutive parliamentary sessions have considered a new draft law to replace the existing one. However, this draft, although it offers an improvement in other respects, continues to maintain its discriminatory character and does not permit people who are not of "Turkish descent or culture" to immigrate to Turkey. Currently, this draft law appears to be dormant, while some parliamentarians are increasingly aware of its incompatibility with EU practice. Furthermore, Turkey does not have the practice of granting permanent residence, while the notion of non-nationals enjoying political rights is not even an issue of debate. Yet, interestingly during the March 2004 local elections, an English resident of the city of Marmaris, popular with European pensioners, complained during an interview on one of the radio stations that he was a tax-payer but was not allowed to vote in the local elections. Just recently, the possibility of acquiring a five-yearly residence permit was introduced for some foreign nationals working in Turkey. Previously, these permits needed to be renewed on a yearly or two-yearly basis. There has also been an improvement in respect to the procedures for obtaining work permits in Turkey, with the adoption of new legislation for foreign workers early in 2003.

Illegal or irregular migration into and particularly through Turkey has increased significantly over the last few years. There are no statistics about the numbers involved. Turkey has come under tremendous pressure to tighten control and sign readmission agreements with EU countries as well as with countries of origin. As the EU tightens its regular immigration and asylum policies third-country nationals from poor Third World countries have been increasingly resorting to illegal migration. A lucrative business in smuggling illegal migrants into Europe has sprung up. This is one area where Turkey has introduced new measures, including the introduction of articles to the Turkish Penal Code making human smuggling and trafficking serious crimes. In this way Turkish legislation has been aligned to international standards determined by the UN Convention against Transnational Organized Crime and its two additional Protocols, including the Protocol to Prevent, Suppress and Punish Trafficking. Increased control and cooperation with EU countries have already culminated in a drop in the number of illegal migrants arrested in Turkey as well as in the numbers of ships captured carrying illegal migrants.[26]

Conclusion

Turkey's handling of traditional or old immigration was closely related to the Turkish state's conception and understanding of Turkish national identity. The laws and the practice with respect to who could immigrate to Turkey were such as to exclude those identities that were deemed by the state unlikely to assimilate or melt into a homogenous Turkish identity. While large numbers of Albanians, Bosnians, Circassians, Pomaks, Tatars, Turks and so on, mostly from the Balkans, were encouraged to immigrate to Turkey, individuals belonging to non-Sunni Muslim minorities, ranging from Armenians and Assyrians to Greek and Jews as well as Kurds found themselves emigrating to Germany and Europe sometimes as "guest workers" and sometimes as asylum-seekers and immigrants. New immigration has a very different composition. Many individuals from neighbouring countries are increasingly entering Turkey sometimes for short-term and sometimes for long term stays. Many are illegally present in the country. There are also large numbers of individuals from distant countries of the Third World crossing Turkey, while some either get stranded there or choose to stay on there. Their presence more often than not is illegal. Some of these individuals are asylum-seekers. Turkey grants them only temporary asylum until the UNHCR can resettle the recognized refugees to third countries, while those whose applications are rejected are either deported or join the ranks of the illegal immigrants. There are also a growing number of foreign nationals, many from EU member states, who are settling in Turkey for employment, retirement and other reasons. The rights of such immigrants are much more limited than what their counterparts enjoy in EU countries.

The Turkish state's position with respect to this new immigration is deeply marked by its conception of Turkish national identity. Yet, the tremendous pace of transformation that the country is going through, especially in relation to efforts to meet the Copenhagen Criteria and harmonize its legislation with the EU *acquis*, are bringing about significant changes in the state's conceptualization of Turkish national identity as well as in its asylum and immigration policies. In these two areas it is possible to talk about policies and approaches that, I would argue, amount to a degree of "post-nationalization". The elements of this "post-nationalization" are evident in the manner in which Turkish officials are much more willing to cooperate with Turkish and foreign NGOs, Western governments, the European Commission and other international organizations, in particular the UNHCR. Furthermore, there is also an effort on the government's part to bring its policies closer to those of the EU. This is most conspicuous in the case of the decision eventually to lift the geographical limitation to the 1951 Geneva Convention. The Turkish public itself is also becoming much more accustomed to an ethnically and culturally diverse society that includes identities that may not easily be associated with a traditional definition of "Turkishness".

Does all this amount to a post-national Turkey? A categorical answer is difficult to give. However, I would argue that the evidence seems to suggest that Turkey is becoming much more post-national especially when one examines its asylum and immigration policies. Naturally, if one looks at where the EU stands on these issues, Turkey still has some distance to go. Yet, can one say that the EU itself or its member countries are actually post-national? Compared to the past, European integration has certainly evolved, and in the area of asylum and immigration the EU is becoming more post-national as common policies are adopted. In turn EU governments that are having to implement these common policies can be said to be more post-national than they once were. A case in point is Germany. Germany was notorious for its restrictive immigration policies, especially in terms of access to citizenship and political rights. This has now changed. In that sense, one can say that Germany is finally leaving behind its Bismarckian definition of national identity.

Lastly, when debating "post-nationalization" in the context of asylum and immigration it should also be noted that these are areas where many European governments face domestic constituencies that are constantly challenging the virtues of diversity and multi-culturalism. Hence, I would suggest that when discussing the question of whether Turkey is becoming post-national or not, it might be useful to bear in mind that identities are constantly being renegotiated and that the EU benchmark which was taken as a reference point to assess where Turkey stands may be slipping backwards. Even if the EU itself may be a post-national institution, not all of its members may in fact live up to a predetermined post-national set of qualities. In that sense if Turkey's transformation is maintained it might just be possible that we may encounter a country that is much more post-national than quite a few current members of the European Union, especially with respect to asylum and immigration.

Notes

Introduction

1 *Yurdcular Yasası. İsviç re'de Cenevre şehrine yakın Petit-Lancy Köyünde Pension Racine'de kurulan İkinci Yurdcular Derneği'nin muzakerat ve mukerreratı,* Istanbul: Yeni Turan Matbaası, 1914, pp. 69-70. For detailed information on Switzerland as the European centre of the Turkist movement see my book *Vorkämpfer der 'Neuen Türkei'. Revolutionäre Bildungseliten am Genfersee (1868–1939)*, Zürich: Chronos, 2005.

2 *Gazi Mustafa Kemal Atatürk, Atatürk'ün Söylev ve Demeç leri*, Atatürk Kültür Dil ve Tarih Yüksek Kurumu, Ankara, 1997, Vol. II, p. 130. Cited in the chapter by Rifat Bali in this volume.

3 See the chapter by Kemal Kirişçi in this book.

4 Atay, Falih Rıfkı, *Mustafa Kemal Mütareke Defteri*, Istanbul: Sel yay., 1955, p. 67, cited in Gülbeyaz, Halil, *Mustafa Kemal Atatürk: vom Staatsgründer zum Mythos*, Berlin: Parthas, 2003, p. 228.

5 See e.g. the photo on one of the first pages of Halide Edib's book *Turkey faces West. A Turkish view of recent changes and their origin*, New Haven: Yale University Press, 1930.

6 *Azınlık Hakları Raporu* of the Commission for Minorities and Cultural Rights (Azınlıklar ve Kültürel Haklar Komisyonu). This commission is dependent on the Prime Ministry's Consultative Committe for Human Rights (Başbakanlık İnsan Hakları Danışma Kurulu); cf. "Avrupa yolunda komik bir kavga" in the Turkish daily *Radikal*, 20 October 2004; "Cumhuriyetimiz tek soya indirgenemez", *Milliyet*, 1 November 2004. There have been many more articles in the Turkish press on this topic, particularly in October and November 2004.

7 A bad example in this respect is Switzerland where, nevertheless, on 14-16 October 2004 the congress was held where most of the contributions in this book were first presented (cf. http://www.hist.net/kieser/bso4).

Chapter 1 (pp. 3-19) – M. Şükrü Hanioğlu
Turkism and the Young Turks, 1889-1908

1 David Kushner, *The Rise of Turkish Nationalism, 1876-1908* (London: Frank Cass, 1977). A Turkish translation appeared two years later, see idem, *Türk Milliyetçiliğinin Doğuşu, 1876-1908* (Istanbul: Kervan Yayınları, 1979).

2 *American Historical Review*, 101/5 (December 1996), p. 1589.

3 See my note in *American Historical Review*, 102/4 (October 1997), pp. 1301-2, and Kemal H. Karpat, *The Politicization of Islam: Reconstructing Identity, State, Faith, and Community in the Late Ottoman State* (New York: Oxford University Press, 2001), p. 474.

4 The official Turkish history textbook for high schools prepared by members of the

Turkish Grand National Assembly and other experts in 1931 contains the following comment regarding Turkism during the reign of Abdülhamid II and in the Second Constitutional Period: "Since Abdülhamid dreamed of uniting the Muslims, he loathed those who spoke about Turkism or Turks even in a literary or scientific sense, let alone those who made any political references. The Committee of Union and Progress started paying attention to Turkism because of the crushing Balkan defeat, because of the fact that Armenian committees with which the Committee had forged an alliance in the past made radical demands and resorted to arms, and because of the national struggles of Muslim nations such as Albanians, Arabs, and Kurds." See *Tarih III: Yeni ve Yakın Zamanlarda Osmanlı-Türk Tarihi* (Istanbul: Devlet Matbaası, 1931), p. 146.

5 Ed[ouard] Engelhardt, *La Turquie et le Tanzimat ou histoire des réformes dans l'empire Ottoman depuis 1826 jusqu'à nos jours* 1 (Paris: A. Cotillon, 1882), p. 33.

6 Roderic H. Davison, *Reform in the Ottoman Empire, 1856-1876* (Princeton: Princeton University Press, 1963), pp. 130-31.

7 *The Memoirs of Ismail Kemal Bey*, ed. Somerville Story (London: Constable, 1920), p. 12.

8 "Zabelezhvaniia vŭrkhu proektŭt za uchilishtata na Midkhat Pasha," *Turtsiia*, nos. 32-33 [March 3-10, 1866], pp. [1-2].

9 P. Baudin, "The Jews and the New Council of State," *The Levant Herald*, August 17, 1876. A decade later in 1885, 99 out of the 22,934 Jewish males (0.44 per cent) living in Istanbul were in state service. This ratio may be considered average for a non-Muslim community as compared to 0.38 for Greeks and 0.58 for Armenians. (See Esther Benbassa and Aron Rodrique, *Sephardi Jewry: A History of the Judeo-Spanish Community, 14th-20th Centuries* [Berkeley: University of California Press, 2000], p. 71). The Jewish complaint, however, centered on the lack of any Jews holding high-ranking offices.

10 Mahmud Celâleddin, *Mir'at-ı Hakikat*, 1 (Istanbul: Matbaa-i Osmaniye, 1326 [1908]), p. 190.

11 See, for example, Ahmed Midhat, "Parlâmentolar," *Tercüman-ı Hakikat*, May 1, 1896.

12 [İshak Sükûtî], "Arnavudlar ve Kürdler," *Osmanlı*, no. 51 (January 1, 1900), p. 1. See also "İttihad Kuvvetdir," *Hak*, no. 7 (December 8, 1899), p. 3.

13 See the first appeal of the CUP distributed in the capital in early October 1895. Başbakanlık Osmanlı Arşivi, Y. PRK. ASK. 107/11 (1313.R.14).

14 Undated [1896?] report prepared by the CUP branch in Egypt, Arkivi Qendror Shtetëror (Tirana) [hereafter AQSh], F.19/60//233/15.

15 Undated [1896] report prepared by the CUP Syrian branch AQSh, F. 19/60//238/621.

16 Dr Mekkeli Sabri to Dr Abdullah Cevdet, Le Mans, June 27, 1931, Private Papers of Abdullah Cevdet.

17 Ahmed Rıza "Mukaddime," *Meşveret*, no. 1 [December 1, 1895], p. 1. In fact, this was nothing other than the repetition of the motto inscribed under the masthead of a popular Ottoman newspaper, *İkdam*, which had started its publication in July 1894.

18 "Bir Arnavud Mektubuna Cevab," *Osmanlı*, no. 76 (January 15, 1901), p. 8.

19 Tunalı Hilmi, *Peşte'de Reşit Efendi İle* ([Geneva], 1317 [1899]), p. 96.

20 M.A., "Osmanlı İttihadı," *Meşveret*, no. 5 [February 1, 1896], p. 1.

21 "Ne Gerek Başına Ligue Var Olsun Türklük," *Şûra-yı Ümmet*, no. 116 (July 15, 1907), pp. 4-5.

22 Dr Bahaeddin [Şakir]'s letter to the Caucasian Muslims, beginning "Aziz Kardaşlarımız" and dated Paris, September 22, 1906/no. 74, *Osmanlı İttihad ve Terakki Cemiyeti Merkezi'nin 1906-1907 Senelerinin Muhaberat Kopyası* (hereafter *Muhaberat Kopyası*), Atatürk Library (Istanbul), Belediye Yazma, Ms. O. 30, ff. 115-6.

23 "Kafkasya'dan Mektub," *Şûra-yı Ümmet*, no. 103 (November 1, 1906), pp. 3-4.

24 See, for instance, Dr Bahaeddin [Şakir]'s letter beginning "Muhterem Din Karındaşlarımız" and dated [Paris], January 3, 1907 [1908]/no. 469, *İttihad ve Terakki Cemiyeti'nin 15 Teşrin-i sânî 1907-28 Mart 1908 Senelerine Ait Muhaberatının Kayıt Defteri*, Turkish Historical Association Library (Ankara), Ms. 130, f. 67.

25 "Me'yus Olmalı mı?" *Şûra-yı Ümmet*, no. 62 (October 24, 1904), p. 1.

26 See [Yusuf Akçura], "Üç Tarz-ı Siyaset," *Türk*, no. 24, April 14, 1904, pp. 1 ff.

27 "Spencer'in Japonlara Vasiyetnâmesi," *Türk*, no. 23, April [7], 1904, p.4. Ahmed Rıza, a leading CUP/CPU member, quoted Spencer's recommendation while criticising European statesmen. See "Réponse de H. Spencer à Barthelot," *Mechveret Supplément Français*, no. 154 (July 15, 1904), pp. 6-7. Spencer had made this recommendation to Kentaro Kanedo in 1892. See *Life and Letters of Herbert Spencer*, 2, ed. David Duncan (London: D. Appleton, 1908), pp. 14-8.

28 Yusuf Akçura, *Üç Tarz-ı Siyaset* (Cairo: Matbaa-i İctihad, 1907), pp. 4, 12.

29 Grey to Lowther, November 13, 1908 (private), PRO/F.O. 800/79.

30 An Armenian journal underscored the importance of this fact, but provided an explanation based upon race. See "Doktor Ishak Sukuti Beyi Mahě," *Droshak* 12, no. 3 /123 (March 1902), pp. 47-8.

31 See Erik-Jan Zürcher, "The Young Turks: Children of the Borderlands?" *International Journal of Turkish Studies*, 9, nos. 1-2 (Summer 2003), p. 280.

32 "Tebligat," *Mizan*, no. 1 (December 14, 1896), pp. 1-2; Mehmed Murad, *Mücahede-i Milliye: Gurbet ve Avdet Devirleri* (Istanbul: Mahmud Bey Matbaası, 1324 [1908]), pp. 192 ff.

33 "Hıristiyanlardan Asker Almağa Dair," *Şûra-yı Ümmet*, nos. 96-97 (August 1, 1906), p. 3.

34 "Londra'dan," *Şûra-yı Ümmet*, no. 50 (April 1, 1904), p. 3.

35 "Abū al-Hudā ve Avanesi," *Şûra-yı Ümmet*, no. 61 (October 10, 1904), p. 2.

36 Dr Bahaeddin [Şakir]'s letter beginning "Kafkasya'daki Müslüman Kardeşleri-mize" and dated Paris, November 23, 1906/no. 215, *Muhaberat Kopyası*, f. 177.

37 "Turcophobie," *Mechveret Supplément Français*, no. 139 (April 1, 1903), p. 3.

38 "Türk," *Türk*, no. 1 (November 5, 1903), p.1.

39 "İfade-i Mahsusa," *Türk*, no. 78 (April 27, 1905), p. 2.

40 "Azerbaycan Türkleri," *Türk*, no. 158 (March 14, 1907), p. 1.

41 "Türkler-Ermeniler," *Türk*, no. 2 (November 12, 1903), p. 2; and "Türkler-Yahudiler," *Türk*, no. 6 (December 10, 1903), p.1.

42 "Bir İfade," *Türk*, no. 134 (June 21, 1906), p. 1.

43 "Türk," *Türk*, no. 1, p.1.

44 The journal called them as the "impotent nations of the East." See ibid. According to the journal the Turks were "the British of the Orient." See Türkmen, "Fezâil-i Millîye," *Türk*, no. 65 (January 26, 1905), pp. 1-2.

45 [Rıza Şakir] "Şecaât Nedir?" *Türk*, no. 163 (May 23, 1907), p. 2.

46 "Kıbrıs Mektubu," *Türk*, no. 81 (May 18, 1905), p. 4.

47 See, for instance, Ahmed Bedevî Kuran, *İnkılâp Tarihimiz ve İttihad ve Terakki* (Istanbul: Tan Matbaası, 1948), pp. 205-7, 216.

48 See Ahmed Lûtfî, *Tarih-i Lûtfî, 8* (Istanbul: Sabah Matbaası, 1328 [1910]), pp.142-4 and 474 ff.

49 Skënder Luarasi, *Isa Boletini: Jetëshkrim i shkurtër* (Prishtina: Rilindja, 1972), pp. 34-6, 44-7.

50 *The Memoirs of Ismail Kemal Bey*, p. 8.

51 "Mawḍû' ta'ammul ilā ikhwāninā al-Sûriyyīn," *Turkiyyā al-fatāt*, no. 3 (January 10, 1896), p. [1]. Despite the Arabist tone of this journal CUP organs praised it in glowing terms. See "Evrâk ve Havâdis," *İlâve-i Meşveret*, no. 7 (March 1, 108 [1896]), p. 3; and "Teşekkür ve Memnuniyet," *Mizan*, no. 167 (March 12, 1896), p. 2324.

52 İbrahim Temo to İshak Sükûtî, December [6], [18]99, AQSh, F. 19/106-3//316/1077.

53 See "Notes et Documents," *Albania*, I, no. 7 (November 15, 1897), p. 120.

54 "Arnavudluk ve Arnavudlar," *Osmanlı*, no. 33 (April, 1, 1899), p. 3.

55 See "Kürdistan Gazetesi," *Osmanlı*, no. 35 (May 1, 1899), p. 4; "İlân," *Osmanlı*, no. 65 (August 1, 1900), p. 8; and "İhtar," *Şûra-yı Ümmet*, no. 1 (April 10, 1902), p. 4.

56 See, for instance, "Bedirhan Bey," *Kürdistan*, no. 14 (April 19, 1899), pp. 2-4.

57 Derviş Hima [Maksud Ibrahim Naxhi Spahiu], "Şehid-i Zîşân Doktor İshak Sükûtî," in Abdullah Cevdet, *Yaşamak Korkusu* (Istanbul: Matbaa-i Cihan, 1326 [1910]), p. 7.

58 See [Abdullah Cevdet], "Paris'e Muvasalat," *Kürdistan*, no. 17 [August 27, 1899], pp. 2-3.

59 See Hoca Muhiddin, *Hürriyet Mücahedeleri yahud Firak ve Menfa Hatıraları* (Istanbul: Selânik Matbaası, 1326 [1908]), p. 5.

60 Dr Bahaeddin [Şakir] and Dr Nâzım to [İbrahim Rahmi Efendizâde] Hayri, Paris, June 2, 1906/no. 27, *Muhaberat Kopyası*, f. 48.

61 Ibid.

62 Undated memorandum [April 1906] from Diran Kelekian to Dr Bahaeddin Şakir, Private Papers of Bahaeddin Şakir.

63 "Küstahlık," *Şûra-yı Ümmet*, no. 75 (May 20, 1905), p. 1.

64 See my study *Preparation for a Revolution: The Young Turks, 1902-1908* (New York: Oxford University Press, 2001), pp. 99-120 and 191 ff.

65 "Arnavud İsyanı," *Şûra-yı Ümmet*, no. 28 (May 13, 1903), p. 2.

66 See Abū al-Hudā ve Avenesi," *Şûra-yı Ümmet*, no. 61, p. 2; and "Arab İsyanı," *Şûra-yı Ümmet*, no. 79 (July 18, 1905), p. 2.

67 See "Fraternité musulmane," *Mechveret Supplément Français*, no. 190 (August 1, 1907), pp. 2-3; and "Uhuvvet-i İslâmiye Cemiyeti," *Şûra-yı Ümmet*, no. 122 (September 15, 1907), p. 4.

68 "Mouvement panislamique," *Mechveret Supplément Français*, no. 148 (February 1, 1904), p. 2.

69 Emile Corra to Ahmed Rıza, Paris, October 17, 1907, Archives nationales (Paris), Fonds Emile Corra, Archives positivistes, 17/AS/23/dr 2.

70 "Une mosquée à Paris," *Le Temps*, May 8, 1898.

71 See my study *The Young Turks in Opposition* (New York: Oxford University Press, 1995), pp. 49 ff.

72 See Hanioğlu, *Preparation for a Revolution*, pp. 40-5, 185-6.

73 Ibid., pp. 240-2.

74 Ahmed Rıza's undated note among his scattered notes in Archives nationales (Paris), Fonds Emile Corra, Archives positivistes, 17/AS/10/dr 7.

75 *Osmanlı İttihad ve Terakki Cemiyeti Teşkilât-ı Dahiliye Nizamnâ mesi* ([Paris], 1324 [1908]), p. 1. The CUP altered this clause slightly when it became a legal organisation after the Young Turk Revolution of 1908.

76 [Mehmed Rıza], "Arz-ı Maksad," *Hülâsa-i Hatırâ t* (Istanbul, 1325 [1909]), p. [iii].

77 See, for instance, *Turkey in Europe and Asia: Oxford Pamphlets 1914*, no. 38 (Oxford: Oxford University Press, 1914), p. 14.

78 See Nordau to Wolffsohn, Paris, November 25, 1908, Central Zionist Archives (Jerusalem), W 96/1.

79 Hüseyin Cahid, "Millet-i Hakîme," *Tanin*, [November 7, 1908]. Many years later, while still accusing non-Turkish ethnic groups of separatism, he staunchly defended his stand. See "Meşrutiyet Hatıraları," *Fikir Hareketleri*, no. 88 (June 29, 1935), pp. 150-1. It is interesting to note that the official history textbook makes a similar reference to the concept: "Fortunately, the Turkish nation, which was this country's hegemon (hakimi) and core element (esas unsuru), set no store by the signature of the Ottoman sultan." See *Tarih III*, p. 153.

Chapter 2 (pp. 20-27) – *Hans-Lukas Kieser* Dr Mahmut Esat Bozkurt (1892-1943)

1   Bozkurt, Mahmut Esat, "Esbabı mucibe lâyihası", in: *Yargıtay içtihadı birleştirme kararları ve İsviçre Federal Mahkemesi kararları ile notlu Meden" Kanun, Borçlar Kanunu tatbikat kanunu ve ilgili kanunlar-tüzükler yönetmelikler*, Istanbul: Fakülteler Matbaası, 1984 (first ed. 1926), p. XXIX, XXX and XXXII.

2   Işıtman, Tarık Ziya, *Mahmut Esat Bozkurt*, Hayatı ve Hatıraları, 1892–1943, Izmir: Güneş Basım ve Yayınevi, 1944, p. 9–10.

3   Işıtman, p. 9 and 84.

4   *Yurdcular Yasası. İsviçre'de Cenevre şehrine yakın Petit-Lancy Köyünde Pension Racine'de kurulan İkinci Yurdcular Derneği'nin muzakerat ve mukerreratı*, Istanbul: Yeni Turan Matbaası, n. d. (1913).

5   For a detailed study of this diaspora see my book *Vorkämpfer der "Neuen Türkei". Revolutionäre Bildungseliten am Genfersee (1868–1939)*, Zürich: Chronos, 2005, and *Osmanische Diaspora in der Schweiz*, thematic issue of Schweizerische Zeitschrift für Geschichte/ Revue Suisse d'Histoire, 51-3 (2002).

6   *Yurtçular Yasası*, p. 37, 48–50.

7   *Yurtçular Yasası*, p. 64–65.

8   *Yurtçular Yasası*, p. 24.

9   *Yurtçular Yasası*, p. 29.

10 *Yurtçular Yasası*, p. 61.

11 *Yurtçular Yasası*, p. 69–70.

12 *Lozan Türk Yurdu Cemiyeti'nin Muharrerat ve Zabt-ı Sabık Defteri*, Library of the Turkish Historical Association (TTK) in Ankara.

13 Cf. Koloğlu, Orhan, *Aydınlarımızın bunalım yılı 1918. Zafer nihai'den tam teslimiyete*, Istanbul: Boyut Kitabları, 2000.

14 97th, 98th and 102th session (4 and 11 May, and 22 June 1919), minutes of the Lausanne *Foyer Turc.*

15 "About the 'Mohammedan Greeks'!", *Turkey,* no. 2, March 1921, p. 6.

16 It was published later: Essad, Mahmoud, *Du régime des capitulations ottomanes: leur caractère juridique d'après l'histoire et les textes,* Stamboul: S.A. de Papeterie et d'Imprimerie Fratelli Haim, 1928.

17 Uyar, Hakkı, *"Sol milliyetçi" bir Türk aydını Mahmut Esat Bozkurt (1892-1943),* Ankara: Büke, 2000, p. 72.

18 The whole speech is reproduced in Uyar 2000, p. 206–212, here 207.

19 Article reproduced in Uyar 2000, p. 162–91.

20 Uyar 2000, p. 35.

21 Uyar 2000, p. 39 and 42; *Gazi Mustafa Kemal Atatürk, Atatürk'ün söylev ve demeçleri,* Atatürk Kültür Dil ve Tarih Yüksek Kurumu, Ankara, 1997, Vol. II, p. 129-132.

22 Uyar 2000, p. 73.

23 Son Posta, 20 September 1930. Cited in Halıcı, Şaduman, Yeni Türkiye'de devletinin yapılanmasında Mahmut Esat Bozkurt (1892–1943), Ankara: Atatürk Araştırma Merkezi, 2004, p. 348. For a similar statement of the Prime Minister at the time, Ismet Inönü, on the Turks' exclusive "ethnic and racial rights" in Asia Minor, see Milliyet, August 31, 1930.

24 Bozkurt, "Esbabı mucibe"â p. XXX–XXXI.

25 Cf. his book *Le Kémalisme,* Paris: Félix Alcan, 1937. Tekinalp (sometimes Tekin Alp), a Turkish Jew who was nine years older than Bozkurt, was no less of a Turkist. He published not only in Turkish, but also in French; in contrast to Bozkurt he abstained from outspokenly racist pronouncements.

26 Uyar 2000, p. 101–102.

27 Uyar 2000, p. 101.

28 Bozkurt, Mahmut Esat, *Atatürk ihtilali,* Istanbul: Kaynak, 1995 (first edition 1940), p.164.

29 Bozkurt, *Atatürk,* p. 107.

30 Bozkurt, *Atatürk,* p. 287.

31 Işıtman, Tarık Ziya, *Mahmut Esat Bozkurt. Hayatı ve hatıraları 1892–1943,* İzmir: Güneş, 1944, p. 63 –64.

32 "Masonluk meselesi, sabık Adliye Vekili Mahmut Esat Beyin Masonlara cevabı I", *Anadolu,* 18 October 1931, cited in Uyar, *Bozkurt,* p. 65.

33 Bozkurt, Atatürk, p. 73.

Chapter 3 (p. 28-34) – *Hamit Bozarslan*
Kemalism, westernization and anti-liberalism

1 E. Copeaux, "La transcendance d'Atatürk", in Mayeur-Jaouen, Catherine (ed.), Saints et héros du Moyen-Orient contemporain, actes du colloque des 11 et 12 décembre 2000 à l'Institut universitaire de France, Paris: Maisonneuve et Larose, 2002, pp.121-135.

2 Bernard Lewis, *The Emergence of Modern Turkey,* London, Oxford University Press, 1968.

3 Niyazi Berkes, *The Development of Secularism in Turkey,* New York, Routledge, 1998 (new edition).

4 Erik-Jan Zürcher, *The Unionist Factor. The Role of the Committee of Union and*

Progress in the Turkish National Movement (1905-1926), Leiden, Brill, 1983.

5   Mustafa Müftüoğlu, *Yalan Söyleyen Tarih Utansın*, Istanbul, Gile Yayınevi, 5 v., 1975-1978.

6   Hülya Adak, „National Myths and Self-Na[rra]tion: Mustafa Kemal's Nutuk and Halide Edip's Memoirs and The Turkish Ordeal", *The South Atlantic Quarterly*, n° 102/2-3, 2003, pp. 509-528.

7   Fikret Adanır, "Kemalist Authoritarianism and Fascist Trends in Turkey during the Inter-War Period", in S. Ugelvik Larsen (ed.), *Fascism Outside Europe. The European Impulse against Domestic Conditions in the Diffusion of Global Fascism*, Boulder, Social Science Monographs, 2001, pp. 313-361.

8   Mete Tunçay, "Atatürk'e Nasıl Bakmak?", *Toplum ve Bilim*, n° 4, 1978, pp. 86-92.

9   Cf. Ernest Gellner, "Flux and reflux in the faith of men", in E. Gellner, *Muslim Society*, op.cit., pp. 58-60 & "Kemalism", in E. Gellner, *Encounters with nationalism*, Oxford & Cambridge, Blackwell, 1994, pp. 81-91.

10 Taha Parla, *Türkiye'de Siyasal Kültürün Resmi Kaynakları*, Istanbul, İletişim, 3 v., 1989-1992.

11 In fact, secularism did preserve the status of Sunni Islam as the state-controlled religion of the nation. Cf. Hamit Bozarslan, "Islam, laïcité et la question d'autorité dans l'Empire ottoman et en Turquie kémaliste", *Archives des sciences sociales des religions*, n° 125, 2004, pp. 99-113.

12 Cf. K. Naci, "Türk Devletinde Halkçilik", ülkü, 3.4.1933.

Chapter 4 (pp. 37-42) – *Fuat Dündar*
The settlement policy (1913-18)

1   Contrary to what is generally accepted, Birinci states on the basis of the original documents in the archives that the date when the Committee was founded is 1895. See Ali Birinci, *"Osmanli Ittihat ve Terakki Cemiyeti kurulusu ve ilk nizamnamesi (1895)"*, Osmanli Encyclopedia, V.2, Ed:Güler Eren, Ankara, Yeni Türkiye, 1999, pp. 401-409.

2   Y.H.Bayur, *Turk inkilabi tarihi*, V.I / I., ed. 2, TTK, Ankara, 1963, p.442.

3   For the role of the Albanians in the Revolution of 1908, see Gazmend Shpuza, *"Arnavutlar ve Jöntürk Devrimi"*, Osmanli Encyclopaedia, V.2, pp.464-472.

4   In addition to Zafer Toprak's excellent study, (*Ittihad - Terakki ve Cihan Harbi: Savas Ekonomisi ve Türkiye'de Devletçilik 1914 – 1918*, Homer, Istanbul, 2003) Zürcher also indicates that between 1916 and 1918, more than 80 joint-stock companies were founded by the Committee. See Eric J. Zürcher, *Modernlesen Turkiye'nin Tarihi*, ed.13, Iletisim, Istanbul, 2002, p.184.

5   Fuat Dündar, *Ittihat ve Terakki'nin müslümanlari iskan politikasi*, Iletisim, Istanbul, 2001, pp.63-64.

6   Dündar, 2001, pp.62-63.

7   Dündar, 2001, pp.64-65.

8   IAMM and AMMU denote the Directorate.

9   See Fuat Dündar, *"Ittihat ve Terakki'nin Etnisite Arastirmalari"*, Toplumsal Tarih XVI/91 (July 2001), pp.43-50.

10 Doktor Friliç and Mühendis Rolig, Türkmen Asiretleri, AMMU Nesriyatindan:2, Kitabhane-i Suud", Istanbul, 1334 and Dr. Friç, Kürtler: Tarih-i ve Içtima"

Tedkik, AMMU Nesriyatindan: 3, Kitabhane-i Suud", Istanbul, 1334.
11 BOA.DH.SFR 54A/51. For all the other similar telegrams see the chapter *"The census"* in Dündar, 2001, pp.84-87.
12 Because of the great number of coded telegrams, and to facilitate reference and save space, we will refer from time to time to the pages of Dündar, 2001, not the numbers of the original documents in the archives.
13 See, for the original document of this order, the annexe in Dündar, 2001.
14 See, for the original document of this order, the annexe in Dündar, 2001.
15 Dündar, 2001, p.101.
16 Kamuran Gürün, Ermeni Dosyasi, ed. 3, TTK, no: VII-79, Ankara, 1985, p.269
17 Hasan Kayali, Jön Türkler ve Araplar: Osmanli Imparatorlugu'nda Osmanlicilik, erken Arap milliyetciligi ve Islamcilik (1908-1918), Tarih Vakfi - Yurt, Istanbul, 1998, p.218.
18 See the documents in Dündar, 2001, pp.123-127.
19 BOA.DH.SFR, 55/117; Dündar 2001, p.134.
20 BOA.DH.SFR, 63/188; Dündar 2001, p.144.
21 BOA.DH.SFR, 77/188; Dündar p.154.
22 Dündar 2001, pp.155-158.
23 Dündar 2001, pp.130-134.
24 BOA.DH.SFR, 82/129; Dündar 2001, p.128.
25 This ordinance was presented to the Council of Ministers on 15 January 1918. See Dündar 2001, p.129. It is important to recall that this Article 3 was transferred to the Law of Settlement of 1935, which was in force until 2004.
26 Dündar 2001, p128.
27 See related documents in Dündar, p.169-170 and H.Yildirim Aganoglu, *Türkiye'de Göç ve Göçmen Meselesi (Balkan harbi sonrasi ornegi, 1912-14)*, unpublished thesis, Istanbul University, Istanbul, 1999, p.42.
28 BOA.DH.SFR, 65,65.
29 Turkmen Asiretleri, p.3.
30 BOA.DH.SFR,60,10.
31 One of the reasons for the reorganization of the AMMU was the settlement of Muslim nomads. According to the Directorate, one million Kurds, one million Turcomans and 3 million Arabs were involved. See TIGMA (Toprak ve Iskan Genel Mudurlugu Arsivi) 272, 12, 37, 21, 1.
32 The answer to a motion by AMMU officials, in the Ayan's parliament. See MAZC (Meclis-i Ayan Zabit Cerideleri), 3,4,2,41,24 March 1918, p.217.
33 Tevfik Ġavdar, "Osmanli Doneminde Nufus bilgileri", Osmanli Encyclopaedia, V.4, pp.551-557, p.556. According to McCarthy, in 1911-1912 , the Muslim population of Anatolia was 14.5 million, while Christians numbered 1.2 million Greeks, 1.5 million Armenians and 220,000 Syrian Orthodox (?) (this last figure including Chaldeans, Jews and others). See McCarthy, Justin, *Muslims and minorities*, New York University Press, New York-London,1983, p.110.
34 Actually, this number should be considered an approximation. Celal Bayar states that in the Aegean region, 1,150,000 Greeks were deported in 1914. (See Taner Akcam, *Insan haklari ve Ermeni sorunu-Ittihat Terakki'den kurtulus savasina*, Imge, Istanbul, 1999, p.183.).

Chapter 5 (pp. 43-49) – Rifat N. Bali
The politics of Turkification

1 The reference work for the Lausanne Peace Treaty is: *Lozan Barış Konferansı Tutanaklar-Belgeler*, (translated by Seha L. Meray), Yapı Kredi Yayınları, Istanbul, 1993. The clauses of the Treaty referring to non-Muslim minorities are nos. 37 to 42.

2 For a study of the process of Turkifying the minorities, the reader is invited to refer to Ayhan Aktar, *Varlık Vergisi ve "Türkleştirme" Politikaları*, İletişim Yayınları, Istanbul, 2000 and Rıfat N. Bali, *Cumhuriyet Yıllarında Türkiye Yahudileri Bir Türkleştirme Serüveni 1923-1945*, İletişim Yayınları, Istanbul, 1999.

3 A. Afetinan, *Medeni Bilgiler ve M. Kemal Atatürk'ün El Yazıları*, 3rd edition, Türk Tarih Kurumu Yayınları, Ankara, 1998, p. 23-24.

4 For the historiography of Türk Ocakları, the reader is invited to refer to the work of Füsun üstel, *İmparatorluktan Ulus-Devlete Türk Milliyetçiliğ i Türk Ocakları 1912-1932*, İletişim Yayınları, Istanbul, 1997.

5 *Vakit*, 27 April 1925 quoted in Füsun üstel, *İmparatorluktan Ulus-Devlete Türk Milliyetçiliğ i Türk Ocakları 1912-1931*, İletişim Yayınları, Istanbul 1997, p. 173.

6 Taha Parla, *Türkiye'de Siyasi Kültürün Resmi Kaynakları, Cilt 3: Kemalist Tek Parti İdeolojisi ve CHP'nin Altı Oku*, İletişim, Istanbul, 1995, p. 27.

7 "Mustafa Kemal'in Adana Türk Ocağ ı'ndaki nutku", *Vakit*, 19 February, 1931.

8 Tekin Alp, *Türkleştirme*, Resimli Ay Matbaası, Istanbul, 1928, p. 63-65. The only study on Tekin Alp is by Jacob M. Landau, *Tekinalp, Turkish Patriot 1883-1961*, Nederlands Historisch-Archaelogisch Instituut, Istanbul, 1984.

9 Rıfat N. Bali, ibid, p. 156.

10 For a study on the Alliance works in Turkey the reader has to look to Aron Rodrigue's *French Jews, Turkish Jews: The Alliance Israélite Universelle and the Politics of Jewish Schooling in Turkey, 1860-1925*, Indiana University Press, Indiana, 1990.

11 For a study of the cartoons in the Single Party period, the reader is invited to refer to the following article: Laurent Mallet, (translated by İrvem Keskinoğlu), "Karikatür Dergisinde Yahudilerle İlgili Karikatürler (1936-1948)", *Toplumsal Tarih*, October 1996, Vol. 6, No. 34, pp. 26-35.

12 Rıfat N. Bali, ibid, p. 287-288.

13 Rıfat N. Bali, ibid, p. 369-377.

14 Hasan-Ali Yücel, *Türkiye'de Orta Öğretim*, Kültür Bakanlığı, Ankara, 1994, p. 25.

15 Rıfat N. Bali, ibid, p. 530.

16 Rıfat N. Bali, ibid, p. 529.

17 *Gazi Mustafa Kemal Atatürk, Atatürk'ün Söylev ve Demeçleri*, Atatürk Kültür Dil ve Tarih Yüksek Kurumu, Ankara, 1997, Vol. II, p. 129-132.

18 Rıfat N. Bali, ibid, pp. 206-225.

19 Rıfat N. Bali, ibid, pp. 226-228. Also Ahmet Yıldız, *"Ne Mutlu Türküm Diyebilene" Türk Ulusal Kimliğinin Etno-Seküler Sınırları (1919-1938)*, İletişim Yayınları, Istanbul, 2001.

20 Tekin Alp, "Türk Kültür Birliği", *Yeni Türk Mecmuası*, Vol. 1, issue 15, November 1933, p. 1239-1250.

21 Fahri Çoker, *Türk Parlamento Tarihi TBMM – IV Dönem 1931-1935*, Vol 1, TBMM Vakıf Yayınları, Ankara, 1995, p. 33-34.

22 For further details on the Capital Tax levy the reader is suggested to consult the following works: Rıdvan Akar, *Aşkale Yolcuları - Varlık Vergisi ve Çalışma Kampları*, Belge Yayınları, Istanbul, 1999; Ayhan Aktar, *Varlık Vergisi ve "Türkleştirme" Politikaları*, İletişim Yayınları, Istanbul, 2000; Rıfat N. Bali, ibid, p. 424-486; Rıfat N. Bali, *The "Varlik Vergisi" Affair – A Study on its Legacy- Selected Documents*, The Isis Press, Istanbul, 2005.

Chapter 6 (pp. 50-56) – *Corinna Görgü Guttstadt* The case of Turkish Jews

1   Details of this policy of settlement can be found in Fuat Dündar: *İttihat ve Terakki'nin Müslümanları İsakân Politikası*, Istanbul , İletişim Yayınları, 2001. Between 1921 and 1929 alone Turkey accepted 719,808 immigrants (in 1927 the total population was 13.5 million); see Soner Çağaptay, *"Reconfiguring the Turkish Nation in the 1930s"*, Nationalism and Ethnic Politics vol. 8, no. 2, Summer 2002, pp. 67-82; in particular p. 71.

2   Details in Soner Çağaptay, *"Kim Türk, kim vatandaş? Erken cumhuriyet dönemi vatandaşlık rejimi üzerine bir çalışma"*, Toplum ve Bilim, No 98, 2003, p. 166 - 185;

3   On 18 March 1931 Mehmet Nasır from Tarsus was denaturalized for having supported the French and Armenians during occupation, Başbakanlık Cumhuriyet Arşivi (BCA): Decision No. 10811 of 18.03.1931 Fon. 30.18.1.2./Place: 18.18.16.

4   BCA: Decision No. 7559/date: 26.12.1928, file 104-23 Fon: 30.18.1.2/place:1.12.29

5   This law was translated into Italian and published in *Oriente Moderno*, 1928, pp. 512-514.

6   Translation from the Italian version in *Oriente Moderno* 1928, p. 513. Articles 7 and 9 regulated denaturalization of those who requested it or those who had acquired a foreign nationality.

7   Çağaptay cites the law not from the Official Gazette but from diplomatic documents, Çağaptay, 2003, p. 177 ff.

8   Gotthard Jäschke, *Die Türkei in den Jahren 1935-1941*. Leipzig: Harrassowitz, 1943, p. 17. I could not find the exact wording of Law No. 2848; Çağaptay, who has written various articles on naturalization, denaturalization, the reconfiguring of the population and the Turkish Nation, does not mention this law. Among the decisions of the Council of Ministers on mass denaturalizations, the *Başbakanlık Arşivi* mentions two (signed by Kemal Atatürk) in 1938. They concern 127 persons who were deprived of their Turkish citizenship because "they had no ties to Turkish culture" ["Türk kültürüne bağlı olmayan 75 kişinin (....)" BCA: decision No. 2/9219 of 07.07.1938 (Fon 30.18.1.2./84.63.18) and decision No. 2/8515 of 07.04.1938 (Fon 30.18.1.2./place: 82.28.16].

9   This was later made more severe with Law No. 4061. In addition, the fees for the revision/confirmation of citizenship were markedly increased several times.

10 Details in Mesut Yeğen, "Citizenship and Ethnicity in Turkey", *Middle Eastern Studies* 40 (No.6), Nov. 2004, pp.51-66, and Soner Çağaptay, "Kim Türk, kim vatandaş? Erken cumhuriyet dönemi vatandaşlık rejimi üzerine bir çalışma", *Toplum ve Bilim* 98, 2003, pp. 166-185.

11 Details in Rıfat Bali, *Türkleştirme serüveni*, Istanbul: İletişim, 1999.

12 Mete Tuncay, *T.C.'nde Tek-Parti Yönetimi'nin kurulması (1923–1931)*. Ankara:

Yurt Yayincilik, 1981, pp. 28-31; the statute explicitly states that the association "Bütün Islâm vatandaşların derneğin doğal üyeleri sayılması" (counts all Muslim subject as natural members).

13 Leyla Neyzi, "Trauma, Narrative and Silence: The Military Journal of a Jewish Soldier", *Turcica*, 35, 2003 pp. 291-313, here p. 298, based on *Türkiye Büyük Millet Meclisi Gizli Celse Zabıtları*. Ankara: TBMM 1920-1921. Non-Muslims were not represented in the Grand National Assembly (TBMM) before 1923.

14 Erik Jan Zürcher, "Ottoman Labour Battalions in World War 1", in: Kieser/Schaller (eds.): *Armenian Genocide and the Shoah*, Zürich: Chronos, 2002, pp. 187-196; Yair Auron, The Banality of Indifference: Zionism and the Armenian Genocide, New Brunswick: Transaction Publishers, 2002, p. 42. Zürcher's research only concerns Armenians. Çağlar Keyder, "Kayip Burjuvazi Aranıyor", Toplumsal Tarih, no. 68; August 1999, pp. 4-11, Istanbul, 1999, reports from Greek sources that these measures were also directed against a large number of Greeks.

15 Aydın Ender, "Ursprung und Vermächtnis des Kemalismus", in Ayres et al., *Türkei - Staat und Gesellschaft*, Frankfurt: isp-pocket, 1987, pp. 68-100, here p. 76, and Ahmet Samim, "Die Tragödie der türkischen Linken", in Ömer Seven (ed.), *Türkei – Zwischen Militärherrschaft und Demokratie*, Hamburg: VSA-Verlag, 1984; pp. 141-153, here p. 150f.

16 As the files I consulted in the BCA.

17 The lists of names are not available for quite a number of denaturalization decisions. In single cases Muslim Turks were apparently deprived of their citizenship. The only example that I know of is the shoemaker Ahmet Talib, who had been living in Germany since 1917; documents in Achmed Talib, *Stationen des Lebens eines türkischen Schuhmachermeisters in Deutschland von 1917 bis 1983. Kaiserreich - Weimarer Republik - Drittes Reich - DDR*, Köln: ÖNEL Verlag, 1997. Documents on Ahmet Talib can also be found in the file of the *Politisches Archiv des Auswärtigen Amtes* (PAAA, Ministry of Foreign Affairs) R 45553

18 Çağaptay/ 2003 pp.607-608.

19 Decision 1745 of 10.08.1922: *"16.4.1338 tarih ve 1514 nolu Kararname ile pasaport verilmemesi kararlaştırılan gayrimüslim Türk tebasına tabiyet varakası dahi verilmemesi"* (Non-Muslims who according to decision No. 1514 should not be given passports should also not get certificates of citizenship) BCA (Fon 30.18.1.1/place No: 5.24..1)

20 BCA: Fon 030.10.00/place: 110.736.12

21 This keyword mainly lists decisions on loss of citizenship (and a few mass naturalizations). The term *"vatandaşlıktan çıkarma"* (deprivation of citizenship) only shows successful appeals against deprivations of citizenship.

22 Article 8 of Law No. 1312 in *Oriente Moderno*.

23 BCA: decision No. 2/9219 of 07.07.1938 (Fon 30.18.1.2./84.63.18) and decision No. 2/8515 of 07.04.1938 (Fon 30.18.1.2./place: 82.28.16).

24 These figures do not include loss of citizenship following the acquirisition of a another nationality!

25 Of the 31 decisions taken in the Cabinet in 1943, 8 concerned Turkish or Muslim individuals. A total of 128 persons were denaturalized because they had taken a different citizenship. These figures are not included in the figures presented above.

26 This number refers explicitly only to Turkish Jews who had registered with the Consulate and still counted as Turkish citizens; Stanford J. Shaw, *Turkey and the*

Holocaust. Turkey's Role in Rescuing Turkish and European Jewry from Nazi Persecution 1933-45, Basingstoke etc: Macmillan, 1993, p. 46 footnote 89.

27 Datenbank Gedenkbuch in Barch = Bundesarchiv Berlin (Lichterfelde), and Isak Behar, *Versprich mir, dass du am Leben bleibst,* München, Ullstein, 2002.

28 These were Drancy in France, Westerborck in the Netherlands and Malines in Belgium.

29 This operation, that resulted in the arrest of some 1,000 well-known Jewish personalities in France, was said to have been carried out in retaliation for antifascist resistance.

30 A detailed report about Rousso in *Milliyet,* 05.07.1992; about A. Saul in *Milliyet* (Turkey edition), 5-9 August 1992.

31 Shaw, 1993, p. 123 ff.

32 A note by Thadden on his talk with Koç from the Turkish Embassy in Berlin (AA Inl. II A dated 22.09.1943) in PAAA R 99446, mentions in particular that the return of "Jews possessing Turkish documents in order, but without any contacts to Turkey for decades" should be prevented!

33 Note of Hahn [the inverted commas imply this was an alias] (D III) dated 17.02.1943 to Pol VII in PAAA99446

34 The lists of names and the countries where the persons were living were only accessible for half of the decisions.

35 Telegram No. 1583 of 12.03.1943 Schleier, German Embassy to Foreign Ministry in PAAA R99446.

36 Onur Öymen, *Die Türkische Herausforderung – EU-Mitglied oder entfernte Verwandte?* Köln: Önel-Verlag, 2001, pp.254-255, seems to be taken from Stanford Shaw, *Turkey and the Holocaust,* 1993, S. 60.

Chapter 7 (pp.57-66) – *Berna Pekesen*
The exodus of Armenians from the Sanjak

1 Research for this paper was carried out in the framework of a project funded by the *Deutsche Forschungsgemeinschaft* on migration movements and settlement policies in Turkey during the inter-war period.

2 See Renée Hirschon (ed.), *Crossing the Aegean. An Appraisal of the 1923 Compulsory Population Exchange between Greece and Turkey* (New York: Berghahn, 2003).

3 On the British and French Mandatory system see the contributions in: *The British and French mandates in comparative perspectives / Les mandats français et anglais dans une perpective comparative,* ed. by Nadine Méouchy and Peter Sluglett (Leiden- Boston: Brill, 2004).

4 On the Treaty of Sèvres see for example Paul C. Helmreich, From Paris to Sevrès. The Partition of the Ottoman Empire at the Peace Conference of 1919-1920 (Colombus, OH: Ohio State University Press, 1974).

5 Youssef S. Takla, "Corpus Juris du mandat français", in: *British and French Mandates,* pp. 63-101.

6 William Stivers, *Supremacy and Oil. Iraq, Turkey, and the Anglo-American World Order, 1918-1930* (Ithaca, NY: Cornell University Press, 1982; Kemal Melek, *İngiliz belgeleriyle Musul sorunu (1890-1926)* (Istanbul, üçdal Neşriyat, 1983); İsmail Soysal, "Seventy Years of Turkish-Arab Relations and an Analysis of Turkish-Iraqi

Relations (1920-1990)", in *Studies on Turkish-Arab Relations 6* (1991), pp. 23-85, hier 27-29; Mim Kemal Ö ke, *Musul ve Kürdistan Sorunu 1918-1926* (Ankara, Bilge Karınca Yay., 1992).

7   Stéphane Yerasimos, "Le Sanjak D'Alexandrette: Formation et Intégration d'un Territoire", *Revue du Monde Musulman et de la Méditerranée*, 48-49, 1988/2-3, pp. 198-212, here 204. The 'National Pact' of 1920 was a programme of the nationalists which stipulated that the integrity of the territory under Ottoman military control on the day of the Mudros Armistice (30 October 1918) was inviolable, implying simultaneously a rejection of all schemes for the creation of an Armenian or Kurdish state. See H.W.V. Temperley, *A History of the Peace Conference of Paris*, vol. VI, (London: Hodder and Stoughton, 1924), p. 605f.

8   Anthony R. De Luca, *Great Powers Rivalry at the Turkish Straits: the Montreux Convention and Conference of 1936* (Boulder, CO: East European Monographs, 1981).

9   Yerasimos, "Le Sanjak D'Alexandrette", p. 206.

10 Cilicia included the cities and hinterlands of Maras, Aintab, Urfa and Adana. The term seems to have been a medieval territorial construct and had no counterpart in Ottoman administrative parlance. See Keith D. Watenpough, "Towards a New Category of Colonial Theory: Colonial Cooperation and the Survivors' Bargain. The Case of the Post-Genocide Armenian Community of Syria under French Mandate", in: *British and French Mandates*, pp. 597-623, here p. 606. On Franco-Armenian cooperation see also Ellen M. Lust-Okar, "Failure of Collaboration: Armenian Refugees in Syria", Middle Eastern Studies 32 (1996), no. 1, pp. 53-69.

11 On French rule, the *Légion Arménienne* and intercommunal conflicts in Cilicia, see the important study by Vahé Tachjian, *La France en Cilicie et en Haute-Mésopotamie. Aux Confins de la Turquie, de la Syrie et de l'Irak 1919-1933* (Paris: Karthala, 2004), passim.

12 On the uprising in Antioch, see Dalal Arsuzi-Elamir, *Arabischer Nationalismus in Syrien. Zaki al-Arsuzi und die arabisch-nationale Bewegung an der Peripherie Alexandrette/Antakya 1930-1938* (Münster-Hamburg-Berlin etc.: LIT Verlag, 2003), pp. 27-40; K.D. Watenpough, "Towards a New Category of Colonial Theory", pp. 604-608.

13 For an eyewitness account, see Georges Boudière, "Notes sur la campagne de Syrie-Cilicie. L'affaire de Maraş (Janvier-Février 1920)", *Turcica* IX/2-X (1978), pp. 155-175. Cf. also Tachjian, *La France en Cilicie, passim*; K.D. Watenpough, "Towards a New Category of Colonial Theory", p. 608

14 For a detailed analysis of drawing boundaries in the Middle East and resulting disputes, see George H. Joffe, "Disputes over State Boundaries in the Middle East and North Africa", in Laura Guazzone (ed.), *The Middle East in Global Change* (London: McMillan, 1997), pp. 58-94. For a discussion of a general typology of spatial boundaries, see Barry Smith, "On Drawing Lines on a Map", in A.U. Frank and W. Kuhn (eds.), *Spatial Information Theory. Proceedings of COSIT 95* (Berlin: Springer, 1995), pp. 475-484; J. R.V. Prescott, *Boundaries and Frontiers* (London: Croom Helm, 1978).

15 Arsuzi-Elamir, *Arabischer Nationalismus in Syrien*, p. 84. See also Michel Gilquin, *D'Antioche au Hatay. L'histoire oubliée du Sandjak d'Alexandrette. Nationalisme Turc contre Nationalisme Arabe. La France, arbitre* (Paris: L'Harmattan, 2000), p. 90.

16 H. Pehlivanlı, Y. Sarınay and H. Yıldırım, *Türk Dış Politikasında Hatay* (Ankara: Asam Yay., 2001), p. 81.

17 Ibid., p. 37. See also M. Gilquin, *D'Antioche au Hatay*, p. 90.

18 On territorial amendments, see Arsuzi-Elamir, *Arabischer Nationalismus in Syrien*, *passim*; further Georges Souren Seraydarian, *Der Sandschak von Alexandrette: Eine völkerrechtliche Untersuchung des Konfliktes.*, Ph. D. Thesis, University of Vienna, 1967; Elizabeth Picard, "Retour du Sandjak", *Maghreb-Machrek* 99 (January-March 1983), pp. 47-64.

19 Ministère des Affaires Etrangères, Rapport sur la situation de la Syrie et du Liban (années 1925 à 1938 (Paris: Impr. Nationale, 1926-1939), as cited by Arsuzi-Elamir, Arabischer Nationalismus in Syrien, p. 25.

20 See Philip S. Khoury, "The Tribal Shaikh, French Tribal Policy and the Nationalist Movement in Syria between the Two World Wars", *Middle East Studies* 18 (1982), no. 2, pp.180-193; Stephen H. Longrigg, *Syria and Lebanon under French Mandate* (London: Oxford University Press, 1958).

21 Kemal Karpat, "The Ottoman Ethnic and Confessional Legacy in the Midde East", in Milton Esman and Itamar Rabinovich (eds.), *Ethnicity, Pluralism and the State in the Middle East* (Ithaca-London: Cornell University Press, 1988), pp. 35-53.

22 Turkish semi-official historiography consequently announced that the Alawites were the descendants of the Hittites and therefore "Turks". Similarly, the *sanjak* of Alexandretta was given the Hittite name of "Hatay" by President Atatürk. See H. Pehlivanlı, Y. Sarınay and H. Yıldırım, *Türk Dış Politikasında Hatay*, p. 90. The Turkish History Thesis declared the Anatolian Armenians to have descended from Turkish ethnic roots. See Soner Cagaptay, "Race, Assimilation and Kemalism: Turkish Nationalism and the Minorities in the 1930s", *Middle Eastern Studies* 40 (May 2004), no. 3, pp. 86-101, here 88f. On renaming of localities in the *sanjak* of Alexandretta see also Werner Arnold, *Die arabischen Dialekte Antiochiens* (Wiesbaden: Harrasowitz, 1998).

23 Arsuzi-Elamir, *Arabischer Nationalismus in Syrien*, p. 209f.

24 Elizabeth Picard, "Les Nationalistes arabes de Syrie et d' Iraq et le Kémalisme: convergence, occultations et influences", in Iskender Gökalp and François Georgeon (eds.), *Kémalisme et Monde Musulman* (=Cahiers du Groupe d' études sur la Turquie contemporaine) (Paris: Fondation de la Maison des sciences de l`homme, 1987), pp. 40-59.

25 Arsuzi-Elamir, *Arabischer Nationalismus in Syrien*, p. 108f.

26 Some authors believe that Ankara was only waiting for the suitable moment to annex the disputed territory. See H. Pehlivanlı, Y. Sarınay and H. Yıldırım, *Türk Dış Politikasında Hatay*, p. 39f.

27 Angora, 23.06.1938, Public Record Office (PRO), Foreign Office (FO), 371/21912; Report of the League of Nations, C.261.1938, Geneva, 20.08.1938, p. 66f., PRO FO, 371/21913; Report of Seiler, Beirut, 13.08.1938, Auswärtiges Amt (AA), Politisches Archiv (PA), 448 (=Sandschak Alexandrette).

28 For general accounts of these developments, see Philipp Khoury, *Syria and the French Mandate: The Politics of Arab Nationalism 1920-1945* (Princeton: Princeton University Press, 1987); Lucien Bitterlin, *Alexandrette, Le "Munich" de l`Orient* (Paris: J. Picollec, 1999); Daniel Pipes, *Greater Syria. The History of an Ambition* (New York: Oxford University Press, 1990); Edward Weisband, "The Sanjak of

Alexandrette, 1920-1939. A Case Study", in R. Bayley Winder (ed.), *Near East Round Table 1967-1968* (New York: New York University, 1969).

29	To the extent that I am familiar with the literature, the exodus and the resulting refugee crisis of 1938/39 have been neglected in research. I thank M. Vahé Tachjian for helpful comments and the following references in Armenian which are unfortunately inaccessible to me: A. Bayramian, "Alexandrette-i sandjak-i hartse yev mitchazkayin tivanakidoutioune 1918-1939" (Antelias: Lebanon: Metsi Tann Kilikioy, 1999); "Houshamadyan Mussa Leran" (Beirut: Atlas Press, 1970).

30	Memorandum by de Chapeaurouge, Beirut, 07.06.1938, AA PA R 104.794 (=Politische Beziehungen zwischen Syrien und der Türkei 1937-38)

31	Seiler to AA, Beirut, 24.06.1938, AA PA, R 104 794.

32	Davis to FO, Aleppo, 10.07.1939, E 5132 and 27.07.1939, E 5503/5132/44, PRO FO 371/23302.

33	Davis to FO, Aleppo, 04.08.1939, E 5640/5132/44, PRO FO 371/23302.

34	"The Turkish authorities tried to persuade them to remain, and the French asked that at least they delay till new homes could be prepared for them in other parts of Syria and Lebanon, but the people were obdurate: go they would, and that immediately. The Turkish and French authorities, seeing it was hopeless to dissuade them, accordingly fell to facilitating the exodus, and within a week it was complete, and that happily without any serious incident." Bridgeman to the Bishop of Jerusalem, Jerusalem, 02.08.1939, E 5056/5138/44, PRO FO 371/23302.; Davis to FO, Aleppo, 10.07.1939, E 5132/5132/44, PRO FO 371/23302.

35	Davis to FO, Aleppo, 04.08.1939, E 5640/5132/44, and 27.07.1939, E 5503, PRO FO 371/23302.

36	Seiler to AA, Beirut, 21.06.1938, German Embassy Ankara 531 (=Syrien, 1936-39); Minutes by J.R. Lockville, 28.08.1939, E 5905/5132/44, PRO FO 371/23302.

37	Bridgeman to the Bishop of Jerusalem, Jerusalem, 02.08.1939, E 5056/5138/44, PRO FO 371/23302.

38	Seiler to AA Beirut, 06.11.1936, AA PA R 102.424 (=Pol. Abt. Länderakten: Syrien, 1936-1938).

39	Seiler to AA, Beirut, 24.06.1938, AA PA R 104.794 (=Politische Beziehungen zwischen Syrien und der Türkei 1937-38).

40	Soner Cagaptay, "Population Resettlement and Immigration Policies of Interwar Turkey: A Study of Turkish Nationalism", *Turkish Studies Association Bulletin*, 26:1 (Spring 2002), pp. 1-25.

41	See Rifat Bali's contribution in this volume.

42	Davis to FO, Aleppo, 08.09.1939, E 5056/5132/44, PRO FO 371/23302.

43	De Chapeaurouge to AA, Beirut, 29.07.1939 , AA PA 448 (=Sandschak Alexandrette) and the unsigned memo dated 15.06.1939, ibid. See also Arsuzi-Elamir, *Arabischer Nationalismus in Syrien*, p. 190.

44	For an overview of forced migrations in Europe, see Eugene M. Kulischer, *Europe on the Move. War and Population Changes, 1917-1947* (New York: Columbia University Press, 1948); Joseph B. Schechtman, *The Refugee in the World. Displacement and Integration* (New York: AS Barnes and Company, 1963) and Norman Naimark, *Fires of Hatred: Ethnic Cleansing in Twentieth-Century Europe* (Cambridge, Mass.: Harvard University Press, 2001).

45	Nelida Fuccaro, "Minorities and Ethnic Mobilization: The Kurds in Northern Iraq and Syria", in *British and French Mandates*, pp. 579-595, here 579-83.

46 See F. S. Northedge, *The League of Nations: Its Life and Tunes 1920-1946* (Leicester: Leicester University Press, 1986).

47 Arnold Toynbee, "The Cession to Turkey of the Sandjak of Alexandrette", *Survey of International Affairs 1938* (London 1941), vol. 1., p. 489.

Chapter 8 (pp.67-73) – Marc Baer
Turkish Nationalism and the Dönme

1   This paper is a condensed version of "The Double Bind of Race and Religion: The Conversion of the Dönme to Turkish Secular Nationalism," *Comparative Studies in Society and History* 46 (October 2004): 682-708.

2   Alexis Alexandris, *The Greek Minority of Istanbul and Greek-Turkish Relations, 1918-1974* (Athens: Center for Asia Minor Studies), 77-104; Erik Zürcher, *Turkey: A Modern History*, 2d ed. (London: I. B. Tauris, 1995), 170-72.

3   Members of this group used the Hebrew term for Believers (*Ma'aminim*); Muslims chose the Turkish equivalent of Conversos or Renegades (*Dönme*). The terms Sabbatean (*Sabatayist*) and Salonikan (*Selânikli*) have also been used. The latter term is not preferred because Muslims of Salonikan origins who are not Dönme are sometimes confused with the group. Likewise, there is a tendency in Turkey to incorrectly use the term "Dönme" to refer to all converts to Islam. I use "Dönme" to denote the descendants of Jewish followers of Shabtai Tzvi who converted to Islam.

4   Some Dönme were pious Muslims. A descendant of Dönme now living in the United States told me his ancestors included Sufi masters of a dervish lodge (*tekke şeyhi*) in Salonika and Arabic calligraphers who decorated mosques.

5   Wladimir Gordlevsky, "Zur Frage über die Dönme (Die Rolle Der Juden In Den Religionssekten Vorderasiens)," *Islamica* 2 (1926): 201-18.

6   Etienne Balibar, and Immanuel Wallerstein, *Race, Nation, Class: Ambiguous Identities* (London: Verso, 1991), 37-106; Ann Stoler, "Sexual Affronts and Racial Frontiers: European Identities and the Politics of Exclusion in Colonial Southeast Asia," *Comparative Studies in Society and History* 34 (1992): 514-51; Talal Asad, *Genealogies of Religion: Discipline and Reasons of Power in Christianity and Islam* (Baltimore: Johns Hopkins University Press, 1993).

7   Gyanendra Pandey, "Can a Muslim Be an Indian?" *Comparative Studies in Society and History* 41 (1999): 608-29.

8   Zürcher, *Turkey*, 198-99.

9   Anthony D. Smith, *Nationalism: Theory, Ideology, History* (Malden, Mass.: Blackwell, 2001), 36-42.

10 Soner Çağaptay, "Population Resettlement and Immigration Policies of Interwar Turkey: A Study of Turkish Nationalism," *The Turkish Studies Association Bulletin* 25 (2001), 3.

11 Ahmet Yıldız, *Ne Mutlu Türküm Diyebilene: Türk Ulusal Kimliğinin Etno-Seküler Sınırları, 1919-1938* (Istanbul: İletişim Yayınları, 2001), 15-20.

12 This hypothesis is based on articles that appeared in the dailies *Vakit* and *Vatan* in the first week of January 1924.

13 *Sebülürreşat* 23, no. 583 (10 Jan. 1924): 174.

14 Ibid.

15 Talat Paşa, *Talat Paşanın Anıları* (Istanbul: Say Yayınları, 1986), 75.

16 *Sebülürreşat* 23, no. 583 (10 Jan. 1924): 174.

17 Gauri Viswanathan, *Outside the Fold: Conversion, Modernity, and Belief* (Princeton: Princeton University Press, 1998), 36.

18 Ibid., 37-39.

19 İbrahim Alâettin Gövsa, *Sabatay Sevi: İzmirli meşhur sahte Mesih hakkında tarihi ve içtimai tetkik tecrübesi* (Istanbul: Lûtfi Kitabevi, 1939), 5; *Sebülürreşat*, vol. 23, no. 585, 10 Kânun-i Sâni 1340 (January 24, 1924), 204-5; and ibid., vol. 23. no. 586, 220.

20 Ahmed Emin Yalman, *Yakın Tarihte Gördüklerim ve Geçirdiklerim*, 2 vols., 2d ed., ed. Erol Şadi Erdinç (Istanbul: Pera Turizm ve Ticaret A. Ş., 1997), ix-xxii. Yalman's nearly two-thousand-page autobiography (Yalman 1997), which is largely based on his writings in *Vatan*, contains neither a single reference to the Dönme nor to the debate of 1924.

21 *Vatan*, January 11, 1924, 1.

22 Ibid.

23 *Vatan*, January 20, 1924, 2.

24 *Vatan*, January 20, 1924, 2.

25 Günay Göksu Özdoğan, *"Turan"dan "Bozkurt"a: Tek Parti Döneminde Türkçülük, 1931-1946* (Istanbul: İletişim Yayınları, 2001), 197.

26 Emin Karaca, *Türk Basınında Kalem Kavgaları* (Istanbul: Gendaş, 1998), 127-29.

27 Ibid., 130.

28 Yalman was able to have a long and successful career as a journalist and vocal patriot, yet was reminded of his Dönme lineage to the end of his life. Incited by vicious anti-Dönme articles in the press, a far-right militant wounded Yalman in a 1952 assassination attempt. Yalman, *Yakin Tarihte*, 2:1589-1621. Despite a lifetime of dedication to Turkey, Yalman is remembered primarily as a Dönme by many rightists and Islamists. In this respect his experience is similar to his contemporary, Moiz Kohen, also known as Tekinalp, the dedicated superpatriot of Jewish origin who devoted his life to the Turkish cause yet is often considered a Jew, but not a Turk. See Jacob Landau, *Tekinalp: Turkish Patriot, 1883-1961* (Istanbul: Netherlands Historisch-Archaeologish Instituute, 1984).

29 Rogers Brubaker, *Nationalism Reframed: Nationhood and the National Question in the New Europe* (New York: Cambridge University Press, 1996), 4-5.

30 Ron Suny, "Constructing Primordialism: Old Histories for New Nations," *Journal of Modern History* 73, 4 (2001), 869.

31 Gershon Shafir and Yoav Peled, *Being Israeli: The Dynamics of Multiple Citizenship* (New York: Cambridge University Press, 2002), 343-48.

32 Ibid., 6-7.

33 Leyla Neyzi, "Remembering to Forget: Sabbateanism, National Identity, and Subjectivity in Turkey," *Comparative Studies in Society and History* 44 (2002), 140.

Chapter 9 (pp.74-82) – *Elise Massicard*
The case of Alevism

Anderson Benedict, *Imagined Communities: Reflections on the origins and spread of nationalism*, London, Verso, 1983.

Ayata Ayşe, " The emergence of identity politics in Turkey ", *New Perspectives on Turkey*, fall 1997, 17.

Benford Robert D., Snow David A., " Framing processes and social movements: an overview and assessment ", *Annual Review of Sociology*, 26, 2000, p. 611-639.

Billig Michael, *Banal Nationalism*, London, Sage, 1995.

Copeaux Etienne, *Espaces et temps de la nation turque. Analyse d'une historiographie nationaliste. 1931-1993*, Paris: CNRS, 1997.

Copeaux Etienne, " Le consensus obligatoire ", in Isabelle Rigoni (ed.), *Turquie, les mille visages. Politique, Religion, Femmes, Immigration*, Paris, Syllepse, 2000, p. 89-104.

Edelman Murray, *Constructing the political spectacle*, Chicago, University of Chicago Press, 1988.

European Commission, *2002 Regular Report on Turkey's Progress Toward Accession*, Brussels, 2002.

Gençkaya Ömer Faruk, "The Politics of Constitutional Amendment in Turkey, 1987-2002," with a revised and updated translation of the 1982 Constitution, in Gisbert H. Flanz (ed.), *Constitutions of the Countries of the World*, Dobbs Ferry, New York: Oceana Publications, Inc., 2003.

Kaleli Lütfi, *Alevi kimliğ i ve Alevi örgütlenmeleri*, Istanbul, Can, 2000.

Massicard Elise, "Les alévis et le discours politique de l'unité en Turquie depuis la fin des années 1980" in Hans-Lukas Kieser (ed.), *Aspects of the political language in Turkey*, Istanbul, Isis, 2002, p. 117-137.

Massicard Elise, *L'autre Turquie: le mouvement aléviste et ses territoires*, Paris, Presses Universitaires de France, 2005.

Massicard Elise, "Alevism in the 1960s: social change and mobilisation", in Hege Markussen (ed.), *Alevis and Alevism, Transformed Identities*, Istanbul, Isis, 2005, p. 109-135.

Navaro-Yashin Yael, "Uses and abuses of State and Civil Society in contemporary Turkey", *New Perspectives on Turkey*, 18, Spring 1998, p. 1-22.

Neveu Erik, "Médias, mouvements sociaux et espaces publics", *Réseaux*, n°98, 1999, p. 17-85.

Öncü Ayse, "Packaging Islam: Cultural Politics on the Landscape of Turkish Commercial Television", *Public Culture* vol. 8, n°1, 1995, p. 51-71.

Robins Kevin, "Interrupting Identities: Turkey / Europe" in S. Hall, P. du Gay (eds.), *Questions of Cultural Identity*, London: Sage, 1996, p. 61-86.

Schüler Harald, " Secularism and ethnicity: Alevis and social-democrats in search of an alliance ", in Stefanos Yerasimos, Günter Seufert, Karin Vorhoff (eds.), *Civil Society in the Grip of Nationalism*, Istanbul, Orient-Institut, 2000, p. 197-250.

Seufert Günter, "The Impact of Nationalist Discourses on Civil Society", in Stefanos Yerasimos, Günter Seufert, Karin Vorhoff (eds.), *Civil Society in the Grip of Nationalism*, Istanbul, Orient-Institut, 2000, p. 25-47.

Sökefeld Martin, "über die Schwierigkeit, dem türkischen Nationaldiskurs zu entkommen: Aleviten in Deutschland und "*Hürriyet*"", in Martin Sökefeld (Hrsg.), *Jenseits des Paradigmas kultureller Differenz*, Bielefeld, Transkript, 2004, p. 163-180.

Tilly Charles, *From Mobilization to Revolution*, Reading, Addison-Wesley, 1978.

Türkiye Birlik Partisi, *Türkiye Birlik Partisi 1966-1978*, Istanbul, Nurdoğ an Matbaası, 1978.

Vorhoff Karin, "'Let's reclaim our history and culture !' - Imagining Alevi community in contemporary Turkey", *Die Welt des Islams*, vol. 38 (2), 1998, p. 220-252.

Yavuz Hakan M. "Media Identities for Alevis and Kurds in Turkey", in Dale

Eickelman, John Anderson (eds.), *New Media in the Muslim World: The Emerging Public Sphere*, Bloomington, Indiana University Press, 1999, p. 180-199.

Yörük Zafer F., "Turkish Identity from Genesis to the Day of Judgement", *in* Kathryn Dean (ed.), *Politics and the Ends of Identity*, Aldershot, Ashgate, 1997, p. 103-134.

Yumul Arus, Özkırımlı Umut, "Reproducing the nation: 'banal nationalism' in the Turkish press", *Media, Culture and Society*, vol.22, 2000, p. 787-804.

Yücel Hakan, *L'organisation alévie-bektachie*, Unpublished M.A. thesis, Istanbul: Marmara üniversitesi, Institute for Social Sciences, 1998.

1   I distinguish Aleviness, which covers the social fact, from Alevism, which desig-
    nates the movement struggling for the recognition of Aleviness.

2   The term *mezhep* refers to the four schools of Islamic law. In Turkish however,
    mezhep often means religious group, i.e. Sunnis on the one hand and Alevis on
    the other.

3   "Siyasi parti kurma hakkı, Anayasanın başlangıç kısmında belirtilen temel
    ilkelere aykırı olarak ve Türk Devletinin ülkesi ve milletiyle bölünmez bütün-
    lüğ ünü bozmak, Devletin ve Cumhuriyetin varlığ ını tehlikeye düşürmek, temel
    hak ve hürriyetleri yok etmek, Devletin bir kişi veya zümre tarafından yönetilmesi-
    ni veya sosyal bir sınıfın diğ er sosyal sınıflar üzerinde egemenliğ ini sağ lamak
    veya dil, ırk, din, mezhep ayırımı veya bölge farklılığ ı yaratmak veya sair her-
    hangi bir yoldan bu kavram ve görüşlere veya herhangi bir diktatörlük türüne
    dayanan bir devlet düzeni kurmak amacıyla kullanılamaz." Siyasi Partiler
    Kanunu, n° 2820, 22 April 1983, art. 5. The English translation of abstracts of this
    law is to be found in Schüler 2000.

4   "Tüzükte üyelik için başvuranlar arasında dil, ırk, cinsiyet, din, mezhep, aile,
    zümre sınıf ve meslek farkı gözeten hükümler bulunamaz". Siyasi Partiler
    Kanunu, art. 12.

5   „Komünist, anarşist, faşist, teokratik, nasyonal sosyalist, din, dil, ırk, mezhep ve
    bölge adlarıyla veya aynı anlama gelen adlarla da siyasi partiler kurulamaz veya
    parti adında bu kelimeler kullanılamaz." Siyasi Partiler Kanunu, art. 96.

6   „Anayasa'da yer alan hak ve hürriyetlerinden hiç biri, Devletin ülkesi ve milleti-
    lyle bölünmez bütünlüğ ünü bozmak, Türk Devletinin ve Cumhuriyetin
    varlığ ını tehlikeye düşürmek, temel hak ve hürriyetkeri yok etmek, Devletin bir
    kişi veya zümre tarafından yönetilmesini veya sosyal bir sınıfın diğ er sosyal
    sınıflar üzerinde egemenliğ ini sağ lamak veya dil, ırk, din ve mezhep ayrımı
    yaratmak veya sair herhangi bir yoldan bu kavram ve görüşlere dayanan bir devlet
    düzenini kurmak amacıyla kullanılmamazlar." Art. 14. For the English text of the
    1982 Constitution, see Gençkaya 2003.

7   Interview with Mustafa Timisi, Ankara, 7th December, 2000.

8   Interview with a former BP executive, Ankara, 12th November, 2000 (author's
    translation).

9   For the ambiguous relation between the Social Democratic parties and particular-
    ist demands in the early 1990s, see Schüler 2000.

10 "Siyasi partiler, laiklik ilkesi doğ rultusunda, bütün siyasi görüş ve düşünüşlerin
    dışında kalarak ve milletçe dayanışma ve bütünleşmeyi amaç edinerek özel
    kanunda gösterilen görevleri yerine getirmek durumunda olan Diyanet İşleri
    Başkanlığ ının, genel idare içinde yer almasına ilişkin Anayasanın 136ncı mad-
    desi hükmüne aykırı amaç güdemezler", Siyasi Partiler kanunu, art. 89.

11   In the end the party was acquitted by the Constitutional Court and was not dissolved.

12   "Anayasanın başlangıç kısmında belirtilen temel ilkelere aykırı olarak dernek kurulamaz; (2) Dil, ırk, sınıf, din ve mezhep ayrımına dayanılarak nitelikleri Anayasada belirtilen Türkiye Cumhuriyetinin varlığ ını tehlikeye düşürmek veya ortadan kaldırmak; (5) Bölge, ırk, sosyal sınıf, din ve mezhep esasına veya adına dayanarak faaliyette bulunmak (6) Türkiye Cumhuriyeti ülkesi üzerinde, ırk, din, mezhep, kültür veya dil farklılığ ına dayanan azınlıklar bulunduğ unu ileri sürmek veya Türk Dilinden veya kültüründen ayrı dil ve kültürleri korumak, geliştirmek veya yaymak suretiyle azınlık yaratmak veya herhangi bir bölgenin veya ırkın veya sınıfın veya belli bir din veya mezhepten olanların diğ erlerine hakim veya diğ erlerinden imtiyazlı olmasını sağ lamak ". Art. 5, Law on Associations n° 29008, 6 October 1983.

13   "Cumhuriyetin Anayasa ile belirlenen niteliklerine ve Anayasanın temel ilkelerine, hukuka, ahlâka, milli birliğ e ve milli menfaatlere aykırı veya belli bir ırk ya da cemaat mensuplarını desteklemek amacıyla vakıf kurulamaz ". Art. 101. For the English translation of the Civil Code, see the website of the Human Rights Law Research Center, Istanbul Bilgi University, http://insanhaklarimerkezi.bilgi.edu.tr/source/51.asp?lid=en&id=0. A similar ban has existed in the Civil Code since 1967.

14   For an overview of the legal struggle of this foundation, mainly with the General Directory of Foundations (*Vakıflar Genel Müdürlüğ ü*), which lasted ten years, see Kaleli 2000: 220-282.

15   Cem houses, cem being the main Alevi religious ceremony.

16   "The creation of an association bearing the name "Alevi-Bektashi" is impossible. The word Alevi is a religious and denominational term; it is impossible to create an association which focuses its activities on Aleviness. Otherwise, other similar religious associations will inevitably be created, which would destroy the indivisible integrity fixed by the Law of the State, the Nation and the country. Besides, it is specified that Aleviness, like all other *mezheps*, enjoys the protection of the law and the Constitution, and is a part of the country's realities, but that everyone should stay in the limits fixed by the law; one can create associations and foundations conducting religious activities amongst others, as long as by using these rights one does not harm the unity and solidarity of the country and the nation". "Alevi-Bektaşi Kültür Derneğ i kapatıldı", *Radikal*, 13rd February 2002 (author's translation).

17   The first version of the 1982 Constitution, adopted during the military regime, mentions separatist threats as the justification for the military intervention: "...following the operation carried out on 12 September 1980 by the Turkish Armed Forces in response to a call from the Turkish Nation, of which they form an inseparable part, at a time when the approach of a separatist, destructive and bloody civil war unprecedented in the Republican era threatened the integrity of the eternal Turkish Nation and motherland and the existence of the sacred Turkish State". ("Ebedi Türk Vatan ve milletinin bütünlüğ üne ve kutsal Türk Devletinin varlığ ına karşı, Cumhuriyet devrinde benzeri görülmemiş bölücü ve yıkıcı kanlı bir iç savaşın gerçekleşme noktasına yaklaştığ ı sırada...")

18   For an analysis of framings and counter-framings during a "critical moment of discourse", when a local event – the Refah City Council's destruction of parts of the

Karacaahmet foundation buildings in Istanbul in 1994 – gave rise to widespread commentary in the mass communication media, see Massicard 2002.

19 The expression "return of the repressed" is used by Robins (1996: 72), and taken over again by Yörük (1997: 122).

20 Which are special editions, and not the Turkish edition plus an European supplement.

Chapter 10 (po. 85-103) – Fatma Müge Göçek
Parameters of a post-nationalist historiography

I would like to thank Burç ak Keskin, Jirair Libaridian, Ron Suny, Erik-Jan Zürcher and participants of the Basel Conference on "Turkey: Towards Post-Nationalism?" for their very valuable comments on this article; the remaining problems in interpretation are of course entirely mine.

Armaoğlu, Fahir. 1964.*Siyasi Tarih 1789-1960 (Political History 1789-1960)*. Ankara: Sevinc.

Artinian, Vartan. 1970. *The Armenian Constitutional System in the Ottoman Empire 1839-1963*. Brandeis University Ph.D. Thesis.

Ben-Yehuda, Nachman. 1995. *The Masada Myth: Collective Memory and Mythmaking in Israel*. Madison: University of Wisconsin Press.

Bolle, Kees W. 1987. "Myth." In *Encyclopedia of Religion*, M. Eliade, ed. New York: Macmillan. Volume 10.

Braude, Benjamin and B. Lewis, eds. 1982. *Christians and Jews in the Ottoman Empire*. Two volumes. New York: Holmes and Meier.

De Certeau, Michel. 1988. *The Writing of History*. New York.

Fuchs, Eckhardt and Stuchtey, eds. 2002. *Across Cultural Borders: Historiography in Global Perspective*. London: Rowman and Littlefield.

Göcek, Fatma Müge. 1996. *Rise of the Bourgeoisie, Demise of Empire: Ottoman Westernization and Social Change*. New York: Oxford University Press.

Libaridian, Gerard J. 1978. "Objectivity and the Historiography of the Armenian Genocide." *The Armenian Review* 31/1-121: 79-87.

White, Hayden. 1978. "The Fictions of Factual Representation." In *Tropics of Discourse*: Essays in Cultural Criticism. Baltimore, MD: Johns Hopkins University Press.

Young, James E. 1988. *Writing and Rewriting the Holocaust: Narrative and the Consequences of Interpretation*. Bloomington: Indiana University Press.

Zürcher, Erik-Jan. 1992. "The Ottoman Legacy of the Turkish Republic: An Attempt at a New Periodization." *Die Welt des Islams* 32: 237-53.

Chapter 11 (pp. 104-122) – Raymond H. Kévorkian
A discourse that legitimizes mass violence

1 AMAE, War Series 1914-1918, vol. 862, report enclosed in the dispatch of the Ambassador at Bern to the Minister of Foreign Affairs, on 28 November 1917, p. 49.

2 Idem.

3 Stepan Astourian, "The Armenian Genocide: An Interpretation", The History Teacher, 23/2 (February 1990), p. 138-140, fn 116-177 and 122-123. Astourian revealed evidence that some other leaders of the CUP, like Sabancalı Hakkı and Hüsrev Sami, were also against the so-called deportations. (Idem, p. 141, fn 124-125).

4   Published in full in *Ikdam*, 25 September 1917. The French translation is attached
    to the dispatch of the French Ambassador at Bern to the Minister of Foreign
    Affairs on 28 November 1917: AMAE, War Series 1914-1918, vol. 862, p. 50-60.
5   Idem. p. 51.
6   Idem. p. 52-53. This discourse is echoed in RLC, "L'Arménie et l'Allemagne", La
    Croix, on 13 October, 1917, *La Suisse*, on 7 October, 1917.
7   Meclisi Mebusan Zabıt Ceridesi [Minutes of the sessions at the Ottoman
    Parliament], 3rd legislature, 5th session, vol. 1, 11th sitting, 4 November 1334 [1918],
    p. 95, 100, 109, quoted by V. Dadrian, *The Armenian Genocide...*, Watertown, 1995,
    p. 7-8 and fn. 1 (in Armenian).
8   Idem. p. 100 and 109.
9   Idem. p. 12-13.
10 Meclisi Mebusan Zabıt Ceridesi [Minutes of the sessions at the Ottoman
    Parliament], 3rd legislature, 5th session, vol. 1, 11th sitting, 18 November 1334 [1918],
    p. 143-161, 109, quoted by V. Dadrian, *The Armenian Genocide according to parlia-
    mentary and XXX sources, op. cit.*, 1995, p. 21-42.
11 Idem. fn. 17. V. Dadrian gives precise information about Sami's criminal activi-
    ties, and about the kidnapping of young women generously offered to his col-
    leagues in Constantinople. Indicted by the Ottoman Martial Court, he was arrest-
    ed and then set free, after he played the fool. He was then caught again and exiled
    to Malta by the British before being tried.
12 Idem, 23rd sitting, 9 December, 1334 [1918], p. 257-258, in V. Dadrian, *op. cit.*, p. 61-
    74.
13 Idem. 11 December, 1334 [1918], p. 286-301, quoted by Dadrian, p. 61-74.
14 Idem. p. 300-301, quoted by Dadrian, p. 70-71.
15 Idem. 25th sitting, 12 December 1334 [1918], p. 305-317, quoted by Dadrian, p. 74-86.
16 Idem. p. 300-301, quoted by Dadrian, p. 86.
17 Service Historique de la Marine (Château de Vincennes), Service de
    Renseignements de la Marine, Turkey, 1BB7 236 (quoted from now on as SHM, SR
    Marine, 1BB7 236). These hearings were published partially in 1933 in the newspa-
    per Vakit, under the title Harp Kabinelerinin isticvabi (Hearing of members of the
    wartime cabinets), and in full, in Turkish transcribed into Latin letters, by Osman
    Selim Kocahanoğlu, *İttihat Terakki'nin sorgunlanması ve Yargılanması* (1918-
    1919), Istanbul, 1998.
18 SHM, SR Marine, Turkey, 1BB7 236, Document n° 1651 B-9, Constantinople, 24
    January 1920; Lieutenant Gobey: p. 3, Annex n° 14, *Ittihat-Terakki'nin sorgunlan-
    ması..., op. cit.*, p. 293-382, contains the full composition of the Commission,
    chaired by Abdullah Azmi, and the dates of the hearings.
19 Idem. p. 7.
20 SHM, SR Marine, Turkey, 1BB7 236, Document n° 1651 B-9, Constantinople, 24
    January 1920, Lieutenant Gobey, Annex n° 15, p. 10.
21 Idem. p. 11.
22 Idem. p. 12.
23 SHM, SR Marine, Turkey, 1BB7 236, Document n° 1687 B-9, Constantinople, 31
    January 1920, Lieutenant Goybet, Annex n° 17, p. 17.
24 SHM, SR Marine, Turkey, 1BB7 236, Document n° 1724 B-9, Constantinople, 7
    February 1920, translated by L. Feuillet, Annex n° 19, Halil Bey, p. 4 and 6, *Ittihat-
    Terraki'nin sorgulanması..., op. cit.*, p. 265-291.

25 SHM, SR Marine, Turkey, 1BB7 236, Document n° 1805 B-9, Constantinople, 26 February 1920, translated by L. Feuillet, Annex n° 20, Said Halim's testimony, p. 18.

26 Idem. p. 19.

27 Idem. p. 20.

28 Idem. p. 21-22.

29 Idem. p. 23-24.

30 Idem. p. 25-26.

31 Idem. p. 29-30.

32 A former *mutesarif* (governor of a district) of Serres, where he took part in the massacre of Macedonians in 1912, Ahmet Şükrü was involved in the murdering of many journalists and Liberal politicians like Ahmet Samim and Hasan Fehmi.

33 SHM, SR Marin, Turkey, 1BB7 236, Document B-9, Constantinople, 3 May 1920, translated by L. Feuillet, Ahmet Şükrü Bey's testimony, p. 21-24; *Ittihat-Terakki'nin sorgunlanması...*, op. cit., p. 171-207.

34 Idem. p. 25, p. 36.

35 SHM, SR Marine, Turkey, 1BB7 236, Document n° 1968 B-9, Constantinople, 15 April 1920, translated by L. Feuillet, Ahmet Nesimi Bey's testimony in front of the 5th Commission of the Ottoman Parliament, p. 1-2, and 10; *Ittihat-Terakki'nin sorgunlanması...*, op. cit., p. 209-251.

36 Idem. p.11-12.

37 Idem. p. 13-18, and 43.

38 SHM, SR Marine, Turkey, 1BB7 236, Document n° 2054 B-9, Constantinople, 3 May 1920, translated by L. Feuillet. İbrahim Bey's testimony, p. 12, p. 27-28; *İttihat-Terakki'nin sorgulanması...*, op. cit., p. 133-169.

39 Idem. p. 27-41.

40 SHM, SR Marine, Turkey, 1BB7 236, Document n° 2000 B-9, Constantinople, 21 April 1920, translated by L. Feuillet, testimony of the former Constantinople commissioner in chief, İsmail Canbolat Bey, p. 7-8; *Ittihat-Terakki'nin sorgunlanması...*, op. cit., p. 417-436. This is a section of the Direction of the Migrants, the Sub-Direction of the Deportees, located in Aleppo, which managed the 25 concentration camps in Syria where many thousands of Armenians died.

41 Krieger, *Documented History of the Massacres of the Armenians of Yozgat*, New York, 1980, p. 51 (in Armenian). The author has published a pioneering work, using an exceptional documentation, especially documents kept in the Patriarchate in Jerusalem, for the first time.

42 Report about the parliamentary sitting in the Constantinople daily *La Renaissance*, n° 13, 22 December 1918, p. 1.

43 Krieger, op. cit., p. 78. As *vali*, he had courageously refused to implement the orders to deport and massacre the local Armenians and had thus been dismissed and replaced. The fact-finding commission included an Ottoman Greek judge and Artin [Harutiun] Mosdichian, a former judge of the Appeal Court of Constantinople. More details on the establishment of the commission are given in Taner Akçam, *İnsan Hakları ve Ermeni Sorunu*, Ankara, 1999, p. 445-446.

44 V. Dadrian, *History of the Armenian Genocide*, XXX.

45 Abstract of Vehip Pasha's testimony, 5 December 1918, read during the first session of the criminal trial of the Unionists on 27 April 1919; *Takvim-I Vakayi*, n° 3540, 5 May 1919, p. 7, 2nd column and complete 12-page handwritten testimony:

Archives of the Armenian Patriarchate of Constantinople, Armenian Patriarchate of Jerusalem Information Office, shelf-mark: L 171-182.

46 *La Renaissance*, n° 307, 27 November 1919, n° 313, 4 December 1919.

47 *La Renaissance*, n° 318, 10 December 1919.

48 V. Dadrian quotes two sessions of this Court in March 1919: one on 8 March, chaired by Fevzi Pasha (*Takvim-i Vekayi*, n° 3493); and the second on 19 March, chaired by Naz"m Pasha (Journal d'Orient, 23 April 1919; *Takvim-i Vekayi*, n° 3503).

49 Reported in *La Renaissance*, n° 113, 12 April 1919, p. 1.

50 Minutes of the fourth sitting of the Unionists' trials: SHAT, Service Historique de la Marine, Service de Renseignements de la Marine, Turquie, 1 BB7 232, Document n° 676, Constantinople, May 1919, Lieutenant Goybet, assistant to the Head of the SR Marine, cross-examination of Ziya Gökalp.

Chapter 12 (pp. 125-135) – *Ebru Bulut*
The social grammar of populist nationalism

1 Michael Billig, *Banal Nationalism*, Sage Publications, London, 1997.

2 However, a new, much more elite-oriented and ethnicist form of nationalism emerged mainly among the intelligentsia in the first half of the present decade.

3 For a detailed analysis of crises as a political instrument see: Hamit Bozarslan, "La crise comme instrument politique en Turquie", *Esprit*, n° 271, 2001, pp.140-151.

4 Ünit Cizre Sakallioğlu argues that in the 1990s Turkish centre-right and centre-left parties should be considered as "cartel parties". They owe their survival neither to their political programme nor their performance in the power. They depend on their proximity to the "cartel" already formed by the state elites. Ünit Cizre Sakallioğlu, *Muktedirlerin Siyaseti*, Iletisim, Istanbul, 1999.

5 Indeed as Serif Mardin suggests, conspiracy theory "often passes for a philosophy of history in contemporary Turkey", "The Nakşibendi Order in Turkish History", in R. Tapper, *Islam in Modern Turkey. Religion, Politics and Literature in a Secular State*, London: I.B. Tauris, 1991, p. 122.

6 Vincent Descombes, "Pour elle, un français doit mourir", *Critique*, 366, 1977, p.1006.

7 Namely the Six Arrows of Kemalism: Secularism, Nationalism, Republicanism, Revolutionism, Populism, and Etatism.

8 Hamit Bozarslan, "'Komplo Teorileri' üzerine Tartışmalara bir Katkı" *Birikim*, n°183, 2004, p.19 -24.

9 David Snow, "Analyse de cadres et mouvements sociaux", *in* Daniel Cefaï and Danny Trom (dir.), *Les formes et de l'action collective*, Ed. EHESS, 2001, pp.27-49; D. Snow, B. Rochford, S. Worden, R. Benford, "Frame alignement processes, micromobilization, and movement participation", *American Sociological Review*, volume: 51, n°4, 1986, pp. 464-481.

10 The Susurluk Affair refers to the following incident: in November 1996, a radical-right militant wanted by the police and a high-ranking police officer were killed in a car accident. A deputy of the True Path Party (DYP) close to Demirel and Ciller, successively leaders of this political party, was the only passenger to survive. In fact, this accident revealed the relation between the mafia, security forces and the political class. But it was instrumentalized to marginalize the Islamist party, which was in power.

11 Bert Klandermans, "Mobilization and participation: Social-psychological expansions of Resource Mobilization Theory", *American Sociological Review*, volume: 49, n°5, 1984, p.587.

12 Perhaps one striking example was a small poster of Atatürk given to every customer in a women's fashion shop during New Year purchases

13 Tanıl Bora, "Nationalist discourses in Turkey", *The South Atlantic Quarterly*, volume: 102, n°2-3, 2003, p. 438

14 Michel Foucault, *Histoire de la sexualité* II (L'usage des plaisirs), Gallimard, Paris, 1984.

15 AKUT: a rescue team founded by a private initiative of mountaineers. This team become famous after the rescue operation after the earthquake in 1999. The whole text of their declaration ran: "Great father, we swear to do all that is necessary in order to protect the Turkish revolution and the Republic of Turkey and to make it progress. We swear to serve the strong Turkey of the future, to be young Turks worthy of you and to advance without any fear on the road you opened. The homeland is in trustworthy hands. Sleep in peace, father of mine". *Milliyet*, 24.11.1999, quoted in Etienne Copeaux, "Le consensus obligatoire", in Isabelle Rigoni, *Turquie: les milles visages*, Syllepse, Paris, 2000, p. 96.

16 For these examples, see Etienne Copeaux, *art.cit.* pp. 89-105.

17 Mauss defines "institution" as "an ensemble of acts or ideas very instituted that individuals find in front of them and who asserts themselves more or less on them. (...) For Mauss, it is a mode of thought as well as a manner of speaking or acting." M. Mauss, P. Fauconnet, "Sociologie" Année Sociologique, vol: 30, 1901.

18 AKP: The Justice and Development Party, led by Recep Tayyip Erdoğan, has been in power since November 2002. It was founded in August 2001 by reformists of the former Islamist Party RP that closed down in June 2001.

19 HADEP: People's Democratic Party, pro-Kurdish, successor of HEP, DEP and at present DEHAP.

20 *Radikal*, 24 October 1999.

21 MGK: National Security Council. It is composed of the President of the Republic, the Prime Minister, the Ministers of Foreign Affairs, Defence, and the Interior, and the five supreme commanders of the armed forces. According to the 1982 Constitution, the government has to "accord priority" to the recommendations of the MGK. However, in 2003, in the constitutional reforms the recommendations of the MGK were defined as "advice" to the government. Thus, they do not have an obligatory character any longer.

22 The Prosperity Party (RP, Islamists) became the first party of the country in the 1995 elections. After months of political instability, the party leader, N.Erbakan, became Prime Minister in May 1996. For the first time in its history, Turkey was ruled by a government led by an Islamist Party. From then on until 28 February 1997, tension between the government and the army increased continuously.

23 Cornelius Castoriadis, *La montée de l'insignifiance*, Seuil, Paris, 1996.

24 Umit Cizre Sakallioğlu, Menderes Cinar, "Turkey 2002: Kemalism, Islamism, and Politics in the Light of February 28 Process", *The South Atlantic Quarterly*, volume: 102, n°2-3, 2003, p. 312.

25 That is, not secularism in its essential nature but its Turkish strong-arm version.

26 Especially the reforms concerning the YÖK (Higher Education Board) or the opening of the university entrance system to students graduated from *imam-hatip*

schools (secondary schools for prayer-leaders and preachers).

27 For instance when the wife of the President of Parliament, who wears a head-scarf, takes part in the welcome ceremony for the President of the Republic after his foreign visits; or the military elites and the President of the Republic "boycott" official ceremonies because of the presence of the veiled wives of some AKP members.

28 Umit Cizre Sakallioğlu, Menderes Cinar, art.cit. p.326.

29 Georg Simmel proposed victory, compromise and fatigue (or lassitude) as factors that provoke demobilization. Georg Simmel, *Conflict: The Web of Group Affiliations*, New York: Free Press, 1964, especially pp. 87-124.

Chapter 13 (pp. 136-146) – *Günter Seufert*
Religion: nation-building or civil society?

1 The other one being the Directorate for Religious Education in the Ministry of National Education, which controls the Faculties of Theology as well as the Preachers' (imam-hatip) Schools and fixes the obligatory religious instruction in school.

2 I. Kara, "Eine Behörde im Spannungsfeld von Staat und Religion", in G. Seufert & J. Waardenburg (eds), *Türkischer Islam und Europa*, Stuttgart, Franz-Steiner-Verlag 1999, p. 209-240.

3 H. Schüler: "Secularism and ethnicity", in: S. Yerasimos et al. (eds) *Civil society in the grip of nationalism*, Würzburg, Ergon-Verlag 2000, pp. 197-250.

4 P. Berger, *The sacred canopy*, Douleday, Anchor Press 1969, pp. 107 and 127f.

5 M. Tunçay, "Der Laizismus in der türkischen Republik", in: J. Blaschke & M.v. Bruinessen (eds) *Islam und Politik in der Türkei*, Berlin (West), Express-Verlag 1984, p. 53-94.

6 See, with a reference to Robert Bellah, Markus Dreßler: *Die civil religion der Türkei*, Würzburg, Ergon-Verlag 1999.

7 G. Seufert *Die Türkisch-Islamische Union der türkischen Religionsbehörde*, in: Seufert/Waardenburg, p. 261-293; G. Seufert: *Turkish state reactions towards the institutionalization of Islam in Germany*, in: J. Malik (ed.) Muslim in Europe, Münster, Lit-Verlag 2004, p. 75-89; S. Kaplan, *Din-u Devlet all over again?* International Journal of Middle Eastern Studies, 01/2001, p. 113-127, and Ö. Altan, *Sanctifying the nation* ISIM Newsletter 21/2003, p. 52-53.

8 M.S. Aydın, "Avrupa Birliği, din ve diyanet", *Islâmiyat* 3/2001, p. 17.

9 A.F. Başgil: *Din ve laiklik*, Istanbul, Fakülteler Matbaası 1955.

10 M.S. Aydın, Avrupa Birliği.

11 See the stance of Atatürk towards the masses according to Metin Heper, "Atatürk'te devlet düşüncesi", in: E. Kalaycıoğlu & Y. Sarıbay (eds), Türk siyasal hayatı: değişim ve süreklilik, Istanbul, Der Yayınları, n.d., p. 245.

12 M.S. Aydın, Avrupa Birliği, p.19.

13 Güncel din" mes'eleler istişare toplantısı I, sonuç bildirgesi, Istanbul, 18 May 2002.

14 Ö. Özsoy, "Individuum und Gemeinschaft und der ‚Andere' im Koran", in: Deutsche Botschaft Ankara (ed.): *Islam und Europa* II, Ankara, Dönmez Offset 2004, p. 10. Idem: Kur'an tarihsel yazıları, Ankara Kitabiyat Yayınları 2004.

15 A. Bardakoğlu, "Din Kur'an'dan ibaret degil", *Radikal* 27 March 2000.

16 Ibid. See also M.S. Aydın, "Dinler ahlak temelinde yakınlaşıyor", Tempo 3 July 2003, p. 18.

17 Bardakoğlu's commitment to a more individualistic reading of Islam has continued during his term of office as Head of the Directorate, see his: "Türkiye'de birey, toplum ve otorite"; manuscript of the speech in Istanbul-Tarabya on 12 June 2004.

18 For the distinction see T. Luckmann: *The invisible religion*, London, Collier/Macmillan 1974, p. 78.

19 M.S. Aydın, in: M. Gündem, "Reform, dinde mi dindarlıkta mı?" Series in *Milliyet*, 20 February 2004.

20 U. Heyd, *The life and teachings of Ziya Gökalp*, London Lzac/Harvill 1950, p. 82 ff.

21 See W.L. King: "Religion", in M. Eliade (ed.) *The Encyclopedia of Religion*, New York 1968, p. 282.

22 A. Küskün: "Ne o, ne de öteki", Tezkire 2/92, p. 30.

23 3 % consider themselves in no way religious and 2 % refuse to comment about their belief, A. Çarkoğlu & B. Toprak, Türkiye'de din, toplum ve siyaset, Istanbul 2002, TESEV Yayınları, p. 42.

24 Kemaleddin Taş, "Türk halkının gözüyle Diyanet, Istanbul, iz Yayınları 1995.

25 Çarkoğlu/Toprak, Türkiye'de din, p. 66 and 68.

26 Op. cit. p. 69 f.

27 23% state that as the natural sciences advance, the content of the Quran is becoming less persuasive (62% against), and 35% say new interpretations of Islam are needed (50% against). Op. cit. p. 14.

28 R. Çakır & F. Çalmuk: *Recep Tayyip Erdoğan*, Istanbul, Metis Yayınları, 2001, p. 178 ff.

29 Ö. Çelik, AKP deputy and Erdoğan's envoy to Israel in autumn 2004, see his: "Beraber yaşama sorunu", *Bilgi ve Hikmet*, 5/1994, p. 16 ff).

30 Official Journal of the European Communities, L 145/44 EN 12 June 2003.

31 O. Oehring, *Cultural rights and freedom of religion for all citizens*, manuscript, Aachen, 2004, p. 2.

32 See in particular the Law of Associations and the articles of the Civil Code.

33 See the numerous contributions of the editor in chief of the daily *Radikal*, İsmet Berkan, in May and June 2004.

34 Commission of the European Communities: 2004 Regular Report on Turkey's progress towards accession, Brussels 6.10.2004, p. 44.

35 Interview with Ali Bardakoğlu, Ankara 27 October 2004.

36 See: Günter Seufert, Müzakere (DİTİB'in Almanya'da din – Müslümanlık tartışmalarındaki yeri), in: Diyanet İsleri Baskanlığı: III Din Şûrası, Tebliğ ve Müzakereleri, Ankara 2005, p. 326-332.

37 H. Hatemi, *Cemaat vakıflarına ilişkin kanun tasarısı*, Istanbul 16 January 2004.

38 Personal communication, 8 April 2004.

Chapter 14 (pp. 147-154) – *Béatrice Hendrich* The emblem of the AKP

1 Faruk Birtek, social scientist at Boğaziçi University (Istanbul), „Yeni bir Parti yok", in: *Radikal*, 16.09.02. - Many thanks to Bruce Grant / New York University for polishing the English version of this text.

2 www.chp.org.tr

3 www.chp.org.tr, 09.11.04.

4   There exist innumberable books and articles on Turkish nationalism. To quote some of the more recent ones: Ayşe Kadıoğlu, "The Paradox of Turkish Nationalism and the Construction of Official Identity", in: MES 4(1996), 177-193; Mehmet Şükrü Hanioğlu, *The Young Turks in Opposition*, New York: Oxford University Press 1995; Béatrice Hendrich, *Milla – millet – Nation: Von der Religionsgemeinschaft zur Nation?*, Frankfurt a.M.: Peter Lang 2003.

5   Yılmaz Altuğ, *Türk İnkilap Tarihi*, Istanbul: Çağ layan Kitabevi 1992 (first publ. 1973), 213.

6   The CHP was re-established in 1992. For the history of the Social Democrat-Republican parties after the last coup d'état see Harald Schüler, *Die türkischen Parteien und ihre Mitglieder*, Hamburg: Deutsches Orientinstitut 1998, 68-94.

7   www.chp.org.tr, 09.11.04.

8   "Yeni bir Parti yok", in: *Radikal*, 16.09.02.

9   For continuity and change in the nationalism of the early CHF/CHP, see further Kemal H. Karpat, "The Republican People's Party, 1923-1945", in: Metin Heper, Jacob M. Landau (eds.), *Political Parties and Democracy in Turkey*, London / New York: Tauris 1991, 42-64, here 51-53.

10 Law No. 2533, 1 96/1. See further the case of the *Halk Partisi* (1989-1991): www.anayasa.gov.tr/KARARLAR/SPK/K1991/K1991-02.htm, 15.12.04.

11 Literally meaning "Party of felicity", "*saadet*" also refers to the Golden Age of the Righteous Caliphs at the beginning of Islamic history, called "*asrı saadet*" in Turkish.

12 Yıldırım Türker, "Çıplak ampulun çiğ ışığı", in: *Radikal* 19.08.01.

13 Aydın Hasan, "Ampul burada aydınlanma nerede?", in: *Milliyet* 16.08.01.

14 Ahmet Turan Alkan: "Ampul", in: *Zaman* 20.08.01.

15 Özgür Ekşi: "SP'li Zengin: Amblem bizden kopya", in: *Milliyet* 16.08.01.

16 Nazım Alpman: "Ampul'ü Erdoğan buldu", in: *Akşam*, 11.11.02.

17 See Günter Seufert, *Neue pro-islamische Parteien in der Türkei*, Berlin: Stiftung Wissenschaft und Politik 2002.

18 See European Court of Human Rights, Case of *Refah Partisi* and others v. Turkey, 31 July 2001; final judgement 13 February 2003.

19 Nazım Alpman, "Ampul'ü Erdoğan buldu", in: Akşam, 11.11.02.

20 See e.g. the 59th government programme, 18.03.03, available on-line at www.akparti.org.tr

21 Yalçın Akdoğan, "Ak Parti ve muhafazakar demokrasi", available on-line at www.akparti.org.tr

22 Beginning of sura 24, verse 35.

23 COM(2004) 656 final.

24 Yalçın Akdoğan: "Ak Parti ve muhafazakar demokrasi", available on-line at www.akparti.org.

25 İsmet Berkan: "İstanbul'un ışıkları", in: *Radikal* 25.01.05.

26 İhsan D. Dağı: *Batılılaşma Korkusu*, Ankara: Vadi Yayınları 2003, 171.

27 CHP Genel Başkanı Baykal: „17 Aralık'ta Brüksel'de Türkiye'ye Verilen, Tam Üyelik Haritasının Güzergahı Değildir", available on-line at www.chp.org.tr.

Chapter 15 (pp. 155-164) – *Gülistan Gürbey*
"Turkey for the Turks" or an open society?

1   Cf.for effects of the EU accession perspective and the reform process: Heinz

Kramer/Hanna-Lena Krauss: "Ein kluger Wegweiser. Der Türkei-Bericht der Europäischen Kommission". SWP-Aktuell 50. Berlin. November 2004; Heinz Kramer: "EU kompatibel oder nicht? Zur Debatte um die Mitgliedschaft der Türkei in der Europäischen Union.". Berlin. August 2003; ibid. "Demokratieverständnis und Demokratisierung in der Türkei". In: *Südosteuropa-Mitteilungen*, 2004/1. Munich, pp 30 – 43; Günter Seufert: "Laizismus in der Türkei – Trennung von Staat und Religion?" In: *Südosteuropa-Mitteilungen*, loc. cit., pp 16 – 29.

2   Cf. on Turkish nationalism Hamit Bozarslan: "Die Büchse der Pandora: Die schwierige Gleichung des türkischen Nationalismus", In: Centre Marc Bloch - Deutsch-Französisches Forschungszentrum für Sozialwissenschaften Berlin (ed.): *Infobrief*, No. 5, 2nd term 1995, pp 31 – 61.

3   In a study carried out on behalf of the Turkish Association of Chambers of Commerce and Stock Exchanges, Dogu Ergil arrived at the conclusion that the state failed to establish national unity, which should only have been established at a political level, because it equated nation with culture and attempted to achieve unity in the field of culture as well. The term "nation" became indicative of the unity of the Turks. The state only allowed for one identity of an ethnic group (Turkish) in its organisation. No structures for maintaining independence were offered in the official political and socio-cultural field. Within the state, based on authoritarian and unitary structures, other groups of the population have no opportunity to preserve their cultural identity. Cf. TOBB: *Dogu Sorunu: Teshisler ve Tesbitler* (The problem of the South-East: diagnoses and prognoses), Ankara, Temmuz, 1995, p 57; Dogu Ergil: "Das Kurdenproblem und Lösungsansätze", in: NAVEND-Kurdisches Informations- und Dokumentationszentrum e.V. (ed.): *Kurdistan heute*, Bonn No. 18, May/June 1996, pp 16 – 19.

4   For more details see Gülistan Gürbey: "Die türkische Kurdenpolitik im Kontext des EU-Beitrittsprozesses und der Kopenhagener Kriterien". In: *Südosteuropa-Mitteilungen*, 1/2004, Munich, pp 44 – 57.

5   In March 2004, RTüK ordered the shut-down of a local station broadcasting from Diyarbakir for 30 days because it had allegedly violated the principle of the indivisibly unity of the state by broadcasting two Kurdish love songs in August 2003.

Chapter 16 (pp. 167-174) – *Eugen Krieger*
Turkey's fragile EU perspectives since the 1960s

1   Cf. for example, Hans-Ulrich Wehler,"Das Türkenproblem", *DIE ZEIT*, No. 38, 12 September 2002; for a political perspective see, for example, Friedbert Pflüger, *Ein Neuer Weltkrieg, Die islamistische Herausforderung des Westens*, Munich, Deutsche Verlags-Anstalt, 2004, pp. 270 f.; Valéry Giscard d'Estaing in "Le débat sur l'identité religieuse de l'Europe entre la Convention", *Le Monde*, 8 November 2002; idem, "Pour ou contre l'adhésion de la Turquie à l'Union européene", Le Monde, 9 November 2002; EU Agriculture Commissioner Fischler,"Die EU ringt um einen Türkei-Entscheid", NZZ No. 212, 11 September 2004; Heinrich August Winkler, "Wir erweitern uns zu Tode", *DIE ZEIT*, 7 November 2002; etc.

2   Ministère des Affaires Etrangères Français, Doc. R/111/60, meeting of the EEC Council of Ministers of 6 February 1960.

3   Under-Secretary of Foreign Affairs Carstens to State Secretary Scherpenberg,

Aufzeichnungen 205-82.00/90.38, 17 July 1959, in Horst Möller and Klaus
Hildebrand, eds., *Bundesrepublik Deutschland und Frankreich, Dokumente 1949-
1963*, vol. 1, *Aussenpolitik und Diplomatie*, Munich, K. G. Saur Verlag, 1997, pp.
731 f.

4   Cf., for example, MP Baade of the SPD faction in the Bundestag during the meet-
    ing of the Foreign Affairs Committee of 9 December 1959, in Karl Dietrich
    Bracher, Klaus Hildebrand, et al., eds., *Quellen zur Geschichte des
    Parlamentarismus und der politischen Parteien*, vol. 13/III, *Der Auswärtige
    Ausschuss des Deutschen Bundestages, Sitzungsprotokolle 1957-1961*, second half-
    volume, Düsseldorf, Droste Verlag, 2003, p. 791.

5   Cf. Can Özren, *Die Beziehung der beiden deutschen Staaten zur Türkei (1945/49 -
    1963)*, Studien zur Zeitgeschichte des Nahen Ostens und Nordafrikas, vol. 5,
    Münster i.a., LIT Verlag, 1999.

6   Premier Ministre, Comité Interministériel pour les Questions de Coopération
    Economique Européenne, Procès-Verbal No. MC/179 de la réunion tenue le 9
    octobre 1959.

7   Ministère des Affairs Economiques, Aide mémoire, Relations économiques fran-
    co-turques et le Marché Commun Européen, 30 September 1959.

8   Ministère des Affaires Etrangères, correspondence No. 945 of the French ambas-
    sador in Turkey, Henry Spitzmuller, to Foreign Minister Maurice Couve de
    Murville, Istanbul, 16 October 1959.

9   French-Turkish talks in Ankara between the Pompidou government and the Inönü
    government of 15-16 July 1963, in *Ministère des Affaires Etrangères, Documents
    Diplomatiques Français*, 1963 II, No. 25, Paris, Imprimerie nationale, 2002.

10 Ministère des Affaires Etrangères, telegram No. 743 from the French ambassador
    to Foreign Minister M. Couve de Murville, 21 September 1960.

11 Ministère des Affaires Etrangères, Documents Diplomatiques Français, 1962 I,
    No. 197, Paris 2002.

12 Cf. the manuscript of the speech in the papers of Emil Noël, EN 1617, in the
    Historical Archive of the EU in Florence.

13 Cf. the copy of Hallstein's speech in the papers of Emil Noël, EN 1617, in the
    Historical Archive of the EU in Florence.

Chapter 17 (pp. 175-182) – *Gabriel Goltz*
The non-Muslim minorities and reform

1   Cf. Fethiye Çetin: "*Yerli Yabancılar*", in: İbrahim Kaboğlu (ed.): *Ulusal,
    Ulusalüstü ve Uluslararası Hukukta Azınlık Hakları*, Istanbul, İstanbul Barosu
    İnsan Hakları Merkezi, 2000, p. 71-81.

2   The status and rights of non-Muslim minorities are derived from the Treaty of
    Lausanne. Although this treaty speaks in general terms of "non-Muslim minori-
    ties" *(müslüman olmayan azınlıklar)*, Turkey recognises only certain non-Muslim
    communities as minorities: the Armenian, Greek, and Bulgarian Christian confes-
    sions and the Jews.

3   For the last up-dating of the law cf. *Resmi Gazete* No. 24990 (11 January 2003): Law
    No. 4778 and *Resmi Gazete* No. 25003 (24 January 2003): *Cemaat vakıfların
    taşınmaz mal edinmeleri, bunlar üzerine tasarrufta bulunmaları, ve tasarrufları*

altında bulunan taşınmaz malların bu vakıflar adına tescil edilmesi hakkında yönetmelik.

4   Cf. *Resmi Gazete* No. 25585 (16 September 2004): *Cemaat vakıfları yönetim kurulu seçimlerinin, seçim esas ve usüllerine ilişkin yönetmelik.*

5   Cf. the changes in the building/construction law (*imar kanunu*) in: *Resmi Gazete* No. 25173 (19 July 2003).

6   Cf. Şükrü Küçükşahin: "*Gizli genelgeyle azınlık devrimi*", *Hürriyet*, 23 February 2004, p.1.

7   According to an article in *Agos* (14 May 2004, p. 1) the restrictions in admitting children of mixed-faith families to minority schools have been lifted by a regulation of the provincial education directorate of the Istanbul governorate. Nevertheless, at the beginning of the school year 2004/5 irregularities were reported.

8   Cf. Otmar Oehring: „Zur Lage der Menschenrechte – Die Türkei auf dem Weg nach Europa – Religionsfreiheit?", *missio* Menschenrechte vol. 20, Aachen 2004, p. 34-38 and idem, Zur Lage der Menschenrechte in der Türkei – Laizismus = Religionsfreiheit?, *missio* Menschenrechte vol. 5, Aachen 2002, p. 25. This situation is about to change slightly. On the basis of the changes made in the building law (cf. fn. 5) the Turkish Supreme Administrative Court (*danıştay*) has overruled on 21 June 2005 a decision of a local administrative court in Ankara stating that churches like mosques have the right to purchase water and energy for free. The mayor of Ankara, Melih Gökçek (AKP), stated on the same day that those who want to build a church in Ankara should apply for public real estate at the Ankara municipality. Cf. „*Kiliseler için "bedava su' yolu açılıyor*", in: *Radikal-online*, 22. June 2005, www.radikal.com.tr/haber.php?haberno=156559 and Muharrem Bayraktar: *Kiliselere 'bedava su!*, in Yeni Mesaj, 28 June 2005, www.yenimesaj.com.tr/index.php?sayfa=yazarlar&haberno=8522&tarih=2005-06-28.

9   Well informed sources in the Turkish EU Secretariat General state that as by July 2005 120 congregational foundations out of 161 have lodged applications with the Directorate General of Foundations with regard to the registration of 2285 properties. Out of these, 341 properties have been registered in the name of the applicant; 471 properties had already been registered in the name of the applicant, thus required no further action; 190 applications had already been included in other applications, thus required no further action; applications regarding 403 properties contained insufficient documentation, and the applicants have been informed accordingly; 880 properties had been registered in the name of public institutions or private persons, thus classified as inadmissible.

10   For a broader overview of the legal situation of congregational foundations cf. among others Yuda Reyna and Ester Moreno Zonana: *Son Yasal Düzenlemelere Göre Cemaat Vakıfları*, Istanbul, *Gözlem Yayınları*, 2003 or Yuda Reyna and Yusuf Şen: *Cemaat Vakıfları ve Sorunları*, Istanbul, *Gözlem Yayınları*, 1994.

11   Cf. Agos, 4 June 2004, p.1.

12   Cf. www.archons.patriarchate.org/news/detail.asp?id=35. On 30 July 2005 the 10th chamber of the Supreme Administrative Court ruled that the orphanage's foundation can't be taken over by the Directorate General of Foundations as "*mazbut*" and sent the case back to a local administrative court in Istanbul where it is now pending. If the local court takes anew a decision not in line with the ruling of the chamber of the Supreme Administrative Court the case will be decided at the

General Council of the Supreme Administrative Court. Cf. *"Vakıf uyumuna yargı desteği"*, in *Radikal-online*, 31. July 2005, www.radikal.com.tr/haber.php?haberno=160158.

13 Cf. fn. 4.

14 Cf. Etyen Mahçupyan: *Türkiye'de gayrimüslim cemaatlerin sorunları ve vatandaş olamama durumu üzerine*, June 2004, www.tesev.org.tr/etkinlik/demokratikleşme_cemaatler.php.

15 Cf. fn. 3.

16 Cf. fn. 4.

17 Cf. Agos, 28 May 2004, p 1.

18 Cf. 5231 *Sayılı Dernekler Kanunu ve Vakıflar Kanunu Tasarısı Taslağı*, in: *Kamu Yönetiminde Yeniden Yapılanma* (6), Ankara, TC Başbakanlığı 2004.

19 Hilal Köylü: *Din notu zayıf*, in: *Radikal-online*, 19 July 2005, www.radikal.com.tr/haber.php?haberno=159051 and Deniz Zeyrek: *'Yasayı da getirin...'*, in: *Radikal-online*, 8 August 2005, www.radikal.com.tr/haber.php?haberno=160877.

20 The Turkish term „*laiklik*" refers to the French concept of "laïcité". That is why in this article the English term "laicism" has been preferred to "secularism".

21 For an overview, cf. the special number of the journal *Birikim: Etnik Kimlik ve Azınlıklar*, No. 71/72, Istanbul 1995.

22 The nationalisation of Islam aims not only at controlling Islam, but also at instrumentalising it to build a homogenous nation, cf. Art. 136 of the Turkish Constitution. Cf. also Niyazi Berkes: The Development of Secularism in Turkey, London, Hurst, 1998 (1968ı), p. 483ff.

23 Cf. Baskin Oran: *Türkiye'de Azınlıklar: Kavramlar, Lozan, İç Mevzuat, İçtihat, Uygulama*, Istanbul, TESEV 2004, pp. 49-66 and İbrahim Kaboğlu (ed.): *Ulusal, Ulusalüstü ve Uluslararsı Hukukta Azınlık Hakları*, Istanbul, İstanbul Barosu İnsan Hakları Merkezi, 2000, pp. 207-275.

24 Cf. Leyla Zana's speech at the European Parliament on 14 October 2004 (MHA News Agency).

25 The draft of a bill on foundations, issued by the Prime Minister's office in October 2004 (cf. 5231 *Sayılı Dernekler Kanunu ve Vakıflar Kanunu Tasarısı Taslağı*, in: *Kamu Yönetiminde Yeniden Yapılanma* (6), Ankara 2004) might be considered a positive sign in this direction; perhaps not the draft itself, because it is criticised harshly by interest groups and the European Commission, but the progress towards more civic participation. Since the publication of the draft, concerned groups have had the opportunity to submit criticisms and proposals. Still, one has to wait and see how far these proposals will be taken into consideration when the bill is drawn up.

26 Cf. the European Commission's 2004 Regular Report on Turkey (COM (2004) 656 final), p. 184.

27 Cf. fn. 8 and 12.

28 Cf. „*Misyoner yayına vize*", in *Radikal-online*, 23 June 2005, http://www.radikal.com.tr/haber.php?haberno=156634.

Chapter 18 (pp. 183-199) – *Kemal Kirişci*
The EU as a vehicle of post-national transformation

1   The author acknowledges that the research for this paper is based on the Boğaziçi

University-Open Society Institute Assistance Foundation joint projection
Immigration Issues in EU-Turkish relations.

2   This literature is vast. Here, two sources with a critical perspective on the issue are
recommended, S. Bozdoğan and R. Kasaba (eds.), *Rethinking Modernity and
National Identity in Turkey* (Seattle, University of Washington Press, 1997), and H.
Poulton, *Turkish Nationalism and the Turkish Republic: Top Hat, Grey Wolf and
Crescent* (London: Hurst & Company, 1997).

3   The fear of conspiracies directed toward Turkey by international actors is often
referred to as the "Sèvres Syndrome". It is the belief that the international community, and in particular the Western world, aspire to revive the terms of the
Sèvres Treaty imposed on the Ottoman Empire after the end of the First World
War and basically divide up Turkey into smaller ethnic states. For an exposé of
this syndrome see D. Jung, *The Sevres Sydrome: Turkish Foreign Policy and its
Historical Legacies* (Chapel Hill, N.C.: American Diplomacy Publishers, 2003).

4   For EU-Turkish relations and the impact of reforms see B. Rubin and A. Çarkoglu
(eds.), *Turkey and The European Union*, (London: Frank Cass, 2003) and M. Uğur
and N. Canefe (eds.), *Turkey and European Integration: Accession prospects and
issues* (London: Routledge, 2004).

5   J. Caporaso, "The EU and forms of state: Westphalian, regulatory and post-modern", *Journal of Common Market Studies*, Vol. 34, No. 1, 1996, pp. 29–52.

6   For a general survey of immigration policies including German and Israel see S.
Castles and M. J. Miller, *The Age of Migration: International Population
Movements in the Modern World*, (London: Macmillan, Second ed. 1998).

7   Castles and Miller note that Turkey's policy "bore some resemblance to Israel's
law of return or Germany's policy towards ethnic Germans in Eastern Europe",
ibid, p. 217.

8   It is not the purpose of this paper to evaluate how post-national the EU's asylum
and immigration policies are. There is a wide body of literature, academic as well
as policy-oriented, that takes a very critical view of these policies in terms of international norms and liberal values. See, for example, A. Geddes, *Immigration and
European Integration: Towards Fortress Europe?*, (Manchester: Manchester
University Press, 2000).

9   The EU has already accepted a series of Council Directives concerning asylum,
immigration and the rights of third-country nationals. Limitations of space preclude their being covered here. But for a detailed and extensive analysis of these
Directives, see P. J. van Krieken, *The Consolidated Asylum and Migration Acquis*,
(The Hague: Asser Press, 2004).

10 Here, too, it should be noted that both the UNHCR and various refugee advocacy
groups have taken a rather critical view as to whether EU Directives concerning
asylum do in fact respect the 1951 Convention. However, this controversy is
beyond the scope of this paper.

11 Immigration was not the only dimension of the Turkish Republic's effort to
build a homogenous national identity. The nation-building process also led to
forced migration and resettlements within the country as well as the emigration of,
for example, the members of the Armenian, Jewish and Greek communities, not to
mention members of other ethnic and religious communities.

12 For a detailed analysis of this see S. Çağaptay, "Kemalist dönemde göç ve iskan
politikaları: Türk kimliği üzerine bir çalışma", *Toplum ve Bilim*, No. 93,

Summer 2002, pp. 218–241, and K. Kirişci, "Disaggregating Turkish citizenship and immigration practices" *Middle Eastern Studies* 36, No. 3, July 2000, pp. 1–22.

13 See for example A. Aktar, *Varlık Vergisi ve Türkleştirme Politikaları* (İstanbul: İletişim Yayınları, 2001).

14 For an emerging literature covering various dimensions of this new immigration see S. Erder, "Uluslararası Göçte Yeni Eğilimler: Türkiye "Göç Alan" ülke mi?" (New Trends in International Migration: Is Turkey an Immigration Country?) in *Mübeccel Kıray için Yazılar* (İstanbul: Bağlam Yayınları, 2000), pp. 235–259, İçduygu, Ahmet and Fuat Keyman, "Globalization, Security, and Migration: The Case of Turkey" *Global Governance* Vol. 6, No. 3, (2000) pp. 383–398, İçduygu, Ahmet, *Irregular Migration in Turkey* (Geneva, IOM, 2003) and E. Zeybekoğlu and B. Johansson (eds.) *Migration and Labour in Europe: Views from Turkey and Sweden* (İstanbul: Şefik Matbaası, 2003).

15 For an assessement of this visa policy see J. Apap, S. Carrera and K. Kirişci, "Turkey in the European Area of Freedom, Security, and Justice". *EU-Turkey Working Papers*, No. 3/August 2004 Center for European Policy Studies, Brussels.

16 İçduygu, 2003, Ibid.

17 B. Kaiser, "Life Worlds of EU Immigrants in Turkey" in Zeybekoğlu and Johansson (eds.) (2003), op cit, pp. 269–290.

18 See Apap et al.

19 The 2004 Turkish Olympic Team included the Ethiopians Elvan Abeylegesse (5000 and 1500 metres) and Tezeta Dangersa (5000 metres), the Belorussian Anzhela Atroschenko (heptathalon), and the Georgian Natalia Nasaridze (archery) out of 14 athletes. The 2000 Olympic Team included the Georgians Ramazan Phaliani, Selim Phaliani and Akın Kakauridze (boxing), and Natalia Nasaridze.

20 It is ironic that there was a time back in the 1950s and 1960s when Turkish national teams included, for example, Greek and Armenian athletes from the once buoyant Greek and Armenian communities in Turkey.

21 Most interestingly, a police official and a member of the Turkish Parliament participated at a UNHCR conference in December 2004 attended by more than fifty participants from various non-governmental organizations and universities in Turkey. They participated in the debates concerning the harmonization of Turkish policy and practice with that of the EU expecially in the area of asylum. Subsequently, in March 2005 the government adopted an Action Plan on Asylum and Migration Legislation. The English version of the Plan can be accessed at http://www.unhcr.org.tr/docs/EU%20Acquis%20Book_Eng.pdf. The document in minute details lays out the tasks and a schedule fot the adoption of the EU acquis in in this area and forsees close cooperation with NGOS and civil society.

22 For an assessment of this progress see K. Kirişci, "Turkish asylum policy and human rights: Adjusting to international norms and EU accession requirements" in Z. Kabasakal-Arat (ed.) *Human Rights Policies and Prospects in Turkey* (University of Pennsylvania Press, forthcoming) and C. Mannaert, "Irregular Migration and Asylum in Turkey". United Nations High Commissioner for Refugees. Working Paper No. 89. May 2003. The last two progress reports prepared by the European Commissions on Turkey's performance towards meeting the EU Acquis have also acknowledged this progress; see *European Union Progress Report for Turkey's Accession 2003* (accessible at http://europa.eu.int/comm/enlargement/report_2003/pdf/rr_tk_final.pdf) and *European Union Progress Report for*

Turkey's Accession 2004 (accessible at
http://europa.eu.int/comm/enlargement/report_2004/pdf/rr_tr_2004_en.pdf).

23 See S. Lavenex and E. Uçarer (eds.) *Migration and the Externalities of European Integration* (Lanham, Maryland: Lexington Books, 2002).

24 The most recent National Program for the Adoption of the *Acquis* (2003) is accessible from http://www.abgs.gov.tr/up2003/up.htm.

25 There are many surveys that show the high level of support for EU membership among the Turkish public. However, these surveys also indicate that the public is distrustful of whether the EU will actually deliver its end of the deal. For an example of such a survey see European Union Survey: "Turkish Public Opinion on the European Union," Research Team: Ali Ġarkoglu, Refik Erzan, Kemal Kirişci, Hakan Yilmaz. (Istanbul: TESEV, 2002). Online at http://www.tesev.org.tr/eng/project/fullreport.php.

26 See Apap et al (2004).

Acknowledgments

This book could not have been made without the invaluable linguistic assistance of Hilary Kilpatrick Waardenburg and the commitment of Thomas Wunderlin (Layout). Many thanks to them. Most of the contributions in this book were first presented at the conference "Turkey: towards post-nationalism?". This conference had been organized by the Swiss Society for Middle Eastern and Islamic Studies (Schweizerische Gesellschaft Mittlerer Osten und islamische Kulturen) and was held in Basel on 14–16 October 2004. We offer our thanks to the sponsors of the conference (Schweizerische Akademie der Geistes- und Sozialwissenschaften, Max Geldner-Stiftung Basel, Freiwillige Akademische Gesellschaft Basel) and to the University of Basel, particularly to the Oriental Institute (headed by Prof. Dr. Gregor Schoeler), for their hospitality and their collaboration with the Swiss Society for Middle Eastern and Islamic Studies. Particular thanks to those actively involved in the organization of the congress: Martha Vogel and Monika Winet (Oriental Institute), and Georg Kreis (director of the EuropaInstitut at the University of Basel).

We are specially grateful to the Swiss Academy of Humanities and Social Sciences (Schweizerische Akademie der Geistes- und Sozialwissenschaften) which has also supported the production of this volume.

List of contributors

MARC BAER is Assistant Professor in the Department of History, University of California-Irvine. He is a historian of transregional religion, the Ottoman Empire, and Modern Turkey.

HAMİT BOZARSLAN is Associated Professor at the Ecole des Hautes Etudes en Sciences Sociales. He is the author, namely, of *100 mots pour dire la violence dans le monde musulman* (Paris: Maisonneuve-Larose, 2005); *Political Contest to Self-Sacrifice: Violence in the Middle East* (Princeton: Marcus Wiener, 2004), *Histoire de la Turquie contemporaine*, (Paris: La Découverte, 2004) et *La question kurde: Etats et minorités au Moyen-Orient* (Paris, Sciences-Po, 1997). He is currently working on the issue of violence in the Middle East.

RIFAT N. BALİ, born in 1948 in Istanbul. Independent scholar. Author of several books and articles on the history of the Jews of Turkey in the Republican period, on anti-Semitism and conspiracy theories, and on the rise of the new bourgeoisie in Turkey after 1980. He is also the author of a bibliography of works published in Turkey on Turkish Jews and a study of the early emigration of Ottoman Turks to the USA.

EBRU BULUT is a PhD Student at the Ecole des Hautes Etudes en Sciences Sociales, in Paris and a Research Assistant at the University of Marmara, Istanbul. She specialises in politics and nationalism in contemporary Turkey.

FUAT DÜNDAR is preparing a PhD at the Ecole des Hautes Etudes en Sciences Sociales in Paris. He has written *İttihat ve Terakki'nin müslümanları iskan politikası 1913-1918* (CUP's settlement policy of the moslems 1913-1918), Istanbul: İletişim, 2001; a work based on extensive research in the Ottoman state archive in Istanbul.

FATMA MÜGE GÖÇEK, currently associate professor of sociology and women's studies at the University of Michigan, Ann Arbor was born and raised in Istanbul, Turkey. She received a B.A. and M.A. in sociology from Boğazici University, and an M.A. and Ph.D. from Princeton University.
The author of *East Encounters West* (Oxford University Press, 1986) and *Rise of the Bourgeoisie and Demise of Empire* (Oxford University Press, 1996), and editor of (with Shiva Balaghi) *Reconstructing Gender in the Middle East* (Columbia University Press, 1994), *Political Cartoons in the Middle East*

(Marcus Wiener Publishers, 1998), and *Social Constructions of Nationalism in the Middle East* (SUNY Press, 2002), she is currently working on a book tentatively entitled *Deciphering Denial: Turkish State and the Armenian Massacres of 1915.*

GABRIEL GOLTZ graduated in Middle Eastern Studies and Political Science from the Free University of Berlin in 2002, after study and research visits to Egypt and Turkey. He was a fellow on the Robert Bosch Foundation's Postgraduate Programme in International Affairs from 2002 to 2003. Since 2004 he has been working as a consultant at the German Embassy in Ankara, Turkey. His chapter in this book reflects the author's personal opinions.

CORINNA GÖRGÜ-GUTTSTADT received her masters in turcology and history from Hamburg University. Her forthcoming book on Turkey and the Holocaust (*Die Türkei und der Holocaust*, Assoziation A, 2006) is based on research in Turkish and European archives and eye witness testimony to explore Turkey's treatment of Turkish Jewish citizens caught in Europe in the eve of the Holocaust.

GÜLISTAN GÜRBEY (Privat-dozent Dr) is a lecturer in the Department of Political and Social Sciences at the Freie Universität Berlin. Her priorities in research and work are: international politics with emphasis on Foreign policy analysis/foreign policy and decision-making processes in foreign policy in defective democracies, conflict research and peaceful conflict settlement, International protection of minorities.

M. ŞÜKRÜ HANİOĞLU is a professor in the Department of Near Eastern Studies at Princeton University. He is interested in the cultural, diplomatic, and intellectual history of the Middle East and Southeastern Europe in the early modern era. His latest publications include *The Young Turks in Opposition* (New York: Oxford University Press, 1995) and *Preparation for a Revolution* (New York: Oxford University Press, 2001). He is currently the Chair of the Department of Near Eastern Stuides and the Director of the Program in Near Eastern Studies and the Ertegün Foundation of Turkish Studies.

BEATRICE HENDRICH holds a PhD degree from the Institute of Oriental Studies at Justus-Liebig-University, Giessen (Germany), where she has been working as Research Fellow at the Collaborative Research Center "Cultures of Memory" on identity and memory culture of Alevis living in Germany. Among her Publications are *Milla – millet – Nation? Von der Religionsgemeinschaft zur Nation? Von der Veränderung eines Wortes und der Wandlung eines Staates,* Frankfurt a. M. 2003, and *Mental Maps, Raum, Erinnerung. Kulturwissen-*

schaftliche Zugänge zum Verhältnis von Raum und Erinnerung, Münster 2005 (co-edited).

RAYMOND KEVORKIAN, historian, Associate Professor at the Institut Français de Géopolitique (Université Paris VIII) and Director of the Bibliothèque Nubar (Paris). Among his publications are *L'extermination des Arméniens. Détruire pour construire une nation turque* (to be published in 2006), *L'extermination des déportés arméniens ottomans dans les camps de concentration de Syrie-Mésopotamie (1915-1916): la deuxième phase du génocide* (Paris 1998) and *Les Arméniens dans l'Empire Ottoman à la veille du génocide* (co-ed., Paris 1992).

HANS-LUKAS KIESER is privat-dozent and lecturer in Modern History at the University of Zurich, specialising in Turkey and the Near East. Among his recent publications are *Vorkämpfer der "Neuen Türkei". Revolutionäre Bildungseliten am Genfersee (1870–1939),* Zurich: Chronos, 2005; *Der Völkermord an den Armeniern und die Shoah / The Armenian Genocide and the Shoah,* Zürich: Chronos, 2002 (2nd ed. 2003); and *Der verpasste Friede. Mission, Ethnie und Staat in den Ostprovinzen der Türkei 1839-1938,* Zürich: Chronos, 2000 (Turkish tr. Istanbul: Iletisim, 2005).

KEMAL KİRİŞCİ is professor at the Department of Political Science and International Relations at Boğaziçi University, Istanbul. He holds a Jean Monnet Chair in European Integration and is also the director of the Center for European Studies at the university. His areas of research interest include European integration, asylum, border control and immigration issues in the European Union, EU-Turkish relations, Middle Eastern politics, ethnic conflicts, and refugee movements. His books include *Turkey In World Politics: An Emerging Multi-Regional Power* (co-edited with B. Rubin) (Lynne Reinner, Boulder, 2001); *The Political Economy of Cooperation in the Middle East* (co-authored) (Routledge, London, 1998); *Turkey and the Kurdish Question: An Example of a Trans-State Ethnic Conflict* (co-authored) (Frank Cass, London, 1997); and *The PLO and World Politics,* (Frances Pinters, London, 1986).

EUGENE KRIEGER earned degrees in Classical Languages and Ancient and Modern History at Basel University. Presently he is assistant dean at the Gymnasium am Münsterplatz, Basel. This paper is a summary of his dissertation, written at the Europainstitut, Basel.

ELISE MASSICARD graduated in Social Sciences and Turkish studies in Paris and Berlin and obtained her PhD in Political Science on the Alevist movement in Turkey and Germany. She is a research fellow at the Centre National de la Recherche Scientifique/Centre d'études de recherches administratives et sociales in Lille (France) and is currently working on the political sociology of contemporary Turkey. She is the author of *L'autre Turquie: le mouvement aléviste et ses territoires*, Paris: PUF, 2005.

BERNA PEKESEN has studied History and Mass Communications/ Journalism in Bochum and Ankara. She is preparing her PhD thesis *Migratory movements and policies of settlement in the Republic of Turkey 1923-1950* (with a special focus on the Jewish communities) at the University of Bochum. Since 2003 she works as a research associate at the Chair for Southeast-European History, University of Bochum. Her more general research interests fall in minority issues, nationalism, Kemalism and international settlement policies in the interwar period.

GÜNTER SEUFERT is a free lanced writer and journalist based in Istanbul. He was trained as a sociologist at the University of Bremen and carried out its Ph.D. research with a grant of the Institute of the German Oriental Society, Beirut & Istanbul. After a postdoctoral research project at the University of Lausanne, Switzerland he overtook a post as senior researcher at the Institute of the German Oriental Society, and worked as the director of the Institute's Istanbul branch in the following years. In 2004 and 2005 he taught as a visiting associate professor at the University of Cyprus, Nicosia.

Index